Praise for *The Small Business Bible*

"A true encyclopedia of all things you need to know about your small business. Keep it close!"

—Michael Gerber, Author of *New York Times* bestseller,
The E-Myth and Chief Dreamer,
In The Dreaming Room LLC

"*The Small Business Bible* is packed with extensive, relevant information for today's entrepreneurs. Steve has provided a comprehensive look at every facet of small business, including up-to-date research on technology, e-commerce, and other growth strategies. Rule #1 for every successful entrepreneur is to put this book on the shelf!"

—Phil Town, Author of #1 *New York Times*
Best-seller, *Rule #1*

"Excellent! Nothing was left out of this definitive guide on how to start and build a successful small business. Whether you are brand new to small business or a seasoned entrepreneur, you can learn something from this book!"

—Hector Barreto, Former Administrator of the Small Business Administration and Chairman of The Latino Coalition

"You might read this book once, but you will reference it for years to come! Steve has done a wonderful job laying out what might otherwise be dry information in an easy-to-understand, lively format. Whatever your business, there is no shortage of actionable, useful ideas in this great book."

—Barbara Corcoran, Founder, The Corcoran Group,
and *Today Show* Contributor

"As the former president of three fast growth companies, I've learned what it takes to start and grow a small business. Steve Strauss' *The Small Business Bible* helps you understand what works and avoid what could be some 'lessons learned the hard way.' Whether you are starting or growing your business, *The Small Business Bible* is highly recommended!"

—Steve Little, The Business Growth Expert and
Author of *The 7 Irrefutable Rules of Small Business Growth*

"Strauss has revamped his classic book with cutting-edge content—from how to green your business to utilizing technology to your advantage. This is a timely, practical, and readable resource!"

—Ken Yancey, Author, CEO of SCORE

The Small Business Bible is required reading for any business owner looking to do things quicker and better. *The Small Business Bible* provides straightforward advice and profitable information for both the startup entrepreneur or the seasoned manager!"

—Gene Marks, Editor of Amazon's #1 Small Business Bestseller,
The Streetwise Small Business Book of Lists

"Whenever Steve has appeared on our show, he has proven himself to be a knowledgeable, entertaining, lively, smart guest! His book has served as a great resource and I highly recommend this great compendium for anyone in the business of small business!"

—J. J. Ramberg, Host of MSNBC's Small Business Show,
Your Business

THE
SMALL
BUSINESS
BIBLE

THIRD EDITION

Everything You Need to Know to Succeed in Your Small Business

STEVEN D. STRAUSS

WILEY

John Wiley & Sons, Inc.

Published by John Wiley & Sons, Inc., Hoboken, New Jersey.
Published simultaneously in Canada.

Library of Congress Cataloging-in-Publication Data:
Strauss, Steven D., 1958—
    The small business bible: everything you need to know to succeed in your
small business / Steven D. Strauss. –3rd ed.
        p. cm.
    ISBN 978-1-118-13594-5 (pbk.); ISBN 978-1-118-22525-7 (ebk); ISBN 978-1-118-23877-6 (ebk);
    ISBN 978-1-118-26339-6 (ebk)
    1.   Small business–United States–Management.   2.   Small business–United States–Finance.
  3.   New business enterprises–United States.   I.   Title.
    HD62.7.S875 2012
    658.02'2–dc23   2011042848

Printed in the United States of America

10 9 8 7 6 5 4 3 2 1

Contents

❧ SECTION I Starting Your Business

PART I Genesis

PART II Opening Up Shop

PART III Franchises

PART IV Home-Based Businesses

PART V Business on a Shoestring

SECTION II Running Your Business

PART I Small Business in the Twenty-First Century

PART II Money

PART III Management

PART IV Technology

SECTION III Growing Your Business

PART I Advertising and Marketing

PART II Your Website

PART III Social Media

PART IV Growth Strategies

PART V Strategies for Small Business Success

About the Author

Steven D. Strauss, often called "America's small business expert," is an internationally recognized author, columnist, lawyer, and speaker. He is the senior business columnist for USATODAY and his column, *Ask an Expert*, is one of the most highly syndicated business columns in the world. Steve is a regular columnist for Yahoo!, SCORE, and many other sites, as well as being a blogger for the *Huffington Post*. He is also the author of 16 books.

A highly sought-after commentator and media guest, Steve has been on ABC, CNN, CNBC, Bloomberg Television, *The O'Reilly Factor*, and the BBC, among others. He is a regular guest on both MSNBC's business show *Your Business* and *ABC News Now* and is regularly seen in magazines and newspapers across the country and around the globe. Indeed, Steve often speaks to groups the world over, including a recent visit to the United Nations. He sits on the board of the World Entrepreneurship Forum and is also a speaker for the United States State Department, speaking in places such as the West Bank, South Korea, Bahrain, Japan, Mongolia, and Jordan. He is also often asked to be the small business spokesperson for companies that wish to reach the small business marketplace.

Finally, Steve too is an entrepreneur. He is president of the Strauss Group, Inc.: the Strauss Law Firm, Strauss Seminar Co., Strauss Syndication, MrAllBiz.com, and TheSelfEmployed.com. He graduated from UCLA, the Claremont Graduate School, and the McGeorge School of Law, and was a Coro Foundation Fellow in Public Affairs. If you would like to get in touch with him, have him speak to your group, or sign up for his free newsletter—*Small Business Success Secrets!*—please visit his website, www.MrAllBiz.com.

Preface

Starting, owning, and running a successful small business is one of the great joys in life. No, there are no guarantees, and yes, there are obstacles. But, if you do it right, if you start the right small business—one suited to your strengths, one that you are passionate about, one that epitomizes your highest dreams and values, and certainly one that allows you to make a nice profit—then there is no telling how far it can take you.

This book will show you how to get there.

But be forewarned: If what you are looking for is a book that will give you the underpinnings of small business theory and expository prose about business assumptions, this is the wrong book for you. Put it down. What you will get instead in these pages are tried-and-true, real-world business tips, skills, examples, and strategies that have been proven to help small businesses grow and that can help *your* small business grow. Written in a friendly, easy-to-understand manner, chock-full of interesting, actual examples, *The Small Business Bible, Third Edition*, contains everything you need to know to have a successful, fulfilling, profitable, and enjoyable entrepreneurial journey.

This third edition greatly expands and updates what was already a very comprehensive book. As we are living through a time when both work and business are changing rapidly, this book can be your guide to what might be some uncharted territory. In this third edition, you can learn what you need to know about important topics such as:

- Social media marketing made easy
- Tapping the growing use of smartphone and app technology
- Facebook for business
- Green businesses
- E-commerce success
- Marketing and advertising today

Covering the simple to the complex, *The Small Business Bible, Third Edition*, allows you to easily and quickly get up to speed on any pertinent subject. Would you like to know how to create a memorable brand for your small business? It is in here. Unsure about small business accounting? Read on. Shoestring marketing? Yep, it is here, too. It is all here. *The Small Business Bible* covers everything you need to know, or might need to know, about starting or running a successful and enjoyable small business. It is not called *The Small Business Bible* for nothing.

As the longtime small business columnist for *USA TODAY,* I have the opportunity to interact with many small business owners. I hear their war stories and learn their secrets, and that is what I want to impart to you in this book: the best tips, hints, and ideas that I have come across. By helping you avoid mistakes, teaching you important and difference-making business strategies, and sharing what works, *The Small Business Bible, Third Edition,* is intended to be your one-stop shop for all things small business. If I have done my job right, yours just got easier because this book should become your indispensable business partner: a well-used, dog-eared friend that shows you the way. Thanks for taking it along with you on your entrepreneurial journey.

—Steve Strauss

Acknowledgments

I would first like to thank my excellent research assistant, Sydney. I would also like to thank my friends and editors at *USA TODAY*—Ray Goldbacher, Ed Brackett, and Matt Trott. As always, I am grateful to all of my pals at John Wiley & Sons for their support. Thank you also to my great brothers Larry and Bruddie. Finally, many, many thanks to my sweet wife, Maria, and my beloved girls, Jillian, Sydney, and Mara.

Starting Your Business

PART

Genesis

CHAPTER 1

In the Beginning

If one advances confidently in the direction of his dreams . . . he will meet with a success unexpected in common hours.

—HENRY DAVID THOREAU

It is a huge step. Deciding to go into business for yourself is one of the most important decisions you will make in your life. Ranking right up there with picking a partner and buying a home, becoming an entrepreneur is one of those life-altering events that will have repercussions for years to come. No, there are no guarantees, and yes, there will be obstacles. But do you know what? If you do it right, if you start the right small business—one that is suited to your strengths, one that you are passionate about, one that allows you to make a nice profit—then there is no telling how far you can go. John Nordstrom, founder of the eponymous department store, said of his roots, "I was not certain what I wanted to do. I started looking around for some small business to get into. Mr. Wallin the shoemaker suggested that we join a partnership and open a shoe store."

ASSESSING YOUR STRENGTHS

Not everyone is cut out to be an entrepreneur. Although there is a common perception that entrepreneurship is exciting, and indeed it is, many other words equally describe the life of the self-made small business person: nerve-wracking, liberating, difficult, challenging, time-consuming, overwhelming, fun, joyous, productive, uncertain—and that's just for

5

starters. Any small business person could expand at length on any one of these adjectives, for all come into play to some degree or another in almost every small business, and often in the same day.

The question is not whether entrepreneurship is right for you, but rather, are you right for entrepreneurship? Can you handle the stress, the freedom, the lack of structure, the uncertainty, and the opportunity that await if you decide to start your own business? This really can't be stressed enough. There is no doubt that being in business for yourself can be great, but if you are not cut out for it temperamentally, it will be a tough road. There is no shame in this. Some people are artists and others are lawyers, some are athletes and others are homebodies, some are entrepreneurs and some are not.

Entrepreneur Defined

Various definitions of an entrepreneur:

- Dictionary.com: "A person who organizes and manages any enterprise, esp. a business, usually with considerable initiative and risk."
- The World Entrepreneurship Forum: "Creators of wealth and social justice."
- One successful entrepreneur (and my favorite definition): "A person willing to take a risk with money to make money."

Which type of entrepreneur are you? To help you decide, take the following quiz. It will help you evaluate your qualifications. As you take the quiz, though, it is important to be perfectly honest. There is no point in answering the questions "right" if the answers are not true for you.

Test Your Entrepreneurship IQ

1. Are you a self-starter?
   a. Yes, I like to think up ideas and implement them. (5 points)
   b. If someone helps me get started, I will definitely follow through. (3 points)
   c. Frankly, I would rather follow than lead. (1 point)

2. How do you feel about taking risks?
    a. I really like the feeling of being on the edge a bit. (5 points)
    b. Calculated risks are acceptable at times. (3 points)
    c. I like the tried and true. (1 point)

3. Are you a leader?
    a. Yes. (5 points)
    b. Yes, when necessary. (3 points)
    c. No, not really. (1 point)

4. Can you and your family live without a regular paycheck?
    a. Yes, if that is what it takes. (5 points)
    b. I would rather not, but I understand that may be part of the process. (3 points)
    c. I do not like that idea at all. (1 point)

5. Could you fire someone who really needed the job your business provided?
    a. Yes, I may not like it, but that's the way it goes sometimes. (5 points)
    b. I hope so. (3 points)
    c. I really can't see myself doing that. (1 point)

6. Are you willing to work 60 hours a week or more?
    a. Yes, if that is what it takes. (5 points)
    b. Maybe in the beginning. (3 points)
    c. I think many other things are more important than work. (1 point)

7. Are you self-confident?
    a. You bet! (5 points)
    b. Most of the time. (3 points)
    c. Unfortunately, that is not one of my strong suits. (1 point)

8. Can you live with uncertainty?
    a. Yes. (5 points)
    b. If I have to, but I don't like it. (3 points)
    c. No, I like knowing what to expect. (1 point)

9. Once you put your mind to something, can you stick with it?
   a. I do not let anything get in my way. (5 points)
   b. Most of the time, if I like what I am doing. (3 points)
   c. Not always. (1 point)

10. Are you creative?
    a. Yes, I have a lot of good ideas. (5 points)
    b. I can be. (3 points)
    c. No, not really. (1 point)

11. Are you competitive?
    a. To a fault. (5 points)
    b. Sure, mostly. (3 points)
    c. Not really, my nature is more laid back. (1 point)

12. Do you have a lot of willpower and self-discipline?
    a. Yes. (5 points)
    b. I am disciplined when I need to be. (3 points)
    c. Not really. (1 point)

13. Are you individualistic, or would you rather go along with the crowd?
    a. I like to think things through myself and do things my way. (5 points)
    b. I am sometimes an original. (3 points)
    c. I think strongly individualistic people are a bit strange. (1 point)

14. Can you live without structure?
    a. Yes. (5 points)
    b. Actually, the idea of living without a regular job makes me nervous. (3 points)
    c. No, I like routine and structure in my life. (1 point)

15. Do you have many business skills?
    a. Yes, I do, and those I don't have, I'll learn. (5 points)
    b. I have some. (3 points)
    c. No, not really. (1 point)

16. Are you flexible and willing to change course when things are not going your way?
  a. Yes. (5 points)
  b. I like to think so, but others may disagree. (3 points)
  c. No, I have a fairly rigid personality. (1 point)

17. Do you have experience in the business you are thinking of starting?
  a. Yes. (5 points)
  b. Some. (3 points)
  c. No. (1 point)

18. Could you competently perform multiple business tasks: accounting, sales, marketing, and so on?
  a. I sure would like to try! (5 points)
  b. I hope so. (3 points)
  c. That sounds intimidating. (1 point)

19. Can you juggle multiple tasks?
  a. Yes. (5 points)
  b. I think so. (3 points)
  c. I don't think so. (1 point)

20. Are you willing to hustle for clients and customers?
  a. Sure. (5 points)
  b. If I have to. (3 points)
  c. I would rather not. (1 point)

21. How well do you handle pressure?
  a. Quite well. (5 points)
  b. It's not my strongest trait, but I can do it. (3 points)
  c. Not well at all. (1 point)

Scoring

80–100: You have both the temperament and the skills to become an entrepreneur.

60–79: You are not a natural entrepreneur but may become one over time.

Below 60: You would be wise to think of another career besides self-employment.

So there you have it. Not only should this quiz help you understand your Entrepreneurship IQ, but also it should give you some insight into the traits and characteristics of a successful, self-employed businessperson: driven, hardworking, creative, energetic, resourceful, confident, and flexible.

Steve Jobs on Entrepreneurs

"I'm convinced that about half of what separates the successful entrepreneurs from the nonsuccessful ones is pure perseverance."

If this describes you (or a close approximation of you), then the next question is, where do you go from here?

RISK TOLERANCE

The quiz that you just took was intended to help you gauge your Entrepreneurship IQ, as well as to show you the traits required to start your own small business. Yes, you will need some business savvy and self-confidence—that's a given. Being creative and hardworking are equally important. But of all the necessary traits, the one that you must have in abundance is a tolerance for risk, because starting your own small business is a risk.

Borrowing money, setting up shop, trying out new ideas—these are all tasks that, although fun and exciting, are also inherently risky. There are no guarantees that your idea or plan will fly. Certainly the goal of this book is to make sure it does, but no matter how much you study and learn, there will always be an element of risk in being an entrepreneur. Would you have it any other way? If your answer is "no," then you definitely have the right stuff. If it is not, if the idea of taking a big risk scares you more than it excites you, then you need to consider carefully whether starting your own business is the best choice for you.

Throughout this book, I will be sharing with you the traits of exceptional small businesses so that you can see what the best of the best do. Here is the first one, and it is good news: great small businesses work to reduce their risk as much as possible. They work at covering every angle so that the risks they take are prudent, calculated risks. Here are a few ways to minimize risk:

- *Know your numbers.* I can't tell you how many entrepreneurs I meet who are in over their heads because they had some idea or whim and dropped a bundle of money on an idea that was not fully vetted. A few years ago, I was involved in an enterprise in which one of the guys decided unilaterally, and impulsively, that the best thing the business could do was to commit to an ad campaign in a major magazine. The campaign was a bust, and the business was stuck with almost $50,000 in advertising debt. Look before you leap.
- *Do your homework.* Do your research. Test the waters. Think it through. Consider worst-case scenarios. Thoroughly analyzing an opportunity or idea before implementing it lessens the chance of investing too much time or money in a bad idea.
- *Incorporate.* If things go south, the corporate shield that protects your personal assets from corporate debts will make a huge difference. If you do not run your business as a corporation or an LLC (limited liability company), you put your personal assets at risk.
- *Have enough insurance.* Just as incorporating reduces your personal risk, so, too, does having adequate insurance.
- *Bring in help.* As entrepreneurs, we like to think we know it all, but we don't. Whether it's hiring someone to free up time for you to do what you do best, bringing in a strategic partner with contacts you don't have, or hiring consultants to figure out how you can improve, getting expert help reduces your risk and makes your life easier.

The upshot of all of this is that great entrepreneurs know their strengths and weaknesses, think ahead, and plan accordingly. That is what you will need to do, too, if you start your own small business—take a prudent, calculated, intelligent risk with a high likelihood of payoff. Just know that risk, even when it is reduced, will still be present because it is the nature of the game.

> **Risks**
>
> "The policy of being too cautious is the greatest risk of all."
> —Jawaharlal Nehru

THE NEXT STEP

Sometimes the idea of starting your own business can be overwhelming. What kind of business should you start? Where will you get the money? How will you find customers? These are all legitimate concerns, and they will be addressed in detail in this book. At this point, however, understand that as you drive down the street, almost every business you see is a small business that is run by someone who, at some point, had never run a business before. But those business owners learned how, found the money, found some customers, and are still around. If they did it, so can you. To join their ranks, you must be willing to do your homework.

Education

The next step is to educate yourself. Most people go into business because they love something and want to do it every day: the baker wants to own her own bakery, the chiropractor wants to start his own practice, and so on. The problem the baker and the chiropractor have is that, although they may know a lot about baking and backs, if they are like most entrepreneurs, they know little about businesses and boardrooms. They may know their specialties, but they do not know everything else that it takes to start and run a successful business. And, problematically, that "everything else" will take up *a lot* of their time. Marketing and advertising, sales and income taxes, hiring and firing, and so on, have nothing whatsoever to do with baking and backs.

The next step, then, is to learn about business in general. Certainly this book will be enormously helpful, and down the road, you will see that nothing beats the trial and error of actually running your own venture. But before you can get to that point, you need to have a general idea of how businesses operate.

Small Business Sites

These sites can teach you a lot about small business:

- www.usatoday.com/money/smallbusiness/front.htm
- Small Business Online Community
- Huffington Post Small Business
- www.TheSelfEmployed.com
- Business Insider
- www.SBA.gov
- www.SCORE.org
- Business on Main
- www.MrAllBiz.com

Even if you passed the Entrepreneur IQ quiz with flying colors, it is probably safe to assume that, although you may have an entrepreneurial bent, you do not know everything you need to know to become successful—which is true for most self-employed people. Therefore, you should begin to brush up on both the subjects that seem interesting to you and the ones that scare you. If finances are not your strong suit, then dig in. As a small business owner, you will inevitably wear many hats. It is not uncommon, especially at the beginning, for the founder of a company to be the president, accountant, marketing wizard, and sales force, all rolled into one. For that reason, it helps to have a broad understanding of what it takes to run a business.

It would also be smart to start reading some business magazines every month. Periodicals such as *Home Business* magazine, *Entrepreneur*, and *Inc.* are chock-full of easy-to-understand articles that will help make you a success.

Free Help!

I would like to really encourage you to check out my website—MrAllBiz. com. There we have all sorts of tools dedicated to helping you succeed in your entrepreneurial journey—everything from courses and CDs to webinars and free e-newsletters.

Experience

Finally, no education would be complete without some practical, hands-on experience. This can take two forms. First, say you want to open an antiques store. You would be wise to start by working at someone else's. If you already have that sort of hands-on experience in your chosen industry, then skip the rest of this paragraph. But if you have never actually worked in a business like the one you want to start, you are *strongly advised* to do just that. Your entrepreneurial dream can wait six months while you gain the sort of experience that will make or break your new business. Working in a business like the one you want to create will teach you things that no book could impart. It is a critical step.

Second, you need to talk to some business owners in your desired field. But remember, if you seek out entrepreneurs in your potential industry in your own town, the going may be tough—they will likely view you as a potential competitor (rightly so) and thus be reluctant to share their insights with you. Therefore, it would be much smarter to go to a nearby town, find a few businesses similar to the one you want to start, take the owners out to lunch, and pick their brains. People love to talk about themselves. Find out everything you can about their businesses:

- What do they like most about their business?
- What do they like least?
- What was the start-up cost?
- How much can you expect to make?
- Where do they advertise?
- If they were starting over, what would they do differently?

No one knows this business (whatever it is) like the owners do. You would be hard-pressed to find better, more pertinent information than the insights you can get from these small business owners, who are already doing what it is you dream of doing.

This informal "MBA" can reap tremendous benefits. By the time you are ready to start your business, you will have a thorough understanding of the risks and rewards of the area you are getting into. Doing this initial research will take time, for sure, but if you follow this plan, you can be assured that when you finally open your doors, you will have reduced your risk as much as possible, and thus your chances of success will be much greater.

CHAPTER 2

Choosing the Right Business

The road to happiness lies in two simple principles: Find
what it is that interests you and that you can do well, and
when you find it, put your whole soul into it—every bit of
energy and ambition and natural ability you have.

—JOHN D. ROCKEFELLER III

When it comes to choosing a small business, there are two types of entrepreneurs. The first is the person who is in love with the idea of starting a very specific business. This person may be a gardener who envisions opening a nursery or a chef who has long dreamed of owning a restaurant. The other potential small business person is someone who is also in love, not with a specific business but with the idea of being his or her own boss. As there are risks and rewards associated with each path, both warrant further discussion.

IF YOU DO WHAT YOU LOVE, WILL THE MONEY REALLY FOLLOW?

There is a saying that goes, "Do what you love; the money will follow." Although this is noble and possibly true, there is more to small business success than simply doing what you love. Don't get me wrong. Doing what you love is indeed the first prerequisite when choosing the right business, but it is just that—a first step.

Live with Passion

What is it that you love? In life, we tend to succeed and perform well when we are engaged in something that we really enjoy. Your business

15

should be no different. Richard Branson did not start Virgin Music because he thought that music would be profitable but because he loved it.

What about you? By now, you know what excites you, what it is that you love most. You know what you like to do, what your passions are, what is fun for you, and how you like to spend your time. Barbara Winter, in her great book *Making a Living without a Job,* says that passion leads to purpose: once you get in touch with those things you are most passionate about, you can begin to create a business of purpose around those things.

That is your first assignment: deciding which of your passions you love enough to start a business around. Remember, your business will become your baby, and like any baby, it will require a lot of love, time, money, and attention if it is to grow strong and healthy. Of those resources, right now, you should be most concerned with time. Your new business will take a lot of time, so pick something that you love doing because you will be spending a lot of time doing it.

Once you know what you love enough to spend all day, every day doing it, you need to figure out what business you could start that relates to that love. Say, for example, that you love plants and gardening, and you have decided that you want to spend every day doing something related to those things. What are your choices? You could, for instance:

- Start a nursery.
- Open a flower shop.
- Start a lawn care business.
- Grow organic vegetables.
- Buy a farm.
- Start a winery.

Getting Inspired

Stuck for a business idea that relates to your passion? Google the keywords of the type of business you are interested in. You might be surprised to see how many different types of businesses other people have created around the same thing.

This is the time for one of those "anything goes" brainstorming sessions. Go for it. Write down any kooky idea that you have. No limits! There are few times in life when the stars align themselves just so and we have a chance, not only for a fresh start, but for a fresh start that is completely of our own choosing. Usually, money is tight, the opportunity passes, or something else conspires to interfere with a brand-new beginning. But if you are at a place where you are reading this and you are ready to start your own business, *and* you have the wherewithal to do so, *and* you can choose any business you want, then savor this moment, for it is rare indeed.

Although it is good and wise to let your mind roam, it is equally shrewd, afterward, to come back down to Earth. What if, instead of gardening, what you love most is nineteenth-century Flemish architecture, and you have decided to become a Flemish architecture consultant? However interesting that may be to you, and although it certainly would scratch your Flemish architecture itch, if you cannot find people who are willing to pay you for your expertise, people who are willing to buy the product you want to sell, you do not have a business, you have a bust. Be realistic—there must be a market for the product or service that you plan to offer.

Assuming, then, that you have decided to pick a business that is a passionate practicality, the last question to be answered is whether you will be able to make sufficient profit from it. There is no sense in starting a business, however much you might love the idea, if you will not be able to make a good living. One reason we go into business for ourselves is the chance to make more money.

Whatever business you want to start, then, whatever product or service you decide to sell, you have to be able to sell it at a price that is high enough to make a profit but low enough that people will buy it. It is not always an easy balance. Why do so many stores in expensive malls go out of business? Because even with a great concept, if their overhead is too high, making a profit is mathematically impossible. Before jumping into a business, you have to crunch some numbers. Do your research. How much does a small business of the type you want to start make? How quickly do they make it? (See Chapter 4, for more information on how to do this.)

Caution!

Too many new entrepreneurs fall in love with their idea and become convinced that it is the greatest thing since sliced bread. *Do not make this mistake.* You must strive to be as objective as possible. Do other people like your idea as much as you do? Ask around. Get feedback. Crunch some numbers. Be a businessperson. Although hunches and intuition are great, you need some objective criteria before making the leap into the land of entrepreneurship.

A Word of Warning

The bad news about starting a business is that good ideas are not very hard to come by. Again, every business you see when you drive down the street was once someone's beloved inspiration. But what did it take to turn that great idea into a successful business? How much time, effort, and money were involved? You can bet the entrepreneur who started that thriving business on the corner probably had no idea how difficult it would be to turn his vision into reality.

Finding a good idea is just the beginning—in fact, it is the easy part. The trick is being able to successfully implement that idea. That is much more difficult. As Thomas Edison said, genius is "1 percent inspiration and 99 percent perspiration." That is as true in business as it is in science. Not only must you come up with a good idea, it must be a good idea that you can move on. That is what you are looking for.

Look around. Are there any businesses similar to the one you want to create? If not, that might tell you something. Maybe your idea is so cutting-edge that no one else has thought of it. Innovative businesses have the chance to become market leaders: Amazon.com was first, Yahoo! was first, Post-it and Pampers were first. Being first gives you something called the first mover's advantage. Simply put, by being first, you have the chance to shape the marketplace. The potential profit from such a business is enormous. The problem, as you may have surmised, is that it usually takes a lot of money to successfully create such a business. If you do not have the drive to do so, or the risk tolerance, or the capital, then you would be best advised to follow and not to lead. Later on, once you have more experience and money, you can innovate all you want, but the beginning of your small business journey may not be the best place to boldly go where no entrepreneur has gone before. Now is probably the time to learn, not to lead.

Consider choosing an idea that others have also successfully implemented. Consider the previous example: books have been written on how to start a florist shop or a nursery; books have not been written on how to tap the Flemish architecture market.

Another advantage of being a follower instead of a leader is that you should be able to find plenty of information that can be of great help to you. In our gardening example, besides books, you could go to SCORE and find some retired florists to help you. You could join a nursery association. You could read trade magazines. None of these resources would be available to you if you chose to invest your efforts in an obscure, albeit possibly fascinating, business or in some cutting-edge business in which you will need to teach consumers about your goods or services.

It is most important, therefore, that you choose a business that you are passionate about but that you can also implement successfully.

IN LOVE WITH ENTREPRENEURSHIP

Now we come to the second sort of entrepreneur—the individual who is more concerned with being his or her own boss than with starting a particular business. Jeff Bezos did not start Amazon.com because he was in love with books. He started it because he discovered that Internet use in the early 1990s was growing at a whopping 2,300 percent per year. Armed with that valuable insight, he analyzed the marketplace and the opportunity and concluded that the best way to tap the commercial power of the Internet was through book sales. Because it was not about the books but rather the opportunity, Bezos is the prototypical second category of entrepreneur.

There is no shortage of people who start their own business because, simply put, they want to be their own boss; that is as great a reason as any. The ability to make your own decisions, the chance to rise or fall by your own ingenuity and hard work, the opportunity to make more money, and the freedom that comes with being a small business person are some of the great joys in life. It is no wonder that many people long to start their own business. When done right, it is special.

Tony Little

If you have ever watched TV, you have probably seen infomercials starring the pony-tailed Tony Little—you know, the ones in which he sells fitness equipment. What you don't know is how Tony became the most unlikely of entrepreneurs. In 1983, when he was a Junior National Bodybuilding Champion training for the Mr. America competition, Tony was blindsided by a bus and almost killed. He suffered numerous lacerations, two herniated discs, a cracked vertebra, and a dislocated knee. His bodybuilding dreams were over.

"I went into a three-year depression," Tony told me. But after seeing a Jane Fonda exercise video, he decided that he could do that, too. So he went to a local television station and pitched a personal training television show, even though he had never done anything like that before. The show was a hit, and a few years later, Tony met the president and founder of the Home Shopping Network. They struck a deal—if Tony could sell 400 videos within four shows, they would work together on more projects. Tony sold all 400 videos . . . in 4 minutes! He went on to sell millions of products and make millions of dollars through his network appearances and infomercials.

When I asked Tony about the keys to business success, he mentioned two things:

1. "Enthusiasm sells!" If you have ever watched one of his shows, you know that is true.
2. "There is always a way to the next level." Tony's life and career are a testament to that.

The question is, what is the best sort of business for you to start? If you want to create a great business, a successful business, then here is a critical tip: *find a business that fulfills a market need.* This sentence should become your mantra. The best businesses find a need—a niche—and fill it. Do that, and almost everything else will fall into place. If you are looking for a business to start, the number one thing to discover is whether that business can sell something that people need. Figure what pain or need the customer has that you can solve.

Here are six steps to take to come to the correct decision and find that great business idea.

1. *Research, research, research, and then do some more research.* Your first step is to analyze both the marketplace and the opportunities that are available. Look around, find some businesses that are doing something that looks good to you, and learn about those businesses. How hard are they to create? How much money do they make? How much money would you need to start the business? The options are many, and there is no shortage of associations and websites that are ready to help you find the right business to start. Among the places you should look are these sites:

    - SBA.gov—"Starting and Managing a Business"
    - Startupjournal.com
    - StartupNation.com
    - FranchiseHandbook.com
    - Money.cnn.com/magazines/business2/startups/index.html

    Look for a business that catches your eye, that seems to have great potential for growth, and that is interesting to you.

2. *Product or service?* When it comes down to it, your business will provide people with a product or a service. Service businesses tend to be less expensive to start, as there is no inventory to buy or products to stock. Whereas product businesses mark up prices on scores of products and profit from the difference, service businesses, such as lawyers, doctors, and consultants, sell time and expertise. An initial decision, then, is which of these businesses best suits your temperament, skills, and goals.

Business Selection Dos and Don'ts

- Do be patient. A good selection process takes time and requires knowledge about the industry, marketplace, and competition.

- Do look for opportunity. As hockey great Wayne Gretzky once said, "Go to where the puck is going, not where it is."
- Don't pick a business that is too challenging. You will be challenged enough.
- Don't pick a business that cannot compete. Find a business, a niche, in which you have some advantage—some "secret sauce"—over the competition.

3. *Analyze your skills and experience.* Suppose you have spent your career doing marketing for major corporations. That is an invaluable skill, and it should be tapped when deciding what business is right for you. Even if it is not a marketing business, you would be foolhardy not to choose a business that does not somehow tap into your well of knowledge and skill. Now, it may be that you are tired of doing whatever it is you have been doing, and that, in fact, is why you want to start your own business. Understandable, for sure. Just be open to the option of finding a business that gives you a leg up on the competition because of your background.

4. *Consider your options.* You could create a business from scratch. You could buy an existing business. You could start a franchise. You could create a home-based business. The possibilities are many. It is important to realize that there are, in fact, a variety of options when choosing a business and learning about the pros and cons of each (read those chapters in this book, research the industry, and speak with people in those sorts of businesses).

5. *Narrow your choices.* Once you have analyzed the market, the opportunities available, your skills and experience, and your goals, you should be able to narrow your choice down to a few types of businesses. The next step may be the most important one. You must— repeat, *must*—go out and find people who own and run these sorts of businesses. Theories and books are great, but nothing beats speaking with someone who lives that business every day.

6. *Start your engines.* Whether you want to start a business because you want to start a business or because you want to spend your time pursuing your passion, it is important to do your homework and to find a niche that fills a market need. Do that, and you are on your way.

CHAPTER 3

Buying an Existing Business

Some regard private enterprise as if it were a predatory tiger to be shot. Others look upon it as a cow that they can milk. Only a handful see it for what it really is—the strong horse that pulls the whole cart.

—Winston Churchill

Starting a business from scratch is a daunting task. You must do everything right, from picking the right business, to giving it the right name, to finding the right location and lease, to getting a business license and insurance—and that is just for starters. It is no wonder that many budding business owners opt to buy an existing business.

Buying someone else's business has several advantages. First, you will not be starting from scratch; the business already exists. Second, you will not have to create "goodwill"—a favorable reputation in the community. That important aspect has already been handled by the current owner. Third, it is quicker—everything should already be in place to hit the ground running. But the main benefit of buying an existing business is that it reduces your risk. A wise man once said that an entrepreneur is "a person who is willing to take a risk with money to make money." As I've mentioned, there is no guarantee that you will make money. A business risk, a calculated business risk, is one thing that makes being in business so fun and exciting.

But notice that I said a *calculated* business risk. Remember, great entrepreneurs are not gamblers—rather, they seek to reduce risk as much as possible. Another way to do that is to buy an established business. Such businesses have a track record: you can look at the books, see how much money it made during the past few years, and have a pretty good idea of how much it will make next year. You simply do not have that sort of information (or comfort) when you create a business from scratch.

FIRST STEPS

Ideally, you will look for a business in an industry in which you have some expertise or one in which your skills are transferable. You also need to consider whether you want a business that is retail or wholesale, product or service, large or small, and so forth. As I discussed in the previous chapter, it is most important to find a business that combines your interests with the ability to make a good living. Can you see yourself working in this business every day, having (for the most part) a good time? That is a key consideration.

Where to Find Businesses for Sale

There are four main sources for finding businesses that are being sold.

1. *Online.* If you type "businesses for sale" into your favorite search engine, you will get a list of sites that broker business sales. Also check Craigslist, under the "For Sale" category you will find a listing called "Businesses." There are many there.
2. *The classifieds.* The Sunday classified ad section of your local paper will have a section called "business opportunities." That section lists small businesses for sale and the price, location, and so on.
3. *Magazines.* At the back of most trade magazines, there is usually a section for business owners selling their businesses. As almost every industry has its own trade magazine, it would behoove you to pick up one and scour the classifieds. If, for example, you wanted to buy a pizza restaurant, *Pizza Today* magazine would be a good place to look.

Sites to Check Out

- Bizbuysell.com
- Businessesforsale.com
- Bizquest.com
- Mergernetwork.com
- Businessbroker.net
- Businessmart.com
- Bizhwy.com

4. *Business brokers.* Although they are not cheap, business brokers can be an excellent resource when searching for a business to buy. A good broker will have access to businesses that you did not know were for sale and can be an important sounding board—giving you feedback and background on the pros and cons of the different businesses you are considering.

Business Brokers

It is not surprising that sellers use brokers. A good business broker can bring in more qualified prospects, weed out the phonies, and garner a better price for the business.

If you are considering hiring a business broker, be sure to find out the following:

- *The broker's experience.* The average age of a business broker is 55, and it is not hard to understand why. Good brokers need to understand finances and financing, business valuation, sales, and so forth. You need someone with experience.
- *Whether the broker is certified.* Look for a broker who is accredited by the International Business Brokers Association as a Certified Business Intermediary.

- *The services provided.* Will the broker value the business for you? Does he or she only negotiate the deal? A good broker should be a financial advisor for your end of the bargain.

Finding a Business Broker

Need a business broker? First, look in the Yellow Pages under "business brokers." Plenty of listings can also be found online. Type "business broker" and the name of your city into your search engine, and see what you get.

HOW MUCH CAN YOU EXPECT TO MAKE?

You know that you can take your money and make about 10 percent each year by investing in a mutual fund. If you can earn 10 percent from a passive investment such as a mutual fund, then what should you expect to earn from an active investment such as an established business? Although it is difficult to put a percentage figure on it, it is not unreasonable to assume that you should expect to make enough to cover the following:

- The business's operating expenses
- Your salary
- Your loan payments on any credit needed for the purchase
- An annual return on your capital

After that, for any business that you are serious about, you need to discover the following:

- *The reasons the business is being sold.* It may be that the owner is ready to retire and wants to cash out. That is a good reason to buy. It may be that the place is a dog and the owner wants to sell his or her problems. That is not a good reason to buy. Although you can expect the owner to paint the rosiest picture possible, he or she cannot legally lie, as that is fraudulent and reason to void a contract. So do your homework. Get some referrals from the owner and call them. Get some trade references and call them. Speak with neighboring businesses. Find out all you can about the business.

- *The competition.* Who are the competitors? How does the current owner deal with them? What competitive advantages would you have if you bought the place?
- *Whether there are nontransferable intangibles.* Some businesses succeed because of the owner—he or she has fantastic contacts, special skills, an "in" somewhere, that sort of thing. You must be sure that you can run the business as successfully when you become the boss.
- *Whether there are any pending changes.* Is the neighborhood stable? Does the government or your potential competitors have any plans for the area?
- *What needs to be changed.* Are the facilities in good condition? Is the decor dated? How is the plumbing and electricity? You certainly do not want to buy the place and then be stuck with major expenses. For this reason (as with a home purchase), any offer you make should be contingent on a successful inspection of the premises.
- *Profitability.* The reason you are looking at an established business is that you want to be able to project your profit and return with some accuracy. The only way to do that is to dig into the books with your accountant. Ideally, you want to see an audited set of books going back at least two years.

Business on a Shoestring

Do you want to buy a business but lack the funds to do so? Then be sure to read Chapter 18 and check out my site, MrAllBiz.com.

Of course, the $64,000 question is the price. How do you know what is a fair price for the business?

BUSINESS VALUATION 101

When it comes to valuing a business, you should consider three basic questions:

1. *What does the business own?* Clearly, a business that has invested a lot of money in assets over the years is more valuable than a business that has not. Assets can take many forms: trucks, equipment, contracts, intellectual property rights, "goodwill," and plenty more. Sellers tend to overvalue goodwill, and buyers tend to undervalue it. It is important, then, to realistically analyze the value of the business in the community.

2. *How much does the business earn?* Again, the same principle applies—a business that makes a profit of $100,000 a year is much more valuable than one that nets $35,000.

3. *Are there any intangibles to consider?* What makes the business unique and profitable? Does it have a great location, a favorable lease, fantastic employees? These are the last things to consider.

These factors should be taken into account and used to determine the value of a business. There are three ways to go about calculating business value. The first is called *price building*. The second method is called *return on investment*. The third is the *multiplier*.

Price building is a valuation method that simply looks at the hard facts—assets, goodwill, leases, real estate, and so on. Essentially, what you do here is list every asset and give it a dollar value. For example, it might look like this:

Bill's Machinery Rentals
Real estate: $125,000
Equipment: $40,000
Inventory: $25,000
Goodwill: $10,000
Total: $200,000

A price of $200,000 may or may not be right for this business. Although it is hard to say, the price builder method indicates that it is (assuming the foregoing numbers, of course).

Business Valuation

Want some help valuing a business? Try visiting Bizcomps.com and Bvmarketdata.com. FastBusinessValuations.com offers a cool, free business valuation tool.

Return on investment (ROI) looks at the business profit per year to help the buyer see the percentage return on his investment. For example, say that Bill's Machinery Rentals is asking $200,000 for the business. Is that fair? Using the ROI method, we would see:

Net profit: $100,000
Business sale price: $200,000
ROI ($100,000/$200,000): 50 percent

Using this method and these numbers the buyer would be getting a 50 percent return on his investment in a year. There are few investments out there that would allow a 50 percent ROI. Thus, a higher price for the business is probably in order.

The last method is the multiplier. Using this method, you would again look at the earnings, but you would then multiply those earnings by some factor—it varies depending on the industry—to get a final price. A factor of 3 would result in a $300,000 asking price. Of course, the battle is what that factor should be.

Yes, all of this is complicated, and that is why hiring a business broker makes a lot of sense. Although you will pay a decent commission, it may be worth it to ensure that you get a good business at a fair price.

GETTING READY TO CLOSE

Aside from pouring over the books, your due diligence will take you on one or more tours of the actual premises. Peek into the nooks and crannies. By this time, you should be aware of both the positives and the negatives of the business, and you should get your questions about the problems answered. Remember that no business is perfect—your job is to decide whether the benefits outweigh the burdens and whether the obstacles can be overcome.

Once you have found a business that you really like, your vetting process must include a final analysis with your lawyer and accountant, even if you have hired a broker. Leases and financial statements are best left to the experts. Speak with customers and suppliers whenever possible. Once your team has concluded that the business is viable, it is time to negotiate a final price and get set for closing.

As you negotiate the final deal, consider adding these provisions to the contract:

- *Link the sales price to customer retention.* Much of what you are buying is the existing customer base. But the clients, especially in a service business, may be more committed to the seller than to the business. Therefore, see whether you can link the purchase price to the number of customers who stay.
- *Have the present owner stay for a while.* This can help with the transition, as well as customer retention. You will pay him or her a consulting fee, but it is usually worth it.

CHAPTER 4

Understanding Your Potential Market

We don't want to push our ideas on to customers, we simply want to make what they want.

—Laura Ashley

This may be the most important chapter in the whole book. Why? Because everything else, from selecting the right business and marketing it to growing and even eventually selling it, hinges on having an accurate understanding of your market. Get this piece of the foundation wrong, and a lot more will go wrong—but get it right, and the world can be your oyster.

THE NEED FOR MARKET RESEARCH

You may be anxious to get started, but you cannot start, not just yet. What you need to do instead is sit back, do your research, and think. It may be that your idea is a winner, but then again, maybe it is not. The key is to analyze your idea and the market for it, and then make sure that you are not the only one who thinks you have a great business idea. A hunch simply will not do. You need hard facts.

Sure, there are businesses that start without going through this step, and yes, some may succeed—but if they do, it has more to do with luck than skill. One purpose of this book is to take luck out of the small business success equation as much as possible. Remember, great

31

entrepreneurs endeavor to reduce their risk as much as possible. Is quitting your job and starting a business fun and exciting? You bet. But you simply cannot do that without having a fairly accurate idea about what your small business is going to be, who your customers will be, why they will buy from you and not someone else, and how much money you can reasonably expect to make. Learn that, and quitting your job becomes much less risky.

The bottom line, then, is that market research is critical. Before you quit your job, before you put your hard-earned money and precious time into an untried business concept, before you risk your and your family's future, it is imperative that you do the work to make sure that your idea is feasible, and if it is not, you must learn what you need to change to make it so.

FIND A NEED AND SOLVE IT

It seems deceptively simple: if people are willing to pay for the product or service you want to sell, your business has a very good chance of success. But this begs the question—are they? Are there people who want or need what you have to sell? What will they pay for it? Why would they choose you? Will your idea fly? If there is no one around who wants your proposed product or service, your business will fail. So before you decide on a business, before you choose a name or get a business license, before you tap your 401(k) or credit cards, you must do your research.

Success Secret

Want to know the secret of successful capitalism? It is amazingly simple. *People will pay you to fulfill their needs or solve their problems.* If you can solve a problem better than anyone else, you will make a lot of money. The catch is figuring out what your customers' needs are.

Is there a market for a coffeehouse in your neighborhood? Why will people choose you over Starbucks? What can you offer that it does not? Market research will tell you. Analyzing the market and industry is a way to gather facts about potential customers and to determine the demand for your product or service. The more information you gather, the greater your chances of capturing a segment of the market. That is why you need to know your potential market before investing your time and money in any business venture—so you don't waste that time or money on an ultimately bad idea.

IS YOUR IDEA FEASIBLE?

The problem for many entrepreneurs is that they fall so much in love with their idea, they become so convinced that it can't miss, that they skip the feasibility analysis stage. Rather than thinking, they start executing. More often than not, such endeavors end with a pile of bills and a hill of broken hearts.

The Three Cs

To avoid that unenviable fate, you need to conduct a thorough analysis of what I call the "three Cs" of your new business: your *company*, your *customers*, and your *competitors*.

- What is your company going to do? What products or services will it provide? How big or small will it be? Retail or wholesale? Where will it be located? How can you best position yourself?
- Who will your customers be? Will you be selling to other businesses or to individuals? Are your customers going to be young or old? Poor or affluent? Men or women? Blue or white collar? How big is the market? What do your potential customers need? Why would they buy it from you? What do they want and will they pay for it? How can you get them to change vendors? How can you reach them? What do they read and watch? The more you crystallize your thinking, the more specific you are about who you are trying to reach, and the more you know about that market, the greater the chance that you will be able to find and entice them to patronize your business.
- Who will be your competitors? What are they doing right and wrong? What are their strengths and weaknesses? How can you capitalize on their weaknesses? Why would their customers leave and come to you? Can you undersell them? Do you want to?

Evaluating a Business

Princeton Creative Research has developed a great checklist for evaluating business ideas. Answer the following questions to evaluate your potential business or product:

- Have you considered all the advantages or benefits of the idea? Is there a real need for it?
- Have you pinpointed the exact problems or difficulties your idea is expected to solve?
- Is your idea an original, new concept, or is it a new combination or adaptation?
- What immediate or short-range gains or results can be anticipated? Are the projected returns adequate? Are the risk factors acceptable?
- What long-range benefits can be anticipated?
- Have you checked the idea for faults or limitations?
- Are there any problems the idea might create? What are the changes involved?
- How simple or complex will the idea's execution or implementation be?
- Could you work out several variations of the idea? Could you offer alternative ideas?
- Does your idea have a natural sales appeal? Is the market ready for it? Can customers afford it? Will they buy it? Is there a timing factor?
- What, if anything, is your competition doing in this area? Can your company be competitive?
- Have you considered the possibility of user resistance or difficulties?
- Does your idea fill a real need, or does the need have to be created through promotional and advertising efforts?
- How soon could the idea be put into operation?

© Princeton Creative Research, Princeton, New Jersey.

There are two possible outcomes of this research. Either you will discover that there is a need for your service, or you will find there is not. All is not lost if it is bad news. It may be that your idea simply needs to be tweaked.

This is what happened to Dave. A computer programmer, Dave decided that he would rather be a small business owner. He looked around, thought about his likes and dislikes, and decided that he wanted to buy a café. He found one that he liked and began to research the area, the competition, the clientele—everything. His research led him to the conclusion that this particular café might be a loser because the lease was not long enough and the drive-by traffic not abundant enough. Undeterred, he started over, found a better café with features that he liked, bought it, and ended up in a business that was not only enjoyable but also provided him with a good living.

Take Two

Before you abandon your idea altogether, see whether you can make it work. Those moments of clarity in which great ideas materialize are not to be dismissed lightly. Insights are valuable, and often you need only track down the right research to figure out how the puzzle pieces may fit together.

The key, once again, is to divorce yourself as much as possible from your love of this idea and to view it as objectively as possible. Put on your skeptical hat and put away those rose-colored glasses. What you need now is 20/20 vision.

WHERE TO FIND THE INFORMATION YOU NEED TO KNOW

There are many resources available that can help you track demographic data, learn about your intended industry, uncover vital information about your potential competition, see whether there is a market for your proposed business, and generally plot your course. Here are your best bets.

Trade Associations

Every industry has a trade association connected to it, and these groups offer a wealth of information. Find groups associated with your idea and contact them. Explain what you are doing and ask about survey data and research reports that are available. Get copies of their publications. Ask whether they have a start-up resource kit available—many do.

Trade Shows

Consider attending the leading association trade show. These shows will put you in touch with hundreds of like-minded individuals—people who are already successfully doing what you want to do. Meeting them and picking their brain can:

- Save you a lot of time
- Tell you exactly who your customers will be
- Provide experienced feedback about your plans
- Let you know how much it should cost to start your business
- Give you a fairly accurate idea about how much you can expect to make
- Warn you of potential pitfalls
- Save your from overly optimistic plans

Trade Magazines

Each industry usually has one or more trade magazines that may or may not be published by the leading trade association. Find the magazine for your industry and get several back copies. You should be able to notice industry trends, mistakes to avoid, potential costs, and much more.

Websites

Aside from the websites mentioned previously, here are a few more that may be helpful at this stage of your entrepreneurial journey:

- www.census.gov: The U.S. Census Bureau offers a lot of free demographic data.
- www.uschamber.com: The U.S. Chamber of Commerce, as well as your own local chamber of commerce, has plenty of resources for new start-ups.
- www.tsnn.com: This is a searchable database of trade shows worldwide.
- www.sba.gov/sbdc: Small Business Development Centers (SBDCs), run with the Small Business Administration (SBA), offer low-cost help to entrepreneurs. You may also find www.SCORE.org a valuable research resource.
- www.inside.com: The home of *American Demographics*, a monthly magazine that offers information on consumer trends, and analysis. This is a pay service.

- www.hoovers.com: Hoover's offers business and industry data, as well as sales, marketing, business development, and other information on public and private companies. This is a fee-for-content site.
- www.marketresearch.com: This site offers over 300,000 market research articles from more than 700 publishers, categorized by industry.

Social Media

Social media is a fantastic tool for conducting free market research. For example, on LinkedIn or Facebook you could join groups related to your prospective business, meet people already doing that business and people already succeeding in that industry, and learn what you need to learn. By searching on Twitter you can also find people in any industry. Connecting with these folks can be invaluable and costs you nothing but time.

Interviews and Experiential Research

Reading is great, but nothing beats actually talking with people who are associated with your potential business. There are two groups of people you need to meet and interview:

1. *Potential customers.* Finding customers for your potential business is not the easiest task in the world, but it must be done. You need to find and meet people who would be willing to pay for the product or service you want to provide. Find out what they like and dislike about their present provider, why they might change, and what would cause them to change—lower prices, a better location, more personal service, or something else.
2. *The competition.* No one knows your potential business better than people who are already running similar businesses. Become their

Stealth Market Research

Looking to find and interview potential customers? Consider going to a competitor's place of business and parking outside unobtrusively. Do not interfere with the business. Simply have a short questionnaire ready and ask people for five minutes of their time. Find out what they think of the business, what they like and dislike, and what they think could be improved.

customer, shop at their store, or use their service. Analyze their strengths, weaknesses, and profit potential.

Hire Some Experts

Find a good MBA program in your area and learn whether it participates in the Small Business Institute program. This program, run by 250 business schools nationwide, assigns graduate students to intern projects, such as market research. For a nominal fee, or no cost, you may get a great team to do some quality research for you. For more information, contact the Small Business Advancement National Center at (501) 450-5300 or SBAER.uca.edu.

Libraries

Of course, librarians are still the keepers of the research key and they can show you where to find plenty of free information. But here is something extra: *The Internet-Plus Directory of Express Library Services: Research and Document Delivery for Hire,* by editors Steve Coffman, Cindy Kehoe, and Pat Wiedensohler, lists 500 libraries nationwide that provide low-cost research services that you can tap into.

Create an Online Focus Group

How do Fortune 500 companies and presidential candidates know which commercials to run, products to pitch, or ideas to share? They use focus groups. A focus group is a group of people who are shown a product or given an idea and asked to comment on it. Find an online discussion group or forum for your industry and ask your questions there.

And again, as indicated, you can do the same thing using social media. All you have to do is ask your networks. Another option would be to post a poll to various groups and tally the results.

Telemarketing and Phone Research

Telephone research is a fairly inexpensive method, costing about one-third less than personal interviews. Using this method, you would hire a telemarketing firm to conduct a survey of a random sample of respondents. The costs associated with this method include the fee for the telemarketer, phone charges, preparation of the questionnaire, and analysis of the results.

Here are some tips when using this technique:

- Tell the interviewee up front how important his or her response is to you and that it will be a short interview (between 5 and 10 minutes).
- Avoid pauses as the respondent's interest drops.
- Keep the questions short and interesting.
- Make the survey answer options consistent.
- If you get more than 250 interviews, you are nearing a good sample.

Direct Mail

Direct mail questionnaires are also inexpensive when using bulk mail, but the response rates are usually less than five percent. The main costs of this method relate to printing of the cover letter and questionnaire, envelopes, and postage.

To increase your response rate, try these ideas:

- Include a congenial letter that explains what you are looking for and why.
- Keep your questions short.
- Limit the length of the questionnaire to two pages.
- Address the letter to a person, not to "occupant."
- Address the letters by hand (tiring, yes, but also effective).
- Include a self-addressed stamped envelope.

PUTTING IT ALL TOGETHER

After conducting all of this research, sit down, sift through it, and analyze the data. You need to get a clear idea of the strengths and weaknesses of your plan. Either you will conclude that there indeed is a market for your proposed business, or you will find there is not. If not, then it is time to go back to the drawing board. Either way, when you start your business, you will have a much better idea about what it will take to succeed, who you are going to be selling to, and what it is they want.

CHAPTER 5

Calculating Your Start-up Costs

Nothing splendid has ever been achieved except by those who dared believe that something inside them was superior to circumstance.

—Bruce Barton

Now we get down to the nitty-gritty. Having come up with an idea that works for you—financially, emotionally, intellectually, marketwise, or however else you define it—the next step is to figure out what it will actually cost to start that business and what level of sales you will need to achieve to sustain it.

ASSUMPTIONS

Figuring out your start-up costs and potential sales is a matter of making educated assumptions. In the last chapter, I suggested that you do a lot of research, much of which will come in handy here. What will it cost to start a business like the one you envision? The numbers you input here will help you figure out how much money you will need and can make, and they will apply equally to the business plan that you will write (explained in the next chapter). You will incur many expenses when starting a business from scratch. Some of these will not be encountered again—the cost of incorporation, security deposits, that sort of thing. Others are ongoing expenses—marketing materials, rent, and so on.

Calculating these costs is a four-step process. The first three steps help you understand how much money you will need for initial start-up

41

costs, the purchase of assets, and monthly expenses. The fourth step helps you understand your potential sales and how much money you will need to break even and earn a profit.

As you calculate these expenses, a word of caution is in order: be conservative, both in your analysis and when it comes time to actually purchase these things. Cash is the lifeblood of any business, but especially a new business. And, as a new business, you won't have the sales or experience to create a steady cash flow to replace what you will be spending. Don't blow it. Don't spend too much. Buy used. Buy from eBay. Horde your precious, precious capital.

> "A business has to be involving, it has to be fun, and it has to exercise your creative instincts."
>
> —Richard Branson, founder, The Virgin Group

Step 1: Calculating Start-up Expenses

Put a realistic dollar figure next to each category:

Creating your legal structure (sole proprietorship, partnership, LLC, or corporation): $

Accountant: $

Building out the space, decorating, and remodeling: $

Licenses and permits from city or county: $

Stationery and logos: $

Marketing and sales materials: $

First month's rent and security deposit: $

Insurance: $

Telephone and utility deposits: $

Signs: $

Internet and website: $

Other: $

Total: $

Step 2: Purchasing Assets

What kinds of assets will you need in order to open your doors?

Real estate: $

Furniture and fixtures: $

Equipment and machinery: $

Trucks and autos: $

Inventory: $

Supplies: $

Other: $

Total: $

Step 3: Ongoing Monthly Expenses

Keep adding—and yes, these numbers can be daunting. But the fact is, starting a business is a fairly expensive proposition. That is why it is so important to be smart and frugal. In this section, you will calculate what it is going to cost to run your business in a typical month.

Rent: $

Utilities: $

Payroll: $

Owner's draw: $

Supplies: $

Insurance: $

Transportation: $

Shipping: $

Legal and accounting: $

Advertising and marketing: $

Inventory: $

Taxes: $

Debt repayment: $

Working capital: $

Other: $

Total: $

Now what do you do? Multiply the last total by 6. That will tell you how much money you need to run the business for six months. Then, add it to the totals calculated in Steps 1 and 2. This will tell you how much money you need to open your doors and to stay in business for six months. It is ideal to have a minimum of six months' working capital in the bank before you start.

Here's an example:

Perry's Pizza Parlor

Step 1. Total start-up expenses: $22,000

Step 2. Assets to be purchased: $15,000

Step 3. Ongoing monthly expenses: $10,000

Start, then, by multiplying the ongoing monthly expenses total (Step 3) by 6—even that is optimistic, as it will likely be more than six months before your revenues will be consistent. The total is $60,000. Adding $22,000 and $15,000 (Steps 1 and 2) to that number, we see that Perry's Pizza Parlor should ideally have $97,000 to get up and running.

Note that I said *ideally.* Not all businesses will have six months' worth of working capital in the bank before they open their doors. Oh well. Although six months' worth is ideal, life and business are not always ideal, and if you will have less than that, it is still possible to make a go of it—it will just be more difficult. Starting a new business is challenging enough, but having a cash crunch from the get-go makes it that much harder. The six-month figure is intended to give you enough of a cushion to get started, open your doors, create some sales, and move forward.

Now the question is, how much pizza will Perrys need to sell to make a profit?

Step 4: Calculating Monthly Sales

Your previous research will tell you how much you can expect to make in this business. The numbers calculated in the preceding steps (especially ongoing monthly expenses) will give you a break-even threshold of sales that you need to achieve. Perry's Pizza, for example, must gross at least $10,000 a month to break even. That means it must earn $333.33 a day. If an average pizza dinner is, say, $30 a table, then Perry's must serve at least 11 tables a day to break even. Anything above that figure is profit that can be earmarked initially to pay off the start-up costs.

Although 11 tables a day may seem doable, it will likely take a while for the restaurant to achieve that level of sales. Building a name and reputation takes time. It is far more difficult and expensive to create a new customer than it is to keep an existing one; the problem for new businesses is, of course, that they have no existing customers, so *all customers* take effort. Having enough money in the bank before you start means that you will have the time necessary to build and grow your start-up.

Thus, it is reasonable to assume that it will take at least six months before Perry's, or any business, begins to make a consistent profit.

> "Reduce your plan to writing. The moment you complete this, you will have definitely given concrete form to the intangible desire."
> —Napoleon Hill, *Think and Grow Rich*

FINDING THE MONEY

In our example, Perry's Pizza should have almost $100,000 in the bank before the doors open. Where will Perry's owner find that kind of money—where will you find that kind of money? The next chapter will explain how to write a business plan that can get you the funding you need, and Chapter 8 will show you where to shop that plan.

I would also strongly suggest you check out one of my recent books, *Get Your Business Funded: Creative Methods for Getting the Money You Need,* in which I discuss this issue at length. I share 25 different and creative ways to get the money necessary to start a business. The money is there; you just need to know where to look.

CHAPTER **6**

Writing a Winning Business Plan

Setting a goal is not the main thing. It is deciding how you will go about achieving it and staying with that plan.

—TOM LANDRY

Having decided on a business that seems both emotionally and fiscally right, the next step is significant: you need to draft a business plan. All of the research that you have done up to this point will now be needed. Maybe you think that you do not want to write a business plan. That is understandable. Writing a business plan is a lot of work. In it, you analyze what you are going to do and how you plan to do it. You crunch the numbers and dissect the competition. You scrutinize risk and ponder reward. It takes a lot of thought and research. So yes, business plans are work, and you may, in fact, be the only person who ever reads yours. But if you are going to create a great small business, one that exemplifies your values and earns a fine profit, then writing a business plan is vital.

THE ROAD MAP

Pilots would never fly from Seattle to Miami without a detailed, well-researched flight plan. The flight plan helps them figure out how they will get from one place to another. It tells them how much fuel they will need, what important landmarks to look for, and how long it will take to get there. It is their blueprint for a successful trip.

Your business plan is your version of a flight plan. It is your blueprint for a successful trip. Creating a business plan forces you to carefully think through your proposed business. It will detail how much money you need to get started and stay aloft, and it will help you understand how to deal with the competition. Writing a business plan will sharpen your marketing ideas, help you understand projected costs and sales, and much more. By analyzing your business thoroughly—both the things you know well and those you do not—you will be forced to really figure out what you are getting into and what it will take to succeed. It is your road map for a prosperous, rewarding journey.

Creating and using a business plan also:

- Helps you avoid pie-in-the-sky projections
- Allows investors and lenders to analyze whether your proposed business is worth their investment dollars
- Helps you identify your market and competition
- Allows you to understand your business better

Business Plans and Established Businesses

Because a business plan projects where the company expects to go over the next few years and how it plans to get there, it can also be an important tool for established businesses. It lets them know whether they are on or off course. Smart businesses create, use, and revise business plans as necessary.

There are two major downsides to not having a business plan. First, without one, your enterprise will be a gamble. It may succeed; it may fail. Who knows? Certainly not you, that's for sure. A well-researched business plan reduces the risk of failure. Second, without a plan, you will never attract an investor. If you require outside funding to get your business started, any investor will want to see your business plan. Whether you plan to approach a bank, an angel investor, or a venture capital firm, a business plan is a prerequisite for obtaining funding.

BUSINESS PLAN ELEMENTS

What exactly goes into a business plan? Appendix B directs you to a model of a complete business plan. Generally speaking, a typical business plan will contain certain standard elements, although not necessarily in this exact order.

Title Page

The title page should include the name of the business, a logo if you have one, the owner's name, the business address and phone number, e-mail addresses, and the business website if you have one.

Executive Summary

The executive summary is the single most important part of your business plan. It is the "greatest hits" of the plan, and it is vital because it is the part that investors will focus on. If they like the executive summary, they will read more, but if they do not, all your hard work will be for naught. If you do not capture the reader's attention immediately with a dynamic executive summary, you've blown it.

The executive summary describes the main points of the plan. Even though your business will be described in detail later in the plan, a crisp three- or four-page introduction captures the attention of potential investors or lenders. It should explain what your business is, who your market is, what is different about your business, why this is a good time to undertake this venture, and why this is a unique opportunity. In addition, the amount of money being sought should be addressed.

> **Write the Executive Summary Last**
>
> Because the executive summary is so important, consider writing it last, after you have thought through the entire plan.

Table of Contents

Next comes a table of contents that lists the section titles and page numbers.

Business Description

In this section, describe exactly what your business is going to be and how you see it growing. Include a description of the products or services you will be selling, your market niche, and so on. Explain how the product or service you will be offering is different from other options on the market.

You also need to show that the market you are planning to tap is large and, ideally, growing. If yours is a local small business, say, that pizza restaurant, then you will need to explain why there is a demand for this type of restaurant in, for example, a 10-square-mile radius. If yours is a national business or an Internet business, then you will need to identify national needs for your services.

You must accurately define the target market for your business. In the case of our pizza restaurant, there may be 20,000 people in the area who would be willing to patronize this type of restaurant. This is called the *feasible market*. You must determine what your share of that feasible market will be. This is called your *market share*.

You must also explain what legal form your business will take: sole proprietorship, partnership, LLC, or corporation.

Make It Yours

Make the business plan yours. Write it in your voice, expressing your passion. Experts can smell a prepackaged, ghostwritten business plan a mile away.

Management

It is impossible to overestimate just how important your management team is to potential investors. Banks and other lenders take seriously the background and experience of the team you have assembled. Obviously, if yours is going to be a solo small business, then you need to document your own skills and abilities. But if you need others to help you run the business, you'd better have a good team in place—and if you have not yet put a team together, now would be the time to do so.

What sort of team, you ask? You may need a director of marketing, an attorney, an accountant, a director of operations, or a director of sales. It all depends on the sort of business you have in mind and what is needed to carry out your vision. Whatever it is, it is important to create a team of qualified people who can impress the top brass. In this section, then, you will list your team members and outline their backgrounds and responsibilities in the business.

Industry Description

This section is where all of your background research—analysis of your ideas and so forth—should be summarized. The information you learned from trade associations and magazines, websites and books, and interviews and meetings can be covered here. Discuss macroeconomic trends and other relevant economic indicators.

Business Planning Software

You do not have to draft a business plan from scratch, and it may not even be a good idea to do so. The model business plan found through Appendix B, for instance, is provided courtesy of Palo Alto Software, using Biz Plan Pro, a very good and easy program to use (and what many consider to be the best business planning software out there, myself included). But even if you do employ a software program, be sure to use your own language and make the plan yours as you write it.

Competition

Include all pertinent information about your competitors, including the length of time they have been in business, their locations, and their average annual sales. How will you beat the competition? Will you offer a better location, greater convenience, better prices, later hours, better quality, better service, or some other advantage? Analyze the following:

- What they do right and wrong
- How customers' needs are and are not being met by your competitors
- How you will lure their customers away

Marketing Strategy

How will you position your goods or services in the market? Are you going to cater to an upscale clientele, other businesses, or another set of customers? What will your pricing strategy be? How will you promote your business? What sort of advertising and marketing do you propose? These are the sorts of questions you must answer. If you already have contacts or contracts with clients, they should be mentioned here as well.

Sales Forecast

When making a business plan, it is important to avoid numbers pulled from out of the blue. Make no mistake about it—you will be tempted to throw in some unrealistic numbers. Why? Because one reason for creating a business plan is to get funding, and one way to get funding is to show your potential for explosive growth, so you may be tempted to create numbers to back that up.

But it is a mistake to do so, for two reasons. First, sophisticated investors and lenders can see through phony numbers, exposing you as a novice, and novices with bad numbers do not get funded. Second, even if your business plan is for your eyes only, inflated numbers can only lead to unrealistic expectations, which, in turn, can lead to business failure when you run out of money before you thought you would.

So you have been warned. It is much wiser to deal in reality, especially when making assumptions about your sales. You need to figure out how much you can expect to sell in the next few years. Yes, of course, you do not know right now, and you will be making some assumptions. All I am saying is that when doing so, err on the side of caution. Be conservative. If you sell more, great. If not, at least your plan served its purpose and warned you. Your honest sales forecast should contain the following figures:

- Monthly forecast for the coming year, both in dollars and units sold
- Annual forecast for the following two to four years, both in dollars and units sold
- The assumptions on which you have based your forecast

Where do you get this information? Time for more research! Analyze potential competitors. Consider their sales, traffic patterns, hours of operation, busy periods, prices, quality of their goods and services, and so forth. If possible, talk to customers and sales staff. Estimate as specifically as possible what your competitors make in a given month. Your sales forecast can be based on the average monthly sales of a similar-sized business operating in a similar market. Second, tap your trade associations and magazines to get an idea of what a typical business in your industry can expect to make.

Estimate your sales, but estimate conservatively. Yours is not an established business but a new start-up. It is highly unlikely that your sales will be as robust as an established competitor for at least a few years.

Finally, include in this section your sales strategy (sales objectives, target customers, sales tools, sales support), distribution plan (direct to public, wholesale, retail), and pricing structure (markups, margins, break-even point).

Financial Analysis

Here you will use your previous analyses to explain how much it will cost to get your business up and running and how much it will cost to keep it going. You will also explain how much money you are asking for and how it will be spent. This section will be based on several financial spreadsheets: balance sheets, profit and loss statements, and cash flow projections. Here again, you will be making financial assumptions, and these assumptions can make or break your business. If you do not understand financial planning, you need to learn it or hire a professional to help you. It is that important.

This financial analysis is often the most difficult part of a business plan for small business people. It is easy to wax poetic about your great idea and how it will make the gang rich. But putting real numbers to those projections is hard work. Even so, you have to do it. You have to crunch some realistic numbers to go along with your realistic plan.

Accounting Software

Computer programs can be of great assistance when it comes time to analyze your business's finances.

Start with an *income and expense statement*. It is what it sounds like—a projection of income and expenses. It should include an opening balance sheet, detailed income projections, operating expenses, and a financial forecast for the next year of operation and for the following two years. It should also include a cash flow forecast of inflows and outflows on a monthly basis for the next year.

Where do you get this information? The usual suspects: competitors, suppliers, trade associations, chambers of commerce, websites, and trade publications.

Next you will need to include a *profit and loss statement*. This is a summary of your projected business transactions over a period of time. It explains the difference between your income and expenses.

Café Coffee
Projected Profit and Loss Statement

Projected Income, Fiscal Year 1	***$187,900***
Projected expenses	
Cost of goods sold	$76,300
Labor	$33,700
Bank fees	$250
Equipment	$4,900
Insurance	$2,800
Marketing	$6,200
Postage and shipping	$1,200
Phone	$2,400
Printing	$1,900
Supplies	$7,200
Taxes	$6,800
Projected total expenses	**$143,650**
Projected net profit	**$44,250**

Tip: A profit and loss statement is also known as a *P&L statement* or an *income statement*.

The *balance sheet* of the business is a snapshot of the venture at a particular point in time. It should include a projection of assets and liabilities.

The *cash flow statement* shows how much cash your business will need, when, and where it will come from. For example, how much inventory will be required, and what will it cost every month? The cash flow statement is important because it forces you to look realistically at the bottom line and determine whether you are going to make enough money to handle your debts.

The financial analysis section of your business plan should also analyze the use of any loan proceeds you are seeking, including the amount of the loan and the term. Finally, you need to disclose your financial situation and how much you will be personally contributing to the venture.

Exit Strategy

Your business plan should conclude with a proposed exit strategy. Your strategy may be a sale of the business or retirement.

Appendix

The appendix should contain the following elements:

- Substantiation documentation and articles of interest
- Names and contact information for your references
- Name of your present bank
- Names of your lawyer and accountant
- Personal net worth statement
- Letters of intent (possible orders, letters of support)
- Insurance coverage (policies, type, and amount of coverage)

THE BOTTOM LINE

Writing is rewriting. Your business plan is no different. You will need to write and rewrite it. But it is a healthy process that will give you a much better understanding of your business, what it will take to succeed, and what risks to expect. It will be a lot of work, but it will be worth it. Either you will get funded, or, at a minimum, you will have learned a great deal about how to make your business fly. Either way, you win.

CHAPTER **7**

Structuring Your Business

The first thing we do, let's kill all the lawyers.

—WILLIAM SHAKESPEARE, *Henry VI, Part 2*

As you begin to build the foundation for your small business, one of the first decisions you will need to make is the legal form that your business will take. You have four options: it can be a sole proprietorship, a partnership, a limited liability company, or some type of corporation. This chapter will help you make that important decision. However, as each business form has its own unique legal and financial ramifications, and although you can theoretically make a choice based on your supposition about what is right for your business, it is better to do so in conjunction with a lawyer and an accountant.

SOLE PROPRIETORSHIPS

A sole proprietorship is the cheapest and easiest form of business that you can start. All you need to do is name the business, get a business license from your city or county, publish a fictitious business name statement in a local newspaper, open your doors, and you are, quite literally, in business. It should cost about $100 to start a sole proprietorship.

Although the good news about sole proprietorships is that they are inexpensive and easy to create, the bad news is not insignificant. The main problem is that, legally speaking, you and the business are one and the same. If something goes wrong down at the shop, you are personally

57

Self-Employment

According to the U.S. Census Bureau, roughly 23 million of the 29 million small businesses in the United States are self-employed, single-person businesses. If this describes you, then you might want to check out my new website just for you—TheSelfEmployed.com. It is chock-full of information and special offers specifically for the solo-business people out there.

---

on the hook. Say, for instance, that you own a pizza parlor as a sole proprietor. One day, one of your delivery boys gets drunk and kills a pedestrian while attempting to deliver a pizza. Because he was drunk, your insurance would not cover the damages. Because he worked for you and was performing a work-related duty, your business would be liable for his actions. And because your business is a sole proprietorship, you personally, and your personal assets (cars, home, retirement), could be tapped to pay the damages from the resulting lawsuit. Obviously, then, starting a business as a sole proprietor is probably not a good idea, legally speaking.[1]

Aside from putting you in legal and financial jeopardy, another problem with this form of business is that it often means you will be working alone. It is not called a "sole" proprietorship for nothing. You will have no partners around to work with or bounce ideas off. Maybe a partnership is the way to go then, you say? Let's see.

PARTNERSHIPS AND LIMITED PARTNERSHIPS

A business partnership is a lot like a marriage. Because you and your partner will be spending an inordinate amount of time together, making decisions together, making individual decisions that will affect the whole, and being together in both good times and bad, you need to think very carefully about (1) whether you really want a partner, and if so, (2) who fits the bill.

---

[1] Throughout this book, I will be giving you legal tips. As I am an attorney, please understand that such tips are based on my real-world experience as a business lawyer. Please also know that the legal tips in this book are just that and should not and cannot be construed as legal advice; *they are no substitute for conferring in person with an attorney who is familiar with your business and situation.*

Legally speaking, a partnership is even more precarious than a sole proprietorship, if that is possible. Why? Because not only are the partners individually liable for the business's debts, just as a sole proprietor is, but also *either partner* can get the whole partnership into debt. When that happens, both partners are legally liable for the debt. The danger is that your partner can make some dumb decisions, sign a bad contract or some such thing, and get the partnership into debt, and you will be personally responsible for that debt.

Another thing to consider is the emotional aspect of having a partner. Do you want a partner? Can you share the power? One nice thing about being a sole proprietor is that you alone are the boss; you have no one to answer to except yourself. But having a partner means, well, you have a partner. You will need to listen to your partner, respect her, defer to her judgment when necessary, and be willing to share responsibility for all decisions and actions. And remember, partnerships do not always work out—best friends who become partners do not always stay best friends.

Conversely, though, there is plenty to be said for having a partner. The first benefit is significant—namely, a partner gives you someone to work with, to share ideas and brainstorm with, and to bounce ideas off of. Also, a partner shares the workload. One bad thing about working alone is that there are too many hats to wear: chief executive officer, head of sales, marketing director, and, too often, receptionist and secretary. Partners help alleviate that burden. Finally, a business partner is someone who shares the financial commitments of the business, and that should be a relief.

It is important to consider carefully the pros and cons of having a partner. Then, should you decide that the benefits outweigh the burdens, you will need to find someone with whom you can work well. Even if you get along swimmingly, be sure to check out your potential partner's background, credit history, and so on. Get some references and call them. This is a very important decision, so act accordingly.

Finally, if you decide to go the partnership route, you are strongly advised to have a partnership agreement, preferably one that is drafted by an attorney. This agreement should spell who will contribute what, who will do what, and, if the partnership ends, who will get what. It is a very important document.

> **Test It**
>
> If you have someone in mind for a partner, it is a good idea to start out working together on a project or two. See whether your styles are complementary and whether you have more fun than problems. After all, one reason you want to start your own business is to enjoy your work more, and your potential partner should add to that.

There are two types of partnerships: general and limited. Whereas in a general partnership, all partners are equal—each can incur obligations on behalf of the partnership, and each has unlimited liability for the debts of that partnership—in a limited partnership, things are different. Usually there is only one person running the show, the general partner. The other partners are called *limited partners.* Limited partners also have limited liability and limited input. They cannot incur obligations on behalf of the partnership, and they do not participate in the daily operations of the partnership. A limited partner is essentially a passive investor.

A limited partner's liability is limited to the amount of his or her financial contribution to the partnership, whereas the general partner has unlimited liability to go along with his unlimited power. This structure allows the general partner the freedom to run the business unfettered and gives the limited partners limited liability if things go wrong. Another important benefit of the limited partnership, aside from the diminished liability of the limited partners and the freedom of the general partner, is that it pays no income tax. Income and losses are attributed proportionally to each partner and accounted for on their individual tax returns. A limited partnership is often the structure of choice for real estate and stock investment groups.

CORPORATIONS AND THE LIMITED LIABILITY COMPANY (LLC)

As you now know, the problem with general partnerships and sole proprietorships is the personal liability that accompanies business debts and other liabilities; these entities do not shield the business owner from legal responsibility. Not so for corporate entities. In fact, one of the main reasons to incorporate is to legally shield your personal assets from business debts. Consider our pizza parlor fiasco. If you had incorporated and one of your drivers had negligently killed someone, only the *business* assets would be at risk. Although still unpleasant, it sure beats having your personal assets at risk. Creditors are limited to the assets of the corporation for payment and may not collect directly from the shareholders.

Pros and Cons of Incorporating

Pros

- The "corporate shield" protects you from legal responsibility and personal liability.
- Corporations are theoretically infinite—they can last in perpetuity. Sole proprietorships and partnerships usually end upon the death, retirement, disability, or bankruptcy of the sole proprietor or partner.
- As the corporation grows, shareholders can continue to share in the profit, but they do not have to stay and run the business. This is not normally true for sole proprietorships and partnerships.
- You may be taken more seriously if your business has an "Inc." behind the name.
- There are many tax advantages to having a corporation, including pension and profit-sharing options.

Cons

- Creating a corporation can be expensive.
- Shareholders have little say in day-to-day operations.
- Corporations are subject to greater government regulation and scrutiny.
- The corporate tax code is complex, is difficult to understand, and will likely require the yearly assistance of a lawyer or accountant.

There are several types of corporations. The two main types are the *S corporation* and the *C corporation* (S and C are subsections of the IRS Code). Although there are many differences between S and C corporations, two stand out.

The first is that C corporations are taxed twice: once when profits are realized and a second time when those profits are passed on to the shareholders. The advantage of the S corporation is that it does not pay a corporate tax at all; instead, its shareholders report profits and losses on their personal tax returns, and therefore profits are taxed only once.

Another difference between the two types of corporations has to do with size. For the most part, C corporations are large, publicly traded businesses. When you see a business whose shares are bought and sold on the New York Stock Exchange, it is a C corporation. In fact, the ability to freely sell shares is one of the main advantages of a C corporation. People who start businesses with an exit strategy of going public typically start C corporations. Although most large businesses are C corporations, some small businesses choose this form of structure as well, for one very good reason: C corporations can deduct 100 percent of the health insurance paid to employees (including yourself).

The double-taxation whammy of the C corporation pushes many small business owners toward S corporation status, which is, generally speaking, intended for and used by smaller businesses. There are certainly more pros than cons to starting your small business as an S corporation:

- S corporations offer limited personal liability.
- S corporations pay no corporate taxes. Rather, profits and losses flow through your individual tax return.
- A sole owner of an S corporation does not have to pay FICA tax—that is, Medicare and the self-employment tax, which together amount to roughly 15 percent on the first $75,000 you earn. That said, an S Corp with employees still must pay the employer's 50 percent share of FICA taxes, while the employee will pay the other 50 percent.

The bad news is that there are restrictions on S corporations: you can have no more than 100 shareholders, and you cannot have any preferred stock.

Advice

Whether to incorporate as an S corporation or a C corporation is a decision that should be made in conjunction with your attorney.

Another type of corporation is called a *professional corporation*. This type is intended for professionally licensed small business owners only, and the professional can be the only shareholder. The types of professionals who can take part in this plan vary by state, but usually lawyers, doctors, dentists, accountants, and psychologists are included. It is important to understand that this type of corporation cannot shield the owner from a malpractice award.

A *limited liability company*, or LLC, is a hybrid that combines the best features of corporations, sole proprietorships, and partnerships. It has become very popular among new entrepreneurs, for several good reasons.

First, and best, like S and C corporations, LLCs protect their owners, called *members*, from personal liability for business indebtedness. Second, like partnerships and sole proprietorships, LLCs are fairly informal. The nice thing about sole proprietorships and partnerships is that they are less structured than corporations, especially with regard to taxes. The tax code is full of detailed rules that apply to corporations. These complicated rules and tax rates create a lot of bookkeeping and legal issues for corporations. Sole proprietorships and partnerships, on the other hand, simply have business profits and losses "flow through" to the individual taxes of the owners. It's much simpler. So, the second advantage of the LLC is that its members can choose to be taxed as sole proprietorships and partnerships are, or they can choose a corporate tax structure if that is more advantageous.

By combining the best of corporations (the so-called corporate shield) and the best of sole proprietorships and partnerships (ease of creation and flow-through taxation), the LLC has become the business form of choice for many small businesses.

LLCs are easy and inexpensive to create (the filing fee charged by your state will be less than what you would pay to incorporate), and they can be formed with only one member (unlike a corporation, which requires officers and a board of directors). Members can use capital or property to buy into the LLC, and they will receive a percentage share of the business that reflects their contribution. When profits are distributed, members will usually get an amount commensurate with their ownership share (again, because LLCs are so flexible, you can even decide to distribute profits unequally if you choose).

There are two types of LLCs. The first is called *member managed.* In this type, all of the owners (there is no limit on the number, but it is usually a half dozen or less) actively run the business. The second is called *manager managed.* Here, the owners have managers running the business. Typically, only members have the right to vote on company issues.

Do It Yourself

There are all sorts of ways to create an LLC or corporation on your own. Check out online sites like RocketLawyer.com, as well as books. Nolo Press puts out some excellent resources, including *Legal Guide to Starting and Running a Small Business,* by Fred Steingold, and *Your Limited Liability Company: An Operating Manual,* by Anthony Mancuso.

LLC laws are state specific, and each state has different requirements. Generally speaking, though, to create an LLC, you will need to file *articles of organization* or a *certificate of formation* with the proper state office and pay a fee. How much? Roughly $75 in most states. After you file the proper documents, you will need to draft your *operating agreement.* In it, you will detail how much the members have contributed, what their percentage of ownership is, how you will run the business, how you will handle distributions, and so on.

Once formed, an LLC can protect you from business liabilities, create an easy structure for running the business, and make tax time easier. All in all, it's a good idea for most small businesses.

Comparing Business Entities

	Protection from Personal Liability	Formalities	Transfer of Ownership	Perpetual Existence	Tax Benefits	Ease of Creation	Cost	Used by Small Businesses
Sole Proprietorship	No	Few	Easy	No	None	Easy	Minimal	Often
General Partnership	No	Few	Difficult (need partner's approval)	No	None	Moderate (a partnership agreement is advisable)	Minimal	Fairly often
Limited Partnership	Limited partners only	Need Partnership agreement	Yes	No	Some	Moderate	Moderate	Rarely
C Corporation	Yes	Many	Easy	Yes	Many	Difficult (usually requires a lawyer)	Expensive	Rarely
S Corporation	Yes	Many	Moderate (must find a buyer)	Yes	Many	Difficult (usually requires a lawyer)	Expensive	Fairly often
Professional Corporation	Yes	Many	No	No	Many	Difficult (usually requires a lawyer)	Expensive	Sometimes
LLC	Yes	Moderate	Easy	Yes	Many	Moderate (may require a lawyer)	Moderate	Often

CHAPTER **8**

Get Your Business Funded

If you would know the value of money, go and try to borrow some.

—Benjamin Franklin, *Poor Richard's Almanac*

The previous chapters were intended to help you put the foundation of your business in place: coming up with your best idea, figuring out what it will cost to create a business, drafting a business plan, and choosing the right legal structure are the basic building blocks of any successful small business. Now you can build on that solid foundation, starting with this chapter. Getting the money to realize your dream can happen only if you have a solid foundation in place; any lender or investor will want to see that those pieces are set. Even if you are going to self-fund the business—through savings, credit cards, or some other plan—this foundation is no less important, as it is the basis for creating a small business that will last.

If you have done the work suggested in the previous chapters, you know exactly how much money you will need to get started and stay open, which puts you far ahead of most new small business entrepreneurs, who have only a vague idea of how much money they will need. The $64,000 question—maybe literally—is where will you find the money to start your business?

There are many, many sources of funding—which is good, because it is highly unlikely that you will secure all of your required funding from one place. Maybe you will combine personal savings and credit cards with an SBA loan and a gift from an uncle. Who knows? While finding

67

the money to fund the dream is always a challenge for an entrepreneur, it is part of the job. Yes, it will be tough, you may get discouraged, and you may not raise as much money as you want; but remember, countless new business owners have found the money to start their businesses, and if they did it, you can, too. Stick with it. If you have a good idea and a solid plan, you can do it.

THE USUAL SUSPECTS

The vast majority of small businesses are started, at least partly, using the entrepreneur's own funds. Indeed, even if you are looking to outside investors, most will want to see that you are sharing some of the financial risk. Yes, tapping your savings for a new, untried venture is a scary thought, but remember, an entrepreneur is a person who is willing to take a risk with money to make money. Risking some of your own money, then, is part of the job description.

Where do you find that money? If you have savings, you will need to use at least some. If you may be getting an inheritance down the road, see whether you can get an advance on it. Many new small business owners use their IRA or 401(k) funds—damn the penalties, full steam ahead. If you still have a stock portfolio, consider selling it. You will have to be creative and a bit bold, but that is likely what will be needed if you are going to make your dream come true.

Commit!

"The moment one definitely commits oneself, then providence moves too. All sorts of things occur to help one that would have never otherwise have occurred. I have learned a deep respect for one of Goethe's couplets: 'Whatever you can, or dream you can, begin it. Boldness has genius, power and magic in it.'"

—W. H. Murray, *The Scottish Himalayan Expedition*

CREDIT CARDS

Another very popular option for funding a start-up company is the credit card. According to one study, almost half of all businesses use credit cards to help with their start-up costs. Again, it is easy to see why this is a popular choice. Credit cards are readily available, you don't need an investor or lender to say "yes," and you can pay it back in installments. The problem is that it is very easy to get in over your head with credit card debt. Before you go running up the cards, charging that new computer and office furniture, some words of warning are in order.

The Credit Card Trap

Excessive credit card debt is one of the most common money problems that small business people face, and it can be a major factor leading to small business failure. Many of us have learned the hard way about the credit card trap. You know what that is, right? Charging or taking cash advances, getting stuck with a huge bill, paying the minimum, and watching the interest grow every month, thus ensuring that the balance is never paid off. It is a trap because you are caught in a predicament that is difficult to get out of, and it ensures that your small business will remain off-kilter.

For example, let's say that you charge $7,000 to get your new business off the ground. Reasonable, no? Let's further assume that you have an interest rate of 17 percent (this is a credit card, after all). How long do you think it will take you to pay off that balance, making a minimum payment of 2 percent? Three years? Let's do a little math. A monthly interest payment of 17 percent on $7,000 is $104. Add that to your balance, and your balance next month will be $7,104. Two percent of that figure is $142—your minimum payment. If you pay only the minimum, it will take (get ready for this) more than 40 years to pay off the entire balance. Don't worry; it gets worse. You'll also end up paying almost $14,000 in interest on your $7,000 balance.

Credit Card Smarts

Getting stuck with excessive credit card debt is one of the worst things that can happen to your new small business. If you do use credit cards to help fund your start-up, you absolutely must get those balances down as quickly as possible. Here's how:

- *Pay more than the minimum.* The first way to avoid the credit card trap is to pay more than the minimum payment due—as much as you can afford. In the previous example, the 2 percent minimum payment amount will go down every month as the principle decreases. However, if you keep paying the original minimum payment of $142 instead of the new, lower minimum, you will cut the time it takes to pay off your credit card debt from 40 years to about 5 years.
- *Do the balance transfer dance.* One of the easiest and best methods of lowering both your monthly credit card payments and your company's overall credit card debt is to transfer the balance on cards with high interest rates to cards with much lower rates—say, 4.9 percent. Look for introductory teaser rates.

Credit cards, although useful and convenient, can kill even the best small businesses. Use them to fund your start-up, but do so with a plan to pay them off as soon as possible.

THE FRIENDS AND FAMILY PLAN

The next most common method of funding your start-up is to find friends and family members who believe in you and your vision and are willing to invest in your new company. Again, this is where your business plan will be necessary. If you can show potential investors a plan that makes sense, the chance of getting them to invest greatly increases. A great thing about this option is that friends and family tend to lend or invest either interest free or at very low interest rates, which makes your job much easier. Especially at the beginning of your venture, capital is precious and must be, if not horded, at least highly respected. You need to keep your overhead as low as possible; low interest on debts helps, and that is why this can be an attractive option.

Example: When Chris Haney and Scott Abbott came up with the idea for the board game *Trivial Pursuit*, they were unemployed journalists with little more than a novel idea. They drafted a business plan and then started talking to everyone they knew about investing in the fledgling company. Finally, they pestered 32 friends, relatives, and former colleagues into investing in the business, raising about $60,000 in the process.

The danger, of course, is that most small businesses are not home runs like *Trivial Pursuit.* Far more likely, you will create a successful business that makes a nice profit and affords you some freedom and a good standard of living. But if that does not happen, if the business does not fly, owing money to friends and relatives for a failed business venture is not a pleasant experience. You have been warned.

BANKS AND CREDIT UNIONS

Of all investments that a bank or credit union can make, lending money to an untried, brand-new start-up is just about the most risky. Home loans are secured by collateral, as are car loans. Loans to existing businesses offer some security because the business has a track record. But the new start-up has none of those things, and so getting a conventional bank loan for a new business is not always easy, especially in the past few years. But the good news when it comes to bank loans is that banks want to lend you money. That is their business, and many are working hard to get money in the hands of their small business customers.

Other entrepreneurs get bank loans for their new ventures every day, and if they did, so can you. Of course, that often means using your home as collateral or signing a personal guarantee for the loan. The problem with a personal guarantee is that incorporating to reduce your personal liability will be a waste of time if you sign a personal guarantee for a bank loan. Then again, entrepreneurs have been known to do almost anything to get the show on the road, and that may be the price you have to pay.

The upshot is that to get a business loan, you need to think like a banker.

THE FOUR CS

When lenders look to extend credit, they are most concerned with the four Cs:

1. *Capacity.* Do you have the ability to repay the loan? A bank will want to see that your business has sufficient cash flow to service the loan, and thus it will ask to see your financial statements. A bank is much more likely to loan to a business that has been around for a while and has a track record. New start-ups with little history fail this test. For this reason, new businesses (and certainly established ones, too) should consider obtaining a loan guaranteed by the SBA.

2. *Collateral.* Can you secure the loan with some sort of collateral? If the answer is yes, then the likelihood of getting a loan is much greater. Just as banks do not make home loans without securing the loan by getting a deed of trust on the property, they also require some sort of collateral to secure a business loan. If you do not have collateral, you will likely need a cosigner who does.

3. *Character.* Does your business have a history of repaying loans on time? Do you have a history of paying on time? Because you will likely be asked to sign a personal guarantee for any business loan you get, your personal credit history is important.

4. *Capital.* How much money do you need, and why do you need it? You'll need to come to the bank with financial statements, a business plan, and a solid explanation for the exact amount you want, how it will be used, and when it will be paid back.

Check Your Credit Reports

Before you apply for any loan, you should know what is in your credit report. Start by getting a copy of your report from the three credit reporting agencies. They joined forces for this purpose and created a single spot to get a consolidated report covering all three agencies (Experian, Equifax, and TransUnion): AnnualCreditReport.com, which is free. You can also get a copy of your business's credit history from Dun & Bradstreet: www.dnb.com.

If you pay an account on time, that shows up on your credit report. If you make a late payment, that will be there, too. A late payment here or there will not affect your ability to get a business loan, but a pattern of late payments will. Charge-offs, judgments, and bankruptcies certainly hurt your cause.

Next, check for errors and outdated information. Anything that is more than seven years old (aside from a bankruptcy) should no longer appear on your credit report. More important, credit reports are rife with factual errors. One billion pieces of credit are reported every month, and along the way, incorrect information ends up on far too many credit reports. The good news is that the Fair Credit Reporting Act mandates that *any* incorrect information on your credit report must be removed once you bring the mistake to the credit reporting agency's attention. Usually this takes a few months, so well before you are going to apply for a business loan, you are advised to get copies of your credit reports and challenge anything that looks fishy.

The Fair Credit Reporting Act

The Fair Credit Reporting Act is a powerful tool that you can use to your advantage. It mandates that incorrect information *must* be deleted from your credit report if *any* part of an account is incorrect. For example, if a legitimately late account *also* has wrong information attached to it (your name is spelled wrong, an account number is incorrect) and you challenge it, the account must be deleted from your report. This is one way people "clean up their credit."

Other Considerations

Aside from the four Cs, banks may also look at two additional factors when determining whether to give you a loan (called *underwriting*). Let's call these the two Es:

1. *Equity.* When you buy a home and begin to make payments, you build equity. If your house is worth $100,000 and you owe $75,000, then you have $25,000 in equity. It is the actual cash value of the property. Well, the same is true for your business. Ironically, one way

to get a business loan is to prove that you don't need one, and the way to do that is to build equity in your business. This can be done by retaining earnings or by receiving a cash injection from an owner. Most banks like to see that your debt is no more than four times your equity. You need equity to make sure your ratios pencil out.

Tip: The amount that your business owes compared with the amount it is worth is called its *debt to equity ratio*. Your balance sheet will help you determine this.

---

2. *Experience.* More relevant to a new start-up, your experience in the business and your experience in the area that the loan is going toward is a final factor that a banker will look at when conducting a lending analysis.

So, do you qualify for a business loan? Let's find out.

1. Do you have a good credit history? ( ) Yes ( ) No
2. Are your taxes up to date? ( ) Yes ( ) No
3. Can the business repay the loan? ( ) Yes ( ) No
4. Does the business have equity? ( ) Yes ( ) No
5. Does the business have little debt? ( ) Yes ( ) No
6. Do you, the owner, have your own money invested in the business? ( ) Yes ( ) No
7. Does the business have collateral? ( ) Yes ( ) No
8. Would you be willing to personally guarantee the loan? ( ) Yes ( ) No
9. Do you have a solid management team? ( ) Yes ( ) No
10. Do you have a business plan? ( ) Yes ( ) No

Scoring

Unless you answered "Yes" to all questions, you may have a hard time getting a loan.
(Courtesy of the Small Business Administration)

SBA LOANS

The U.S. government knows how important small businesses are to the U.S. economy. Therefore, it created and funds the SBA, whose mission is to help the country's small businesses succeed. One way the SBA accomplishes that goal is by guaranteeing certain loans made by lenders to small businesses. By acting as a guarantor, the SBA reduces the risk to the lender, and so many more small business loans are made. What you want to do, then, is find a bank or credit union that deals with SBA-guaranteed loans.

SBA Backgrounder

The Reconstruction Finance Corporation was a loan program created by President Herbert Hoover to help businesses hurt by the Great Depression. When Franklin D. Roosevelt was elected to the White House in 1932, he adopted and expanded the program. However, during World War II, many small businesses were unable to compete against large corporations and their government contracts, so Congress created the Smaller War Plants Corporation in 1942. Like its predecessor, this corporation provided loans to entrepreneurs and businesses. After the war, the corporation was dissolved and the U.S. Commerce Department's Office of Small Business assumed some of its responsibilities. Finally, in 1952, President Dwight D. Eisenhower signed legislation to create a full-time small business agency—the Small Business Administration.

There are many SBA loans and programs. Following are the main ones.

7(a) Loan Guaranty

This is the granddaddy of them all. The 7(a) is the SBA's bread-and-butter loan program. Not only can a 7(a) loan be used for start-up purposes, but it is flexible enough to be used for working capital, equipment, furniture, and real estate. The length of the loan can range from 10 to 25 years. Current loan limits are $5 million. For more information, go to www.sba.gov, "Loans and Grants."

7(m) Microloan Program

This program is smaller. The terms of the loans are shorter, and the amounts that you can borrow are less. Here, you can get up to $50,000 for working capital or for the purchase of furniture, supplies, inventory, fixtures, or equipment. You cannot buy real estate with these funds. Note, too, that the loans are not made through traditional lenders— instead, nonprofit organizations that have experience lending and offering business assistance make the microloans.

504 Certified Development Company Loan Program

This program offers long-term, fixed-rate loans for real estate and machinery purchases or for modernization and expansion. The usual 504 deal requires that the small business contribute at least 10 percent of the funds; a private lender will fund approximately 50 percent, and the 504 loan secured from a certified development company covers 40 percent. The 504 share of the deal can go up to $1.5 million (and up to $2 million in some cases).

Express Loans (Community Express, Patriot Express, SBA Express)

Express loans are what you would expect—quick loans. Decisions are made in 36 hours. Loans for less than $25,000 require no collateral, and loans can go as high as $350,000.

Export Loans

The SBA has three different export loan programs: Export Express, Export Working Capital, and the International Trade Loan Program.

SBA Help

The SBA has one other program that you should know about if you are looking for start-up capital. The Loan Prequalification program will analyze your loan package, up to $250,000, before you take it to a lender. An SBA-designated liaison will review your application, offer suggestions, make corrections, and help strengthen your submission.

The SBA has all sorts of loan packages, so you should check out both their website and your local SBA lender to learn more.

EQUITY FINANCING

Going into debt, or *debt financing,* is one way to fund a business. The other is called *equity financing.* Many growth-stage small businesses use equity financing to finance expansion plans. As the term implies, equity financing occurs when you sell part of the business in exchange for capital. The deal can take many forms, from selling shares in a corporation to adding a partner to adding members to your LLC. As in the start-up stage, equity financing often comes from nonprofessional investors such as family members, friends, business associates, or industry colleagues.

The other form of equity funding comes from professional investors known as venture capitalists (VCs) and angel investors. VCs are typically groups of wealthy individuals or financial institutions, and most specialize in a few industries that the members know well. In Silicon Valley, for example, the lion's share of VCs are former computer executives who want to invest in new high-tech start-ups. Angels are individuals who want to invest in growth opportunity businesses. VCs, although certainly on the lookout for the Next Big Thing, more often look to invest in companies that are three to five years old and have a solid plan and sound management team in place able to execute that plan. VCs will look at and listen to hundreds of pitches and plans before investing in the cream of the crop.

ANGEL INVESTORS

Angel investors are, as the name implies, blessed people who invest in start-up ventures. Typically, angels are individuals who have made a lot of money themselves and are looking to reinvest some of their capital. Usually they have made their money in a particular industry and prefer to invest their funds in that industry.

Where do you find angels? Usually they are found through networking. Speak with your lawyer and accountant. Check with stockbrokers, real estate agents, bankers, customers, sales reps, and industry colleagues.

You will need to be persistent, as you never know where that angel may come from. It is also possible to find angels online by doing a Google search. Of course, finding an angel will not be easy, but again, it is possible. If and when you do find one, here are three steps that can help you get a deal:

1. *Prepare your elevator pitch. Elevator pitch* is business jargon for a proposal that can be explained in about 30 seconds—the length of time you might ride in an elevator with an investor. Your elevator pitch must be intriguing, intelligent, short, and powerful, and it should motivate someone to want to know more. Because the first thing you will do when approaching any potential angel is to pitch your idea, you need to have a snappy one ready.
2. *Do your homework.* If your pitch works and you get a meeting, you must come prepared. Of course, your business plan must be flawless—that's a given. Equally important, though, is having some background knowledge about the potential investors. How did they make their money? What are their backgrounds? What else have they funded? Learn all that you can about the investors before going to the meeting. Pique their interest, show potential, and create rapport. Be enthusiastic and know your business plan inside out.

> **Angels and Mentors**
>
> Many angels like being mentors, and they may be willing to use their own contacts to help you find additional funding or assistance. Ask.

3. *Follow up.* If the meeting goes well, make sure to get some references from the angel for other deals he has done. Call the references and make sure the angel is easy to work with and legitimate. If everything checks out, then congratulations are in order!

VENTURE CAPITAL

If an angel investor is an individual with a lot of money, a VC firm is a group of similar people with even more money. VCs can be made up of family members, investment banking firms, professional investors, or some other group that is looking to invest in businesses with big potential. But understand that most VCs are interested in businesses that need at least $250,000, and even then, the possibility of landing VC money is remote at best. A VC firm may receive more than 1,000 proposals a year, and the vast majority are rejected. The qualities that VC firms look for are uniqueness, growth potential, and a strong management team. Unless yours is a small business with huge potential, you would be best advised to look for funding elsewhere.

DEALING WITH INVESTORS

When a business wants to bring in an investor, whether it is a family member, an angel investor, or someone else, there are several ways to do the deal, depending on the legal structure of the business.

Sole Proprietorships and Partnerships

If the business is a sole proprietorship or a partnership, the money could be considered a loan that will be repaid by an agreed-upon time at an agreed-upon interest rate. Alternatively, you could say that the investor is buying a part of the business and will receive a percentage of the profits every month. This is something to be negotiated.

Corporations

When a company is a corporation (either an S or a C corporation), the two basic methods for raising revenue are the sale of debt and the sale of equity. The sale of debt is a deal whereby the invested money is considered a loan. These are called *debt securities.* Some investors like debt securities because they take precedence over equity securities. That is, in a risky start-up, if something goes wrong, the investor's loan is legally protected and given higher legal priority than your ownership interest.

One reason you might want to structure the investment as a debt security is taxes. If you simply sell this investor's stock, when he or she is repaid, it will likely be considered a dividend. When your business pays someone a dividend, it is not deductible on the business's taxes. If you structure the deal as the sale of debt (a loan), however, your repayments are considered interest payments, and thus they can be deducted from the business's taxes. By structuring the deal as a loan, then, your business would pay less in taxes.

The second method for structuring the deal is simply to sell your investor's shares of the corporation, called a *sale of equity* or a *sale of securities*. Many investors like this option because it gives them an actual ownership interest in the businesses. The sale of common stock to an investor carries with it the right to participate in earnings and the right to vote on the board of directors. This is the most common type of corporate financing arrangement.

How much stock should the investor receive? It is impossible to say. It depends on the size of your business, the amount of money he is investing, how much authority you want him to have, and so on. You will need to discuss this with your lawyer.

LLCs

If you own an LLC, things are a bit different. LLCs do not have "shares" of stock, as a corporation does. Instead, its owners are called members, and you sell membership shares. If you want to sell your investor shares of your LLC, you are certainly free to do so. However, if you do, this may change the structure of your LLC. Recall that there are two types of LLCs. Most are member managed: the owners—the members—manage and run the business. The other management structure is called manager managed; this means the owners have managers who help run the business. The nonmanaging owners (presumably your new investors) would simply share in the LLC's profits.

It is important to understand that in a manager-managed LLC, only the named managers have the right to vote on management decisions and act as agents of the LLC. Your investor would be akin to a shareholder in the corporation, except that he wouldn't have the right to help pick a board of directors, nor could he sit on the board. Why? Because LLCs don't have boards of directors.

CREATIVE FINANCING

If getting the money you need is important to you—and it is usually a big issue for most small business people—then I would urge you to pick up my other book, which discusses this issue in detail, *Get Your Business Funded: Creative Methods for Getting the Money You Need.* In it, I share 25 different ways to fund a business. The following are some of the creative ideas from that book that you might want to check out:

Crowdfunding

Crowdfunding is an idea that really could happen only in the Internet age. What you do is this: Google the term "crowdfunding" and locate one of the sites that specialize in this (IndieGoGo.com, Kickstarter.com, etc.) On these sites, you can list your business or project and ask the crowd to help fund you. The amount individuals invest is usually small, $100 or so, but by getting a lot of people to do that, you can raise some serious capital.

But here's the best part: you do not pay them back in cash. Instead, you give some benefit of your business in return. For example, say you are opening a sandwich shop. You list your business on your crowdfunding site, and offer, say, to name a sandwich after someone for a month in exchange for $100. The upshot is that you can raise money, give a benefit, and not go into debt (as you would using credit cards for instance) or have to barter away equity (as you would with a VC for example).

Business and Business Plan Competitions

Many communities and a lot of colleges host competitions, seeking to find the best businesses in their area and give them a leg up (and jump-start their local economies) by rewarding the winners of the competition with money ($100,000 winners are not unheard of), in-kind contributions, and other help. Google "business plan competition" and your city and region and you should find some. Again, the benefit is that you do not go into debt using this option.

Microfinance

The term *microfinance* is usually thought of in the context of the third world, where, for example, a farmer might get a loan of $100 to buy a cow and become more self-sufficient. Well, microfinance has come to the west, only here you add on a zero or two.

The SBA has microloans up to $50,000. ACCION USA and Grameen Bank are also players in this field for smaller sums. The good news is that your credit need not be perfect to get a microfinance loan.

Partners

Finding a partner with the money when you provide the great idea and sweat equity is a tried-and-true business funding option.

CHAPTER **9**

Getting Help

In times like these, it helps to recall that there have always been times like these.

—PAUL HARVEY

As exciting as it is, starting a new business can easily be just as overwhelming. There will be days—many, in fact—when you will be the president, chief financial officer, marketing genius, and receptionist . . . and that is just before noon! Even worse, you will need to understand not only the part of the business that you love but everything else, too—advertising, law, insurance, team building, and so on. Of course, buying this book (thank you very much!) is one way to get up to speed, but happily, there are others. In this chapter, we will explore the resources you can tap to get the help you need. You are not alone.

SMALL BUSINESS ADMINISTRATION (SBA)

What would you say if I told you that there is an agency in the federal government with a multibillion-dollar budget whose sole function is to help you succeed? That would be a pretty good partner to have, wouldn't you say? Well there is, and it is. According to my friend Hector Barreto, former head of the SBA, it is the agency's job to "advise, counsel, assist, and protect America's small business." It does so in a variety of ways:

- In its field offices throughout the United States, the Virgin Islands, Puerto Rico, and Guam, the SBA offers classes, counseling, and a variety of programs designed to help small businesses succeed.
- As discussed in the previous chapter, the SBA's loan guarantee program enables entrepreneurs to obtain loans with very favorable rates.
- After a natural disaster (such as Hurricane Katrina) or other major calamitous events (such as September 11), the SBA helps small businesses with disaster assistance.
- By helping entrepreneurs learn more about bidding on contracts, the SBA provides much needed contracting help. Its program, called Business Matchmaking, helps small businesses bid on and get contracts with the federal government and private industry. See www.business-matchmaking.com.
- The SBA's recently redone website, www.sba.gov, is full of great and useful information.

Why Small Businesses Fail

According to Hector Barreto, small businesses fail because:

- They are undercapitalized
- The business is a bad idea
- The owner lacks the drive and commitment to see the venture through
- The owner is unprepared
- The business has poor employees
- The owner does not know how to use technology to his or her advantage
- The owner does not know what he or she does not know and is unwilling to learn it

---

The SBA is a super resource that can help any new business.

SCORE

SCORE is an amazing organization. Made up of business executives and entrepreneurs, SCORE is an all-voluntary organization that offers free, confidential counseling and education on almost any subject you can name. Need help with a marketing campaign? SCORE can help. Opening an auto repair shop? A SCORE volunteer probably has done that, too. SCORE matches you up with a counselor who will give you as much help as your business needs, and if that counselor cannot help you with a specific problem, there is another SCORE counselor who can. It is amazing that you can get so much help, absolutely free. SCORE's counseling sessions take place at your business, in any one of SCORE's nearly 400 offices around the country, or of course, online.

SCORE also offers a variety of small business workshops, both in its offices and online. In a typical year, SCORE offers about 7,000 workshops and seminars to approximately 150,000 people. Some are free, whereas others usually cost less than $50. And how about this: even though there are about 10,000 SCORE volunteers nationwide, the organization is staffed and run by only 14 people. Everything else is done by volunteers. It is an incredible organization and a great resource.

SCORE Tips

The SCORE website (SCORE.org) is bursting with useful business tips, like this one, for example:

Seven Keys to Growing Your Business

1. The product must satisfy an immediate need.
2. Offer good quality at a fair price.
3. Be careful with your money.
4. Cash flow is essential.
5. Guard your cash carefully.
6. Maximize your marketing.
7. Selling is the core skill of a successful business.

SMALL BUSINESS DEVELOPMENT CENTERS

Small Business Development Centers, or SBDCs, are an offshoot of the SBA intended to provide management and technical assistance to small business owners. There are 63 SBDCs around the country, and each is tied to a lead organization that sponsors the center and helps run the program, such as a university or nonprofit organization. There is also a network of smaller centers and satellite locations in each state, and these, too, are associated with universities, community colleges, or nonprofits.

Like SCORE and the SBA, SBDCs offer counseling and other assistance to entrepreneurs. Volunteers come from chambers of commerce, the legal and banking communities, academia, and SCORE. SBDCs also use paid staffers. Assistance can range from helping small businesses with financial issues and marketing to production, organization, and even engineering and feasibility studies. SBDCs make a special effort to work with minority and economically disadvantaged entrepreneurs, as well as with veterans, women, and the disabled.

MENTORS

Having a mentor is one of the best ways to learn more about how to run a business. A business mentor can open doors, teach skills, and give valuable feedback. No doubt it is a good deal for you. But it is often equally satisfying, if not more so, for the mentor, as he or she can see the experience make a difference. It is a chance to give back. Maybe you are asking yourself, "Hey Steve, that sounds great, but I don't know anyone who would or could mentor me. Where would *I* find one?" Good question. Here are a few good answers:

- *Ask.* Finding a mentor is often the result of simply having the chutzpah to ask someone whom you admire whether she would be willing to mentor you. Or just ask around. Tell people that you are looking for a mentor; you may be surprised at how willing people are to help. Speak with business associates, friends and relatives, other entrepreneurs, people at your place of worship, or even members of online communities.

What to Look for in a Mentor

You want someone whom you respect, who has something to teach you, and who has some connections with people you'd like to meet.

- *Pay.* If someone knows what you want to learn but is disinclined to be your mentor, for whatever reason, consider buying his or her time. Is it ideal? No, but it may still work. For instance, what about approaching that person and offering a fee for a few days of consultation and six months of telephone follow-up? Explain that you think the relationship could help you get your business off the ground and that you respect his or her time, and therefore you are willing to pay for it. You may suddenly find yourself with the best mentor that money can buy, especially if you are not in a competing business.
- *Click.* There are many places online where you can find a mentor: SCORE, the National Association of Women Business Owners, the Initiative for a Competitive Inner City, and SBDCs are a few.
- *Social Media.* LinkedIn is an especially good resource for finding the right person to help you take your business to the next level, mentors included.

MRALLBIZ.COM, THESELFEMPLOYED.COM, AND OTHER WEBSITES

There is no shortage of websites that want to help you succeed in your new business. And, if I can offer a shameless plug here, my main sites, MrAllBiz.com and TheSelfEmployed.com, are two of the best. Like this book, MrAllBiz is organized into three main sections: *Start Your Business*, *Run Your Business*, and *Grow Your Business*. But it also offers resources that can be found only online: video, audio, podcasts, e-books, my daily blog, and plenty more. I am confident you will get a lot from visiting the site. Similarly, if you are a solopreneur, TheSelfEmployed.com should prove to be a great resource for you—articles, videos, forums, special deals—the whole enchilada.

There are many other sites that you might want to check out as well:

- *USA Today Small Business.* Of course, I am biased toward the site of my paper, but for good reason. Here, you can read lots of columns, blogs, and get small business news you can use (Usatoday.com/money/smallbusiness).
- *Business Insider.* This is an excellent resource (www.BusinessInsider.com).

- *Harvard Business Review.* This is another excellent choice for ideas and strategies that work (www.HBR.com).
- *Business Week.* Although *Business Week* is known for its excellent coverage of big business, its small business treatment is significant, too. At this site, you will find plenty of articles profiling entrepreneurial ideas (www.businessweek.com/small-business).
- *Inc.* Both the magazine and the website are chock-full of useful ideas. As the website says, "*Inc.* delivers advice, tools, and services, to help business owners and CEOs start, run, and grow their businesses more successfully. You'll find information and advice covering virtually every business and management task, including marketing, sales, finding capital, managing people, and more" (www.inc.com).
- *Entrepreneur.* Although not as useful, in my opinion, as *Inc., Entrepreneur* is both a magazine and website that can be of some help (www. entrepreneur.com).
- *Small Business Online Community.* This site, run by Bank of America, is an excellent place to meet other entrepreneurs online and get excellent success strategies and content (as I write for this site as well, my bias comes through here too, but even so, objectively, it is a great resource) (http://smallbusinessonlinecommunity.bankofamerica.com/index.jspa).

MAGAZINES AND TELEVISION

Finally, there is plenty more help available from the mass media. Aside from the magazines already mentioned, you may also want to check out *Home Business* magazine, *Forbes Small Business,* and *Business 2.0.*

There are also a couple of television shows that are very good; for instance, MSNBC's *Your Business* is an excellent show that features profiles of small businesses, roundtable discussions, interviews, and strategy segments. It is very entertaining and informative.

Opening Up Shop

CHAPTER **10**

Location, Location, Location

Nothing focuses the mind better than the constant sight of a competitor who wants to wipe you off the map.

—Wayne Calloway

Now comes the fun stuff. Although the matters discussed in the previous section—drafting a business plan, finding the money, and so on—are necessary prerequisites to starting a successful small business, they really cannot be described as fun. But the things you will do now should be quite enjoyable. From finding the right location to outfitting the office or shop, you should take pleasure in the actual process of physically creating a business.

NOT ALL LOCATIONS ARE CREATED EQUAL

Not every business needs a great location. It depends on the type of business you have, the brand you are creating, the amount of foot traffic you require, and the amount of money you have to spend. A business in which you will be going to your customers' locations rather than vice versa certainly does not need a terrific location—house cleaning or pool care businesses, for example. Wholesale businesses, warehouses, and factories also do not need great locations. Out-of-the-way locations can be a wonderful, inexpensive choice for many businesses. Opening in a redevelopment area, for example, may afford you tax breaks.

The first consideration then, is how important traffic will be to your business. If your business is going to be a retail store catering to the public, especially if there are going to be a lot of spur-of-the-moment drop-in customers, then a high-profile, high-traffic location is vital. A convenience store needs a great location with a lot of traffic, but a chiropractor does not.

Location Checklist

You will want to consider the following when looking for a good location:

- *Population.* Are there enough people in the immediate area and in the broader region to support your sort of business? What has been the fate of similar businesses in the area?
- *Traffic.* If your business will depend on drive-by traffic, then you need to be located in a center of activity or on the route to or from there. Is the location served by public transportation? Is it on a major thoroughfare?
- *Competition.* Where is the competition in relation to the store? Having too many competitors nearby can be a problem.
- *Visibility.* The location probably needs to be visible from the highway, not set back or otherwise easily missed.
- *Signs.* Good signs can make a big difference. Make sure that there are no legal or lease restrictions precluding you from erecting a noticeable sign.
- *Facilities.* What are the facilities like? Is there enough parking? Is there a bathroom for the public? For your staff? What about outdoor lighting and landscaping?
- *Landlord.* Get some references. Is the landlord responsive and easy to work with, or is he or she impossible?
- *History.* Avoid locations with bad reputations, such as those where businesses move in and out every few months, because you will have to spend a lot of time overcoming preconceived notions about the place.
- *Rent.* Rent, although obviously a concern, should not be the sole and deciding factor. Yes, you need to keep your overhead low, but locating your business in a cheap, bad location is also a path to failure.

Finally, whatever location you choose, be sure that it is zoned for your type of business. You might want to consider a few other things:

- Can employees and suppliers get there easily?
- Is there an adequate shipping and receiving area?
- Are there any environmental issues to consider?
- Is it wired for the Internet?
- Is there room to expand?

Example: Sam is a retailer who likes to locate his stores across the street from major malls. He figures he gets the benefit of the mall's advertising and pull without having to pay mall rent.

NEGOTIATING THE LEASE

Negotiating a lease with a landlord is like any other negotiation. It is important to know at the outset what you want and what you can afford. Remember, *everything is negotiable.* If you are negotiating lease terms, understand that you are a valuable commodity to a landlord. It is no easy task for a landlord to find a qualified commercial tenant. He or she probably wants you as much as you want the space. Accordingly, you may be in a more powerful position when negotiating a lease and can ask the landlord for concessions and changes to the lease, if required.

Negotiating a good deal on your lease requires that you know the rental history of the area. What are similar spaces renting for? What is the vacancy rate in the area? If it is high, you can negotiate a good deal because the landlord really needs you. If the space has been empty for a while, you need to find out how long and why. The more you know, the better the deal you will be able to negotiate.

When presented with a lease, you must go over it with your lawyer. The lease will be drafted by the landlord's lawyer for the landlord's benefit, so you need your attorney to figure out what is fair and what is not. Although you might be presented with a preprinted lease that seems as if it cannot be changed, it can. The essence of contract law is that both sides must agree to all conditions. That, in fact, is why a contract is also called an *agreement*. If the lease contains provisions that you and your lawyer do not like, negotiate to change them. Always remember, *everything is negotiable*.

Verbal Promises

Any verbal promises made by the landlord *must* be made part of the written lease or they will be unenforceable.

IMPORTANT LEASE ISSUES

When analyzing the lease and the space, first consider the square footage listed in the lease. Because your rent is normally tied to the location's square footage, you might want to have an architect measure the usable space that you will be renting—often, it is less than what the landlord says or the lease indicates. The landlord will typically include spaces such as closets, bathrooms, and hallways as part of the square footage, yet these are not office space. Other issues to consider:

- *Rent.* When negotiating a long-term lease, ask for a few months of free rent.
- *Length.* The term of the lease must be long enough to establish your business but not so long that you cannot move or close up shop if things do not work out there. A year or two, with an option for a renewal, is probably about right for starters.
- *Assignments and subleases.* Negotiate for the right to assign or sublet your space so that if you need to get out, you can. With an assignment, the new tenant is totally responsible for the rest of the term, whereas a sublet keeps you financially on the hook until it is over. Either way, the landlord will probably want the right to review (or refuse) the person you pick, and that is a reasonable request.
- *Gross or net?* A gross lease is one in which the landlord pays the insurance, taxes, utilities, and so forth. If it is a net lease, you must be very clear about what is and is not included. Who pays for heating and

airconditioning? Who pays for security, cleaning, and parking? Who pays for repairs?

Triple Net Lease
A *triple net lease* is one in which the renter pays, in addition to rent, all operating costs and expenses for the property, such as security, mainte-nance, taxes, and insurance.

- *Escalation charges.* Be sure to restrict any "escalation charges" in later years. These are costs incurred by the landlord for expenses such as increased property taxes, property and business insurance, and so on. Although you will be asked, you *do not* have to agree to share these costs.
- *Signs.* Broach the subject of signs early, long before you sign any agreement. Signage restrictions can be deal breakers.
- *Utilities.* Under some leases, the business must purchase the utilities from the landlord. Be sure that the lease grants you the right to audit the utility bill so that you can ensure the landlord is not defrauding you.
- *Renovations.* Your landlord may agree to help or otherwise contribute to renovations that you require before move-in. Why? Because doing so increases the value of the building and helps lock you into a multi-year lease.
- *Restrictive covenant.* You may require a restrictive covenant to prevent competitors from opening similar businesses nearby. For example, if you are located in a mall, you might want to prevent the landlord from renting to another business like yours.

It is imperative that you review the proposed lease with your lawyer. Above all, try to cultivate a good working relationship with your landlord. That will go further toward working out problems than a dozen letters from your lawyer.

CHAPTER 11

Branding 101

Customers must recognize that you stand for something.

—HOWARD SCHULTZ, FOUNDER, STARBUCKS

Gene Simmons of the rock band KISS once remarked that although he liked being in a rock-and-roll band, he loved being a rock-and-roll *brand*. What did he mean by that? Think about KISS for a moment. What images and feelings come to mind? Probably that distinctive KISS logo, the white makeup, the outrageous shows, the wild stories. KISS carefully cultivated that bad-boy image, and it's worth a fortune to them. That is what Simmons meant: having a band is great, but it's the brand that pays the bills.

BRAND NEW

What comes to mind when you think about Rolls-Royce, Nike, or Apple Inc.? Each business evokes very clear thoughts, feelings, and images. Each has a strong corporate identity, or *brand,* associated with its name, and that is no accident. These companies have spent a lot of money getting you to conjure up specific images and feelings when you think about their businesses.

This begs the question, what do you want people to think of when they think about your new small business? The idea of creating a brand for your small business is really quite important. Maybe you think that doing so is beyond your reach, that branding is a concept for the big boys. Think again. Branding is something that you can—and should—do, too.

One concept that you will see repeated throughout this book is that you could not have picked a better time to start or own a small business. A variety of factors have come together to make this a new era for small business, an exciting time full of potential. It used to be that big businesses had an advantage over small businesses because of their greater resources. Bigger used to be better. But no longer. Little is the new big. Three things have changed the landscape in your favor:

1. *A change in thought.* What the business world has come to see is that smaller is quicker, more innovative, more entrepreneurial, and better able to adapt to change. Bigger can be slower, plodding, boring, and bureaucratic. More and more, people see the power of small.
2. *The information/computer/technological revolution.* This revolution means that small businesses can look much bigger than they actually are, and no one ever need know. Between computers, laser printers, smartphones, apps, faxes, websites, and software, any small business can look big.
3. *A growing market.* More and more, big businesses are seeing the power and market potential of small businesses, and they are catering to that market. Ideas and tools that were once considered the private domain of large businesses are being offered to and used by small businesses. Evidence: Staples, Greatland's 1099 and W-2 services, Microsoft Outlook, and FedEx Express.

Small Business Stats

There are roughly 29 million businesses in the United States. Of those, according to the U.S. Census Bureau, 23 million have no payroll. Of the 6 million businesses with payrolls, 99 percent are small businesses with fewer than 100 employees, and most of those have fewer than 10.

The era of little has arrived, and branding is the first of several ideas in which you will see that strategies once confined to the corporate boardroom can be applied equally on Main Street.

CREATING A BRAND THEY'LL REMEMBER

If you want to succeed in business, you too will need to create an identifiable brand. Boiled down to its basics, a brand is the essence of what makes your business unique. It combines your name, logo, and purpose into an identifiable whole. It is your image based on reality. Your brand represents your business identity, your unique position in the market. Are you the friendly lawyer, the holistic market, the geeky computer consultant, or what? Without a brand, you may find that instead of being all things to all people, you are nothing to no one. A brand is a hook to hang your hat on so that people will remember you. Nike? That swoosh, and the phrase "Just Do It" come to mind. That is the gold standard we are aiming for.

You begin to create a brand by carefully thinking about what your business will be, what makes it unique, who your customers will be, and what it is they will want. Creating a brand is vital because many other decisions will hinge on this one. Your name, logo, slogan, website, social media handles, even the location you choose and your pricing structure depend on the brand you are trying to create. A discount motorcycle warehouse will put things together far differently than a Harley-Davidson showroom will.

Your Name

What you choose to name your business will have as much to do with extending your brand as anything else. Because you will not have the sort of budget required to create brand awareness in the general public, as large companies do, one of your best chances for creating a favorable image is to do so through your name. If you are creating a restaurant, the name *Aunt Suzy's Food Emporium* creates a much different image than *Susan's Brasserie*.

When naming your business, you have two choices. Either you can choose a name that describes exactly what the business is and what benefits it offers, or you can choose a name that has nothing to do with the business at all. The latter describes names such as Xerox, Amazon.com, and Kodak. Although interesting, the problem, of course, is that if you don't have enough money to get people to remember the name of your business, instead of a memorable, quirky name, all you will be left with is a quirky name.

The other option is almost always preferable for the small business. This process involves thinking about the benefits your business offers the public and naming your business after that. Examples here include Jiffy Lube, Baja Fresh, or Quickee Mart. Choosing a name that creates awareness of your business benefits can go a long way toward creating a brand that people will remember.

There are two important things to consider when naming your business. The first is the image and brand you want to create. The thing about a successful brand is that there is consistency across the board—the image, colors, location, logo, and pricing all reinforce one another. If you are creating an upscale Italian design store, your location, prices, and *name* must all reflect the image you are trying to create. Maria's Discount Italy probably won't cut it, but Maria's Casa de Italia might.

The second factor is the benefit that someone would derive from patronizing your business. The best name is one that combines the image you want to create with a perceived benefit: think of Netflix, Discount Warehouse, or Speedy Linguine.

Logos and Catchphrases

A graphic image that reinforces your name builds your brand. Ideally, it says who you are and what you do. A logo can be a symbol (Target's target), a graphic interpretation of your business name, or both. Either way,

it needs to concisely convey the image you want to present to the world. Here is my logo:

Steve Strauss
Small Business

When choosing a logo, the essential quality is that it graphically represents to the world who you are and what is unique about you. Accordingly, choosing a logo is akin to naming your business: you want a logo that is distinctive, memorable, and laden with benefits.

When creating a logo, again, you have two options: you can do it yourself or hire someone to do it for you. Doing it yourself will probably require you to use a graphics program that offers clip art, pictures, and photographs. It is important that you do not use material that is copyrighted in your logo design.

Free Logos

You can find some free logo generators online. Check out www.cooltext
.com and www.logogenerator.com.

It is probably better to hire someone to create a logo for you. Prices vary—you could pay anywhere from $100 for a student's services to $10,000 for a professional. You might be surprised at the great quality and affordable prices you will get from graphic arts students. A cost of $1,000 for a quality, professional logo is reasonable to expect.

One way to add even more value to your logo is to incorporate a slogan. You want your catchphrase to reinforce your desired image, and the benefits you offer should be encompassed in that catchphrase as part of your overall branding strategy. If you are sensing a theme here, you're right. For example:

- IBM: Think
- Carpet World: Elegance Underfoot
- BMW: The Ultimate Driving Machine

These three things—your name, logo, and catchphrase—are the holy trinity of your brand, and they all are equally essential.

Next, you want to pick colors and fonts that reinforce your emerging brand. A computer consultant would be smart to use a `modern-looking` font but would be unwise to use an 𝕺𝖑𝖉 𝕰𝖓𝖌𝖑𝖎𝖘𝖍 font. Self-evident, for sure, but important to remember nonetheless. The font you choose and the colors you pick will be used to represent your name, logo, and slogan in all of your printed materials. This tapestry of decisions should create a unified, interwoven theme that reinforces the brand you are working to create.

EXTENDING YOUR BRAND

Once you have your name, logo, slogan, font, and color ready, it is time to get the word out. All are combined to create your graphic materials. Your name, logo, and slogan should appear on your stationery, business cards, envelopes, mailing labels, website, invoices, and receipts—in short, *everything*.

Your Website

As much as anything else these days, more than most things actually, your website is vital to creating and sustaining a great brand. It is often where people go first when checking you out and so you want it to reflect the brand you are trying to create. The look and feel of the site must be considered integral to your brand. It not only must contain your name, logo, colors, and catchphrase but must be your main vehicle for extending those branding choices.

Social Media

Your social media efforts, as explained later in this book, are just as vital to your brand these days as your website, signs, business cards, and all the rest—more so, maybe, because that is where the eyeballs are. When people find you on Facebook or Twitter or LinkedIn or YouTube or wherever, you want to be sure that what they find is the business personality you are trying to perpetuate. You do that by branding these sites as well—with your name and logo, with your colors and catchphrase, and especially with what you post. Your online social media posts are now a vital part of any brand strategy.

BRANDING SECRETS

You get the idea. You want to create a consistent theme that reinforces the image you intend to create. But branding goes even beyond that. Because your brand is based on both how you *want* to be perceived and how you actually *are* perceived, it follows that the other half of brand building is creating positive perceptions based on substance and style. But how?

Make a Promise and Keep It

Your brand is your promise to your customers. Decide what that promise is, what you want to come to mind when they think of your business, and keep that promise. Volvo promises safe cars. Nordstrom promises great customer service. What does your business promise?

Do What You Do Best, Again and Again

A brand is a promise that boils down to "If you buy this product, you know what you will be getting because our company stands for X, Y, or Z." For example, Volkswagens are affordable, Walmart is inexpensive, that sort of thing. This kind of branding takes time, and it derives from a company doing what it does best and then making sure everything else it does supports that value proposition. Consistency is key.

Offer Superior Customer Service

This is a theme that will be discussed in more detail later in the book, but suffice to say that all your hard work creating a cool brand will be a waste of time and money if it isn't reinforced by happy customers. Customers should find it easy to work with you or buy from you.

The Dot-Com Brands

You cannot get by on brand alone. That was the lesson of the dot-com boom and bust. Take Pets.com, for example. The high-flying start-up burned through millions of dollars and soon went out of business because it focused far more on branding than it did on business. Its once-famous sock puppet was interviewed by *People* magazine and appeared on *Good Morning America,* but the company soon learned that creating an identifiable brand is not the same as creating a valuable business.

The bottom line is that you want to constantly reinforce the image you are creating through your actions. Remember, the two keys to establishing a strong brand are developing a specific identity and then communicating that identity consistently. Do that, and your small business will be off on the right foot.

CHAPTER **12**

Products and Inventory

Products are made in the factory, but brands are created in the mind.

—WALTER LANDOR

Needless to say, the type, quality, and style of the products you stock go hand in hand with the brand you create. The question now is where to find those products and how best to keep them on hand. Although stocking the store may initially seem like a needle-in-a-haystack chore, it need not be. With a bit of investigation, you can find the right suppliers.

IT'S ALL IN THE BUYING

John owns a very successful antique shop in California. In fact, it is so successful that John works only six hours a day, four days a week, and he still makes a nice six-figure income. His store is usually busy, and it is not hard to see why. It is full of fascinating old knickknacks, doodads, odds and ends, and other items that he buys from a variety of sources: dealers, antique shows, garage sales, classified ads, and estate sales are the most common.

When asked about the secret of his success, John answers quickly. "It's all in the buying," he says. John loves shopping for things to put in his shop, but he won't buy anything, no matter how much he likes it, unless he can get it for the right price. He knows that if he pays too much, no matter how interesting the item is, it will take up valuable space in his store—space that could be occupied by products that sell for nice profits. He also knows that if he can get the right item for the right price, selling it won't be a problem. John is convinced that the reason for his success is not how well he sells but how smart he buys.

It's all in the buying could be the motto for this chapter. It is as sound a small business principle as you will hear. Your caveat is this: as you start to make decisions that will build your brand, don't forget that the name of the game is making a profit. Buy low and sell high. The key now is to find the right suppliers that will help you buy low.

FINDING THE RIGHT SUPPLIERS

There are many existing channels for buying merchandise; you just need to tap into them. Here are your best bets.

Referrals

The problem with speaking to people in your community who have a business similar to the one you have or want to start is that they may view you as a competitor and therefore be reluctant to help you. It is probably wiser then to find people in a neighboring area and speak with them. They can tell you who their suppliers are and the names of the suppliers' representatives. Call the reps and have them come to your home or store to show you their line.

Sales Reps

Manufacturers, wholesalers, and distributors employ traveling agents and representatives who sell their products. Some of these reps sell products for a single company; others represent several companies that sell similar products. A sales rep for the gift industry, for example, may represent the lines of many different manufacturers that create products sold in a gift store: stationery, cards, candles, picture frames, soaps, magnets, and so on. Sales reps travel with their wares and visit the shops of potential and current clients. They will suggest new products, show samples and catalogs, take orders, and even help install specialty equipment or displays. By some estimates, there are more independent sales reps than any other type of home-based business.

Trade Shows

Trade shows are perhaps the best place to find products and suppliers for your business. Trade shows are presented by people in the business for people in the business. By attending, you will make invaluable contacts, see the latest trends, meet potential suppliers, learn the lingo, and get a crash course in your industry. By wandering the aisles, finding the products you like, and then talking with the rep in each booth, you will begin to establish yourself. To find a trade show in your industry, log on to www.tsnn.com.

Trade Magazines

Pick up a copy of the trade magazine(s) for your business and look at the ads. They want to sell to you. Call the companies whose products you like, and again, get them to send a rep to meet with you.

Trade Associations

One of the nice things about contacting your trade association is that it may have a list of overseas contacts who sell what you are looking for, and those products likely will cost less.

Go to the Source

If you know which product you want and who makes it, then go online and get the company's contact information. Call the company up and ask for the sales department. Explain who you are and what you are doing and ask to meet with the rep in your area.

MEET THE REPS

If you already have an established business, then meeting with reps should be simple. They know that you know the program. But if yours is a new business, the challenge is to get reps to take you seriously, to see you as a viable contact. Most reps are overworked and don't have much time to waste, so be sure to present yourself professionally. If you are new to business, it may be that the company or the rep will want to see letters of credit, references, or something similar. The rep wants to be sure that you will be able to pay for what you order, in full and on time. Of course, the vendor wants your business, but business is business. Finding vendors is a matter of creating relationships as much as anything else, and you need to establish relationships with your potential vendors and their representatives.

Sometimes, without any trade references, getting your foot in the door and proving your mettle is difficult. This is especially true if you are trying to establish trade credit and want the vendor to sell to you net 30. If you find the big manufacturers difficult, start with a smaller company or a local vendor. If you start small, establish yourself and build some trade credit and trade references. Then you can expand and attract the bigger manufacturers.

Net 30

Paying for items 30 days after the invoice date is called Net 30.

When meeting with company representatives or independent sales agents, you want to be sure to get samples of the products they are offering. Sometimes these will be free, sometimes not. Pay if necessary. Take the samples and make sure that they are the quality and style you want. The important thing is that you find products:

- That you can afford
- That customers will want
- That build your brand

Remember, *it's all in the buying!*

INVENTORY CONTROL

You need to order enough stock in enough variety to respond to the needs of the many different types of customers who will be coming into your store. Remember that cars, for example, come in all shapes, sizes, and price ranges for a reason. It takes all kinds of people to make the world go 'round. If you stock your store only with items you like, then you are losing the chance to sell to people who are unlike you, and rest assured, there are plenty of those out there. You may not like stuffed kitty cats, but someone else does.

How much product do you need? First, the shelves must look full. Second, although it might sound trite, you need enough product to meet the normal demands of your business. A store with a track record can look to previous years' sales, but a new start-up must use the figures calculated in the business plan. (I told you it was important!) Once you know how much you need, you should order that amount and a bit more, maybe even 10 percent more. This is enough of a cushion should a vendor deliver late or should some *force majeure* (act of God) cause your shipments to arrive late.

Inventory Control Software

One way to keep track of inventory is by searching for and purchasing a good inventory control software program.

This leads us to reorders. After a while, you will get a sense of the rhythm of your business. You will know how long it takes supplier X to deliver product Y, and you will order accordingly. But especially in the beginning, you need to be all over this. If you have 50 stuffed kitties and sell 5 each week (a 10-week supply), and if it takes 2 weeks to get them delivered, you need to reorder when you have three weeks worth of product left so that you never run out. Running out of inventory is a rookie mistake and one that can easily be avoided with just a little bit of planning.

The flip side of a lack of inventory is having too much inventory. This can be an especially nasty problem if you sell perishable goods or seasonal items. Excess inventory slows your cash flow and costs you money by taking up space for items that would otherwise be selling.

What do you do when you have too much product on hand? The time-honored thing to do is to have a sale. *Sale* is one of the two most powerful words in business (*free* being the other). The good thing about a sale is that it brings people in the door for the sale items, and they just may stick around and buy other items that are not on sale. The bad news is that you are losing money on sale items that you need to move because you didn't practice smart inventory management.

Cash Flow and Inventory Control

One of the most important concepts in business is the 80–20 rule, which holds that 80 percent of your sales will come from 20 percent of your customers. Know who those customers are and treat them right, and your continued success is almost assured.

The 80–20 rule applies to inventory as well. Of your sales, 80 percent will likely come from 20 percent of your products. It may not be—in fact, it probably won't be—your most expensive items. Rather, it will probably be the less expensive items that are turned over again and again that will account for 80 percent of your sales. Those vital 20 percent products are the lifeblood of your business, accounting for much of your cash flow. Obviously, if you don't always have enough of those products, you will be severely hampering your cash flow.

You may not be able to afford everything you want for the store when you want it. But if you know which products account for 80 percent of your sales, you will be able to prioritize accordingly.

Tracking Inventory

Depending on how much inventory you stock, you may need an inventory control system. Such a system can tell you what you need to order, what sells best, and whether an employee may be stealing from you. Your system might be manual, although these days it is far more common to have a computerized system. Accounting programs such as QuickBooks and Microsoft Office Accounting have inventory tracking control systems as part of their standard functions.

Manual Inventory

With a manual inventory control system, each item in the store is tagged. The tag is removed when the item sells, the used tags are itemized (so that you know what has sold), and then checked against the physical inventory (so that you know whether anything is missing).

A sophisticated inventory control system will allow you to know exactly what sells, compare it with what else sells, let you know when to reorder, and help you figure out which products are the most profitable. Another option is to invest in a point-of-sale (POS) system. POS software creates up-to-the-minute inventory records from the point of purchase.

Tip: You may want to check with your trade association to see whether industry-specific accounting and inventory systems are available for purchase. Most industries have these now. Although they are more expensive, because they are specific to your industry, they make a lot of sense for your business. In that regard, they are sometimes better than off-the-shelf products.

Whatever system you choose, it is important to understand that software today is very powerful and can give you much more than a mere recitation of what sold and what did not. Now, you can get sophisticated reports that help you analyze sales data, chart sales by month, compare sales by price (or any other variable, for that matter), keep track of accounts receivable, calculate sales taxes, and generally run your business very effectively.

If you buy the right products at the right price and keep track of what you need and when, your small business will be the better for it. And always remember, *it's all in the buying.*

CHAPTER 13

Savvy Pricing Strategies

If you really put a small value upon yourself, rest assured
that the world will not raise your price.

—ANONYMOUS

How much should you charge for your products or services? 'Tis a question that vexes many an entrepreneur. Of course, you want to charge enough to make a healthy profit, but not so much that you drive customers away. The price you charge is also an important aspect of your brand. Thus, you may need to tinker a bit before you find that perfect price.

THE PSYCHOLOGY OF PRICE

You expect to pay more for a BMW than a Volkswagen because of the brands those companies have created (among other reasons). BMW aims to sell fewer products at a higher price to a wealthier and more discriminating audience. Volkswagen goes for high volume and less profit per sale. Both are valid strategies, and both work.

The price of your product carries with it great psychological impact. When you pay more, you expect more; you expect more from a car that costs $50,000 than you do from one that costs $20,000. It is no secret that there is a direct correlation between price and quality in the minds of consumers. Your task is to use that mind-set to your advantage.

For example, products with even-numbered prices are generally considered higher quality than those with odd-numbered prices. A stereo

113

selling for $200 is thought of as better and higher quality than one selling for $179.99. If you are seeking to sell high-end items, then consider pricing them with an even number. If you are looking to be the low-cost leader in your area, then use .99 to your advantage. So the first thing to consider when pricing is the type of consumer you are trying to reach, which relates to the brand you want to create.

Odd Numbers

Odd numbers work. One study found that merchandise sold better in lots of three for $5.31 ($1.77 each) than $1.69 each. A price of $3.33 might also catch someone's eye.

Determining Your Optimal Price

Your optimal price is one that affords you the most sales at the greatest profit. Determining your optimal price is a five-step process.

1. *Figure out your minimum price.* If you are selling widgets, you need to know what it costs you to sell one widget. This includes your actual cost to buy or manufacture that widget, plus a proportional cost of your overhead—rent, labor, shipping, insurance, and so on. Once you know what it actually costs you to buy and sell a widget, then you will know the minimum price you must ask for that item. Charge anything less, and you will go out of business. Anything more is profit.

2. *What is the focus of your brand?* Is yours a gourmet boutique market or a produce warehouse? The gourmet store can charge more, but the produce warehouse will sell more. You can sell a lot for less at a lower profit, or less for a lot at a higher profit, or something in the middle.

3. *Analyze your competitors.* Price is not the only factor that consumers look at when making purchasing decisions, but it is a factor. You absolutely have to know what your competitors are charging and take that into account. Maybe you want to undercut them, which works. Maybe you want to match them while offering some incentive. That works, too. Either way, remember that capitalism is cutthroat. You have to be cognizant of what your competitors are doing and offer something better—whether it is price, service, location, or something else—if

you are going to succeed. When analyzing a competitor's prices, be sure to note whether your products are superior, inferior, or similar. Which of your competitors seem to be doing the best? Ask yourself whether price is the reason. If not, what is? Can you beat them on price? If so, that's good.

4. *Set a price.* Knowing the minimum you must charge, knowing what your competitors charge, and knowing the image you want to portray allows you to set your prices accordingly.

5. *Test, test, test.* Your first price is not your last price. Especially at the beginning, you will need to tinker a bit. If you have a product that you are selling through other stores, for example, test one price in one store and another price in another store. Try an ad in one paper at one price and another in a similar paper at a different price. Compare the results.

Testing

Even small business owners who have been in business for a long time should occasionally test new prices for old products. You never know, there may be a hidden gold mine in your store simply awaiting your discovery.

Product pricing is part art, part skill, and all perception. A customer will pay a particular price for your product if he perceives that it is worth that price. If not, you will never make a sale. Why do Ralph Lauren Polo shirts cost almost $100 when a similar shirt without the pony logo costs $25? Perceived value. Why can't you sell a bruised tomato, even for a dime? Perceived value. You need to find that magic equilibrium point at which customers perceive value and you perceive dollars.

Fear Not!

Too many small businesses do not raise prices for fear of losing customers. That is a mistake. Inflation is real. What it cost you to produce and distribute a product five years ago is not what it costs today, if for no other reason than inflation has made your dollars worth less. Raise your prices and see what happens. The worst thing is that you lose some sales and have to drop your prices again. The best thing is that extra revenue begins to come in the door.

GAS WAR!

Some people reading this book will remember a time when gas stations at the same intersection would engage in a "gas war." One station would drop its price per gallon to, say, 59.9 cents, and the station across the street would go down to 58.9 cents. This would go on for a while, and people would flock to the stations to get cheap gas, a Coca-Cola glass set, or some such thing—but I digress.

The problem with the gas war mentality is that all of your hard work—coming up with a great idea, drafting that darn business plan, finding just the right spot, building a brand, all of it—is reduced to selling your stuff for less. Unless you can really compete on price, and want to, don't make the mistake of thinking that you can simply charge what your competitors charge (or less) and all will be fine. McDonald's is the cheapest because it can afford to be and because that is its business plan, ditto Walmart. Is that *your* business plan?

Customers look at a variety of factors when deciding where to buy. Sure, price is a big factor, but it is not the only one and often is not the dispositive one. Think about your own purchasing decisions. How often do you buy solely because you found a product for less? Probably not very often. Starbucks is certainly not the cheapest place to get a cup of coffee, but it is the most popular. Its customers have reasons beyond price for frequenting that establishment. What is it that your customers want? Give them want they want, and then worry about price.

Let's say that you are a lawyer with a wills and trusts practice. Yes, you can charge what the trust mill across town charges, but you probably don't want to, and you certainly don't have to. There are all sorts of consumers shopping for a wills and trusts lawyer. The ones who go for the mill probably have fewer assets and fewer concerns. But if you open up shop in a nicer part of town and charge more, if the brand you are trying to create is excellence and quality legal work, then you can charge more. Perception creates price. If clients perceive you as a great lawyer who does good work, you can charge commensurate fees. You will attract better clients with interesting legal matters who have more resources to pay higher fees. Price is not what they are worried about—finding someone who can save on estate taxes is. In this scenario, competing on price means that you will get stuck with a lesser practice.

There are several other reasons why competing on price is often a bad idea:

- *You will not make enough money.* This is especially true for a service business. It takes time and costs money to maintain your office, travel to see clients, buy insurance, and so forth. You simply have to be able to charge enough to cover your monthly nut and earn a profit to boot. Remember, too, that it is unlikely you will bill 40 hours a week—you simply can't if you are going to run the business, too. You have to charge enough to make a good living.
- *You will attract customers who care only about price.* If that is the sort of customer or client you want, fine, but if it isn't, then avoid the gas war.
- *You will not get good customers.* The flip side of the previous point is that by focusing on low prices, you may drive away quality customers who care about more than just price.

Of course, you want to be competitive, but offering a fair, reasonable price is different from offering the lowest price—much different. But what if the price that you think is fair differs from what a customer or client thinks is fair? Should you negotiate your fees or prices? It depends. If you have a sofa in your furniture gallery that has been sitting there for a year, you would be silly not to negotiate a lower price and move the merchandise. On the other hand, you don't want to get into the habit of negotiating every time you quote a fee or name a price. The best advice is to be judicious, and avoid negotiating if possible, but do so if you must. It is probably better to get less and secure the sale than to be rigid and get nothing.

How to Get Customers to Pay More for Your Services

- *Offer a flat fee.* Customers like knowing exactly what the cost will be, and often they will pay more for that peace of mind.

(continued)

- *Offer a free consultation.* A free half-hour session builds rapport, and rapport means work. If you get the gig, you can always build that half hour back into your fee (or not).
- *Start small.* Offer to do a smaller project first to build confidence. Once the customer likes you and your work, you can charge more.
- *Guarantee your work.* Guarantees build confidence, and confidence means higher fees.
- *Build a brand.* People love brands and are willing to pay more for a brand.
- *Become an expert.* Similarly, people are willing to pay more for advice and help that they consider to be a step above. By becoming an expert in your field (via your posts, articles, speeches, appearances, etc.) you will be able to charge more.

THE LOSS LEADER

The loss leader is a tried-and-true pricing strategy that keeps old customers, attracts new ones, and increases sales. Sound good? You bet, but it comes with a price—if done incorrectly, you can lose a lot of money.

The loss leader is a pricing strategy that attracts consumers to your business by offering them sharp discounts on specific items or services—that is, goods or services that you sell at or close to a loss. Often, the sale price will not even cover the costs of your advertising, overhead, and the product itself. The idea is that by taking a loss on the sale (hence the term *loss leader*), you are leading people into your store with the intent of having them buy not only the bargain but also things that are not discounted.

When you see an ad for a great sale somewhere, that store is using the loss leader strategy. It is hoping to lead you into its establishment with the discounted ad price and then sell you something more expensive. Customers may buy the discounted item, or they may not. The important thing is that they are visiting the business.

Once they get there, the rest is up to you. When they buy other products, you make up for the loss that you are taking on the sale item. For example, say you own a convenience store. By advertising a name brand product like, say, Coca-Cola, on sale for less than the normal price, you will definitely attract people into your store. Once they come in and locate the Coke, you could have alongside it some chips and dip, or other items that upsells them into buying more and therefore compensates for your loss on the cola. The loss leads to a bigger sale.

Other than bringing customers in the door, a loss leader is also used for other reasons.

Moving Unwanted Merchandise

If you have stock that is not moving or that you otherwise want to get rid of, a loss leader can move it. People love a bargain.

Attracting New Customers

New customers can learn about your business when they hear about the sale. For example, the book store could buy a lot of teen novels, discount them, and thereby attract the always desirable younger shopper with disposable income.

Building Your Brand

Earlier, I said that if you do not want to be known as a discount shop, do not compete on price. However, the opposite is now true. If you would like to be known as the low-cost leader, then a loss leader strategy will help associate your business with low prices. It is important, though, that you don't just sell junk at a discount. That is probably not the sort of brand you want to create.

Creating Repeat Customers

Once people find your store and see how well they are treated, what good prices you have, and the friendly staff who wait on them, they will likely come back again and again.

The loss leader is a time-honored business strategy that works, but to make sure it works for you, two precautions are necessary. First, you need to be sure that the lost profit can be countered by the sales of other goods or services. If you price a product or service too low and people don't buy anything else, the loss leads nowhere. It's no longer a loss leader—it's just a loss. Second, be sure that you actually have the discounted item for sale, at the price you advertise it. Not having it (unless you sell out), or not having it at the price you mention in the ad, is fraudulent and illegal.

As long as you do not price the item too low (and thereby take too large a hit in the process) and you take care of the customer once he or she comes into your store, the loss leader can be a very smart pricing policy. Use it to build your customer base and your reputation.

PART

Franchises

CHAPTER **14**

Selecting the Right Franchise

In business for yourself, not by yourself.

—RAY KROC, FOUNDER OF THE FIRST McDONALD'S FRANCHISE

Starting a business from scratch is akin to baking bread from scratch. It takes trial and error, as well as several bad batches, before you figure out what works. On the other hand, starting out by buying a franchise is like getting a good recipe right from the start. Because the franchisor has already baked some bad loaves and has learned how to avoid repeating those mistakes, because the trial-and-error stage has already been handled by someone else, and because you will be buying, among other things, that expertise and wisdom, purchasing a franchise reduces the risk inherent in entrepreneurship. There is less chance that you will burn your bread and a greater chance to make some dough when you buy a franchise.

FRANCHISE BASICS

There are both pros and cons to buying a franchise. Let's consider each.

Franchise Terminology

The *franchisor* is the company offering its name and business system to the buyer, or *franchisee*. The business that the franchisee buys is called the *franchise*.

Pros

Maybe the best part of buying a franchise is that you are buying into a proven system. Here is how it is supposed to work: Say that somewhere, some business owners created a successful business that they believed could be duplicated—that is, the reasons and methods for their success could be systematized and taught. So the business owners reduced their success to a step-by-step plan. That system, that business model, is the franchise. The idea is that if you do what they did, you will get the same results that they got. A good franchise, then, is a systematic way of doing business whereby you agree to do things the franchisor's way and are allowed to use its business name, logo, system, and so on. The first benefit of franchising, therefore, is that, theoretically, you reduce your risk of failing because you are buying a proven system.

Tip: To learn more about franchising, visit the International Franchise Association's website at www.franchise.org, as well as FranchiseHandbook.com.

Note that I said that you *theoretically* reduce your risk. That is true only if you buy into the right system. Not all franchises are created equal. You really need to do your homework before buying a franchise. This piece of advice will be reiterated several times throughout this chapter, but it bears repeating: the very best thing you can do before buying any franchise is to talk to current franchisees. See how they like the system and the franchisor. Discover how much money they make (as opposed to what the franchisor might represent). Find out whether they would buy into the system again, knowing what they know now.

The second benefit of buying a franchise is that you should get plenty of help. Ray Kroc put it best: you might be in business *for* yourself, but with a franchise, you are not in business *by* yourself. When you start a business from scratch, you are on your own, whereas when you start a franchise, the franchisor is there (or should be) to help you succeed. It offers expertise in a wide variety of areas. A good franchise system trains you to be a successful businessperson. Furthermore, there will be other franchisees in the system with whom you can learn from and work. That, too, should be a great resource.

The last benefit of franchising is that you will get assistance with your advertising and marketing, and with bigger franchise systems, you will get the benefit of their national advertising campaign.

Cons

Although the benefits of buying a franchise are significant, the downsides should not be minimized. The first is that it can be fairly expensive to buy a franchise. When you buy a franchise, you are buying the franchisor's name, logo, goodwill, expertise, system, and training. That can be worth a lot, especially for a well-known franchise. This is not to say that all franchises are expensive—there are many that are quite reasonable—but be aware that if you want to buy a name-brand franchise, you will pay for that name.

The second major drawback to franchising is that you will have less independence as a franchisee than you would have as a regular entrepreneur. The system is the system, and you will agree in your franchise contract to run your business according to the system, even if you don't agree with it in principle. An ice cream franchisee who does not want to give away free cones one summer evening every year has to do so if the franchisor says so. Because the franchisor trusts you with its brand and goodwill, you are supposed to do things its way.

This brings us to the last shortcoming of franchising. You will be in an unequal relationship with the franchisor. The very nature of the business arrangement, as well as the contracts you sign, puts the franchisor in the power position. This is difficult for many franchisees, especially when something does not go right. There have been many lawsuits against franchisors that the franchisees feel are overreaching and domineering. Then again, there are plenty of franchisors that are easy to work with.

The thing to take away is that there are good franchisors and bad franchisors. It is in your best interest to do plenty of research so that you can rest assured the company you decide to partner with is a good one.

RESEARCHING THE FRANCHISE

When starting your franchise analysis, start globally, then narrow it locally. By that I mean begin by looking at the universe of franchises available—there may be franchises that would be perfect for you, if only you start out thinking broadly. After that, narrow down the choices to the ones you like best and think would work well in your area.

Begin by picking up a copy of the *Franchise Handbook,* or go online to www.FranchiseHandbook.com. The *Franchise Handbook* is a quarterly publication that lists most franchises, what they are about, and what their fees are.

It is also a good idea to attend a franchise expo in your area. These are held fairly regularly, and the *Franchise Handbook* site lists many of them. The problem with an expo, though, is that only a few franchisors out of the hundreds available will be there. But even so, it gives you a chance to get some face time with actual franchisors.

Questions to Ask

When speaking with franchisors at a franchise trade show, you want to learn several things:

- What is the total investment required?
- Does the franchisor offer financing?
- What sort of training and support can you expect?
- What sort of advertising does the franchisor do?
- Are there some current franchisees with whom you could speak?

After looking at the franchise universe, you can begin to narrow the choices down to a few industries that you like best and seem to have the most potential. Which ones best match you, your skills and interests, and your financial wherewithal? Does there seem to be a market for that type of business in your area?

As you narrow your choices, start to contact those franchisors that seem like the best and request information. Visit their websites. But you certainly cannot only rely on those materials alone to make your decision. Find franchisees of the franchisors you like best and speak with them. *The most important thing you can do in this process is to talk to current and former franchisees.* They can tell you what the franchisor is like to work with, what to be concerned about, and a whole lot more.

What to Look For

Of course, you want a franchise that will be interesting and lucrative, that is a given. Although you can never be guaranteed of that, there are traits that good franchisors have in common that you should know about:

1. *There is plenty of support.* The best franchise systems are ones in which the franchisor sees its relationship with franchisees as a partnership. The former head of Pizza Hut, Steve Reinemund, put it this way: "Franchisees are only as successful as the parent company and the parent company is only as successful as the franchisees." That is the attitude you want to see. Support can mean many things. It means extra assistance during difficult times. It means good communication at all times. It means superior training and materials. The franchisor may help you select a location for your business, negotiate your lease, finance the fees, or provide other services. Support is an attitude that says the franchisor is only as successful as the franchisee.

Good Idea

Get all promises of support in writing.

What kind of support should you expect? This is typical:

- Local and national advertising
- Support and feedback from a field representative
- Updated operating manuals

- Continuous training for you and your managers
- Communication: newsletters, Intranets, and e-mails are the most common

2. *Advertising is key.* Not all franchises are dependent on advertising, but enough are that this is an important distinction. New customers must come from somewhere, and a superior franchise system will help you get those new customers with its advertising campaign.

3. *The franchisor is flexible.* The nature of franchising is that there are processes and procedures to follow. That sort of uniformity is one of the things that makes franchises attractive—customers know what to expect. And although that is good, franchise rigidity is not. You want a franchisor that understands creativity and independence are part of being an entrepreneur, even a franchised entrepreneur. Good franchisors know that it is franchisees that often come up with the breakthrough idea. The Big Mac was invented by McDonald's franchisee Jim Delligatti in 1968. Avoid the rigid franchisor.

4. *The franchisor keeps up.* An offshoot of the foregoing point is that a flexible franchisor should also be a modern one. Tastes and values change, but not all franchises do. Look for a franchise system that puts money into research and development, constantly testing new products and ideas.

5. *The franchisor has a solid reputation.* Checking with past and current franchisees certainly helps, but don't stop there. Do an online search. Go to the library and find articles discussing the franchisor. Contact the Federal Trade Commission to see whether there have been any complaints about the franchisor.

6. *The franchisor is fairly large.* A large number of franchises is a good sign; it indicates that the business model works and that the franchisor has a successful, established business. This is not to say that newer franchises with fewer units are bad, only that they are less tried and true. A smaller, newer franchise is a bit more of a gamble, and one point of buying a franchise is to reduce risk.

7. *The franchisor is franchisee friendly.* Buying a franchise is a long-term investment, so you'd better be sure that the franchisor is a company that you can work with.

NARROWING YOUR CHOICES

All of this research should enable you to narrow your choice down to a select few franchisors. At that point, it is time to set up some face-to-face meetings. At these meetings, a few things should occur. First, every question you have asked should get an answer. Get a feel for the franchisor, its system, and whether you are compatible; the last thing you want to do is to invest a lot of money and make a long-term legal commitment to a franchisor whose values and modus operandi are different from yours.

What to Ask

By the time you have narrowed your choices down to a select few franchises, you should have a slew of questions for each franchisor. Yes, you may be very excited and might be ready to get started, but slow down. Now is the time to be prudent and thoughtful, to be, well, a businessperson. You will want to discover:

- The total fees you will have to pay, for what, and when. Is financing available? If not, does the franchisor have a relationship with a lender you can talk with?
- Will you need to buy real estate? Will the franchisor help you find a location? Does it offer architectural blueprints for building the store? Does it have a deal with contractors with which you can work?
- What sort of equipment is required? Do you buy or lease it? What are the initial and ongoing inventory requirements? Which suppliers are used?
- How extensive is the training program? How long is the initial training, where does it take place, and when are follow-ups?
- What sort of advertising and marketing support does the franchisor offer? How much is the advertising fee?
- What sort of research and development program is offered?
- How long is the initial franchise agreement, how long is the renewal, and which party has the option to renew? Can you sell or assign your franchise if you desire?

How Much Can You Really Make?

You certainly want to ask how much money you can reasonably expect to make. But do not be surprised if the franchisor is not willing to tell you. If the franchisor says, for example, "You will make $80,000 a year," and you do not, then what? You might sue the franchisor for misrepresentation. Thus, most franchisors are tight-lipped about potential profit—of all things! You can gather this information during your research phase as you interview other franchisees.

The FDD

Franchise law used to be dominated by a document called the UFOC—the Uniform Franchise Offering Circular. That document has now been replaced by its successor—the FDD, the Franchise Disclosure Document, a name that better reflects the document's purpose.

The FDD must be given to any potential franchisee within 14 calendar days of the signing of any contract (previously, under the UFOC, the document had to be delivered at the first in-person meeting at which the subject of buying a franchise is discussed, or at least 10 business days prior to the signing of any franchise contract requiring payment by the franchisee to the franchisor). The smart potential franchisee will ask for this critical document much earlier in the process.

The FDD contains extensive information about the franchise and is intended to both give you a chance to learn about the franchise and to make a rational decision.

The FDD

Not only must you get the FDD at least 14 days before signing any contract, but you also must receive a copy of all contracts at least five days before signing.

The FDD, although written in legal gobbledygook, is nevertheless a wealth of information. There are 23 standard items in the document. The important areas to concentrate on are these:

- *Number 2.* This section discusses the experience and background of the directors, officers, and managers of the franchisor. Know thy franchisor!
- *Number 3.* This section examines the litigation background of the franchisor, as well as the people listed in Number 2. Beware of excessive lawsuits or regulatory actions by government entities. In particular, be on the lookout for lawsuits by franchisees against the franchisor.
- *Number 4.* This section will list any bankruptcies for either the business or the people mentioned in Number 2.
- *Numbers 5, 6, 7, and 10.* This is where you learn about the monetary commitment. Franchise fees, ongoing royalties, and the estimate of the total investment can be found here. Number 10 discusses whether financing is available.
- *Number 11.* This section is critical. It discusses the franchisor's obligations to you, such as training and so forth.
- *Number 19.* This section is not required by law, but if it is present, it will discuss potential profits.
- *Number 20.* Also important, this section details the number of franchisees who have entered and left the system recently. It also lists the names, addresses, and telephone numbers of current and past franchisees. That alone makes the FDD very valuable.
- *Number 21.* This is the section to review with your CPA. Here you will find three years' worth of audited financial statements.

Additionally, under the FDD, franchisors must disclose how many franchises over the past three years were sold, terminated, or transferred. That too makes this a very valuable document.

FEES

Typically, four costs are associated with buying a franchise. The first is the franchise fee. This is what you pay to buy into the system, use the franchisor's logos, get trained, and so forth. The franchise fee might be as little as $2,500 for a small, unknown franchise, or it might be $50,000 for a well-known outfit. Second, you will pay an ongoing royalty of 3 percent to 6 percent of gross sales per month to the franchisor.

Third, expect to pay some monthly or quarterly fee for the advertising pool.

The last cost is usually the largest one. It is the amount that it will cost you to build out the store (if it is a retail franchise) in accordance with the franchisor's mandates. Again, this could be minimal, or it could be $500,000 or more. Why so much? Here are some of the things you may have to pay for:

- *Real estate.* You may have to buy land and a building. You may also have to put down security and utility deposits.
- *Design fees.* You may need an architect to draft plans for your store.
- *Construction fees.* This can include everything from constructing the building to remodeling to landscaping.
- *Equipment and fixtures.* You may need to buy tables, chairs, telephones, display counters, computer systems, and cash registers.
- *Décor.* Signs, pictures, lighting, and interior design may be required.

Other costs associated with opening your doors might include the following:

- *Inventory.* You have to stock the shelves.
- *Insurance.* You will need workers' compensation, liability, property, and other insurance.
- *Labor costs.* Your staff may be required to get initial training from the franchisor.

Costs

Costs vary widely. McDonald's states that a potential franchisee must have at least $175,000 of his or her own cash on hand to even begin discussions and the franchise fee alone is $45,000. Estimates are that a new McDonald's costs between $1 million and $1.8 million. For Subway, the franchise fee is $15,000 and capital requirements range between $114,800 and $258,300. For ServiceMaster the fees are as follows: franchise fee: $24,900 to $79,200 and capital requirements between $47,860 and $161,125.

THE FINAL DECISION

Do not be intimidated by the costs listed here. Constructing a stand-alone restaurant franchise is an expensive proposition, but the vast majority of franchises are not stand-alone restaurants. There are literally hundreds of choices out there. If you do your homework, you can find one that has a solid reputation, offers a fair return on your investment, is interesting to you, and is affordable. Good luck!

CHAPTER **15**

Secrets of Franchise Success

The secret of success is to know something nobody else knows.

—Aristotle Onassis

Running a successful franchise—indeed, running any successful business—requires several traits and abilities. Yes, working hard and working smart count a lot, but there are other equally important factors that go into the franchise success equation. Some, such as strong sales skills, are obvious. Others, such as exceptional employee relations, are not. In this chapter, the secrets of the best franchisees are yours for the taking.

SURVEY SAYS

Fred Berni is the president of Dynamic Performance Systems Inc., a company that helps franchisors select successful franchisees. Franchisors have a vested interest in finding strong franchise candidates, according to Berni, because unsuccessful franchisees create franchisor aggravation, employee morale problems, unflattering media exposure, and possible lawsuits. Thus, franchisors want to find and recruit potential franchisees who have a high likelihood of success.

In an effort to help his clients, Berni and a staff of psychologists undertook a survey of hundreds of franchisees over a period of several years in many different industries. Asking more than 600 questions covering a wide range of attitudes, personality traits, and skills, the study examined how and why successful franchisees differed from less successful ones. The purpose of the study, Berni says, was to "find a way to identify which candidates had the greatest likelihood for success, identify whether personality characteristics could predict performance, and identify what the mystery 'other factors' are."

According to Fred Berni

"Some years ago, I became aware of the frustrations that franchise professionals had in predicting how well a particular candidate would eventually perform. My clients told me, and research backed their claims up, that personality seemed to have no great track record in predicting performance. Obviously, there must be other factors in place of, or in addition to, personality at work here. So I decided to find out what these other factors were."

—Fred Berni, www.franchise-profiles.com

The results were illuminating, to say the least. The first interesting finding the survey uncovered was that, as Berni says, "Attitudes, not personality, are the best predictors of franchisee performance. Beliefs drive results." Berni's survey found that successful franchisees shared many common core values and attitudes. Although a franchisee's personality and skill set were important, these qualities paled in comparison to having the right attitude and values. "Initially, we were somewhat surprised to learn that preexisting skill sets had no predictive value. Upon further reflection, though, this makes perfect sense. After all, every franchisor trains candidates in those skill sets necessary to actually run the business."

Just what are those attitudes and values that make a difference, that separate the excellent from the mediocre franchisee? Hang on, because the results are illuminating. (These results are reported in order of importance.)

Successful Franchisees Involve Their Employees in the Business

Perhaps the most fascinating fact is that the way a franchisee treats employees is *the single most important factor in determining franchise success*. The survey found that:

- Successful franchisees truly believe that their employees are a valuable business asset, not a burden or a business expense.

- Successful franchisees manage in a participative, as opposed to a domineering, style.
- Successful franchisees treat employees with decency and respect.

As a result of such enlightened thinking, franchisees who treat their employees right tend to have less staff turnover, fewer hiring expenses, more contented employees, a happier workplace, and thus more loyal customers. Happy employees offer better customer service, which, in turn, translates into increased profits. Conversely, if your employees think you are a jerk, will they go out of their way to make a customer happy? You know the answer. In other words, your employees figure if you do not help them, why should they help you?

Successful Franchisees Are Optimistic

Having a positive outlook on life generally and on the franchise in particular were found to be major factors in franchisee success. It is not difficult to figure out how this attitude translates into day-to-day activities. If valuing employees creates happier employees, which, in turn, equals happier customers, the same will be true for positive, optimistic franchisors. That positivity filters down to all areas of the business, shedding light on everything and everyone associated with the business.

Successful Franchisees Are Moderately Independent

Yes, the nature of the franchisor–franchisee relationship means that independence is not a paramount virtue. But surprisingly, it is those franchisees who are, in fact, somewhat independent—those who have ideas and try them out, who think for themselves, and who are self-determining— who are most successful. The best franchisees strike a balance between following the system (you did buy the system for a reason) and being entrepreneurial. Balance is the key. The good news is that you do not have to be a corporate clone to be a successful franchisee. Nice, huh?

Successful Franchisees Are Adept at Sales and Marketing

This trait is linked to independence. Franchisees who are most successful do not wait for business to appear or for their franchisor to roll out a new marketing campaign. The most successful franchisees work at becoming knowledgeable businesspeople. They learn new marketing tricks and try them out. They schmooze and sell. They network and pitch products. In other words, they know that sales is a game, and it is a game they enjoy playing.

Another aspect of this finding is that the best franchisees sometimes take off their manager hat and do not expect their staff to do all the selling. Excellent franchisees are out there in the store, talking to customers, making suggestions, and making the sale, too, knowing that if they have a "selling attitude," their employees will, too.

All of these traits are not just amorphous attitudes. They are beliefs that create actions that promote success and sales.

Successful Franchisees Are Social

Business is a social game, and the best franchisees know that. No, you cannot help whether you are an introvert or an extrovert, but just know that being extroverted and gregarious directly affects the bottom line. Employees like you better, and relationships with customers are strengthened.

Franchise Tip

Are you introverted by nature? Do you find selling difficult? Too bad! If you want to succeed in your franchise, you will need to lead by example. Fake it till you make it. Your staff will take their cues from you. If they see you are quiet, that will become the corporate culture of the business.

The upshot of all of this is that the franchisees who are most successful know that people come first. If they treat their people right, other things fall into place. It is the franchisee who is dictatorial, resentful, restless, or negative who has the least chance of success.

OTHER FACTORS

Aside from the traits, attitudes, and actions listed in the previous section, there are several other factors that foster franchisee success.

Follow the System

This does not contradict the finding that independence is important. Of course, independence is important. If you were not independent, you would never have gone into business for yourself. But you bought into your franchise for a reason, and evidence shows that successful franchisees follow the system.

Becoming a franchisor and creating a successful operating system is no small feat. Not only must franchisors create a successful business to start with, but they also must be able to reduce that success to a repeatable, teachable system. By the time you buy your franchise, the hood on that system has been up many times, and the engine that is the system has been tinkered with, analyzed, fine-tuned, turbo-charged, and perfected. Mistakes have long since been made, funny noises have been fixed, and the bugs have been worked out. The system is what it is for some very good reasons.

If you do what the franchisor did, you should yield the same results— that is the plan. If you want to do things your own way, then starting a business from scratch and becoming a prototypical entrepreneur would be a better choice. But if you are at a place where you have already gone a different route and bought a franchise, then it would behoove you to follow the program.

Be a Jack of All Trades

Clay Werts is a no-nonsense man with salt-and-pepper hair who has been a very successful franchisee for more than two decades. An owner of three Baskin-Robbins franchises, all popular, Werts has some strong beliefs— learned in the trenches—about what it takes to make it in the franchise game. He is, first of all, a big believer that a franchise owner must be a jack of all trades but master of none. Why is that? Because running a franchise requires many different skills—promotion, management, finance, and so on. Being able to handle all the different facets of the business is critical.

To illustrate his point, Werts talks about a couple he once knew who owned (notice, past tense) an ice cream store not far from his. The husband was the king of promotions and the wife the queen of ice cream decorations. Yet they went out of business within a year. According to Werts, although the couple did two things well, that was all they did well.

The couple was especially bad at cash management. The money they made in the summer was not saved for the inevitable downturn that an ice cream shop has in the winter. Cash management is as important as marketing and as important as a beautiful product. You have to do several things well to stay in business, Werts insists.

Location, Location, Location

Clay Werts is also a big believer in the power of having a good location. You can stay in business if you have a great location, he says, even if you are not the best businessperson. But if you have a bad location, no matter how good a businessperson you are, your possibilities are limited.

What is his final piece of advice for franchise success? "Think big," he says. "If you are an optimist, are willing to take a risk, and work your tail off, anyone can make it."

Learn Advertising and Marketing

Superior franchisees are proactive when it comes to creating business. They accept the challenge of finding new customers—they almost relish it. Of course, they like and benefit from the franchisor's efforts, but they know that they cannot rely solely on what the franchisor does. "If it's to be, it's up to me," might be their motto.

Too often, franchisees fail to advertise sufficiently, or they waste advertising on an unfocused approach that does not zero in on the people who are ready, willing, and able to purchase their products or service. Instead of marketing to a specific audience, these franchisees instead target a broad audience in an attempt to reach everybody, usually reaching nobody.

Tip: One famous advertising executive once remarked that the best ad he had ever seen read, "Farm fresh eggs available today." The tight ad conveyed a feeling ("farm fresh"), the product (eggs), and a call to action (fresh today only).

The way to avoid this unenviable fate is easy. You must know your target market. You have to know who your customers are; what they like to watch, read, and listen to; what they buy and why; and how you can fill those needs. Once you know this, picking the vehicle to deliver your message to that market becomes much easier. Knowing your audience up front and actively and consistently marketing to that audience is a hallmark of successful franchisees.

Repeat: Location, Location, Location

We have all seen them—McDonald's, Pizza Hut, Taco Bell, Olive Garden, and Hardee's lined up in a row down the street like so many dominoes. And then you pull into the mall, visit the food court, and there they are again—Sbarro, Dairy Queen, Subway, and Edo, all awaiting your business. Why is that? Don't they cannibalize each other's business by being so close together? The surprising answer is usually no.

By building near each other, many successful franchisees have found that rather than fostering competition, being close builds business. There can be a synergy when you locate your franchise near other franchises— you create a destination. But to succeed in this environment, your business has to be good—very good—because if it is not, the competition will eat you alive. The competition is tough, yes, but having a busy location is worth it.

The moral of the story? Whether your franchise lends itself to a cluster model or some other model, for the retail franchisee, location makes a big difference.

PART

IV

Home-Based Businesses

CHAPTER **16**

The Home-Based Business

There's no place like home.

—DOROTHY

Working from home is an attractive option to many. By avoiding the overhead of an office, working from a place you enjoy, and chucking the rat race, working from home can indeed be great—and don't forget that easy commute to the extra bedroom. But having a home-based business is not all milk and honey, not by a long shot. Your chances of small business success increase when you work from home, because you have lower overhead expenses. Nevertheless, there are challenges aplenty when you work from home. Here we explore the promise and problems of the home-based business.

MAKING THE DECISION

There are two types of home-based businesses. First, there is the home-based business that is started with the intention that it will remain a home-based business. Because working at home can be easy, pleasant, and inexpensive, many people start their business from home because that is where they intend to stay for the long haul. Second, there is the home-based business that is started with the intention to move out as soon as it is economically feasible. These entrepreneurs know that the start-up phase of a business is critical: money is usually tight, and starting a venture from home allows them to earmark their precious capital for things other than rent and commuting costs. It, too, is a smart strategy.

Whether you already have a business that you are considering moving into your home or you are thinking about starting a home-based business from scratch, know that it takes a certain temperament and an iron will to be successful at it. Do you make the cut? Let's find out. Take the following quiz. For every "yes" answer, give yourself 5 points. For every "no" answer, give yourself 0 points.

Are You Ready to Be a Home-Based Entrepreneur?

1. Do you have the space at home to create a private office?
2. Are you self-disciplined enough to work when your family is around?
3. Do you have, or can you get, the technology required to run a modern home-based business—a separate phone line, high-speed Internet, cell phone, and fax machine?
4. Are you willing to work alone, cut off from colleagues and associates?
5. Are you self-disciplined enough to avoid going to the refrigerator, television, or Internet throughout the day?
6. Does your business model lend itself to working by yourself at home?
7. Are there distractions at home—noisy neighbors, loud babies, or intrusive friends with nothing to do but pester you?
8. Will your customers take you seriously if you work from home?
9. Are you excited about the possibility of working from home?
10. Does your family support your plan to work from home?

Scoring

30 and higher: You have both the temperament and support necessary to work from home.
20–30: You might be able to start a successful home-based business, but be sure to line up all your ducks.
Less than 20: Working from home is not for you.

The Home Business Boom

It has never been easier or more popular to work from home. Thanks to technological advancements, home-based entrepreneurs have all the tools they need not only to succeed but also to look like a pro in the process. Computers, laser printers, websites, digital voice mail, and the like, allow any home-based entrepreneur to look and act like a sophisticated operation. Moreover, attitudes have changed so that working from home is more often viewed with envy than with curiosity, as in days past. Combined, these changes in technology and attitudes have created a seismic shift in how work is done, meaning that more and more people are moving their office into their home.

If present trends continue, within 10 years, one out of every three households will have someone working from home. *Entrepreneur* magazine estimates that almost $500 billion is generated each year by home-based businesses. In a recent survey, it was reported that almost 25 percent of all home-based businesses had a yearly gross income between $100,000 and $500,000.

So yes, these days, working from home has a bit of cachet. It is hip. It is also smart. One of the main advantages of starting a business from home, either initially or over the long term, is that it dramatically reduces your overhead, which is significant. One trait that successful small businesses have in common is that they keep a close eye on the bottom line. That is not to say they are cheap—*frugal* might be a better word. These businesses know that if spending gets out of hand, profits are hard to maintain. So a home-based business makes a lot of business sense, because major expenses such as rent, labor, and travel are almost nonexistent. Therefore, the potential for success is greater.

Tip: If you are starting and running a home-based business, then I suggest you check out my new site just for you: TheSelfEmployed.com. There you will find special offers from partners, great content, tips and strategies, and a community of like-minded people.

Pros and Cons

Just as there are pros and cons associated with buying a franchise, so, too, are there pros and cons to running a home-based business.

Pros

First, because home-based businesses are less expensive to operate, starting a home-based business is practical and doable. Finding the funds to buy an expensive food franchise, for example, is a very difficult task. But starting a small business from home is very, very affordable. Moreover, not only is your rent less, but also there is less mileage put on your car, less need to wear expensive clothes, and significant tax deductions available.

Second, people who work at home tend to like working at home. They are a happy lot. A *Prevention* magazine survey found that home-based businesspeople say that they eat healthier, have more free time, exercise more often, and have a better sex life than they did when they were employees. The survey also found that those who work from home spend more time with family. Mothers or fathers with school-age children are available more often.

Finally, working from home is a very flexible option. Because your office is just down the hall, it is easy to make a work schedule that works for you. You can work when you want—if that is at midnight when you cannot fall asleep, well, bully for you.

Many businesses you know started out as home-based businesses:

- **Microsoft**
- **Apple**
- **Disney**
- **Amazon.com**
- **Xerox**
- **L. L. Bean**

Cons

I said earlier that working from home requires discipline, a fact that I know from personal experience. Having worked both inside and outside the home, I personally like working outside better, as the detriments of working from home are not insignificant.

The first problem is that there are a lot of distractions when you work at home, distractions that are not present when you work in an office outside the house. If you have children, the good news is that when you work at home, you see your kids a lot. The bad news is that you see your kids a lot. Crunching to meet that deadline or taking that important phone call is more difficult at home because, frankly, those around you do not always realize that even though you are at home, you are also at work. If you do not mind being interrupted, that is good because you *will* be interrupted.

Second, home-based businesses require self-discipline in many areas. If you want to sleep in, you can. If you want to work in your bathrobe, you can. It is easy to find yourself watching too much television, playing too much golf, or surfing the Internet too often. Goofing off: Who would have thunk that would be a home-based business hazard? Conversely, instead of working too little, it is just as easy to work too much when you work at home. Your office, after all, is right down the hall. Why not put in a couple of extra hours and get that project out the door? Workaholics need self-discipline, too.

Home-Based Home Run

Bette Nesmith was a single mother who worked as a secretary at a bank during the 1950s. She was a lousy typist, making far too many typos, but she was a fine artist. Seeing her artistic abilities, the bank asked her to paint a Christmas scene on its windows each year. One year, while painting the holiday scene, she made a mistake. She painted over it, as artists do, and thought to herself, "I wish I could paint over my typos when I type." Then she realized that she could! Nesmith brought some tempera paint to work and began painting over her typos. After a while, she decided that this revolutionary idea would make a great business, so she started one out of her house. At home after work, Nesmith began to experiment with different combinations of paint and, in the process, invented Liquid Paper.

Finally, a nice thing about going to a regular office every day is that there are people with whom to interact and socialize, and that simply does not happen when you work at home. Meeting new people, sharing ideas, hearing the latest joke—you give all of that up when you open your own home-based business. Yes, you may hire employees down the road, but when you start out at home, you are usually alone.

TAKING THE PLUNGE

If you decide that a home-based business is right for you, it is vital that you do it right. First, do not make the mistake of thinking that you can get by cordoning off some space in the living room. You can, but it will not work for long. You need a separate room, both because your work will require it and because you will need it psychologically to reinforce the fact that you are *at work*. Not only that, if you want to claim the home office deduction on your income taxes, you need to have a room that is devoted solely to the business.

Start by picking the right room. Now, it may be that there is no choice to make, that you have but one room available. If, however, you do have a choice, try to pick a room that:

- Has plenty of space
- Has enough electrical outlets
- Has a view
- Is off the beaten path of the house
- Is private

You need room for a desk, a chair, a computer, a phone, a file cabinet, storage, bookshelves, and workspace for assembling materials, stuffing envelopes, that sort of thing. If you will be meeting customers, you need enough room for chairs or a couch and a table. Depending on your business, you may also need space for employees, a waiting area for clients, or production facilities.

Equipping the Home Office

To set up your home office, you will need the following:

- *Electrical.* If possible, install extra outlets, and if you do, install them at desk level. If your office is going to use a lot of equipment, consider installing a separate circuit breaker.
- *Telephone.* You may need two phone lines, one for the phone and one for the fax machine, if you anticipate faxing much. (This is in addition to your regular home phone line.) Certainly your cell phone can work too as a business line.
- *Internet.* You will need a DSL, cable, or wireless Internet connection.

Once the office is ready to go, so are you. After that, starting your home-based business is not much different from starting any other business. You need to get a business license, decide on an image and a brand, begin to market yourself, and so on. One difference, though, has to do with getting the right insurance.

Insurance

The mistake that many new home-based entrepreneurs make is thinking that their homeowner's insurance will cover them should they have a loss and need to make a claim. In fact, some homeowner's polices specifically exclude businesses from coverage. So, the first thing to do is review your policy and see whether your home-based business is covered. If not, call your insurance agent and find out what it takes to get covered.

The other mistake is to avoid telling your carrier about your home-based business, figuring that if you ever need to file a claim, the company will never know the difference. The problem with that thinking is twofold. First, if you have a lot of computer equipment, business software, inventory, or other signs of a business, the insurer probably will figure it out. Second, if your insurer concludes that you do, in fact, have a home-based business, and your claim includes business losses, it can legitimately deny the claim for the business losses. It is better all around to pick up a home-based business endorsement that specifically covers your business.

CHAPTER **17**

Successful Home-Based Business Strategies

We are built to conquer environment, solve problems, achieve goals, and we find no real satisfaction or happiness in life without obstacles to conquer and goals to achieve.

—MAXWELL MALTZ

For those who have done it, creating a successful home-based business is a true accomplishment: carving out a niche in a competitive world and doing something that you love, where, when, and how you want, is most certainly something to be proud of. What does it take? What distinguishes excellent from mediocre home-based businesses? Like many endeavors described in this book, it requires both attitude and strategy. Model both, and you are on your way.

BALANCING ACT

There is a direct correlation between creating a thriving home-based business and striking the proper work–home balance. Working from home requires not only that you find a balance but also that the people around you do, too. As I discussed in the last chapter, you need to learn, fairly quickly, when and how to take your work hat on and off. When you work at home, there is a fuzzy line that is too easy to cross. By setting down some ground rules, you give your work the rigor that it may lack but certainly deserves:

- *Create a schedule and keep to it.* Sure, you can deviate—that is half the fun. But deviating from your schedule should be the exception, not the rule. By sticking to a schedule, you signal—both to yourself and to the world—that although you are at home, you really are at work. If you take it seriously, others will, too.
- *Dress appropriately.* When you work at home, it is too easy to make every day casual Friday. Although you certainly do not have to wear a suit to the office, you need not be a slob either. By dressing professionally, you are saying, with deeds and not just words, that your home-based business is the real deal.
- *Keep your office separate.* To the extent possible, your office should be *your office.* If it doubles as a children's playroom or the laundry room, not only is it hard to get work done but also the delicate work–home balance will be out of whack.

When you take your home-based business seriously, when you create boundaries and parameters, others will, too, although it may take a while and some training. People who do not work at home often quietly resent those who do, and certainly they think you have plenty of extra time on your hands when you work at home. Visions of lazy afternoons and mid-day naps dance in their heads.

Your ground rules are the antidote. Your rules may be that when your door is closed, no one can bother you, or that from 10 to 11 o'clock, you return phone calls and should not be disturbed. It could be that your entrepreneurial friends who also make their own schedules know that you *can* be bothered on Wednesday and Friday afternoons, when you take time off. The point is, it is your business, and growth will come easier when you and those around you know and follow the rules, whatever you deem them to be.

GROWTH STRATEGIES

There comes a time in the life of many home-based businesses when it seems like it is time to move up and out of the house. But if you have grown accustomed to the place, accustomed to the pace, how do you leave the creature comforts of home and still grow? The answer is, you don't have to. Here are some simple ways to continue to grow and still work in your slippers when the mood strikes.

Use an Executive Suite

Executive suites are offices that you can rent by the hour, day, week, or month and share with other small businesses. They are fully furnished, have secretaries and receptionists on hand, and offer all the amenities (conference rooms, Internet access, copy machines, and so on) of your own full time, out-of-the-house office but at a fraction of the cost. Most are located in beautiful, modern downtown offices, so you are assured of impressing clients.

Fees vary depending on your needs. For example, you may want to continue to work at home and simply use the address of the suite on your stationery. That works. Most suites offer an affordable virtual office option (a couple hundred dollars a month, tops) that allows you to use their address, have them receive your mail, have them answer your phone (transferring the calls to you at home), and get a few hours of conference room time, too, for meeting with clients. The more office time you need, the more you pay. These are great places to meet clients and make an impression.

By utilizing an executive (or professional) suite, you can put a shiny external face on your home-based business if you so desire, and at a very affordable price.

Example: Regus Business Centers offer executive suites at more than 400 locations worldwide in incredible, state-of-the-art buildings. They offer fully furnished offices, the ability to pay only for the time you use, a professional staff, a prime business address, and high-tech, wired conference rooms. Best of all, once you are part of the system, you can use any office in any one of their other locations. If, say, you rent a virtual office in Manhattan and have to go to Los Angeles to meet a big client, all you need to do is call your New York office and have them book you a room in the Southern California office of your choice. Check out www.regus.com.

Rent the Space You Need

Many successful home-based businesspeople continue to run their business out of their home while renting the space they need to grow. Barsahrin Travis is a yoga teacher. She used to hold sessions in the quiet living room of her house, but when her classes grew too popular, she decided to rent space at a nearby dance studio. She continues to manage her thriving business from home but uses space outside the house to grow.

It may be that you need warehouse space, a place for inventory, a location for your workshops, space for employees—the reasons for wanting more room are varied. The important thing is not to think of it as an either/or situation. You can continue to work from home *and* rent space and continue to grow. You do not have to move out of the house to get bigger.

Remember, too, that it is fairly easy to access your computer remotely; working in one place and logging on to another computer (back at home, for example) is easy. The latest version of Windows offers this sort of interface, as do websites such as www.GoToMyPC.com. Having a small business server also allows you to remotely access your office, which makes having two workplaces much easier.

Get Help

When you face the happy dilemma of too much growth and not enough room, another option is to contract with another company or individual to handle the overflow for you. Yes, hiring people as employees or independent contractors to do work that you could do yourself costs money, but that is what businesses do—they segment duties and hire staff to handle jobs. It is a sign that your home-based business has reached a more mature stage of development.

Aside from taking those duties off your hands, the other benefit of hiring help is that it frees you up to concentrate on matters that are more important. At the risk of sounding redundant, far too many small business people spend far too much time working *in* their business and not *on* their business. You have only so much time, and when you spend it stuffing envelopes or filling orders or collecting past-due invoices, you take time away from doing something else—and that something else is usually a better, smarter use of your time. Hiring staff enables you to have more free time to think bigger and plan better.

Go Virtual

If you do not want the expense and responsibility of hiring employees and finding space for them to work, consider hiring a virtual assistant. Virtual assistants are independent contractors who work from their own home or office, handle duties for you, and communicate with you via telephone, fax, e-mail, or messenger service. Virtual assistants have become quite the rage of late.

According to the International Virtual Assistants Association, "A Virtual Assistant (VA) is an independent entrepreneur providing administrative, creative and/or technical services. Utilizing advanced technological modes of communication and data delivery, a professional VA assists clients in his/her area of expertise from his/her own office on a contractual basis."

VAs are especially good at handling pesky administrative duties such as collections, marketing, travel planning, research, and accounting. They might even help create your website, prepare your newsletter, or schedule appointments. VAs are affordable—typically less than $50 an hour. You pay only for the time you use. Best of all, by hiring a VA, you get all the advantages of having an assistant without the associated overhead— no employment costs or taxes, no rent for office space, nada.

VAs can really help your business grow. Good ones are committed to your success, knowing that if they do well, you will do well, and if you do well, they might do even better.

Tip: For more information on hiring a virtual assistant, contact AssistU (www.assistu.com) or the International Virtual Assistants Association (www.ivaa.org).

GET PAID WHAT YOU ARE WORTH

A problem for many small, home-based businesses is that they set their prices when they first open their doors and fail to raise them—ever. Afraid of driving away customers, these businesspeople get stuck in time, charging and getting paid amounts that are years out of date. So how do you raise prices, earn what you are worth, and keep customers in the process? There are five steps to take.

1. *Decide on a reasonable amount.* If it has been awhile since you last raised your rates, you may be out of touch with what the market will bear. What are your competitors charging? That is a good place to start. Like Goldilocks, you do not want to be too hot or too cold. You want to be just right (unless what you offer is qualitatively different). Decide on an amount that you think is fair and reasonable.

Flat Fees

Do you hate hourly billing? Consider the beauty of the flat fee. When you charge a flat fee, you can estimate your hours and bid the job accordingly. Clients love flat fees because they know exactly what the job will cost. You have an incentive to get the work done faster (your flat fee will be the same), and you do not have to spend all that time adding up every quarter hour you spent on a project.

---

2. *Give clients reasonable notice.* Whether you intend to raise your rates $10 an hour, 25 percent, or whatever, you need to give your clients advance warning so that it is not a shock and so that they can plan for it. When you tell them, be businesslike. Do not apologize, and do not explain. Confidence is key. People raise their rates—that is a fact of business. You are good at what you do, and you deserve to raise your rates, too. Be sure to explain that your new rates are in line with the norm in the industry. If you do feel the urge to explain the rate hike, you can always say, for instance, "My fees are still reasonable, and I have not raised them in years. I have to keep up with my overhead" or "I decided that I need to raise my rates 10 percent every other year."

3. *Test.* This is an optional step. If raising your rates makes you nervous and concerned that you will lose clients, consider trying it out on a few clients for starters. Discover their reaction. If it works, then roll out fee increases across the board. If not, retreat!

4. *Handle resistance.* Clients who voice their displeasure will need a little extra TLC. Explain how much you do for them and how much extra you do that is gratis. Make sure they understand that your new fees are not out of line, and besides, if they switched to someone new, it would require time and training, and that would eat up any savings they might get. Reiterate all that you do. Explain that you dislike raising your rates but really have no choice; based on your long-standing working relationship, you hope they will understand. If they still balk, consider giving them a perk—maybe another 60 days at the old price. That might work.

PART

V

Business on a Shoestring

CHAPTER 18

The Shoestring Entrepreneur

> I am an optimist. It does not seem too much use being anything else.
>
> —WINSTON CHURCHILL

Starting and growing a business on a shoestring may not be the optimal choice, but if you are an entrepreneur at heart, it still beats working for "The Man." Indeed, starting on a shoestring puts you in good company. It is safe to say that most start-ups begin without as much money as the owners would like, but they get off the ground anyway. But understand this, too: although starting and growing a business on a tight budget is possible, it is not easy. Doing it successfully requires several things: the right attitude, OPM (other people's money), and frugality.

THE RIGHT STUFF

Although many start-ups do not have optimal funding, a shoestring start-up is a different animal. Starting on a shoestring means that, rather than having less than optimal funding, you have little or no funding at all. It means really starting from scratch. But you can do it. Countless others have done it.

To do it right, you need to begin your bootstrap entrepreneurial journey with a grounded understanding of what it will take. There are five rules of the road to follow:

1. *Know that fortunes have been made on minuscule beginnings*. Peter Hodgson borrowed $137 to buy the goop he would rename Silly Putty.

Arnold Goldstein, author of *Starting on a Shoestring,* began his first retail discount store, containing roughly $100,000 of merchandise, using only $2,600 of his own money. Real estate is one way you could start on a shoestring right now. By obtaining a 10 percent loan from the Federal Housing Administration (FHA), you could buy a $150,000 duplex for $15,000 down. That is amazing. Even without 90 percent of the money needed, you could start a real estate business. There are ways to do it. If others have done it, you can, too.

2. *Understand the difference between good debt and bad debt.* When you do not have enough money, you usually have to go into debt to start or grow a business. But it is important to understand that not all debt is bad debt. Bad debt is unmanageable. Credit card bills that you cannot pay are bad debt. But debt that helps you get ahead in life—start a business, buy a home, or finance a college education—is good debt. Most millionaires start out in debt, but it is good debt. No, it is not ideal, but if you have a plan to pay it back, start-up debt can be good debt for you, too.

3. *Serve the market.* Every successful business must serve a market need. Whatever your shoestring idea is, it had better be a darn good one. Shoestring entrepreneurs rarely get second chances. Tapping friends and family to help finance your dream can happen only once. Invest in only your best, most commercial idea, or suffer the consequences.

4. *Shoestring businesses require creativity.* Improvising, making do, juggling, and borrowing from Peter to pay Paul will be necessary if you have to start or want to grow a business on a limited budget. Hire students. Buy some software and learn how to design your own website. Ask for free help. You will have to be highly energetic and very creative if you are going to succeed in this sort of endeavor.

5. *You gotta believe.* Northwestern University once conducted a survey of successful shoestring entrepreneurs and discovered that most of them had never owned a business before, had little business education, and, even though they did not have enough money, started a business anyway. Essentially, they did not know enough to realize that they should have been afraid. You have to have the same chutzpah. To be successful, you will need to be out there raising money, selling, projecting a confident image. If you are afraid or unsure, stop right there and make a U-turn. Do not pass Go and do not collect $200. Shoestring entrepreneurship is for the hearty alone.

OTHER PEOPLE'S MONEY

There are two types of shoestring operations. The first is started on a shoestring without borrowing any money at all. Maybe you have $500 or $1,000 or $2,500 and want to start a business on your own but do not want to take on any debt. Usually, such ventures begin as part-time home-based businesses that grow incrementally. It is possible to make a go of it, but the margin for error is so slim that it makes the possibility of succeeding very small. Nevertheless, that sort of shoestring entrepreneur will find some useful tips later in this chapter, and especially in the next chapter.

The second type of shoestring entrepreneur is one who wants to start a business without much of his own money or who wants to grow his existing business but lacks the funds to do so. These entrepreneurs will have to get some funding somewhere. They will have to use other people's money. The challenge is finding that other person with the money.

Brainstorm!

Jay had a great idea for a business. He would create the world's most unique treasure hunt. In this James Bond adventure, Jay would hide several diamonds somewhere in his city, create clues hinting at where they were located, write a background story for participants, and hire actors to play parts in the scenario. Jay figured that people would pay a lot of money for the chance to find the diamonds and act out their movie hero fantasies. The only problem was that Jay had little money. Undaunted, he wrote the script, asked some friends to play the parts, spent what little money he had creating a nice brochure . . . and then ran out of money. He finally put a little classified ad in the paper, hoped that a few people would sign up, and then he could use that money to buy the diamonds. One person called.

Finding that money is a two-step process. First, you will need a solid business plan. No investor will put money into your idea based on the idea alone. You will need facts and figures to back up rosy rhetoric. You need a business plan.

Then you must go out and start knocking on doors. Funding a start-up without your own money is a numbers game. You will likely need to talk to *a lot* of people before getting the money you need. Begin with friends, family, business associates, and professional colleagues. Most of these people will want to see that you are investing in the business, too, figuring that if you are unwilling to take a financial risk, why should they? If you have no money to put into the business, you have to be up front about that. Explain that your time, effort, and expertise will be your investment, and that is worth a lot. If you have some money to invest, do so. Even a little bit can impress. Try not to get discouraged. Remember, it is a numbers game. Chris Haney and Scott Abbott spoke with more than 100 people before getting 32 to invest about $2,000 apiece to fund their business based on a game they had just invented, called *Trivial Pursuit*.

Understand that, armed with a business plan, a good idea, a winning smile, and little else, you represent both peril and promise for would-be investors. The peril is that you could take their money and lose it on some untried scam. The promise is that you could take their money and make them wealthy with your great idea. Your challenge is to prove that the latter is far more likely to occur than the former.

Be Professional

The key to winning over any investor is to look like a pro. If you talk big without having the facts to back you up, you will look foolish. You have to be a businessperson. Draft a business plan. Have your elevator pitch ready. Know your market. Know your numbers inside out. Know thy competition. Be able to defend your plan of action. Explain with conviction why your plan is a great opportunity for the investor.

The friends and family plan works sometimes, and sometimes it does not. If it does not work for you, here are a few other viable shoestring funding sources.

Locate a Partner

Many partnerships begin because one person has the idea, skills, experience, or opportunity and the other has the money. If you have the desire and passion to start a business or need to grow your present business but lack the funding to do so, then teaming up with the right partner—one who has money—is a very real way to fund the plan. Of course, you will have to give up half your equity, but that is a small price to pay to live your dream.

Here is an example: Chester Carlson was an inventor by nature. When he landed a job in a patent office that required him to duplicate detailed patent applications by hand, he decided that there had to be a better way to re-create them. So at his workshop at home, Carlson began to tinker and fiddle. He eventually figured out a process that would allow him to reproduce documents electronically. Carlson then spent the next few years trying to sell his invention to companies such as General Electric, RCA, and IBM. He had no success. He was an inventor, not a salesperson.

Then a man named Joe Wilson heard about Carlson's invention. The president of a small photographic company called Haloid, Wilson went to see Carlson, saw a demonstration of the process, and said, "Of course, it's got a million miles to go before it will be marketable. But when it does become marketable, we've got to be in the picture!" Wilson and Carlson decided to become partners—Carlson had the invention, and Wilson had the money. Haloid eventually pumped $100 million into Carlson's invention before taking it to market and naming the machine, and the company, Xerox.

The question you probably have is, where can I find that magic partner? There are several sources:

- You start by networking. Speak with your lawyer, accountant, and other business associates. Talk to friends, family, colleagues, and people where you worship. Get the word out. Networking works.
- You should also speak with suppliers and distributors, as they may know people in the field who are looking for an opportunity. Consider speaking with people in your line of work who have retired. They may want to get back in the saddle or become a passive investor or partner.
- Conduct a Google search.
- Post an ad on Craigslist.
- Put the word out via Twitter and other social media.
- Put an ad in the paper under the section "capital needed." Scour the "capital available" section as well.

Online Resources

The web is a fine place to find a business partner. Try these sites:

- www.businesspartners.com
- www.PartnerUp.com
- www.PartnerBinder.com

When speaking with potential partners, you will get the money you want *only if* the partner gets what he or she wants. It may be that the partner wants a say in day-to-day operations. It may be that he or she just wants a monthly cut of the profits. Here, then, is another winning concept from the desk of the successful small business person: *ask investors what they want and give it to them.* Your partner might want to be a 50–50 partner, as Joe Wilson and Chester Carlson were, or your partner might want to be a "silent" partner who merely wants to invest in return for a share of the company. You will get what you want if your partner gets what he or she wants.

Supplier and Distributor Financing

Distributors and suppliers want your business, and they know that by offering you some financial assistance, they may be able to turn you into a long-term repeat customer. Your job, then, is to show them that if they lend you some money to get started, they will get your continued business. This happens more often than you might think.

Suppliers and distributors will want to learn about you, visit your business (if you have one), and check your references. Like any lender or investor, they need to be convinced that you will be able to pay them back. The key to success is preparation. You need a solid plan showing how helping you will help their bottom line.

Franchisor Financing

There are many franchisors that offer some degree of financing. Although financing 100 percent of a franchise is not unheard of, 50 percent or so is more typical. According to the International Franchising Association, roughly 33 percent of all franchisors offer some type of financing. Some franchisors offer interest-only loans, others offer loans that require no payment for the first year, some finance everything, and others finance the franchise fee only. It all depends on you and the franchisor. You need to ask.

It is also true that most franchisors have relationships with lenders, so that may be another possibility. Other alternatives include franchisor loan guarantees or working capital loans. Finally, many franchisors have relationships with leasing companies that might be able to finance the equipment needed to run the franchise. As this can be a major expense, do not overlook this possibility.

Free E-Book!

Log on to my site, TheSelfEmployed.com, mention this book, and you will receive a free e-book—*The Best Zero-Cost Shoestring Marketing Tricks, Ever!*

Other Options

As mentioned in other chapters, venture capital firms and angel investors may also be a possibility. And do not forget SBA-guaranteed loans.

The Deal

When structuring any finance deal with a potential investor in your shoestring business, work to make the deal a win–win situation. When structuring a loan or investment deal, keep these points in mind:

- Ask for more money than you need. If the investor balks and negotiates down, it will not be a crisis, and if not, you will have more than enough.
- Make sure it is your company that takes out the loan. You incorporated, right?
- Get the interest rate as low as possible. Everything is negotiable.
- Work to get as much time as possible to repay the loan, with no prepayment penalty.

GRAND OPENING

Shoestring entrepreneurship extends well beyond financing. You have to be vigilant about keeping your expenses to a minimum in every area.

Rent

Rent is one of the biggest expenses a business has, so minimizing your rent is imperative. Avoid the high-profile location and its high-profile rent. Instead, think like a shoestring businessperson: Rent a smaller space than you would like. Rent in an out-of-the-way location. Start a home-based business if you must. Just do not blow your dough on rent.

Business Incubators

Another low-cost option is to start your business in a business incubator. Business incubators are partnerships among public, private, and nonprofit organizations that work to promote entrepreneurship and small business growth. They do this by providing inexpensive space from which new businesses can be launched. Incubators usually offer free (or very inexpensive) administrative service assistance, legal help, business planning, financial advice, and so forth. As the name indicates, they are places that nurture, or incubate, a business while it learns to spread its wings and fly.

Although all business incubators work to launch successful businesses, each is unique. In Silicon Valley, for example, many business incubators foster computer-oriented start-ups, whereas in Wisconsin, incubators may foster dairy and farming-related businesses. It depends on the region and the incubator.

Business Incubators

There are many benefits to be derived from starting your business in a business incubator:

- Reduced rent
- Financial and business assistance and expertise
- Shared services
- Contacts

You can find out what types of incubators are available in your area by contacting the National Business Incubation Association (www.nbia.org).

Equipment

Shoestring entrepreneurs are always looking for a bargain. They buy furniture, equipment, and fixtures used, and if you are shoestringing, you should, too. The Yellow Pages are a good place to start. The Internet is a bargain hunter's paradise; eBay is but one of many places to look. Newspaper and magazine classified ads are a great resource.

If you cannot find what you need used, many manufacturers will finance up to 90 percent of your new purchase, preserving your precious capital. Consider leasing any fixtures or equipment you might need.

INVENTORY

Stocking the shelves of your store when you have a small budget is also possible. How do you do that, you ask? It is similar to a method mentioned earlier: you need to find suppliers that will give you their goods on credit. There are thousands of wholesale product manufacturers, suppliers, and distributors looking for business. One way for them to get it is to stock your shelves without requiring an up-front payment for the goods. They are paid when the goods sell.

Start by preparing a powerful package that proves your pluck, thereby inducing them to want to work with you. It should contain your business plan, stationery, letters of reference, the name of your lawyer and banker, and so on. Anything that gives you legitimacy helps your cause. Explain how much inventory you need, the terms you propose, and how and when you will pay it back. You need to convince the supplier that you are likely to become a new client who will be buying their goods for many years. That is what works.

After you have the package ready, you need to contact the sales rep from the supplier, manufacturer, or wholesaler whose products you want to purchase. Present the package to each one and ask for an appointment with the company's credit manager or regional sales manager. You stand a pretty good chance of success if you have a good package, a decent credit rating, and some trade references.

If the supplier agrees to stock your shelves for no money down, you will need to agree to continue to buy from the company for the term of the loan. You will also need to agree to grant the supplier a security interest in the merchandise, meaning that if you default or go bankrupt, the supplier gets its merchandise back.

Tip: When negotiating the terms of the deal, *do not* agree to buy from one manufacturer exclusively. For you, that should be a deal breaker.

You may get most of the product you need from one supplier, or it might take many suppliers lending you small amounts. Either way, the plan is to get the shelves stocked without investing a lot of your capital up front.

When you are doing business on a shoestring, you do whatever it takes.

BUYING A BUSINESS WITH NO MONEY DOWN

Is it possible to buy a business with little money of your own? Maybe. It is akin to buying a small piece of real estate without a lot of money. Remember that $150,000 duplex? Using a 10 percent loan obtained from the FHA, you need only $15,000 to buy it; the bank secures the loan with a lien against the property and loans you the rest. That is called *leverage*—with the asset securing the loan, you can leverage a small amount of money to make a large purchase. Leverage can be applied to the acquisition of a business, too. The secret is to find a willing seller who is open to some creative financing.

If you can get a conventional bank loan, great. Existing businesses have track records and assets (accounts receivable, autos, machinery, and so forth), so getting a bank loan is certainly possible. However, if you cannot get a bank loan, you still might be able to buy the business using seller financing. Sellers are often willing to finance some or all of the purchase.

Sellers need buyers, and if your purchase is made contingent on seller financing, the seller just might do it. Buyers are not always easy to find.

Of course, the seller will want to secure the loan with the ability to foreclose on the business and take it back if you default. That is fine. If you agree to that (and you should), then getting the seller to finance your purchase is very realistic. The optimal plan would be to combine bank and seller financing. Say, for instance, you want to buy a furniture store that is worth $100,000. It may be that the bank will finance half if the seller finances half, and away you go!

But what if the seller is willing to finance, say, 40 percent, and the bank will only match that amount? What if you need additional creative financing options to swing the deal? Where do you find that $20,000? There are several choices:

- *Debt financing.* Business sellers include in the asking price the amount they need to pay off their business debts. If you agree to assume those debts, you can reduce your down payment by that amount. Are you willing to assume $20,000 of the seller's debt?
- *Inventory financing.* When you buy a business, you also buy its inventory. If you are short $20,000, find out whether the owner will agree to liquidate $20,000 in inventory. You then reduce the purchase price by that amount. Similarly, the owner could sell a business asset worth $20,000—a truck, machinery, or even a piece of real estate.
- *Broker financing.* The majority of all business sales are done through a broker. Find out whether the broker is willing to reduce his or her commission to keep the deal alive.
- *Supplier financing.* Check with the business's suppliers. They may agree to loan you the $20,000 if it means they will continue to have a major account.

There are many ways to finance a business purchase with no money down. Creativity and a willing seller are all that is required.

CHAPTER **19**

Marketing on a Shoestring

Sell to their needs, not yours.

—Earl G. Graves

There is no doubt that big corporations have resources and abilities not shared by their small business brethren. They have budgets that we can only dream about, experts to do their bidding, even managers to manage their managers. Likewise, we have attributes they do not. Small businesses are far less bureaucratic. We are resourceful. We are nimble and quick. I would venture to say that the only area in which small businesses actually envy big businesses is with regard to their budgets. One ad in the *Wall Street Journal* might cost a Fortune 500 company $100,000. What kind of marketing could you do with $100,000? But fear not. Marketing need not cost a fortune. There are scores of ways to market on the cheap, look big in the process, and even the playing field.

THE SHOESTRING GROUND RULES

Marketing need not cost a fortune to reap tremendous rewards, but first, you have to know the ground rules.

Shoestring Marketing Takes Commitment

If you are like most small businesses, you have one or two or three tried-and-true marketing methods. But shoestring marketing means that you will try, and eventually adopt, several more methods. If three methods allow you to net $150,000 a year, what might you be able to make using six methods? To become a shoestring marketer means that you will try out many methods, test them, see which ones work best, and then add the winners to your marketing repertoire. This will take time, as you must run an ad or test a marketing method several times before learning whether it is effective. As a marketing campaign generally takes three to six months to produce results, commitment is required.

Shoestring Marketing Requires Consistency

To build a brand, people must hear a consistent message from you. Eventually, they will know that you are the "King of Big Screens" or that "You won't be undersold!" or whatever it is that you promise your customers. But to create that image, your marketing—shoestring and otherwise—must be consistent.

Consider the electronics store that spent a ton of money on a television campaign that lasted a week. The owner got results for about two weeks. He then tried a small, inexpensive ad *every week* in the Sunday entertainment section. It became his bread and butter. It created profits. Consistency is key.

Shoestring Marketing Requires Creativity

In the next section, you will find many inexpensive ways to market your business. Again, for this plan to work, you will need to try several and see which ones generate the best results. Try some that are foreign to you. Be creative.

Shoestring Marketing Must Be Measured

The only way to know whether your shoestring marketing campaign is working is to measure the results, and so you must create ways to measure your campaigns. Your benchmark might be sales during the same month last year. It might be the number of calls you receive in response to a flyer. Whatever the case, you need to create a starting spot so that you can decide which methods garner the best results.

So this is the plan: Read through the many ideas listed here and decide which ones might work best in your business. Set some benchmarks to test them against, and then try some out. Then try some more.

Be patient. Be creative. Watch the bottom line, and then decide which techniques should become additional tools in your marketing tool chest.

MAJOR MEDIA METHODS

Many shoestring methods allow you to advertise on television, radio, or in newspapers or magazines at a great discount.

Co-Op Advertising

Co-op advertising is a cost-sharing arrangement between a manufacturer and a retailer whereby the retailer places an ad that is partially or fully paid for by the manufacturer. The catch? The manufacturer's product or name must be mentioned in the ad. For example, Stuart ran an expensive ad every month in a fitness magazine that read, "The Bike Castle—Where Bikes Are King!" Near the bottom of the ad, it said, "Featuring Trek Bikes." Trek paid for much of that ad. That is co-op advertising. Similarly, when a convenience store advertises a certain product, you can bet that company helped pay for the ad.

Collectively, manufacturers earmark approximately $30 billion annually to help small businesses stretch their advertising dollars, yet surprisingly, much of that money goes unused. An obvious way to stretch your advertising dollar is to find out whether any of your suppliers offer co-op funds. Having your suppliers pay for your advertising is an excellent way to grow your business without spending much money.

Buy Remnant Space

Near press time, magazines and newspapers may have unsold advertising space, called *remnant space*. If you are flexible, willing, and able to buy at the last moment, you can pick up remnant space for a song. The same principle applies to unsold radio and television time. Call your local media outlets and ask about remnant space possibilities.

Overnight Radio

One inexpensive way to build your business is to use overnight radio advertising. In major media markets, advertising during drive time (7 to 9 A.M. and 4 to 7 P.M.) can run anywhere from $250 a minute to a whopping $1,000 a minute. At those prices, the repetition you need to create a successful campaign may be unaffordable. Overnight ads, on the other hand, cost much, much less and still can be very effective, even though they certainly reach a far smaller audience.

Kristy Hicks is a radio account executive who explains that many large news talk stations have nighttime or overnight ratings that rival the ratings of many smaller stations during their drive time, but this time is sold at a fraction of the cost. For a recent client, for example, she was able to get overnight 60-second spots at a major station for $10 a minute in a major market, and the audience size rivaled smaller stations' drive time audience. This is not atypical. Overnight spots are usually undersold at most stations, and they can be had at a great discount.

Secrets to Success

Kristy Hicks says that an effective overnight radio campaign requires three elements:

- *A compelling message.* You have to be selling something that people want to buy.
- *Frequency.* Repetition is the key.
- *Consistency.* Hicks points out that we all know the famous radio tagline "We'll leave the light on for you!" because Motel 6 never fails to use it. That is the power of consistency.

Cable Television

Whereas broadcast television is often cost prohibitive, cable television, especially late at night, is not. And the great thing about cable is that you can target your market very specifically by advertising on the exact stations your market watches. An overnight cable television ad might run as little as $25 a spot.

Newspapers

Advertising in the newspaper can be expensive and even though circulation is down, it still can be very effective if done right. Here are a few ways to reduce your costs:

- Cut the size of your ad in half and save 50 percent. Double the size of your headline. If you then buy a premium placement (about 15 percent extra), you still save 35 percent and have an ad that might really get noticed.
- Consider advertising with an insert only in the neighborhoods and ZIP codes that purchase your goods. You do not have to buy the whole region. You will save 50 percent or more.

Classified Ads

Both magazines and newspapers have classified ads (especially the Sunday paper), and the best thing about them is that they reach people who are shopping and ready to buy. If you test an ad and it works, ask for a frequency discount when buying in bulk. You can have as much success with a classified ad as you can with a display ad at a fraction of the cost. Tip: Have a snappy headline!

> ### The Rate Card
>
> When media reps quote you their rates, they quote from their *rate card*. Remember the rule that everything is negotiable. The rate card *is* negotiable.

Craigslist

The online equivalent today of classified ads, Craigslist is an amazing, and amazingly cheap, way to market your business and sell your wares. Many of the ads are free, and those that are not are cheap. It is the go-to place for people looking for a bargain, and who are looking to buy something *now*.

> ### 800 Numbers
>
> A very affordable option, 800 numbers increase your response rate by 30 percent to 700 percent.

Publicity

It does not take much money to get free publicity, but what it does take is a great press release or press kit. If you can convince a radio or television station or a magazine or newspaper that your business is newsworthy, and then get them to do a story about it, bingo! That free publicity is worth its weight in gold. You can parlay it into more business and reproduce that story for years to come, building credibility in the process.

PRINT TECHNIQUES

There are many other ways to market your business with little money yet get big results using the printed word.

E-Newsletters

Another good way to promote your business is through e-newsletters. They demonstrate how much you know about your field and do so in a low-key, informative way. Then, when a recipient needs someone with your expertise or products, he thinks of you. Although e-newsletters are all the rage, physical newsletters should not be forgotten either.

Consider also advertising in other e-newsletters. It's very cost-effective and you reach a highly specific, qualified audience.

Testimonials

Satisfied customers can be one of your best sales tools. Ask customers to write a testimonial on their letterhead and then include these letters in your marketing materials and promotions. Testimonials lend credibility to your advertising offerings. They also are great to use in sales presentations. My standard speaking contract states that if the meeting planner is happy with my speech, he or she will write a letter of recommendation

Tip: Post testimonial videos of happy customers on your website. They will get clicked a lot and are highly credible and effective.

within two weeks after the event. I then send these letters to upcoming prospective speaking clients.

Flyers

Five thousand flyers at 3 cents each costs $150. Hire a student to put them on cars downtown. The key to a good flyer is to offer cheap prices and emphasize benefits, benefits, benefits!

Coupons

Most coupons are never redeemed. Even so, creating a coupon costs almost nothing, and if your brand stresses low costs, coupons, even unredeemed, build your brand. And if they are redeemed, you drive more business your way. To be effective, coupons must offer at least a 15 percent discount. (Note: Because deal-of-the-day discount coupon websites are both a way of selling coupons and such a trending issue, they are given their own treatment later in the book.)

Invoice Coupons

Try adding a coupon to your invoices to sell more products to existing customers.

Personal Letters

President George H. W. Bush is said to have written more than 10,000 thank-you letters and credits that, at least partially, with getting elected president. Cost? Not much at all. In this era of instant communication, people really remember an actual letter. Consider writing a letter to your current customers, offering them a special discount, sale, or something else as a way to thank them for their business. Then hire some students to address the letters by hand.

ACTIONS

There are plenty of other low-cost marketing tricks you can try.

Barter

There are two forms of barter. Using the traditional method, you and another vendor agree to trade goods or services. More often these days, barter is done through a barter exchange that acts as an intermediary. The exchange issues "barter bucks" to you when you do something for someone else in the group. You can then use those bucks to purchase goods or services from anyone else in the group. As with everything else, the Internet has changed barter, too. Online barter exchanges have cropped up across the Internet, and they are great places for small businesses to get started. A good virtual barter exchange should keep track of transactions, act as an intermediary, issue the currency, handle the paperwork, and keep its fees to a minimum.

Barter

According to the International Reciprocal Trade Association, almost half a million small businesses use commercial barter exchanges every year, generating more than $10 billion in sales.

Barter offers several benefits:

- *You can get rid of excess assets.* Store owners have excess inventory, restaurants have empty tables, chiropractors have free hours, and so on. Barter allows you to move assets and products that are not being used.
- *You create new customers.* Barter exposes new people to your business. By joining a barter group, you may find that people who bartered for your goods or services may become regular clients.
- *Barter saves money.* When you use your time rather than your money, you save money.

Contests

A contest can generate interest and free publicity for your business. For example, a restaurant might have a yearly contest to see which customer can eat the most of its famous "Flaming Chicken Wings." Not only would this generate interest among its clientele, but also a local newspaper might pick up the contest as a fun human interest story.

And these days, contests may be even better online. Having a contest on your Facebook page, or a Twitter contest linking to your website is a great way to generate buzz and make a sale.

Networking and Social Networking

Having a good elevator pitch can create opportunities out of humdrum real-life encounters. Beyond that, social networking, of course, is a marketer's paradise, so I would suggest that if this interests you, jump ahead to those chapters later in the book that discuss Facebook, Twitter, LinkedIn, and the rest in full detail.

Demonstrations

Demonstrating your product at a mall, trade show, or other high-profile location usually leads to sales. Infomercials are nothing but 30-minute demonstrations.

Samples

When the car dealer lets you take the car that you are considering buying home for the night, what is that? It is a free sample. Gourmet grocers set out free food all day, as does Costco. Why? Free samples are inexpensive loss leaders that create sales. What can you offer for free?

Seminars

Seminars are a good way for service businesses to introduce themselves to potential customers, build rapport, and entice people to want to know more. Seminars are used by many professionals—doctors offering Lasik eye surgery or lawyers who create living trusts are common. Although not the most inexpensive option, seminars can be a very lucrative marketing mechanism.

Become the Expert

When you become known as an expert in your field, whatever your field, you will find that the world will beat a path to your door. Consider the following:

- By being the expert, you immediately distinguish yourself from the competition.
- By being the expert, you immediately offer your clients something of value that competitors cannot, and do not, offer.
- By being the expert, you can charge more for your services.
- By being the expert, you become the first choice.

How do you come to be known as an expert? Pick something that you know or do, something that you are passionate about, and begin to devote more energy to it. Then, share your analysis, ideas, and insights with colleagues and the public.

How else can you become known as an expert? Draft a press release, have a television or radio segment produced about you, or have a newspaper article written about you. Write an article for the local paper or for a trade journal. Advertise as "specializing in . . . ," like the car dealer whose ad reads, "Specializing in customers with credit problems."

Befriend a Concierge

The job of the concierge at a hotel or office building is to offer services to guests. Get on the concierge's list, and he or she becomes your marketing arm.

Offer Free Consultations

Free consultations usually lead to paying clients.

Be a Good Citizen

By sponsoring a youth sports team, coaching a team, or donating your services to charity, you begin to create a positive reputation in the community. What about sponsoring a segment on your local public broadcasting television or radio station? That certainly can be a chic method. All of this will (eventually) lead to more sales.

The Internet

Because Internet marketing is such a dynamic, powerful tool (pay per click, social media, etc.), I give it a chapter all its own. See Chapter 43.

EXAMPLES

Many of the options listed here are intended to whet your appetite. There are simply so many ways to market your business, many of which are underutilized by most small businesses, that it would be a shame if you stubbornly stuck to the same few techniques. Try a few of these out and see if you do not experience increased sales as a result.

Seasons Travel
Gross Sales Per Month: $4,000
Marketing Budget: 7.5 Percent of Gross ($300/month)
Monthly Shoestring Marketing Plan

Method	Cost	Analysis
Personal letters	Effectively $0	Only takes time
Brochures	$600 yearly to $50/month	Always on hand
Classified ads	$ 20	One newspaper, once a week
Craigslist	$ 20	Basic listing
Newspaper display ads	$ 100	One paper, once a week
Direct mail	$ 10	Postage
Public relations	$ 50	Cost of materials
Circulars	$ 50	Cost of materials and payment to put on cars
Total	**$300**	**Consistency is key**

Larry Allen and Associates, Attorneys at Law
Gross Sales Per Month: $20,000
Marketing Budget: 15 Percent of Gross ($3,000/month)
Monthly Shoestring Marketing Plan

Method	Cost	Analysis
Yellow Pages (physical book and online)	$ 500	One large ad
Internet Pay-Per-Click campaign	$ 1,000	Two medium weekly ads
Radio	$ 750	Always heard on the news talk station
Direct mail	$ 250	Three mailings a year
Free seminars	$ 450	Four times a year, amortized
Website	$ 50	Design and promotion, amortized
Total	**$3,000**	**High profile**

SECTION II

Running Your Business

PART

Small Business in the Twenty-First Century

CHAPTER **20**

Our Flat World

This is Globalization 3.0. In Globalization 1.0, which began around 1492, the world went from size large to size medium. In Globalization 2.0, the era that introduced us to multinational companies, it went from size medium to size small. And then around 2000 came Globalization 3.0, in which the world went from being small to tiny.

—THOMAS L. FRIEDMAN

Let me say up front that I have never lost a job because it has been outsourced, and I am sincerely sorry for anyone who has. That said, in bigger terms, I think that globalization is good for the world, and it's good for small business. Here is why: in a world that is increasingly fragmented and discordant, globalization creates bonds. It offers hope, fosters democracy, bolsters the middle class, creates new markets, and creates jobs, both here and abroad. And, according to Dan Griswold in *Trading Tyranny for Freedom: How Open Markets Till the Soil for Democracy*, "economic integration promotes civil and political freedoms directly by opening a society to new technology, communications, and democratic ideas . . . By promoting faster growth, free trade promotes political freedom indirectly by creating an economically independent and politically aware middle class." He adds that "nations that have [opened] themselves to the global economy are significantly more likely to have expanded their citizens' political and civil freedoms." The bottom line is that, even with its obvious flaws, globalization helps small business.

GLOBALIZATION AND SMALL BUSINESS

For most of recorded history, small business did not change much. Intrepid entrepreneurs, seized with an idea, set about turning it into reality: they raised capital, found a location, stocked the shelves, and hunted for customers in their area. This was as true in ancient Persia as it was in colonial America as it was in Southern California in the 1960s, when my dad opened his first carpet store. Although he and his partner eventually grew that single store to become a nice chain of 16 stores or so, the idea was the same as it had always been: they sold carpet to people in their area.

But in this new, wireless, 24/7, networked, global e-conomy, everything has changed. Sure, you can be like my dad and every other small businessperson who came before him and sell your products or services in your little area—but why? The fact is, there are more markets available to a small businessperson today than at any time in recorded history. Between the Internet, the fall of communism and corresponding rise of capitalism across the globe, and new technologies that are turning the world from, as Thomas Friedman says, "small to tiny," there are incredible opportunities to grow your business in ways my sweet dad could never have dreamed.

This is the biggest single transformational event to ever occur in the history of small business. Read that sentence again, because not only is it true, it means a lot to your small business.

It used to be that the only businesses capable of operating outside their region were large multinational corporations—the IBMs, Nikes, and East India Trading Companies of the world. But no longer. Today, any entrepreneur armed with a computer, an Internet connection, and a good idea can become a global player. There has never been a better time to own a small business. The opportunities are incredible.

Little Is the New Big

Not long ago, Big was big. Back in the 1960s, 1970s, and 1980s, television was dominated by the Big Three networks, the automobile industry was run by the Big Three automakers, and the telecommunications industry was controlled by Ma Bell and the Baby Bells. Chevron's acquisition of

Standard Oil in 1984 was the largest merger in history. Politically, two giant superpowers ruled the globe.

But all that began to change in the 1990s, when we saw the breakup of the Soviet Union, the rise of capitalism in China, and the beginning of the Internet revolution. Suddenly, there were billions of new capitalists and consumers and radically new ways to reach them. Suddenly, Little was big. With millions of people selling to millions more online, with capitalism spreading across the globe, and with technology making it easier to do more with less, small business came into its own. That we are now experiencing the golden era of small business cannot be disputed. Can small business compete in this global marketplace? You bet. Little is the new Big.

THE WORLD IS FLAT

To understand how best to take advantage of this brave new flat world, you'd better understand just what it is and what it means. Although Friedman's book and phrase are useful touch points, the idea is bigger than a book. It is nothing less than a transformation of how the world in general, and, for our purposes, the business world in particular, operates.

When Friedman says "the world is flat," what he means is that the playing field is leveling out. Advantages that one country or person may have had in the past are being made less important by new trends and technologies, especially the Internet and global capitalism. Today, the world increasingly has access to the same tools and information. The Internet has made the same information available to everyone. The playing field is leveling out. Whereas my dad once had an advantage because his market was affluent Southern Californians, now anyone anywhere can access that same market. The playing field is leveling out.

According to Friedman, Bill Gates has a useful take, putting it this way: twenty years ago, would you rather have been a B student in Poughkeepsie or a genius in Shanghai? Then, the answer was easy—you would rather have been a B student in Poughkeepsie. But today, "It's not even close. You'd much prefer to be the genius in Shanghai because you can now export your talents anywhere in the world." Friedman has his own take: "When I was growing up, my parents told me, 'Finish your dinner.

People in China and India are starving.' Now I tell my daughters, 'Finish your homework. People in India and China are starving for your job.'"

,Whatever the case, there is no doubt that both the business of the world and the world of business are undergoing a radical transformation from the local to the global, the independent to the interconnected, the round to the flat. It is an incredibly exciting, albeit equally challenging, time to be a small business owner. The world awaits.

Microbusiness

Whether it is Muhammad Yunus winning the Nobel Peace Prize in 2006 for his groundbreaking microloan bank or Kiva offering loans, grants, and small business know-how to the developing world, microbusinesses are radically changing the world. Throughout history, people have devised systems to help the poor, whether it be religion, charity, or communism. But it turns out that the greatest thing ever invented to help someone out of poverty is a small business. The most recent example: The capitalist revolution in China has pulled hundreds of millions of people out of poverty in a generation—the single greatest antipoverty program ever.

RISKS AND REWARDS IN THE NEW WORLD

For the entrepreneur, this changing world is one of both risks and rewards. The risks are clear everywhere you look. The collapse of communism and subsequent rise of capitalism throughout the world, especially in the former Soviet Union, China, and India, means that you have far more potential competitors, that more people are now seeking the same dollar. In addition, international trade agreements such as NAFTA have made international trade far easier. And if yours is, in fact, a business that can be done remotely, the truth is that people and businesses are increasingly looking to buy goods and services from parts of the world where costs are far lower.

Although the challenges are real and should not be underestimated, the potential rewards dwarf the risks. Not only are you competing with entrepreneurs across the globe, *but they are competing with you, too.* You probably cannot undercut them insofar as fees go, but that does not mean you do not have definite advantages that they do not have. You speak the universal language of business, English. You likely have a great education that, even with that online access to education, is still hard to replicate. You have access to great products and give great service. These are not insignificant things.

Maybe even more important, all of this flattening means that you have many more places where you can sell your products and services; there are markets available to you that have never been open before. That is the main thing—the important thing:

- There are virtual markets such as eBay or your website.
- There are physical markets outside your immediate area.
- There are markets in other countries.
- And finally, there are now literally billions of new consumers with access to capital and to the Internet who can become your customers.

The upshot is that this interconnected e-world is one of opportunity, if only you can see it and take advantage of it. Here's how.

THE WORLD ENTREPRENEURSHIP FORUM

For the past few years, I have been privileged to be a member of the Board of an international think tank called the World Entrepreneurship Forum (WEF). Founded in 2008 by EMLYON Business School and KPMG, joined in 2011 by ACE (Action Community for Entrepreneurship, Singapore) and NTU (Nanyang Technological University, Singapore), the WEF aims at finding entrepreneurial solutions to our world's problems. It promotes the entrepreneurial spirit in all fields of society and encourages all forms of entrepreneurship, integrating economic and social objectives.

For people interested in how to best shape the world of tomorrow, on affecting this flat world, and how entrepreneurship can have a positive and influential role in that world, the WEF is an organization that is worth noting, following, and maybe even joining. Why? Consider that the World Entrepreneurship Forum acts as:

- A global think tank proposing recommendations and developing global actions to tackle our world's problems in an entrepreneurial way

- An international network of entrepreneurs supporting the development of entrepreneurial spirit in society (personally, this is my favorite part—meeting entrepreneurs from Africa, Asia, South America, etc., and seeing what we have in common, and what we do not, is fascinating)
- A center of entrepreneurship identifying and proposing the next practices in the field of entrepreneurship

The think tank focuses on four main issues in which it seeks to challenge and influence the world of tomorrow:

1. Creating innovative and high-growth companies to create millions of jobs around the planet
2. Developing entrepreneurship at the bottom of the pyramid to alleviate poverty and create new markets
3. Shaping entrepreneurial cities to become tomorrow's centers for innovation
4. Implementing entrepreneurial education to disseminate an entrepreneurial mind-set, skills, and competencies throughout society on a lifelong basis

And it does all of this with an eye on sustainability and human rights. It is no wonder then that the WEF calls itself, and rightly so, "A worldwide think tank devoted to the entrepreneur, creator of wealth and social justice."

If this is of interest to you, please contact me via my website, MrAllBiz.com, to learn more.

SUCCEEDING IN A FLAT WORLD

If you want to take advantage of all of these new markets, of all of this internationalization of business and the reduction of business borders, then you have to look and act like a global player. Even if you are a microbusiness, the good news is that, thanks to another remarkable effect of the computer/technology/Internet revolution, no one ever needs to know how small your business is if you do not want them to know. Between your website, e-mail, computer hardware and software, mobile phones, and more, any small business can look big and professional. Even if your venture is nothing but a laptop in your spare bedroom, you can look like a global player.

How great is that? When my dad had one little 900-square-foot carpet store in Los Angeles, he put the "small" in small business. Today, he would have had a gorgeous website selling carpet from all over to all over. This is a radically different—and better—business model. (I keep mentioning my dad in this chapter because it really helps illustrate just how different business is today compared with even a generation ago. I also hope it serves as a whack on the side of the head—if you are still doing business the old fashioned way, stop it! There is a world of opportunity out there.)

The first tip for succeeding in a flat world is to look big but act small. This is the advice that Friedman gives in his book, and it is spot-on. In an online world, people cannot look you in the eye to see what kind of person you are, they cannot come to your store to see how great it is, all they can do is judge you by your site, so you need to have a great one. Your website can look as elegant, impressive, and professional as that of any large corporation without costing a fortune. And not only can you offer as many products as they do, but because you are smaller, you can offer more personal customer service. So online you can win, and win big, no matter how small your business, but only so long as you do it right and look like a pro.

There are two ways to tap the global market. First, as I will discuss in greater detail later in the book, you can do it through e-commerce. Second, as I discuss here, you can do business with companies in other countries (although even that does necessitate a great website as well). So first, you have to decide whether yours will be a strictly e-business site or whether your website will be merely an entree into doing business in and with another country.

Here are the steps to take for doing international business in a flat world:

- *Do your market research.* As always, I recommend that you think before you leap. A little research—figuring how your business translates internationally—will save you a lot of time and money down the road. Here are some places to start:

- The U.S. Department of Commerce, International Trade Administration (www.commerce.gov), has approximately 2,500 trade experts in 70 countries who help you learn about international commerce.
- For free global trade exporting help, check out www.trade.gov or call 1-800-USA-TRAD(E).
- *Prepare.* Get your site ready. Does it need to be translated into a foreign language? Will your marketing materials translate? How are sales done in the countries you have targeted, and what special etiquette rules should you know? You better find out before you go. (I learned the hard way when I was speaking in Mongolia that drinking Genghis Khan Vodka, *lots* of Genghis Khan Vodka, is expected of new business associates!)
- *Decide how to distribute your product.* You can sell online, of course, but you could also hire a fulfillment service, hire foreign agents or representatives, hire a foreign distributor, or even set up a joint venture. If you decide to work with a foreign business associate, keep in mind that you will want to find a partner who has a track record of selling to the companies or consumers you are targeting and who can speak both languages.

The secret to winning in this flat, global economy, then, is to play to your strengths, not compete against theirs. It means looking big but playing small. It requires offering up something unique and superior. In short, winning the game involves embracing the global economy, not fearing it. The days of running a mom-and-pop brick-and-mortar small business selling carpet to folks in the neighborhood are over.

Or at least they should be!

CHAPTER **21**

The Green Business

> The message to the business community is there need not
> be any conflict between the environment and the econ-
> omy. We will find the way not only to reconcile those but to
> find new profits and new opportunities as we do the right
> thing.
>
> —AL GORE

Whether we are talking about Al Gore winning an Oscar and the Nobel
Peace Prize in the same year or continued reports of the melting of the
polar ice caps, there is no doubt that climate change is changing the
world. For the small business interested in this trend, this means one of
two things: either you can take your existing business, green it up, and
make it more environmentally friendly (often called creating a *sustainable
business*), or you can start a new business intended to capitalize on
the green marketplace. Either way, you can do well by doing good. This
chapter explores both options.

GREEN BUSINESS OVERVIEW

Just what constitutes a green business? Broadly, sustainable businesses
operate in ways that minimize their environmental impact by:

- Reducing waste
- Conserving natural resources
- Reducing, reusing, and recycling
- Preventing or minimizing pollution

199

- Operating more efficiently
- Selling green products
- Supporting other ecofriendly businesses

Creating a sustainable business can be as simple as instituting a recycling program in your office or as complex as, say, creating a carbon-neutral airline. Nature Air was started in 2001 in Costa Rica with one plane and 17 employees. Today, it has become one of Central America's premier airlines and runs a sustainable business by donating 2.7 percent of its pretax revenue to saving Costa Rica's rainforest, thus making it a carbon-neutral business (a cost it does not pass on to its customers). Says Alex E. Khajavi, founder and CEO of Nature Air, "Nature Air is proof that a sustainable business model is good for business."

Carbon Neutral Defined

According to the *Oxford American Dictionary,* "Being carbon neutral involves calculating your total climate-damaging carbon emissions, reducing them where possible, and then balancing your remaining emissions, often by purchasing a carbon offset: paying to plant new trees or investing in 'green' technologies such as solar and wind power."

GREENING YOUR BUSINESS

No matter how big or small your business, you can do your part to help the planet by making your business green. Indeed, whether yours is a microbusiness (a business with no employees—usually a sole proprietor, consultant, or freelancer) or the biggest small business possible (under the SBA definition, a "small" business with—get ready for this—499 employees), making your business more environmentally friendly need not be difficult.

For example, Elysa Hammond was hired by the energy bar company Clif Bar to be the company's "corporate ecologist." She took several simple steps to make the company greener:

- The company switched to 100 percent postconsumer recycled paper.
- Desk-side recycling was instituted.

- Waste was either recycled or composted, resulting in an 80 percent reduction.
- The company bought wind energy credits to offset its energy use.
- Most important, product packaging was redesigned, allowing Clif Bar to eliminate 90,000 pounds of shrink-wrap yearly.

Many of these are steps that any small business could institute. So no, it is not that difficult—rather, it's a matter of making the commitment and then following through on that commitment. Here are some ways.

Change Your Lightbulbs

By now, we have all seen those curly new bulbs that are coming out, and they do make a big difference. Called compact fluorescent lightbulbs, or CFLs, they use 66 percent less energy than regular bulbs. Although they are a tad more expensive, over the long term, CFLs save money and the environment because they last 13 times longer than normal lightbulbs.

REDUCE YOUR PAPER CONSUMPTION

Cutting back on paper use helps the environment in several significant ways. First, it protects forests. Reducing paper consumption also cuts landfill use and associated energy costs that go into getting that paper to the landfill.

You can reduce your paper use by setting your copier and printer to do two-sided printing. You can edit on screen to cut back on paper drafts. You can circulate memos by e-mail. And you can turn used paper into scratch pads.

Make Your Office Ecofriendly

- Eliminate unnecessary reports and out-of-date forms.
- Avoid using fax cover sheets whenever possible.
- Use lightweight paper or paper with at least 25 percent postconsumer recycled content.
- Use e-mail and voice mail instead of snail mail when appropriate.
- Turn old file folders inside out and reuse them.
- Shred newspapers and use for packaging.
- If your office is small, combine your recyclables with those of nearby small offices.

Buy Green Products

Green and other "bio-based products" are recycled, low impact, or made of materials that come from plants rather than petrochemicals. An example of a bio-based product is a "tree-free" paper currency that Crane & Co. is creating for the U.S. Treasury out of 75 percent recovered cotton and 25 percent flax. These days, ecofriendly products can be obtained in almost any hue: recycled plastic binders, checks, envelopes, and pads using recycled products and printed with soy ink, green printing supplies, and much more. Although finding or buying green products might seem like an expensive or daunting task, our old friend the Internet has made it easy. There are several great directories of green businesses that sell everything from environmentally friendly travel to green office products. You can find your own green suppliers here:

- www.greenpages.org
- www.greenpeople.org
- www.EcoBusinessLinks.com

You might also want to check out electronic equipment bearing the Energy Star label. This is a voluntary Environmental Protection Agency (EPA) program that allows companies whose products are environmentally friendly and use less energy than standard products to market those products with the Energy Star label. And don't doubt that these products can make a huge difference: according to the Energy Star website, "If just one in 10 homes used Energy Star qualified appliances, the change would be like planting 1.7 million new acres of trees."

Although there is much to be said for all of these sorts of products, not surprisingly, they come with downsides. First of all, they generally cost more—sometimes a lot, sometimes a little. Availability may be an issue, and often there is not a lot of choice, as this is such a new industry. But if your commitment is green, the benefits outweigh these sorts of concerns.

Travel Green

Of course, telecommuting and teleconferences are easy, inexpensive ways to reduce the impact of your travel, but there is plenty more that you can do.

Green Pens

Ian LeBauer was looking at all of the pens he owned and wondered why pens, as disposable a product as there is, are made from plastic, as non-renewable a material as it gets. And so the Goodkind Pen Company was born. Not only are the pens made from wood rather than plastic, but they also use a nontoxic, non-petroleum-based ink and recycled steel and brass ink cartridges. The company also uses recycled packaging for shipments.

First, you can offset your travel emissions by purchasing *green tags* to cover your airline and other travel. Also called *renewable energy certificates,* green tags support new energy technologies in an amount that you choose (in this case, an amount related to the distance you travel). By buying green tags, you reduce the environmental effects of burning the coal, gas, and other fossil fuels related to your travel. And because airline travel in particular is one of the most carbon-heavy things any of us can do, donating to the development of new technologies and alternative energy by purchasing green tags is a great way to reduce your carbon footprint. For example, if you were to fly from San Francisco to New York and back, you would be responsible for 2.46 metric tons of carbon dioxide. According to www.CarbonCounter.org, a tax-deductible green tag purchase of $29.52 would offset that.

Alternative Transportation

You can make your office less auto dependent by creating a safe storage area for bikes and by encouraging employees to rideshare or use public transportation.

You can also reduce your company's auto impact by joining the nation's only environmentally friendly auto club. The Better World Club, co-founded by its president, Mitch Rofsky, is one such business. It offers the same nationwide services as AAA, and often at a lower price—24/7 emergency roadside assistance and towing, flat tire and lockout service, jump-starts, and so on. The Better World Club also incorporates many environmental and social initiatives, such as:

- Dedicating 1 percent of gross revenues to environmental cleanup and advocacy
- Pioneering carbon offsets in the travel industry
- Pioneering the nation's only roadside bicycle assistance
- Discounting fees for owners of hybrid cars
- Offering discounts on ecotravel
- Treating domestic partners as joint members

Maybe it's no surprise then that the club has an 80 percent renewal rate and membership is growing.

Reduce Your Waste

It is estimated that the average office employee generates a half pound of paper waste every day. But if that half pound were recycled, it would save the equivalent of one pound of greenhouse gas emissions. Waste reduction also makes good business sense, as it can save your business money through reduced purchasing and waste disposal costs.

There are all sorts of ways to reduce this waste: Use incoming shipping boxes for outgoing packages. Use durable or biodegradable towels, tablecloths, napkins, plates, and glasses. Recycle paper and junk mail. Instead of throwing away unused supplies, and food, donate them to charity. Install faucet aerators and low-flow toilets in restrooms.

You may also want to check out the WasteWise program. This EPA program is free and offers assistance to help you develop, implement, and measure your waste reduction activities. WasteWise will audit your office's waste output and offer strategies specific to your office. After that, it will help you track your office's success at reducing your waste.

So yes, there really are many ways to make your business greener.

I'm Dreaming of a Green Christmas

What about greening up your office holiday activities? Instead of buying new gift wrap, use the Sunday funnies. Instead of bubble wrap, use popcorn. Don't use plastic at your holiday party. Save packing material, wrapping, ribbons, and boxes for use next year.

TAPPING THE GREEN MARKETPLACE

How hot are green businesses? Very hot!

- "Sustainability will emerge from this financial crisis as a global mega-trend offering business opportunities similar to those that arose during the information age. Your task right now as an entrepreneur is to immediately begin educating yourself and prepping for this opportunity" (Entrepreneur.com).
- "The reality is that green businesses and the low carbon economy are on track to achieve their biggest breakthrough sometime around 2015" (BusinessGreen.com).
- Graduate schools of management are offering sustainable business courses, and some are even offering entire programs dedicated to the green business revolution.
- Maybe the fastest-growing supermarket chain in the country is Whole Foods.
- According to John Doerr of the investment firm Kleiner Perkins (whose investments include start-ups Amazon.com, AOL, and Google), "Green is the new red, white, and blue."
- Hybrid cars such as the Toyota Prius, the Nissan Leaf, the Ford Fusion, and the Honda Fit comprise a hot trend in the automotive industry.

So maybe it is no surprise that according to the SBA (SBA.gov), "A growing number of large and small businesses view these global environmental problems as business opportunities. Why? Because there are major profits to be made by those that develop solutions to these pressing issues."

So yes, there is no doubt that there is a market for the right green business. The question is, can you make a go of it in what is undoubtedly still a niche, if growing, market? If you can, the good news is that green consumers are willing to pay more for green products; witness the cost of organic produce and hybrid cars. The challenge for the green entrepreneur is that, although green consumers are willing to pay higher prices, few consumers make their buying decisions based primarily on the environmental impact of a product.

Example: In 1996, husband and wife Thomas Fricke and Sylvia Blanchet launched ForestTrade, a company that sells organic, sustainably produced spices and coffee. In light of consumers' growing desire for organic foods, the business model made sense. It also made sense environmentally, as it would promote rainforest conservation. Today, ForestTrade works with more than 5,000 small-scale farmers in Indonesia and Guatemala who manage almost 100,000 hectares of sustainable rainforest land, and ForestTrade's business is booming.

THE GREEN CONSUMER

Green buyers put a premium on—and are willing to pay more for—environmentally safe, organic, and healthy products made by sustainable, socially responsible businesses. According to Conscious Media and Lifestyles of Health and Sustainability, about 15 percent of this 65 million-strong market are "hard-core" green consumers, meaning that environmental friendliness is their main purchasing criteria. More than convenience, more than price, these consumers base their buying choices on their values and patronize companies that they perceive as sharing those values. If you can show these consumers that you do indeed share their values (by what you sell, how you do business, the donations you make, and so on), then you are in the game.

Here are a few tidbits that you need to know about the green consumer:

- Green consumers appreciate value.
- They tend to have an intellectual bent, allowing you to make rational arguments to win their loyalty.
- Mostly, they are middle- to upper-middle-class consumers.
- By and large, environmental concerns are more important to people younger than 30 than to those older than 30, but again, that is just a generality.
- Buzzwords that strike their fancy: *recyclable, biodegradable, environmentally friendly, organic, local, reduce, reuse, sustainable, compostable, bio-based,* and, of course, *green.*

The Hybrid Car Consumer

One of the most recognizable green products out there is the hybrid auto-mobile. Just who buys hybrids? According to JD Power and Associates:

- Hybrid car buyers are among the most highly educated of all car buyers
- They make more money than the average car buyer
- They are more likely to be female
- Many want to make a statement with their purchase
- They tend to be a few years older than the average car buyer
- They plan to keep their car longer than the average driver
- They are willing to pay more for an environmentally friendly product
- They personally want to do something to help the environment

But as time goes by, it won't be just these 15 percent hard-core environmental consumers who will be shopping this way—probably we all will, to some extent or another, because global warming, climate change, and the environment will only grow in importance. The latest Green Gauge Report found that 87 percent of consumers are "seriously concerned" about the environment. Therefore, people are discovering that they can make a difference by changing how they shop and what they buy. This means that the green marketplace will continue to evolve and grow. It also means you have an incredible opportunity. Help them help the planet.

There are plenty of resources available to help you better understand the green marketplace. Some that you might want to check out are:

- Lifestyles of Health and Sustainability analyzes the market vis-à-vis health and fitness, the environment, sustainable living, and social justice (www.lohas.com).
- The Natural Marketing Institute reports on the health and wellness marketplace (www.nmisolutions.com).
- The Organic Consumer Trends Report analyzes the organic consumer market and makes growth projections. Although a hard copy of the report will cost you a whopping $7,500, plenty of the information is available for free from the Organic Trade Association (www.ota.com/organic/mt/business.html).

- The Hartman Group studies and reports on consumer behaviors in the sustainability, health, environmental, and wellness markets (www .hartman-group.com).

As you analyze the market and consider your business options, keep in mind that whatever your green business idea, it must be not only good for the environment but economically feasible as well. If no one is willing to pay $18 for a bar of your organic soap, you will end up with a lot of leftover soap. So, as with any business venture, the first job for the green entrepreneur is to listen to and serve the marketplace. Yes, there are opportunities, no doubt about it. The secret is to marry your passion to one of those opportunities in such a way that it allows you to help the planet and your pocketbook at the same time. It is no small order. Artists can dream up a painting and paint it, but green entrepreneurs must not only dream up a pretty picture, they have to figure out how to make a profit with it to boot.

According to Mitch Rofsky of the Better World Club, the key is to find your niche:

- *Be unique.* As they say, "niche and grow rich."
- *Advertise and market in the right places.* "You have to advertise in places where people who see what you offer will want it," says Rofsky. For the Better World Club, that means outlets such as *Sierra* magazine and NPR's *Car Talk.*
- *Don't forget, it's still a business.* Your first job is to break even, and then to make a profit. Offer competitive prices if you can and exceptional customer service.

Businessweek's Hottest Green Start-ups

- *Solar.* The industry is projected to grow to $75 billion by 2016. In 2010, solar patents were second only to fuel cell patents in the clean energy area.
- *Clean energy technology.* In 1999, clean energy technology made up less than 1 percent of the total venture capital investments. By 2005, that number had quadrupled. In 2010, global clean energy finance and

investment grew to almost a $250 billion industry, up 30 percent from the previous year.
- *Organic food.* Organic food is expected to grow 11 percent annually in the foreseeable future, according to the Organic Trade Association's Manufacturer Survey.
- *Green building.* Green construction is expected to grow five times over today's business. "The value of green building starts was up 50 percent from 2008 to 2010 (to $71 billion) and represents 25 percent of all new construction activity in 2010," according to Construction.com.
- *Advanced fuel technologies.* Many venture capital firms are putting their investment dollars into things such as ethanol, biofuels, and hydrogen.

So, in one sense, we are back at square one. To succeed with a green business, you must do what any entrepreneur does: Find an idea that you are passionate about, and run it by your friends, family, and advisors to see what they think. Do some research to determine the viability of the idea. Draft a business plan. Get funded. Start your business. It's the same path we all take, but for you, my environmentally conscious friend, the difference is that you will be tapping an emerging market and helping to make the world a better place. Kudos.

CHAPTER **22**

The New Consumer

When in doubt, predict that the present trend will continue.

—MERKIN'S MAXIM

In the last chapter, we saw how environmental concerns are causing customers to reevaluate their purchasing preferences. But it's not just ecoshoppers who are changing the small business marketplace; it is the marketplace itself that is shape-shifting. Whether we are talking about the aging baby boom generation or the trendy Generation Y, the fact is, today's small business market is not your father's Oldsmobile. It is a whole new world out there.

Consumers become your customers for a variety of reasons: it could be that you have better prices, you are more convenient, you have better products, or you are a nice person. All may be true, but increasingly in this new millennium, other considerations are coming into play. Business is changing rapidly. It used to be that everyone wanted to sell to the all-important demographic of middle-income consumers aged 25 to 54 because they had the most money to spend, but that paradigm's expiration date has lapsed. Today, new customers are growing in importance. If your small business is going to succeed, you need to understand who they are and what they want so that you can give them what they are looking for.

Specifically, in this chapter, we are going to look at three groups of potential new customers: Baby Boomers and members of Generations X and Y.

THE AGING BOOMER CONSUMER

Today, four generations of people make up your potential customers:

1. *Traditionalists.* Born before 1946, these elderly people value loyalty, respect authority, and are generally conventional.
2. *Baby Boomers.* The Baby Boom generation was born between 1946 and 1964. Now the grown-ups they once scorned, Baby Boomers have money and authority but still like to think of themselves as unconventional iconoclasts.
3. *Generation X.* Born between 1964 and 1979, Gen Xers generally dislike hierarchy and authority. They are informal, well educated, savvy, and cynical.
4. *Generation Y.* Born after 1980, this generation, also called the "Millennials," has lived lives of relative abundance and comfort. Individualistic and autonomous, they also are incredibly technologically literate.

Boomers Today

Let's begin with the Baby Boomers. Yes, we all get tired of hearing about the Boomers (hey, even I get tired of it, and we're t-t-t-talking 'bout my generation!). But you won't be bored once you realize just how much money this massive, soon-to-be-retiring, affluent generation can generate for your business.

The Baby Boom generation, once known for its youth, non-conformity, and self-absorption, is young no longer. The youngest of the bunch are over 50, and the oldest are having hot flashes and getting ready to cash their Social Security checks. Never content with the status quo, Boomers are entering old age with the same gusto they harnessed to take on the Vietnam War, est, and personal fitness. The only difference is that now they have the time, money, and position to reinvent old age, just as they reinvented adulthood.

The question for the entrepreneur is how to most effectively tap this huge, aging market numbering 77 million. Traditionally, businesses avoided older consumers, opting instead to sell to people aged 25 to 54, believing

---

The Vespa

Vespa motor scooters reentered the U.S. market in 2000 after an absence of 15 years. Although the plan was to sell to 20-something Gen Yers, almost immediately Vespa found an unexpected market selling to nostalgic Baby Boomers. Fully 25 percent of Vespa USA sales are to adults older than age 50.

---

that they were the ones who had the money and were open to trying different products. But that simply is not true for the Boomer generation. According to Yankelovich Inc., today 67 percent of consumers older than 50 do not think it is "risky" to buy an unfamiliar brand. The reason for their flexibility? "This group grew up in a time when novelty and experimentation were higher on the priority list than during the prior generation," says Yankelovich president J. Walker Smith. That attitude means a 50-year-old Baby Boomer is more than willing to try that new product or service.

But the bad news is that the recent financial downturn we all lived through affected the Boomers and their portfolios significantly. While they still have money, they have less money than they ever anticipated and are reacting accordingly. As such, the question then becomes, what should you be selling to them? Needless to say, it must be something that speaks to where they are in life and how they want to live:

- *Active "retirement."* Baby Boomers are not retiring in any traditional sense of the word, certainly not as their parents did—with a gold watch and a "thank you very much." Instead, many retiring boomers are viewing their empty nest years as a time to experiment—to start new businesses, partake in exotic adventure travel, that sort of thing. The key to marketing to this segment is to position your business, service, or product as an extension of this exciting new stage of life.
- *Nonretirement.* More than a few Boomers lost their jobs in the economic downturn and have no plans at all now to retire because they can't afford to. They will keep on working (if they even found other jobs), so your job could be helping them get through this unexpected turn in their lives and careers.

Baby Boomer Retirement Statistics

The average life expectancy for Baby Boomers is 77.4 years. According to a survey conducted by Merrill Lynch & Co., only about 20 percent of Baby Boomers saw themselves stopping work altogether after the age of 50.

- *Healthy living.* Of course, being healthy is important to anyone who is getting older, but it is especially important to a generation whose mind-set is focused on being young at heart, if not young for real. Between Jane Fonda exercise videos, jogging, yoga, and personal fitness, the boomers have taken healthy living and exercise to a whole new level. Not only do they want to be healthy, they want to remain healthy, so one way to cater to them is to show how your products and services offer yet another way to soak up that elusive fountain of youth.
- *Financial stability.* There is sure to be a significant market catering to older Americans who want to revive their nest egg, or at least keep it, let alone seeing it grow.
- *Making a splash.* Whether it is starting a second or third career, joining the Peace Corps, or helping a child start a business or buy a home, you can be sure that the Baby Boom generation will want to continue to have an effect on the world around them.

Boomers Put ``Old" on Hold

Washington Post—When the first Marine Corps Marathon took place, in 1976, the oldest runner to finish the race was 58 years old. On the race's 30th anniversary, the oldest finisher was 82. So who's "old" these days? The 60-year-old with twins in preschool? The 65-year-old launching a second career? The 70-year-old with no gray hair, no wrinkles, and great cleavage? The cliché that "60 is the new 40" may be overdoing it, but it captures a sense that Americans—particularly the 78 million baby boomers born from 1946 through 1964—are approaching their later years with different plans and expectations than their parents and grandparents did.

GENERATIONS X AND Y

When it comes to understanding the new consumer, at the other end of the spectrum are the alphabetical generations: X and Y.

- *Generation X* makes up just under 20 percent of the U.S. population. Born between 1965 and 1979, they are now starting families and buying the houses that the aging Boomers are selling.
- *Generation Y*, born between 1980 and 1994, is more populous than Gen X, making up fully one-quarter of the U.S. population.

Growing up after Watergate and coming of age during the two Iraq Wars, both Gen X and Gen Y are suspicious of big institutions in general and of the government and the media in particular. Independent, self-directed, and technologically savvy, reaching them is a challenge because they take everything with a grain of salt.

Other things to know about Generations X and Y:

- Unlike earlier generations, equality of the sexes at work and at home is a given for them.
- They tend to delay marriage until their late 20s.
- They have little brand loyalty.
- They consider themselves entrepreneurs. Even if they don't start their own business, they have entrepreneurial careers.
- Even more than Baby Boomers, Gen X and Y parents dote on their children excessively and spend accordingly.

The Tech Factor

When Irongate Land Company in Chicago wanted a name for the new condos it was developing to sell to Generation X and Y customers, it turned to the marketing agency Torque for help. The name that Torque came up with for the development, 33Six, was "based on that age group's fascination with and dependence upon technology-based gadgets like cell phones, the Blackberry and Internet connections."

So, how do you sell to a group that is inherently distrustful and cynical? The secret is to use those qualities to your advantage. Of course, you must avoid any hint of a hard sell—nothing would turn them off more. What they want is authenticity. They are not going to trust what they read, what your brochure says. They want to see and understand for themselves the value of a product or service. They need to feel in control and smart, need to see the benefits, and need to understand how your product will benefit them specifically. You may also find that non-traditional marketing is a better way to reach them: word of mouth, viral campaigns, Internet marketing, and other new media strategies work.

The other important thing is to reach them where they are: online. More than almost any other generation, Gens X and Y spend time on the Internet, networking, shopping, reading, watching videos, meeting, and gaming. That means you have to be there, too. One especially potent way to reach them is through the plethora of social networking sites out there like Facebook, LinkedIn, and so on. The savvy marketer who wants to tap the Generation X and Y market will have a significant online social networking presence.

Moreover, according to "The State Of Consumers And Technology: Benchmark" by Charlene Li, "Gen Yers—who came of age with computers and broadband, iPods, and iPhones (among other things) stand apart from older generations because of their hands-on approach to the web. Marketers trying to anticipate future consumer trends should tune in to Gen Yers. As these do-it-yourselfers become a primary consuming audience, they will carry with them their cross-channel shopping enthusiasm, active blog usage, and reliance on the information-scouring powers of Google."

The essential thing, then, to understand about selling to the new generation of younger adults is that they are web-savvy, and, not only do they see through the spin, it turns them off. Your pitch to them has to take all of this into account.

PART

II

Money

CHAPTER **23**

Accounting Ease

There's no business like show business, but there are several businesses like accounting.

—David Letterman

Business accounting is a way to keep score. If one purpose of a business is to make a profit (certainly there are many others—to create value, find meaningful work, live your dream, make the world better, and so on), then proper business accounting helps you know how well you are doing. No, it is not glamorous, but it is important. Remember, there are two parts to your business: doing the things you love and doing the things you must. Accounting falls into the latter category (unless, of course, you are an accountant).

ACCOUNTING BASICS

Accounting is the general process of tracking your income and expenses and then using those data to examine the financial status of your business. Your basic accounting tool is the *general ledger.* It is the place where you keep track of all of your business's financial transactions. That information is then used to create financial statements such as *balance sheets* and *income statements.* An *accounting period* is a set amount of time during which a business's financial reports can be compared with one another; it may be a month, a quarter, or a year. One year in a company's financial life is called a *fiscal year.*

219

The general ledger comprises four basic categories: assets, liabilities, income, and expenses. All general ledger entries are double entries— debits are kept on the left and credits on the right—and for every financial transaction in your business, the debits and credits flow from one side of the ledger to the other. When you sell an item, for instance, you record the sale (credit) on one side, but you also have to debit your inventory on the other side. For every debit, there must be an equal and offsetting credit. When debits and credits are unequal, your books don't balance. All debits and credits either increase or decrease your account balance.

Accounting History

Double-entry accounting dates back to the fifteenth century. The first written ledger comes from a 1458 manuscript by Benedetto Cotrugli, which Franciscan monk Luca Pacioli included in his seminal work *Summa de Arithmetica, Geometria, Proportioni et Proportionalita*, printed in Venice, Italy (on a Gutenberg press), in 1494.

Each area that feeds the general ledger has its own subledger containing details about what is going on. For example, daily sales and payments are recorded in the accounts payable and accounts receivable subledgers and, correspondingly, increase cash and decrease inventory in the general ledger. Many different accounting software programs are available today. It is much easier to understand how a general ledger works if you buy a program such as QuickBooks, as it will walk you through the process and do much of the work for you.

Tip: When organizing the accounting department of your small business, it is optimal to hire at least two people. The problem with having a single accounts payable and receivable person is that having one person write checks and then reconcile the checking account is asking for trouble.

Your ledger will be the basis of your basic financial reports, which will be generated by your software program or by your accountant. Financial reports, such as profit and loss statements, are important because they are a snapshot of the financial health of your business. For instance, your income ledger will tell you how much money you brought in this month, but you will know how much profit you made only when the income ledger is compared with your expense ledger. Your accounts receivable ledger will tell you whether your customers are paying on time and whether you have enough money coming in to pay your bills. Financial reports, therefore, give you an overall picture of the fiscal condition of your business.

BUDGETING

Would you ever get into your car with a bag over your head and drive away? Of course not. How would you know whether you had enough gas, or had the car pointed in the right direction, or had an emergency light flashing? Your eyes and the car's dashboard give you the feedback necessary to get where you want to go, and safely. In financial terms, running your business without a budget is like driving a car with a bag over your head. How will you know whether you have enough money to expand? How can you tell whether you are on track to accomplish your sales goals this year? Can you afford another employee? Your budget will tell you. Without a budget, you can't see whether you are headed in the direction you planned on going.

All too often, small business people have no clear financial idea of how they will get where they want to go, and it is not hard to see why. Most of us view budgets as a necessary evil at best, and something to be avoided at worst. The traditional view is that a budget is a restrictive plan that forces you to deprive yourself of what you want. The good news is that a budget can be much different.

It helps to rethink the word. Instead of the word *budget*, substitute *plan* instead. A good plan is a guide, not a noose. A reasonable, intelligent plan is a business tool that allows you to allocate your resources to your greatest benefit. Creating a plan lets you control your business's cash flow instead of it controlling you.

Creating a budget need not be a complicated or time-consuming task. The key is to figure out how much money you have available to spend and where you want to spend it. It is a matter of digging through your records to see how much is coming in, where it has been going, and then deciding *where you would rather have it go*. That's really all a budget is—a business plan that allows you to put your money to its best use.

Your budget will have two categories: *projected income* and *projected expenses* (again, any good accounting program will walk you through this). In the income category, you conservatively estimate how much you can expect to make next year from all sales and other sources of income. Look at what you made last year and extrapolate from that. If you are new to business, what does your business plan say? Be realistic. If you paint too rosy a picture, you can easily get in over your head and spend money that never materializes. If you make more than your projected income, great. But if you make less, watch out!

As far as expenses go, consider every expense that you have, such as advertising, auto, insurance, lease payments, taxes, phone, utilities, inventory, equipment, payroll—any and all expenses that you anticipate will be borne by the business next year.

Once you see your projected income and expenses on paper, you will know exactly how much you need to make every month in order to keep things afloat and how much you will have left over. You will be far less tempted to indulge in business expenses that are not part of the plan. By having a budget, you will ensure that your expenses do not exceed your income and that your money goes where you think it can best be used.

CASH FLOW

Cash flow is like oxygen to your business. Without it, your business will suffocate and die. One more reason to create a budget, then, is to ensure that you will have adequate cash flow. I can't say this any more plainly: without consistent, sufficient money to buy inventory, pay bills, handle payroll, and pay yourself, you will go out of business. Preserving and defending your cash flow, therefore, is critical.

Aside from creating a budget, here are three more ways to control your cash flow:

1. *Live by the rule.* Without cash flow, your business will suffocate and die.
2. *Create cash flow projections.* You need to know how much money will be coming in and when. Realistic cash flow projections are key. What do you expect your cash balance to be in six months? Always know that number.
3. *Keep the pipeline open.* Clients or customers you create today may hire you, but it may be a few months before you finish the work and send out a bill, and it may be another month or two before they pay. You have to keep creating clients and doing work today to keep the cash flow spigot open.

Tip: Always project three to six months ahead when it comes to cash flow. If you will need money in six months, you *must* create new business within the next three months. That way, you can do the work or sell the product, bill it, and get it paid within six months.

A cash flow crunch is usually the result of poor planning. All businesses have business cycles, and they must be planned for. Starbucks knows that coffee sales go up in the winter and down in the summer. In the summer, then, the company introduces cooler drinks to keep the cash flowing. The same should be true for you. You must know your business cycle, know when you can expect times to be good and bad, and plan accordingly.

If you do run into a cash crunch, there are two things you can do. First, receive your receivables. Allowing clients to pay net 30—that is, 30 days after purchase—is a common business practice. But anything more than that is bad business. If you consistently have outstanding invoices, change your terms. Accounts receivable are the lifeblood of your business, representing your business's cash flow and liquidity. Getting your receivables current can bring in immediate cash.

Getting Accounts Paid

- Assign an employee the task of contacting all accounts receivable older than 30 days, and get a specific date when the debt will be paid. Have the employee call again on that day if the money is not received. Once a receivable is more than 60 days old, you have a real problem. If you are a sole proprietor, you must prioritize this task.
- Institute a new policy—giving customers 30 days advance notice—that a surcharge of at least 10 percent interest will be charged on all invoices more than 30 days old.
- Inform your customers that all outstanding balances must be made current before any new product will be sent out.
- If necessary, hire a lawyer or a collection agency to commence collection activities.
- As a last resort, you can always sell the debt. The money owed to you is a commodity and can be sold like one. Collection agencies buy bad debt every day, albeit at a sharply discounted price.

The other option for dealing with a cash crunch is to get a loan. Sometimes you simply need a short-term infusion of cash to keep things going until business picks up again. A prudent loan with a plan to pay it back can be a smart solution to a short-term cash crunch.

HIRING AN ACCOUNTANT

Not a few small business owners have a hard time dealing with the financial aspects of their business. They may be great innovators, have plenty of enthusiasm, and be the best salespeople around, but ask them to create a balance sheet, and watch their eyes glaze over. Even the most powerful accounting software is useless if you cannot input or understand the data. Sometimes—nay, often—hiring an accountant is smart business.

Although accountants cannot guarantee your success, they can be an important adjunct to your business. Their basic services include keeping track of how much your business owes and how much it is owed, creating financial statements (such as balance sheets, income statements, and cash flow statements), and reconciling bank statements. Beyond that, a CPA might do the following:

- *Handle taxes.* A good accountant can save your business thousands of dollars through proper tax planning.
- *Do your payroll.* Payroll is often outsourced.
- *Handle audits.* An accountant might prepare an audit for a small business whose potential investors require audited books.
- *Deal with the IRS.* The other sort of audit, the unwelcome one, is another area in which accountants can come in handy.
- *Offer business and financial planning.* A CPA can help with succession and estate planning or help value the business for sale purposes.

Where do you find a good accountant? Referrals are the best source. If you know someone who has a good bookkeeper or accountant, find out whether he likes his accountant and why. Get referrals from friends, business associates, your banker, your attorney, and other entrepreneurs you know. After you get a few names, set up some appointments and conduct an interview to learn key information:

- *What's their experience?* You want someone who deals with small businesses, especially those in your field.
- *Is timely service delivered?* Numbers are constantly coming in from your business, so make sure that you will get reports at least monthly.
- *Who will service the account?* Will it be the person you are meeting with, or some junior accountant whom you do not know?
- *What services can you expect beyond reporting?* Will the accountant handle your taxes, payroll, or what?
- *Will you get business consulting as well?* A good accountant should become a valuable member of your team, helping you in areas where you are weak.
- *How much will it cost?* You should know fairly accurately how much time the accountant will put in each month and what you should expect to pay.

Because your accountant should become a dependable business advisor, you want one whom you can trust and with whom you get along well and feel comfortable. Independent accountants or small accounting firms can provide personalized service, whereas a "Big Five" firm offers more services and lends prestige to your company. This, in turn, may help you raise capital, establish credit, and open doors.

Cutting Accounting Costs

Accountants are professionals, and their fees are not inexpensive. Even so, there are a few ways to keep your accounting costs down:

- *Keep great records.* Keep receipts organized. Keep your ledger legible and up to date. Have your records automated, if possible.
- *Handle the small stuff.* The stuff that you can do, do.
- *Use a bookkeeper.* If all you need is someone to do the books, a book-keeper is much less expensive.

CHAPTER **24**

Making a Profit

It is no secret that organized crime in America takes in over forty billion dollars a year. This is quite a profitable sum, especially when one considers that the Mafia spends very little for office supplies.

—Woody Allen

The name of the game, of course, is making a profit, and there are many factors that go into the equation: overhead, markup, and what the competition is doing, for starters. In this chapter, we will examine how to make a consistent profit and what to do if you are not.

COMPUTING YOUR PROFITABILITY

As a concept, profit is easy to understand. It is the difference between what it costs you to make or buy your product and what you earn from selling it. It is when you break down this seemingly simple concept that things get a little complicated. When it comes to profit, there are four components to understand: gross profit, net profit, profit margin, and markup.

Gross Profit and Net Profit

The *gross profit* on a product sold or service rendered is computed by taking the money you brought in from the sale and subtracting the cost of goods sold (COGS). *Net profit* is your gross profit less taxes and interest. Net profit is the same thing as earnings or net income.

227

> ### Cost of Goods Sold
>
> COGS represents the costs you actually incur in making the product or service. For a product, it includes raw materials, labor, and other directly associated costs. For a product that you sell, it is your wholesale costs.

Computing Your Profit

Keeping a running tab on profitability helps you stay focused and gives you an early warning sign of trouble ahead. Let's say that you run a child care center. To compute your profit, you must figure out your total costs to take care of each child, including such things as:

- Rent
- Labor
- Food
- Insurance
- Utilities
- Advertising
- Auto
- Other

Let's assume that your total overhead every month is $5,000. If you care for 10 children, then your expenses per child would be $5,000 divided by 10, or $500 per child. That is your break-even point per child per month. Now let's assume that you gross $8,000 a month, meaning that you charge $800 per month per child ($800 × 10 children = $8,000). Your gross profit per child is $300, and your total gross profit is $3,000. Is that good or bad? It depends on your *profit margin*.

Profit Margin

While your gross profit is expressed as a dollar amount ($3,000), your gross profit margin is expressed as a percentage, computed as follows: gross profit divided by sales equals gross profit margin. In the preceding example, the gross profit would be $3,000 divided by $8,000, or

38 percent. That is good. Any business that makes a 38 percent profit is doing something right. Again, good accounting software will help you calculate these numbers quite quickly.

Markup

Knowing your markup is critical to understanding your profitability. Like your gross profit margin, your markup is also expressed as a percentage: sales price minus cost to produce divided by cost to produce. In the case of the child care center, it would look like this: $8,000 (sales price) minus $5,000 (cost to produce) equals $3,000. That $3,000 divided by $5,000 equals 60 percent. So the markup for each child is 60 percent—again, quite impressive.

This begs the question, how much should you be charging for your goods or services?

PRICING

Just how important is selecting the right price? It could mean the difference between success and failure. The wrong price can put you out of business. Finding that magic number requires careful thought and planning. In the foregoing example, you know that you must charge at least $500 per child per month to break even. The trick is to come up with a higher price that gives you a good profit while still attracting customers.

Get Educated!

The financial aspects of running a small business are often confusing. Classes at your local community college can teach you even more. Other places to look for continuing adult education business classes are chambers of commerce, websites, and private training companies.

There are two schools of thought when it comes to pricing products and services (above the break-even point): If you are more interested in growing rapidly and capturing a larger share of the market (your *market share*), then you need to price your goods as low as possible because the laws of economics dictate that a lower price will attract more customers. Volkswagen sells far more cars than Mercedes, but Mercedes makes more money per car. If you are going for a broad customer base, then you need to figure out, often by trial and error, a price that people will consider a bargain but will still allow you to make a profit.

However, if dominating the field is not your business model—if you are more interested in increasing profits—then you need to go with a higher price. It has to be near the competition's price yet high enough for you to live on. It's not always easy to figure out, and it takes time.

Add into this equation the brand you are attempting to create. As I discussed earlier, a big part of how people perceive your business is what you charge. Two lawyers may do the exact same sort of work, but the one who charges $350 an hour will be perceived as better than the one who charges $150 an hour. Yes, she will get fewer clients, but they probably will be better clients.

Follow these five steps to determine your fees and prices:

1. *Determine your break-even point.* Start by calculating your break-even point using the formula mentioned earlier.
2. *Identify your customers and brand.* Are your customers middle class or wealthy? Is your brand upscale or not? Do customers want a bargain, or is quality more important?
3. *Learn what the competition is doing.* Again, people look for bargains. If you can afford to beat the competition, all else being equal, you *will* get business.
4. *Don't set your price too low if you want to grow.* The best source of cash for growth is a healthy gross profit margin.
5. *Test, test, and test some more.* Finding the right price will require trial and error. Tinker.

INCREASING YOUR PROFIT

You can improve your profits in three ways. First, you can sell more. Second, you can increase your prices. Third, you can reduce your overhead. That's it.

Sell More

Of course, the best way to increase your profit is to sell more. Easier said than done, you say? Maybe, but the entire next section of this book is devoted to the many different ways to grow your business. You are probably selling more today than you were five years ago. The trick is to duplicate what you have done right, continue to do that, be sure to add some new profit centers, and read Section III.

Increase Prices

Many small business owners are afraid to raise their prices for fear of driving away customers. That fear may or may not be warranted. When you use price as the primary gauge of your services, then other factors, maybe more important ones, get left out of the equation—things such as quality, personal service, convenience, and speed. McDonald's and Walmart emphasize low prices because that is their business model, and unless it is yours, too, then constantly worrying about fees and prices is likely a mistake.

Instead, you need to decide what it is you offer that is best and emphasize that. If price is not critical, then raising your prices is a smart way to increase profits. Think again about Mercedes—it does not fight on the cheapest-is-best battleground. Rather, it emphasizes quality and makes a handsome profit in the process.

Because you are your own boss, you set the prices. When is the last time you raised your prices? Although you should be concerned about driving away clients if you do, it is still worth a shot. If your fears are valid, you can always lower your prices again. But if your fears are ungrounded, you will be giving yourself a well-deserved raise.

Raising Your Prices

If you run a service business, consider testing a price increase on a few customers first. If they do not balk, then you can roll out your price increases across the board. If they do object, you can always roll back your prices.

Reduce Your Overhead

The tried-and-true way to increase profit margin is to decrease costs. When a Fortune 500 company lays off 1,000 employees, it is utilizing this strategy. Of course, the risk is that by cutting costs, you may cut into the very thing that brings in business. That is a real danger, and that is why firing employees usually is not the answer. So what is?

You have to figure out a way to reduce your overhead and, more important, to encourage employees to care about keeping costs down, because it is often your employees who hold the key to cost overruns. If you can get them committed to saving, then staying consistently profitable is much more likely.

Other ways to reduce your overhead:

- *Cut back on available supplies.* One of the things employees love about being employees is that they can nab pens and send FedEx packages without paying for them. However, if costs are an issue in your workplace, you simply must put a stop to excess waste in this area.
- *Rent out space.* If you have unused workspace, you may be able to rent it out to another small business.
- *Give incentives.* Because employees are on the front lines, they may see waste that you do not. Rewarding them for suggesting cost-saving measures that you can implement is a smart strategy.
- *Buy in bulk.* Sam's Club, Costco, and other warehouse clubs are savings bonanzas for the small business owner. Costco's executive membership, which costs about $100 a year, allows you to shop earlier and offers you the chance to buy low-cost insurance, telephone service, lines of credit, and much more.
- *Buy used.* Instead of purchasing new furniture, for instance, buy used.

Help from the Post Office

The U.S. Postal Service offers many services geared toward the small business owner. Go to www.usps.com/business/business-solutions.htm.

- *Rethink phone service.* Many carriers have great deals; you should not be paying retail any more. Maybe you don't even need a landline at this point; many small businesses are ditching them. Another increasingly popular option is VoIP: using your Internet lines as phone lines.
- *Review insurance coverage.* The coverage you bought a few years ago may be outdated and overly expensive. Call your broker and get him to give you new quotes from several different insurers. Nonsmoker and good driver discounts should be explored.
- *Requests for proposals.* Your tried-and-true vendors may have gotten a little lazy, taking your account for granted. Shop your needs to some new vendors and see whether they can save you some money.

These are just a start—of course, there are many other ways to reduce overhead without affecting the bottom line.

PAYING YOURSELF

A question that many small business owners have vis-à-vis profitability is how much they should be paying themselves. When figuring out how much to pay yourself, the most important thing to consider is your business's financial condition. Before you can decide how much money you can safely pull out of the business each month, first you need to figure out how much money your small business needs—its needs come first. If you bite the hand that feeds you, it will bite you back. Thus, you need to calculate your break-even point and go from there. Knowing how much is coming in and going out allows you to figure out how much you can realistically afford to pay yourself. How much is that? Only you can say for sure after seeing your budget. As you decide, beware of paying yourself too much or too little because either could trigger a tax audit. Let's say that you own a C corporation with $600,000 in profits (that is, taxable income). You might decide that it makes sense to pay yourself a hefty six-figure bonus. Although surely you deserve it, if your annual income is significantly higher than the average for chief executive officers (CEOs) in your industry, the IRS may conclude that the bonus was a sham transaction intended to reduce corporate profits and reduce taxes. Similarly, if your S corporation does not pay you enough, that too could trigger an audit.

Many small businesses start out as sole proprietorships or partnerships. As a sole proprietor, you can pay yourself whatever you want; it depends almost entirely on how much profit you make, how much money your business needs, and thus what you can afford to pay yourself. Partners must consider one another's desires when determining how much they will be paid.

The same is true for LLCs that have more than one owner, with one caveat: you can make a distribution of profits legally, *only if* doing so does not impair the solvency of the business.

Bottom line: Remaining profitable takes constant attention to detail. Keeping track of your margins and then increasing business or reducing costs as necessary is what is required.

CHAPTER 25

Insurance

The superior man, when resting in safety, does not forget that danger may come.

—Confucius

The idea of insurance is a contradiction—you buy something that you hope you will never need. But even so, you sure are glad it is there when you need it.

TYPES OF INSURANCE

When you own a small business, the array of potential insurance products can be overwhelming. Which types of insurance are really important?

Health

Employees consistently rank health benefits among the most important fringe benefits of employment. Because it is so important and so complicated, this issue is covered extensively in Chapter 28.

Business Owner

Business owner insurance is also known as *catchall* coverage. It is a basic policy that provides protection from fire, other mishaps, and some liabilities.

Property and Casualty

Just as you insure your house against property loss, so, too, must you insure your business for the same. Property insurance protects your business against physical damage or loss of business assets. It is used when troubles such as fire, theft, explosion, or vandalism damage or destroy your equipment, inventory, or building.

Consider insuring the following:

- Buildings and structures, whether leased or owned
- Equipment, whether leased or owned
- Inventory
- Machinery
- Cars and trucks
- Computers, printers, fax, and phone equipment
- Furniture and supplies
- Money and securities
- Important papers, books, and documents
- Signs, fences, and other outdoor property
- Intangible property such as goodwill

How much should you expect to pay for property insurance? It depends on your claims history, the insurer, what you want to insure, the type of structure, whether you have any protective safety measures, and the location of your property. As with the rest of your insurance needs, you need to shop around, as rates can vary widely.

Liability

Also known as *comprehensive general liability,* or CGL insurance, this type of policy has two functions. First, if someone is injured because of your negligence or the negligence of one of your employees, the policy pays the claim. Second, if you are sued for damages related to the policy, the policy will pay the cost of your attorney. Needless to say, in this litigious society of ours, liability insurance is almost a must.

Workers' Compensation

Workers' compensation insurance is required in every state except Texas. Note, however, that not every employer is required to carry it; in some states, small businesses with few employees (typically fewer than five) are not required to carry workers' comp insurance. Check with your state insurance commissioner's office.

Like CGL insurance, workers' comp does two things. First, it covers medical bills and lost wages for injured employees. Second, if an employee is injured or killed on the job, it protects the owner against claims by the injured employee's family. Additionally, you can buy extra coverage to protect your business from claims of sexual harassment or discrimination.

Rates for workers' comp depend on how long you have been in business, your state, and the number of claims you make. Rates are usually set for three years, after which time the insurer compares the number of claims submitted against those of similar businesses. If you have fewer claims, some insurance companies will give you a refund. One way to reduce your premium, then, is to have a good safety record. Your insurer may require that you follow the guidelines of the Occupational Health and Safety Administration or classify your employees, as insurers base premiums, at least in part, on the risk of injury for different job classifications.

Workers' Comp

It can be difficult for small businesses to obtain affordable workers' compensation insurance. In response, some states have created risk-sharing pools for such companies. Do not expect to find many discounts, however, as this is an insurance of last resort.

Errors and Omissions

Called *E and O insurance,* errors and omissions coverage is for service businesses, offering protection if you neglect to do something and thereby cause a customer or client damage. For example, a physician's medical malpractice insurance is a type of E and O coverage.

Business Interruption

Business interruption insurance (BII) is designed to cover the loss of income if normal business operations are disrupted by damage caused by a fire, flood, or other disaster. BII is intended to cover loss of income directly related to the loss of physical property. Thus, if your location is vital to your ability to make money, then business interruption insurance is important. A service business probably does not need BII, as services can be performed most anywhere, but a factory would definitely need business interruption insurance.

Keyman

As the name indicates, this sort of policy insures your business against the death of a key employee, be it the CEO, vice president of sales, or someone else. Think about it: What would happen to your business if a key employee died? For some small businesses, the company would die, too. There are two important things to understand about keyman insurance:

1. If your top management is thin—that is, if one or two people are responsible for keeping the ship afloat—then keyman coverage is critical.
2. Buy as much coverage as your business can afford. Accurately estimate what it would cost the company if the key men or women on your team were to vanish, and buy a policy for that amount if you can afford it.

Auto

If your business makes deliveries or if you provide employees with company cars, then auto insurance is a must. Although you may be tempted to purchase the minimum coverage required by your state, that is not enough—the point of insurance is to protect your business. If your driver kills someone in an auto accident, a minimal $25,000 policy will equal bankruptcy. For an established business, $1 million in liability coverage is probably right. A better way to keep premiums down is to increase your deductible.

Life

Why are you in business for yourself? Surely, one reason is that you want to create financial stability for your family. What if something happens to you—what will become of your dream then? Without adequate life insurance, it probably will turn into a nightmare. Beyond that, many banks require that the owner of the business have life insurance before they will loan the business money.

When shopping for life insurance, you will be faced with a decision: term or whole life policy? Buying a whole life policy is like buying a house: as you pay the premium, you build equity in the policy. Buying a term policy is like renting: it is cheaper, but you build no equity. In this case, renting is probably better than buying, as rates for term life insurance are amazingly affordable. Even though you will not be building equity, the money you save is usually better spent in other areas of your business.

Tip: Premiums for business insurance are tax deductible as a business expense, although life and keyman insurance premiums are not deductible if the business is the beneficiary of the policies.

BUYING INSURANCE

The list of potential insurance products is a bit daunting, and no one is telling you that you must buy all of them. Sure, it would be nice, but as in the rest of your business, choosing what sort of insurance you really need is a matter of weighing the risks and rewards. There is a finite limit on what you can realistically do, and sometimes you simply must marshal your resources to the best of your ability and hope for the best.

To save as much as you can on your insurance costs, it is important to know the difference between an insurance agent and an insurance broker—it is a distinction that can save you money. An agent represents a single company. He may be able to get you a good deal, but only within the company that he represents. A broker, on the other hand, represents many different insurers and thus has the ability to shop around to many different insurers and find the best deal out there.

Tip: A great place to go and compare rates and policies is EHealthInsurance .com.

The second way to reduce the cost of your premiums is to take the highest deductible that you can reasonably afford. Needless to say, it has to be an amount that you can *actually* afford. There is no point in taking a $5,000 deductible if your small business will be unable to absorb the difference.

Another way to make insurance payments more manageable is to create a payment plan that works for your budget. Fortunately, insurance companies are quite flexible when it comes to the payment of premiums. You can pay monthly, quarterly, or yearly. Find yourself a good insurance broker and go over your needs. He will be able to guide you in making the right decisions and obtaining the right coverage for your business.

EXCLUSIONS

Whatever policy you look at, be sure that you understand what the exclusions are. Exclusions are claims that the policy does not cover, and every policy has some. Some policies have many. There is nothing worse than having a loss, thinking that you are covered, and then discovering that the type of loss you suffered is specifically excluded in the fine print of your policy. For example, a property loss policy will likely exclude losses resulting from theft by an employee. So before you sign, be sure you know what is covered and what is not.

The Four Parts of Any Insurance Policy

1. *Declarations page*. This names the policyholder, explains what is insured, and lists the maximum payout by the insurer.
2. *Insurance agreement*. This section sets out the responsibilities of both sides under the insurance contract.
3. *Conditions*. This section details exactly what is covered and under what circumstances.
4. *Exclusions*. This area details what is not covered.

MAKING A CLAIM

The time may come when you suffer a loss and need to make a claim against your carrier. Insurance companies are sticklers for details, and if you do not follow their procedures to the letter, you may find that they will deny your claim, and legitimately. You can do a few things to ensure that your insurance works for you.

Before Making a Claim

Be sure you have excellent records that are kept in a safe, secure spot, preferably off site. All receipts, backups of important files, and backups of computer data should be readily accessible so that you can get to them easily. Similarly, it is a good practice to make a video of your premises and property every year. Spend some time documenting what you have and where. Then put the tape with your other vital records in a secure location. It will be invaluable if you ever need it.

Keep Good Records

A main reason for keeping good records is that it speeds up the claims process. The longer it takes you to gather the information your insurer needs, the longer it will take to process your claim; also, the longer it takes to process your claim, the longer it will take to get that check.

After a Loss

When you have suffered a loss, follow these steps when making a claim:

- *Report the incident immediately.* Tell your agent or carrier about the problem as soon as you can. Some policies require notification within a certain time limit, meaning that your insurer can deny coverage if notice comes in too late.
- *Protect your property from further damage.* If you are filing a property loss claim, policies often require that damaged property be kept safe from further damage.
- *Provide documentation.* If you have receipts, copy and provide them. If you made that video, get it out.
- *Communicate and cooperate.* The easier you make it for the adjuster, the easier it will be for you.

CHAPTER 26

Get a Handle on Taxes

To you taxpayers out there, let me say this: Even though income taxes can be a pain in the neck, the folks at the IRS are regular people just like you, except that they can destroy your life.

—DAVE BARRY

Taxes are one of those things that almost every entrepreneur hates dealing with. So, I will make with you the same deal that I make with the readers of my weekly *USA TODAY* column whenever I write about taxes: give me just a bit of your time, and I will make this as painless as possible—and maybe save you some money in the process.

TAX BASICS

The amount that you or your business will pay in annual taxes depends on several factors: the legal form of your business, how much money it made during the year, what your expenses were, how sharp your accountant is, and how much you personally know about the tax system. Here is what you need to know about taxes if you run a small business.

Deductions

You already know that you can deduct "ordinary and necessary" business expenses to reduce your taxable income. That's the easy part. Travel, supplies, inventory, labor costs—all are deductible from your federal income taxes. The real question is, Are there any loopholes you can use?

- *Entertainment.* It used to be that you could deduct up to 80 percent of all legitimate entertainment expenses, but the limit now is 50 percent. The good news is that almost any entertainment activity that relates to your business can be deducted: a round of golf, an important dinner, a game or concert, or even a day on a boat. The important thing is to keep good records, including all receipts, and to be able to prove that the expense was actually related to business. It is not a bad idea to write whom you were with on the receipt before filing it away.

App of the Day: Sick of keeping every receipt, losing some, being unable to read others? Then check out a great app called Concur Breeze (www.Concur.com). With this cool tool you can take a picture with your cell phone of the receipt, throw it away, and have the receipt automatically entered into an expense report. Ditto your credit card expenses.

- *Travel.* As you know, travel expenses that you incur for business are 100 percent deductible. However, if your family joins you on your business trip to Orlando, their expenses are not deductible. The loophole is that if you stay an extra night or two to get a discounted airfare, the extra costs for your hotel and meals are deductible.
- *Automobile.* There are two methods of calculating your vehicle deduction. The *standard mileage* method allows you to deduct 55.5 cents per mile that you drive the car for business, as well as business-related tolls and parking expenses. The *actual expense* method permits you to deduct your total expenses for gas and repairs, plus depreciation. Then, you need to multiply your expenses by the percentage of business use. For example, if your total expenses are $10,000, and you use the car 40 percent for personal use and 60 percent for business use, your deductible auto expenses would be $6,000. Keep a log of when the car is driven and for what purpose.

- *Business losses.* Business losses can be deducted against your personal income. If the amount that your business lost is more than your personal income, the extra loss can be applied to future income taxes.
- *Loans and credit cards.* Interest on loans, purchases, or advances can be deducted as a business expense.

Tax Tip: The following expenses are tax deductible for your business:

- Professional association fees
- Business gifts
- Bank charges
- Magazines and books
- Losses due to theft
- Commissions paid
- Website development
- Parking and tolls
- Seminars
- Bus fare

- *Charity.* Sole proprietors, partnerships, LLCs, and S corporations can pass through charitable contributions to the owner's personal tax return. C corporations may claim any charitable deduction for themselves.
- *Taxes.* Sales taxes on items that you buy for the business are deductible. Fuel and excise taxes are often overlooked deductions. Property tax and local assessments are deductible. Employment taxes that you pay are also deductible, although the self-employment tax paid by individuals is not deductible, and neither is federal income tax paid.

Small businesses lose audits when they have poor records. The important thing is to keep all receipts, cancelled checks, credit card statements, and so forth. If you do keep good records and you are ever audited, your chances of success—of not getting hit with an extra assessment and fine—will be much greater. Keep good records!

Keep Track of Mileage

If you have a hard time keeping track of your business mileage, here is a tip for you: CarCheckup is a small device that plugs it into your car. When you drive, it records your speed, miles, and so on. If you leave it plugged in all day, it will record start and stop times and the distance of each trip. Then, when you need to make a mileage log, simply remove the device from your car and plug it into your computer. You can then download your data onto carcheckup.com and the program will crunch the numbers for you.

Employee Taxes

Employees and taxes go hand in hand. When hired, your employees need to fill out a federal W-4 form and an Immigration and Naturalization Service Form I-9. As you begin to pay them, you will need to deduct a variety of taxes from their paychecks.

- *Social Security.* Social security taxes (also known as FICA) must be withheld from each employee's pay. You match the amount withheld and pay it to the federal government.
- *Medicare.* Medicare must also be withheld. You need to match and pay this amount.
- *Unemployment tax.* You need to withhold, match, and pay this tax.
- *State income taxes.* These taxes are withheld.

W-2s and 1099s Made Easy

Whether you are an independent contractor, or a business with employees and hire contractors, 1099s and W-2s are part of your life, and probably a confusing part at that. Here is some good news for you: check out Greatland .com. Greatland is the leader in 1099 and W-2 reporting, with all of the forms and software you may need to take what is often a confusing issue and make it much simpler.

Taxes and payroll are not easy issues for most small businesses, which is why businesses often outsource this task. There are all sorts of different companies that offer these services, and even software that helps you do it yourself, and it would behoove you to check these out. Additionally, from personal experience, I can attest that both Bank of America's Easy Online Payroll and its Full Service Payroll are excellent services that can help any small business get a handle on payroll.

Sales Taxes

Unless you live in one of the five states with no sales tax (Delaware, Montana, New Hampshire, Oregon, and parts of Alaska), if you sell a product, you will owe your state tax money. What you will owe varies greatly; not only does the amount vary by state, but also some states tax services in addition to products. You need to check with your state tax board to see whether the rules apply to you. If your service or product is subject to your state's sales tax, you need to register with your state's tax department, track taxable and nontaxable sales, and then include that information with your state tax return.

Sales Tax

There are two exceptions to the sales tax rules. First, resellers—such as wholesalers and retailers with a resale license—do not owe sales tax. Second, sales tax need not be paid on sales to tax-exempt organizations such as public schools and churches.

Deadlines

When you own your own small business, you need to be aware of tax deadlines beyond April 15:

- Corporations must file their returns within two and a half months of the end of their fiscal year.
- Quarterly estimated taxes are due four times a year: April 15, June 15, September 15, and January 15.
- Sales taxes are due quarterly or monthly, depending on what state you are in.

- Employee taxes may be due weekly, monthly, or quarterly, depending on the number of employees you have.

Quarterlies

Quarterlies should be paid by any small business that expects to pay at least $500 in taxes for the year. You are supposed to pay either 90 percent of the tax that you expect to owe or 100 percent of the previous year's tax.

Property Taxes

If your business owns real estate, it will owe property taxes. Moreover, if you lease property, your lease may require you to pay the property taxes. In some leases, the owner pays the base-year taxes—an amount equal to that owed the year before the lease was signed—and the lessee (you) pays any increases. In most places, the tax rate on commercial property is significantly higher than that on residential property.

TAX TIPS

All small business owners want to save on their taxes. The question is, how? There are many strategies you can adopt to help reduce your tax bite. But don't wait until December 31 to take action. Some advance planning can go a long way toward reducing Uncle Sam's take come tax time.

Set Up a Retirement Account

Self-employed entrepreneurs can divert pretax dollars into different types of retirement savings accounts and thereby reduce their yearly taxable income.

- *Keogh plans.* A Keogh retirement plan allows self-employed taxpayers to contribute significant sums (up to $49,000) every year to a tax-free account. Keoghs are fairly complicated to create, and the assistance of

a financial advisor is required. However, there are several benefits to starting a Keogh retirement plan:
- Contributions are deducted from gross income.
- Taxes are deferred until the money is withdrawn.
- Interest earned is also tax deferred until withdrawn.
- Contribution amounts are more liberal than those for IRAs.

- *Solo 401(k)*. This plan is great because of its high contribution limit. Like a Keogh, a solo 401(k) allows you to contribute up to $49,000 a year into your retirement account, but with this type of account, the amount you can contribute rises as you get older.
- *SEP IRAs*. A simplified employee pension individual retirement account, or SEP IRA, is a plan that allows you to contribute and deduct up to 20 percent of your income into a tax-deferred retirement account. SEPs are indeed simple: they can be created in a few minutes at a bank or brokerage house with no professional help, and no annual government reports are required. They beat regular IRAs because they allow for larger contributions.

Roth IRAs

You may be tempted to set up a Roth IRA as well. Although a Roth IRA is a good choice for retirement purposes, it does little good for your business, as contributions are not tax deductible.

There is one important thing to understand about your retirement plan: if you do set up a Keogh, solo 401(k), or SEP, you have to offer it to your employees as well. This means you will likely need to make contributions beyond your own. Therefore, you should consult with an employee benefits professional before setting up any sort of retirement plan for you and your employees.

One last bonus for creating a business retirement plan: you can get a tax credit of up to $500 for the first three years of the plan if you have fewer than 100 employees.

Lease Your Property to Your Business

If your business uses property that you personally own, you can save on business taxes by leasing the property to the business. The lease expense to the business is tax deductible, and the income you generate personally from the lease income is not subject to Social Security tax. You can then take any applicable depreciation allowance for the leased property.

Tip: Got a shoebox full of receipts? Then check out Shoeboxed.com. This great service allows you to send them your physical paper receipts and logs so that the tedious work of entering and scanning your receipts is done for you. Shoeboxed enters your data onto secure servers for you to review at your leisure.

Use the Tax Laws

The Jobs and Growth Tax Relief Reconciliation Act of 2003 offered plenty of help for the small business owner. The best part of the bill is the generous change with regard to the rules for depreciating business expenditures. Previously, equipment and business assets had to be depreciated over a five- to seven-year time span. Under the new rules, however, you can now depreciate and deduct 100 percent of the cost of almost all new and used assets in the year in which you buy them. Previously, the deduction topped out at $25,000, but now you can depreciate up to $100,000 for any asset acquired after May 5, 2003.

Reexamine Your Business Structure

If you have been in business for a while and are making a profit, it may be smart to change your legal form of business. For instance, a growing S corporation may want to become a C corporation so as to take advantage of benefit programs that are limited to C corporations, such as group-term life insurance and various health insurance options. A newly profitable sole proprietor may want to form an LLC to get personal liability protection or an S corporation to reduce self-employment tax.

Pay Your Quarterlies

Make sure that you are paying your quarterly estimated taxes on time and in sufficient amounts to avoid penalties and interest down the road.

Delay Your Receivables and Accelerate Your Expenses

At the end of the tax year, if your business expects to have significant income from accounts receivable, consider delaying those receivables until after the first of the year. Doing so will reduce your business's net taxable income for the year. Similarly, if you anticipate a large tax bite at the end of the year, you might consider accelerating some expenses into the current tax year. Expenses that can be accelerated include corporate charitable contributions, 60 percent of health insurance premiums for yourself if you are self-employed, year-end employee bonuses, and any other tax-deductible expenses you are planning on making.

Deduct Your Home Office

If you use part of your home for business, you may be eligible for the home office deduction. Here are the rules: (1) your home office must be used "exclusively and regularly" for your business, and (2) the area must serve as your principal place of business or the place where you meet with customers in the normal course of business. If you pass that test, then you can deduct a proportional share of your mortgage payments, insurance premiums, utility expenses, and so on.

SURVIVING AN AUDIT

Even if you know your tax law and do everything right, the chances of getting audited are greater for you than for the public at large. Why? Because small businesses are audited more than any other entity. If you do get that dreaded letter and have to attend a tax audit, here is what you should do.

Get Some Help

If you have a CPA consider hiring him or her to help you prepare for and attend the meeting. Your accountant should be your financial business advisor, and this is when you need him or her most. If you can't afford an accountant, you must do on your own what the accountant would do: prepare. You need to look at the return(s) in question and be able to substantiate (with those good records you were advised to keep) what is in the return. You, or you and your accountant, need to prepare all documentation for the audit.

Be Organized

Make sure your receipts are organized, your canceled checks and credit card receipts are in order, and all logs and other records are ready. Having your ducks in a row builds credibility. The success of your audit depends on your ability to document your income and expenses. You will want to have ready for the auditor bank statements, cancelled checks, receipts, invoices, sales slips, petty cash vouchers, printouts of electronic records, bills, checkbook registers, ledgers, journals, appointment books, and any other physical documentation of your records. Without adequate records, the IRS auditor can legally make assumptions about your income and deductions.

Prepare Your "Listed Property" Records

Equipment that has both personal and business use, such as computers, cell phones, and autos, is called "listed property." You must provide the auditor with business records of your listed property.

Prepare Your Travel and Entertainment Records

Travel and entertainment expenses must be proved by written record (see IRS Code § 267). One way to document these expenses is with an appointment book or log.

As you can see, winning an audit is much more likely if you have a practice of maintaining records, keeping receipts, and chronicling what you do.

PART

Management

CHAPTER 27

Hiring and Firing

Getting fired is nature's way of telling you that you had the
wrong job in the first place.

—Hal Lancaster

It is oft said that your employees are your most valuable asset, but that may
not necessarily be true. It would be nice if they were, and sometimes they
are, but, simply put, employees are also a lot of work. Hiring them, dealing
with the myriad issues and troubles that arise, letting go of the problem
ones—employees take plenty of time and effort. So as you go about dealing
with them, especially the hiring and firing part, there are a few things you
should know to make things easier and to keep you out of hot water.

EMPLOYEE OR INDEPENDENT CONTRACTOR?

It is not surprising that you might want to hire people and call them independent contractors. Although an employee and an independent contractor often perform similar duties, your obligations toward an independent
contractor are minimal compared with an employee:

- You need not provide an independent contractor with workers'
  compensation insurance.
- You need not match an independent contractor's unemployment
  insurance payment.
- Most important, you need not pay any portion of an independent
  contractor's Social Security or Medicare taxes.

So yes, it would be nice to hire independent contractors to do the job of
employees (many employers do), *but only* if they are really independent

contractors. There are two main distinctions between an employee and an independent contractor. First, employees have to follow direction, whereas independent contractors are truly independent—they get to decide how, when, and where they work. Sure, you can oversee what they do and approve or disapprove of the project, but you cannot control the process of when and how they do the work. Second, employees are exclusive—that is, they work for only one company, and certainly never work for competitors at the same time. Independent contractors, on the other hand, offer their services not just to one business but to the public at large. Indeed, they often work for several similar businesses at the same time. That is why they are called *independent contractors*—they must be independent.

You may be tempted to save money and hassle by saying that a position calls for an independent contractor, but if the worker is really an employee (because he or she is not truly independent), the results can be severe. If you get caught (and you will probably get caught—employees resent this tactic), not only will you owe back taxes, interest, and penalties to the federal government, but also you may owe money to the employee for lost benefits. On top of that, you will likely get in trouble with your state's labor department. All in all, taking this shortcut is a mistake to avoid.

HIRING EMPLOYEES

Hiring employees should be a fairly enjoyable process. (In fact, most of your small business should be fairly enjoyable—that is a big reason why we are in business for ourselves. But I digress.) Finding and hiring the right people is a chance to implement your vision for your business. You get to locate the types of people you would like to work with and the types you think your customers would like dealing with. As much as you look at background, education, skills, and intelligence when hiring, you should equally consider personality and compatibility. You spend plenty of time with your employees, and you want to make sure that yours will be an enjoyable place to work.

Finding and hiring good employees, therefore, is one of the most important things that you can do as a small business owner. Employees help set the tone, employees do the work, employees deal with customers, and employees are the ones on the front lines. If they blow it, they give you and your business a bad name, and conversely, if they do things properly, you all win.

Preparation

Before hiring anyone, you need to have a very clear idea of what the position will entail. Write a job description that includes duties, hours, responsibilities, and so on. This will help you focus on the qualities that you want in an employee. Based on the job description, consider how much schooling and experience the person should have, what sort of people skills are necessary, what you want from the employee, and so on. Some of this can be gleaned from an employment application.

Sample Employment Application

PERSONAL INFORMATION

Name:

Address:

Phone number:

Social Security number:

Position applying for:

When are you available to start:

EMPLOYMENT INFORMATION

Please list your employment for the past three years:

Date: Employer/Supervisor: Address/Phone #:   Duties:

Special skills and qualifications:

Other:

EDUCATION

School: Years of attendance: Did you graduate?:

REFERENCES

Please list three references:

Name: Relationship: Years Acquainted: Address/Phone #:

Dated: _____Signed:_____

After receiving the application and weeding out the undesirables, you should prepare an interview questionnaire that you can use as a guide for the interview. You will need to explore the candidate's background, experience, qualifications, ideas, intelligence, and references. Be sure to include open-ended questions that require the applicant to explain things. You should have several questions ready regarding each important attribute for the position.

Finding Qualified Applicants

Once you know what you want from an employee, you need to find a stable of potential candidates to interview for the position(s). Of course, a help wanted ad in the classifieds, in your window, or on a site such as Monster.com can draw a pool of applicants, but don't overlook other options:

- *Craigslist.* Especially if you are looking to hire a Gen X or Gen Y employee, this online classified ad marketplace will yield a bonanza of applicants. (Using it to hire an assistant got me well over 100 *qualified* applicants!)
- *Temp agencies.* The best thing about hiring a temp is that you can test-drive an employee before making a long-term commitment.
- *Seniors.* Older workers usually have an excellent work ethic, and they are responsible and eager to please.
- *State employment agencies.* Every state has job placement programs. If you tap this resource, the state not only will post your job listing on state job boards but also may prescreen applicants for you.
- *Colleges.* Universities are a good place to find smart, inexpensive part-time employees.

Interviewing

With all interviewees, you need to discover whether they are responsible, why they left their previous jobs, whether they can take direction, if they have ever been fired, why they want this job, and their qualifications for the position. Also, as mentioned, as much as you want someone who meets your qualifications, do not overlook the applicant's personality and how well you may or may not get along. Be sure to get references and a resume.

Your interview should be straightforward, but not predictable. Be sure to ask some questions that (1) the applicant is not ready for and (2) will force thinking on the fly. To the extent you can also get into a conversation and not just a Q and A session, do so; it should reveal some interesting information.

Discrimination in Hiring

When interviewing candidates, avoid asking questions about race, sex, color, national origin, religion, finances, or disabilities. Concentrate on job-related questions.

Coachability

It is hard to overestimate just how important the employee-hiring process is. A good employee may be a new profit center or simply another pair of valuable hands—selling, helping, assisting clients, and boosting morale. On the other hand, the wrong person can steal, create havoc, anger customers, and hurt sales. Worse, if fired, an unscrupulous employee might even sue for wrongful termination (that is, illegal termination), even though you were legally and morally correct in letting him go.

Therefore, you cannot be too careful when interviewing potential employees. Of course, honesty, intelligence, skill, and affability are important. You can garner much of that information from resumes, references, and interviews. Knowing what people did in the past is a pretty good indication of what they will do in the future. Really, that is rather standard stuff. Most small business owners have a pretty good sense of what they are looking for in an employee. You know about checking references.

However, one area that is often overlooked is something I call *coachability,* and it is vital to making a smart hire. Coachability is an employee's ability to take direction and make changes, to listen and adjust, to think and respond. Just as not everyone is cut out to be an entrepreneur, not everyone is cut out to be an employee.

Running a small business and hiring the right employees is not unlike running a sports franchise. There are good teammates and bad teammates. There are employees who make everyone around them better and those who hog the ball. As in sports, uncoachable employees can ruin your team. You have to stock your business with employees who are willing to do things your way, who listen, who can take constructive criticism, who are willing to try new things, who are adaptable and positive—who are coachable.

So, when interviewing prospective employees, be sure to find out what kind of teammate they have been and will be. As much as skill and smarts, their coachability can make or break your season.

Hiring

"Always choose attitude over experience. When I hire people I make a habit of never looking at their resume because most people spend most of their life in the wrong job. I never hire complainers or excuse makers because they'll find a way within my company to do more of the same. People with a can-do attitude are a pleasure to work with."

—Real estate millionaire Barbara Corcoran

NEW EMPLOYEES

Whenever you hire new employees, there are several agreements that you may want to consider having them sign.

- A reasonable noncompete agreement if the employee might learn things that could be used against you later
- A nondisclosure agreement to prevent employees from disclosing confidential trade secrets
- An assignment of inventions or "work for hire" agreement if the employee will be involved in creative endeavors

You should also have an employment contract, as it is a good way to memorialize your agreement with the employee. It is critical that the contract state clearly and boldly that "nothing in this agreement is intended to guarantee employment or alter the fact that [name of the employee] is an at-will employee." This document helps clarify your relationship with the employee, but it is also an important defense in any future litigation. The agreement should cover the following:

- *Compensation.* This section details the employee's base salary and benchmarks for bonuses or commissions.
- *Job description.* Explain *in detail* what is expected of the employee, including hours, duties, sales quotas, everything. Be expansive and explain that other responsibilities may be added later on.
- *Benefits.* Your benefits package should be explained. You should reserve the right to change the benefit plan.
- *Stock options.* If you offer stock options as part of your benefits or incentive program, the process by which they are attained and exercised needs to be explained.
- *Arbitration.* Litigation is expensive, and many employers have mandatory arbitration clauses in their employment agreements.
- *Immigration status.* Employees must verify that they are citizens of the United States or have the proper work visa.

Both you and your employee need to sign the contract, and you should keep a signed copy in a safe and secure place.

You may also consider having an employee handbook that explains important policies and procedures, such as workplace safety, antidiscrimination policies, handling of complaints, discipline, sick leave, and vacation policies. This handbook should also reiterate that workers are considered at-will employees.

The Family and Medical Leave Act

If you have 50 or more employees, you are required to abide by the Family and Medical Leave Act. The FMLA mandates that eligible employees must be given up to 12 weeks of unpaid leave during any 12-month period to care for a new child (including adopted children), to care for an immediate family member with a serious health problem, or to take care of the employee's own serious health problem.

LEARNING FROM NEW EMPLOYEES

If you are a good employer, you do a lot of listening. Employees are one of your very best resources for learning how to improve your business; they will see things that you miss. However, on the totem pole of valued employees, new employees are usually near the bottom. That may be a mistake. New employees can give you a perspective that more entrenched employees lack or have lost.

After employees have been with you for a few months, consider giving them a survey to fill out; the results will probably be illuminating. For example, your survey might look like this:

1. Name:
2. Position:
3. Please describe your job:
4. What are the most important things you do in your job?
5. What is the best part of your job?
6. What is the worst part?
7. What would you change about your job?
8. Does the job reflect what you were told during the hiring process?
9. What improvements could be made to our hiring process?

"IT JUST ISN'T WORKING OUT"

You may be tempted to implement a probationary period of, say, six months when you hire new employees. You should avoid this. Why? Because by creating a probationary period, you are implying that different rules apply before and after the probation. You do not want that. You should have one set of rules for everyone, whether it is their first day or tenth year.

You may also be tempted to fire an employee when things go wrong. It is far better, and helps you avoid litigation, to document problems first. Yes, it is true that an at-will employee can be fired at any time, but creating a paper trail can only help you. Document every transgression in writing. Give the employee a letter explaining what he or she is doing wrong and what can be done to reverse course, and have the employee sign it.

Firing and Discrimination

Remember, you cannot fire, without repercussions, an employee because of discrimination or retaliation or an employee who has a long-term contract.

To avoid an ugly and expensive wrongful termination suit, here is a checklist of things to consider before terminating an employee. Of course, not all items will apply to all employees, but this gives you an idea of issues to consider prior to firing.

- Analyze whether the problem is the fault of the employee or your business procedures. If this is how you run your business, firing the employee will not solve the problem.
- Make sure that you have documented the employee's transgressions in writing.
- If you have a grievance or complaint procedure, be sure that it has been followed.
- Determine whether similar employees have been treated similarly to the employee in question. Disparate treatment equals litigation.
- If the employee is a member of a protected class (disabled, minority, elderly), be sure that the reason for the termination is valid and double-check to make sure the problems with the employee have been documented.
- Make sure the employee is not being fired in retaliation for the exercise of a legal right.
- Make sure the employee does not have a contract for continued employment, either written or implied.

If you determine that firing the person is the best course of action, it is best to do so in the morning, usually midweek, although late on Friday afternoon may work well, too. Break the news in the employee's office or in a conference room, and endeavor to do so gently. Make it brief and dignified. If you are concerned that the employee might become violent, have a security guard ready nearby (hire one for the day if necessary).

Just Cause Employees

The opposite of an at-will employee is a just cause employee. Employees with long-term employment contracts (such as tenured teachers) are just cause employees. As the term implies, these employees may be legally terminated only if there is a just cause. Just cause may refer to illegal behavior, excessive absenteeism, insubordination, sexual harassment, or serious incompetence. Firing a just cause employee requires investigation, notice, and hearings.

After the employee has left the premises, you may need to change the locks or access codes if the employee had security clearance. Finally, write a disengagement letter to the employee afterward, handling any necessary housecleaning matters and reiterating what happened in the termination meeting.

A necessary part of small business, letting employees go can and should be done in a way that minimizes your risk.

CHAPTER **28**

Pay and Benefits

Nothing is more pleasing and engaging than the sense of having conferred benefits. Not even the gratification of receiving them.

—ELLIS PETERS

People work for many reasons, and compensation is just one of those reasons. To create and sustain a successful small business, you need to take into account the many benefits that people derive from work. From the noble (the desire to make a difference) to the mundane (the need for health insurance), work means different things to different people. Although pay is the main way you compensate employees for a job well done, it is by no means the only way. What you want is to create the conditions that foster a happy, productive workplace:

- *Happy employees work better.* They are respected, and in turn they give respect.
- *Happy employees are engaged.* When people are forced to do the same thing over and over again, lethargy cannot help but creep in. The great managers mix it up and play to people's strengths, not just the job's requirements or description.
- *Happy employees have a stake.* Ideally, they have a financial stake in the business, but it can also be an emotional one; they buy into the vision. Employees who believe in the business are typically satisfied people.

In this chapter, a smorgasbord of benefit options is offered for your consideration. Remember, great benefits foster grateful employees.

WHAT IS REQUIRED?

By law, you are required to give employees only certain benefits, although they are probably not the ones you might think. You must:

- Pay them at least the prevailing minimum wage
- Provide workers' compensation insurance
- Withhold and match FICA taxes
- Pay unemployment taxes
- Have employees work no more than 40 hours a week, or pay overtime, unless they are exempt employees
- Give employees time off to serve in the military, to serve on a jury, or to vote

Exempt from Overtime?

According to the Fair Labor Standards Act, certain employees are exempt from overtime and minimum wage requirements. These employees, who typically hold executive, administrative, professional, or outside sales positions, are compensated on a salary basis regardless of the number of days or hours worked.

You are not required to give employees benefits such as:

- Bonuses
- Health insurance
- Paid vacation time
- Sick leave
- Retirement plans
- Stock options
- Life insurance
- Time off on legal holidays

Of course, although you are not required to offer such benefits, if you want to create a place where people want to work, a place that is special, and a place that engenders loyalty, you will want to provide some or all of these benefits.

The quality of your benefits package is something that employees will look at when deciding whether your business is a place they want to work. And because the quality of the employees you attract has a direct impact on the quality of your business (and the quality of your bottom line), offering a full benefits package is an important criterion to consider, albeit an expensive one.

BONUSES

Money is a mighty motivator. For that reason, bonuses can be a valuable incentive. Bonuses can be structured in two ways. First, individual employees can be given benchmarks to hit, and a sliding-scale bonus can be offered as the employee hits each goal. Because this sort of system works best for sales staff, another sort of bonus plan may work better companywide. Under the second system, goals for the entire business are communicated to all employees, and as the company hits those goals, a pool of bonus money is created. Each goal reached fills the pool more, and at the end of the year, the pool is divided equally. Goals could be sales, reduced overhead, or less shrinkage.

Shrinkage!

Not just a term from *Seinfeld*, *shrinkage* refers to a reduction in inventory caused by accounting error, employee theft, customer shoplifting, administrative error, or vendor fraud or mistake.

This system has several advantages. First, it helps teach your employees about business, and the more they know, the less likely they are to waste. Second, it gives everyone a stake in the outcome, not just your salespeople. Third, it creates a sense of teamwork and helps employees feel invested in the business.

STOCK OPTIONS AND OWNERSHIP

Another trait shared by successful small businesses is that they often give employees a stake in the business—an ownership share. Rather than being just another place to work and draw a salary, a small business that offers employees part ownership creates committed entrepreneurs. As a result, employees are more motivated, more dedicated, and more conscientious. And the possibility that the business could hit it big, and thereby make the employee rich, is another powerful motivator.

There are three types of stock ownership plans:

1. With a *stock option plan,* your business awards the option to buy company stock at a specified price, and the employee has a certain amount of time to exercise the option and become a part owner of the company. Approximately 10 million employees in public and private businesses hold stock options at any one time.
2. An *employee stock ownership plan* (ESOP) is a sort of retirement plan akin to a 401(k), although in this case, instead of creating a diversified portfolio, the retirement funds are invested in the stock of the employer. In this scenario, the company contributes cash to buy its own stock (usually from the owner), which is then shared among the employees. There are significant tax benefits available under this plan. It is estimated that about 8 million employees invest in ESOPs.
3. An *employee stock purchase plan* allows employees to buy stock at a discount (usually around 15 percent). Employees can then sell the stock for a profit or simply hold on to it.

Creating an ESOP

For more information on creating an employee stock ownership plan, contact the National Center for Employee Ownership at 510-208-1300 or visit www.nceo.org.

OTHER RETIREMENT PLANS

For employers and employees alike, the most popular employer-sponsored retirement plan is the 401(k), as contributions are tax deductible for employers and tax deferred for employees. Participation is optional, although employees today know they need to fund their own retirement and appreciate the opportunity to do so. As a small business owner, the question you must answer is whether you can afford to match funds contributed by employees. It is expensive to match employee contributions dollar for dollar, even if the dollars are tax deductible.

Investments made by 401(k) contributions can be handled by employees or by the plan administrator; know, however, that with a 401 (k), the more options you give your employees, the more expensive administration will be. Expect administration costs to be at least $1,000 per year, as reports must be filed with the IRS, the U.S. Department of Labor, plan participants, and so forth.

To set up a 401(k) or other tax-deferred retirement, you need to speak with a financial planner or accountant.

HEALTH INSURANCE

Employees consistently rank health insurance among the most important benefits supplied by an employer. The problem for the small business owner is that the cost of insuring employees continues to rise at frightening rates. And unlike larger businesses, which can pass on or absorb increases to some degree, small businesses have neither luxury. What are you to do? There are options, but no great answers. Some are better than others, but in all honesty, most options for reducing health care costs involve cutting benefits or shifting costs to employees. Although such measures may help keep costs down, they do not make for a happy workplace.

The first and easiest thing to do is shop around. There are all sorts of plans to choose from, with varying degrees of cost and coverage. Online, www.eHealthInsurance.com is a great site for comparing health plans. You should also speak with an insurance agent or broker. The plan you bought a few years ago may have cheaper alternatives today. Remember, too, that an insurance broker can shop your needs around to many different providers, whereas an agent works exclusively with one company. By shopping, you can compare quotes for scores of different plans.

Shopping for Insurance

What is it that you require? Your health insurance plan can be comprehensive or minimal, expensive or not. First, consider the extent of coverage that you require. An inexpensive plan that covers little is probably a waste of money. You likely want a plan that at least covers expenses such as:

- Doctor and hospital visits
- Catastrophic injury and illness
- Prescriptions and wellness

You may also want a plan that includes things such as:

- Vision and dental benefits
- Maternity and obstetrical care
- Counseling and alternative treatments

But, as you well know, the more you offer, the more it will cost.

Tip: Even if you cannot afford to pay for benefits such as vision and dental care, you can offer them to your employees on a voluntary basis as additional coverage they can purchase. Aflac, for example, has some great voluntary insurance programs that are worth checking out.

The other consideration is cost. When analyzing insurance coverage, you need to take into account three factors: the monthly premium, the yearly deductible, and the price of co-pays. A high deductible means lower monthly premiums but probably less coverage. It's a tough trade-off, and the truth is, you probably cannot afford as much insurance as you would like to offer your staff. But, by the same token, you must also realize that employees consistently rank good health insurance as one of the benefits they appreciate most. If you want to attract great employees, you need to offer them as much coverage as you can possibly afford.

Options

You have several basic options for health insurance:

- *Traditional health insurance.* This type of insurance allows employees to pick any doctor or specialist they want. They must meet a yearly deductible, and there is usually a cap on out-of-pocket expenses. This is the most flexible yet most expensive type of plan.
- *Health maintenance organizations.* HMOs direct employees to providers within the system. The primary care physician is the gateway to all other medical care. Co-pays are small, and deductibles are not usually required.
- *Preferred provider organization.* A PPO allows employees to see any health provider they want, but if they choose a doctor outside the system, their co-pays are higher.
- *Point of service.* With a POS plan, as with an HMO, employees have small co-pays and are encouraged to see doctors in the network. If they go outside the network, they must meet a deductible and pay a percentage of the fee.

Two other health care options may also be worth considering:

- *Health savings accounts.* HSAs are sort of like IRAs for medical care. They are made up of two parts. The first is a health insurance policy that covers expensive hospital bills. The second is an interest-bearing investment account into which employees contribute money tax free; the money is then withdrawn to pay for medical care. If employees do not use the money they save (if they have no medical need to), the money accumulates with tax-free interest until retirement, when they can withdraw it for any purpose.

Tip: To learn more about health savings accounts, go to www.hsainsider.com.

- *Health purchasing alliance.* Instead of joining one health plan, you join an alliance of many health plans, all of which are jointly administered.

Because the plans compete for your health care dollars, you get the best possible prices and can shop for coverage options in one place.

Finally, you should find out whether your business is eligible for discounted health care plans from an association. Chambers of commerce often offer this, as do trade associations.

Alternatives

Aside from shopping for the right plan, there are a few other things you can do to reduce your small business's health care costs. First, if health care costs are choking you, then undoubtedly you have considered cutting back on your plan. If, for example, your plan offers disability and vision benefits, you may have to cut those. Unpleasant, yes, but at least your employees will still be covered in the areas where it really counts. And no, I certainly do not enjoy advising you to cut employee benefits, but I also understand that health care costs are a major concern for many small businesses, and cutting benefits is better than cutting jobs.

Also, if you have a plan that requires co-pays, as most do these days, you can reduce your premiums by increasing employee co-pays: the higher the co-pay, the lower your premium. Similarly, you can increase prescription co-pays: by increasing the amount your employees pay for their prescriptions, you can reduce your premiums.

Whatever you choose to do, it has to be thoughtful and decided with your employees. Because health care is so important, you must carefully weigh your need to control costs against your employees' needs for adequate health care.

The Bottom Line

You want to create the best benefits package you can in order to give your employees what they deserve. Doing so in an affordable way is the challenge. Here are a few steps you can take:

- *Choose a policy that everyone can live with.* No, it may not be ideal, but by purchasing a decent, if basic, policy—whether it is an HMO or POS or whatever—at least you are doing more than many small businesses.

- *Offer voluntary extras.* By offering your staff the chance to purchase voluntary insurance products through their employment, you are increasing the value of their benefits packages without affecting your bottom line.
- *Consider tax savings.* Programs such as flex plans and HSAs can help your employees pay for their health care costs with pretax dollars. They will appreciate that, too.
- *Take advantage of changes in the law.* As we all know, health care law changed radically with the passage of the Affordable Health Care Act of 2010. That law, should it withstand legal challenges, will have far-reaching effects on your ability to purchase health care for your company. Be sure to do your research once the litigation ends to see how it might help you with choices, state insurance exchanges, tax credits, and so forth. Check out EHealthInsurance.com to stay up to date.

HOLIDAYS, SICK LEAVE, AND VACATION

Time off work for holidays, sick leave, and vacation is not a right that employees have but a benefit that you offer. Legally, according to the Fair Labor Standards Act, you are not required to give paid time off for holidays, illness, or vacation. But just because you don't have to be a good employer does not mean that you shouldn't. If you want to recruit great people, you have to create a great place to work, and this is one place to start.

The Traditional Method

Small businesses usually set up a leave policy whereby employees get x number of sick days, y number of holidays, and so forth. You simply decide how many sick days and vacation days each employee is to get per year, whether they will be paid days or not, put it in writing, and let everyone know. Typically, new employees get about 16 days off per year, allocated evenly between vacation days and sick days. Most employees expect a paid week or two off per year.

> **Days Off**
>
> Most employers provide paid holidays for New Year's Day, Memorial Day, Independence Day, Labor Day, Thanksgiving Day, Christmas Eve, and Christmas Day. When it comes to other religious holidays, the norm is to allow employees to take the day off without pay or to use vacation time. Most small businesses also allow four paid days off to attend to a death in the immediate family.

Innovative Options

Consider this new idea: pool these types of leave into a bank of hours that employees can use as they see fit. For example, instead of giving employees 11 holidays and 5 vacation days a year, you might decide instead to give everyone 100 hours each year to use how and when they want.

This sort of plan has many benefits. First, it promotes honesty. Employees can schedule days off without having to call in sick. Also, it respects employees as adults, in effect telling them that you trust them and that you assume they know best how to balance their personal and work lives. Employees are responsible for their choices. They may use a half day here, a full day there, and a week for vacation, or they may save their time for sick days.

Another innovative option is the flex holiday plan. At the beginning of the year, create a list of major holidays (there may be 25 or more): everything from Christmas Day to St. Patrick's Day to Kwanzaa and Presidents' Day should be on the list. Employees can select any 11 holidays. This plan also respects employees as adults and allows them to decide what is important.

Intangible Benefits

Benefits can take many forms. Aside from offering options such as health and retirement plans, you can also create policies that will be appreciated by your staff—policies that are every bit as much of a benefit as money.

For instance, your small business could be family friendly, allowing employees to leave when family commitments arise. You could welcome employees' children when they come to the store or office. I know of one office that encourages employees to bring in their dogs every day. You could offer job sharing so that a new mom can have her job and care for her baby, too.

What else could you do to make your workplace better? The great thing about innovative policies is that employees appreciate them as much as anything else you offer, yet the policies may not cost nearly as much as other, more expensive benefit options.

CHAPTER 29

Training and Motivating Your Staff

Help me help you!

—Jerry Maguire

Some employees are hired, trained a bit, and expected to do their jobs competently. Others are hired, trained properly, expected to do their jobs competently, and the training continues. Which do you think will be more effective? Right. Even so, it is understandable when a small business owner fails to properly train his or her employees. After all, training takes time, and time is our most precious commodity (other than cash flow!).

Making the mistake of spending too much time working *in* our business rather than *on* our business is something that all small business owners are guilty of. It is easy to get so lost in the day-to-day minutiae of your business that you miss the big picture. Training and motivating employees is one way to counteract that. It ensures that your plans and vision are being carried out, even when you are busy doing other things.

TRAINING

Good training creates better employees. The type and extent of the training that you offer will vary depending on your goals. It may be as simple as explaining a new policy and showing employees how to implement it, or it might be a several weeklong process whereby employees learn a new

277

skill from scratch. Either way, adequately training your staff is vital to the continued success of your small business.

Example: Nancy Clark owns two retail dance apparel stores, so it is physically impossible for her to be in both places at once. Therefore, she is a big believer in proper training: she spends up to a month training new employees before allowing them to work on their own. During the training period, which she conducts during regular store hours, Clark makes sure new employees learn everything from opening and closing procedures to knowing the merchandise to operating the cash register. Clark trains her staff "from the ground up," so that when a problem arises, the employee is able to handle it. "Thorough training creates knowledgeable staff, and that in turn creates a well-run business," says Clark.

To be most effective, employees' training should begin the day they start work and cover everything they need to know. By creating a training process that covers all the bases, you create better employees—which, in turn, allows you to concentrate less on problems and more on the areas of your business that you enjoy. Your initial training may cover many areas; here are a few you might want to cover:

- *Philosophy.* Employees should understand your way of doing business.
- *Brand.* Teach your employees what your business is all about and what you want the company "personality" to be.
- *Policies.* Overtime, vacation, sexual harassment, workplace safety, and other policies need to be explained.
- *Operations.* How do employees operate the alarm, the lights, the point-of-sale system, the computer, and so on? Employees also need to know how to restock the shelves, how to handle a complaint, and other issues.
- *Expectations.* To know what to do, employees need to be taught what you expect of them.

Many small businesses spend the bulk of their training on the one issue that is both the most important and often the hardest for employees:

sales. Sales training not only gives employees a valuable skill but also offers you a chance to teach your troops your way of doing business. Your sales training should cover these topics:

- *Attitude.* Is your staff to be friendly, chatty, professional, or reserved? Some small businesses want their employees to be aggressive, whereas others want them to be almost invisible. What say you?
- *Products.* Employees need to learn about your product line, why you sell what you do, how it ties in with what you are trying to accomplish, and how that fits the needs of customers.
- *Money.* How should employees handle cash sales, credit cards, and checks?
- *Operations.* Employees need to know how to handle returns, refunds, and so on.

The Shadow Knows

One of the best ways to train new employees in the art of sales is to have them shadow your best salesperson for a few days.

Ongoing Training

If employees want more out of their work than just a paycheck, what are those other things? One of them, to be sure, is additional skills. Today's workforce is so mobile and forward-looking that one of the best things you can do to create loyalty is to train your employees well and add to their skill sets. By doing so, you will increase your employee retention rate and create a better business. *Inc.* magazine puts it this way: "Make 'train to retain' your company mantra."

Beyond retention, there is much more to be gained from adopting an ongoing training program:

- You create a stronger, more business-savvy workforce.
- You build loyalty.

- You create a stronger "bench," that is, a better pool of people to promote from within.
- You reduce layoffs; rather than letting someone go, additional training may solve the problem and avoid the hassle of having to train someone new from scratch.

As I have said repeatedly in this book, small businesses can learn plenty from larger businesses. KPMG is one of the world's largest accounting firms, and the company is dedicated to ongoing training. According to its literature, "Our training doesn't stop between the major events of an individual's career. We offer an ongoing program to help keep KPMG people sharp and up-to-speed. These additional training programs include technical updates, industry conferences, and enabling skills training. For you, this thorough, comprehensive and continual training process helps ensure that your skills and abilities always fit perfectly with the teams you join."

Ongoing training can take many forms. The most popular are additional computer skills, financial management, technical training for individual occupations, and career path training. And no, none of these need cost a fortune.

Pop Quiz!

The California Chamber of Commerce conducted a survey of 100 of the most successful small businesses in that state. One of the questions it asked was this: The real key to business success is . . .

A. Hard work and perseverance
B. Fine products and service
C. Advertising
D. Knowing the fundamentals of business
E. Employees

What was the most popular answer? E—Employees.

Training Managers

Regular employees are not the only ones who need adequate training—managers do, too, maybe more so. Managing people is not a skill that always comes naturally, and so the more you can help your managers help your staff, the more successful everyone will be. The good news is that managers are already motivated to succeed—otherwise they would not be in the position they are in. Managers need to be taught how to coach, as that, essentially, is their job. They need to prod, push, and praise just so, in order to bring out the best in your people.

How do they do that? There are four traits you can teach that will help any manager be more successful:

1. *Listen.* Is it true that Ernest Hemingway was referring to managers when he said "Most people never listen"? Probably not, but he could have been. Managers are wont to talk a lot—too much, usually. If you can get a manager to listen to what your employees are saying, your employees will begin to listen to what the manager has to say. Respect breeds respect.
2. *Ask.* No one likes being told what to do, and this is even truer as employees get older. Managers will get far more from your staff if they avoid barking orders and ask for help instead.
3. *Be reasonable.* Of course, a manager has to be assertive and get the job done, but we all know that you get better results with honey than you do with vinegar.
4. *Prioritize.* Great leaders set priorities and enlist the people around them in getting those priorities accomplished.

The One Minute Manager

Maybe the best management book ever written is *The One Minute Manager.* In it, authors Ken Blanchard and Spencer Johnson explain the value of one-minute goals, one-minute praise, and one-minute reprimands. It works this way: managers create a one-page set of goals for each employee, summarizing the top 20 percent of tasks for that employee (here we go again—that
(*continued*)

20 percent is said to correspond to the top 80 percent of productivity). The employee then gets to work, and the manager follows up—consistently—giving either one-minute behavior-based (not personal) praise or reprimands. Praise keeps employees going in the right direction, whereas reprimands help them move toward the right direction.

Training Techniques

Properly training your staff and managers need not be boring. People learn best when they are engaged. Accordingly, any small business that is looking to improve its training should consider doing something more than lectures alone. For example, you might try these techniques:

- *Shadowing.* Sending people into action with already trained employees is a fast way to get someone up to speed.
- *Videos.* People recall what they see. Videotapes can be a very effective training method for employees and managers alike. Videos can teach people how to sell, how to open and close, how to spot and deal with potential theft, how to motivate, and so on.
- *Role-playing.* Staff members can take turns pretending to be the thief, the reluctant customer, or the irritated patron. You can then show them the proper way to handle these situations.
- *The Internet.* Online training is a booming business, and convenience and low cost are just two reasons. Do a search and discover how many options there are.
- *Review.* Have staff contribute botched sales calls or success stories to the class to use as examples.

The bottom line is that your commitment to training and education can retain employees, help them provide better service, boost morale, and yes, increase sales. All in all, it is a pretty good idea.

MOTIVATION

There are two ways to motivate employees: with money and without money.

Money Motivators

It is no secret that money motivates employees, you know that. Holding sales contests, offering bonuses, dangling raises—these are tried-and-true ways to motivate people. The benefits package you offer is a similar motivator, but this begs the question: Why does it take money to motivate an employee?

The answer is that the possibility of making more money transforms the employee into an entrepreneur, and entrepreneurship is based on the premise that hard work and ingenuity will be rewarded. Isn't that how you think? "If I implement that plan, we could increase sales by 10 percent!" Well, that is precisely what an employee thinks when offered a money motivator. "If I sell more than anyone else this month, I win that trip to Hawaii!" So the secret to motivating with money is to tap into this mind-set for mutual benefit.

First, you can always link an employee's pay to performance. That is exactly how commissioned salespeople work. Similarly, you could link bonuses to desired outcomes. For example, you might offer your director of operations a nice bonus if he can reduce overhead by 10 percent for the year. A manager might get 10 percent of any increased revenues for his store for the month. There are many ways to structure such a compensation program.

When creating a money-motivated system, it is important that the reward be linked to an outcome that the employee can control. The director of operations can directly affect overhead, but he or she cannot increase sales, so a reward based on increased sales would not work for him or her. If the reward is based on overall company performance, the employee will be motivated to try harder only if he or she can affect that performance. As long as the reward and the desired action are linked, the motivation will be there.

Contests

Contests are an excellent way to build excitement and create desired behaviors and outcomes. Successful contests use realistic and achievable goals, are limited to a short period of time, have desirable prizes, link rewards to performance, and have uncomplicated rules.

Motivation on a Shoestring

Employees who are disengaged are so for a reason. The Gallup Organization's annual survey of employment found that employees are unmotivated when they do not know what is expected of them, when they feel stagnant in their work, and when they do not feel appreciated. People lose enthusiasm for a job when it becomes boring and routine, when bosses are clueless, and when their employer seems to care more about money than people.

If you want to motivate employees without money, the first thing you need to do is engage them. You need to learn what excites a problem employee and begin to foster that. This individualized approach is the opposite of what many managers do—notice the problem and try to fix it. That motivates no one. What motivates people is feeling appreciated as individuals and contributing what they have to offer.

There are many simple ways to motivate people, to have them feel appreciated, without spending a lot of money:

- *Show appreciation.* Thanking employees for a job well done is so simple yet so effective. Thanks can take many forms. It could be a pat on the back from a manager, a call from the president, a special parking spot for a week, a night out with your team, increased territory, a massage and facial, or a round of golf. FedEx inscribes the names of special employees' children on the nose of new planes to thank the employee for a job well done. How often do you see a plaque naming the employee of the month?
- *Recognize employees.* Letting everyone know that a team member did a great job works wonders. A survey conducted by the Minnesota Department of Natural Resources found that for 68 percent of employees, being appreciated is important to job satisfaction. At Blanchard Training in Escondido, California, praise from customers and managers is reprinted in the company newsletter. What about sending a press release regarding an accomplishment to your trade journal?
- *Ask for input.* Listening to employee ideas and taking action on them makes people feel as if they are part of a team and that what they say makes a difference. At Grumman Corporation in New York,

employees whose suggestions are implemented receive gift certificates. Fel-Pro in Skokie, Illinois, has a yearly drawing for $1,000 for all employees who participated in the employee suggestion program.

- *Offer freebies.* Employees who do something above and beyond the call of duty can be given an afternoon off, a gift certificate to Nordstrom, or tickets to a sporting event. At H. B. Fuller Company in St. Paul, Minnesota, employees get a paid day off on their birthday. Mary Kay Cosmetics gives the birthday girl a lunch voucher for two.

- *Make your business a special place to work.* What about having a massage therapist come by every other week for complimentary 15-minute back massages at employees' desks? What about an in-house yoga class? Have a yearly picnic with spouses and children. Organize a rafting trip down the river. None of these ideas costs a lot, but all would be appreciated, and appreciation *is* motivation.

Be creative. Take suggestions. Employees are much more motivated when they enjoy their workplace. A few changes can reap tremendous rewards.

Top 10 Employee Rewards

According to Michael LeBoeuf, author of *The Greatest Management Principle in the World*, the top 10 rewards for good work are:

1. Money
2. Recognition
3. Time off
4. Ownership shares
5. Favorite work
6. Promotion
7. Freedom
8. Personal growth
9. Fun
10. Prizes

CREATING AN EXCEPTIONAL CULTURE

Training and motivating your staff can take you only so far. At the end of the day, what will make a difference—as much as anything—is the culture of your small business. All businesses have a culture—some by design, most by default. A negative culture is created by employees who feel unappreciated, by workplaces that are unharmonious, and by managers who are incompetent.

On the other hand, if you communicate a sense of direction, of mission, if you foster teamwork and cooperation and fun, you begin to create a positive culture, a place where people want to work. Your corporate culture should be a reflection of your goals and ideals. Creating this sort of culture allows employees to act appropriately, to understand what it is you are trying to accomplish, and to implement that vision in their own unique way. It gives work meaning. It gives employees direction. And in the end, it boosts profits.

How do you create a superior culture? You start by having a mission.

The Mission Statement

We have all seen them: mission statements that were seemingly created by force at some corporate retreat, prominently displayed, cockeyed, on a wall somewhere, meaning nothing to anyone. But a real mission statement, if done correctly, can be a very effective business tool because it tells you, your employees, and your customers what your business is all about and where it is headed. Knowing your mission also helps everyone understand how their daily activities and policies are helping or hurting the cause. Thus, it not only keeps you focused but also helps employees understand what is expected of them.

You can create a mission statement by answering the following questions:

- What personal values do you want to be embodied in your business?
- What qualities and characteristics should be exemplified by your business?
- What resources are at your disposal?
- What is your niche?

- What is your grand vision for your business? (Think big!)
- Based on your values, vision, characteristics, and resources, what is the purpose of your business?
- Which of your personal qualities do you want to be infused in the business?
- How can your business best serve your clients, family, employees, and investors?
- How much money do you want to make? What are your markets? Who are your customers? What is your responsibility and commitment to them?
- Are you willing to commit to your mission, your vision, and your dream? Are you willing to pay the price, whatever that is?

Based on your answers, based on your values, dreams, plans, niche, resources, and market, draft a mission statement of 50 to 400 words that incorporates any or all of these. Make it large and bold and fantastic—something you believe in with all your heart. Surrender to your purpose.

(The Mission Statement exercise is adapted with permission from the Speaking Success System by Burt Dubin. See www.speakingsuccess .com.)

Mission and Culture

A mission statement that you actually believe in is the first step toward creating a superior corporate culture. Here are a few more things that you can do to create a valuable business culture:

- *Have clear goals and values and live by them.* Businesses usually set goals but just as often lose track of them. Successful small businesses, however, have a plan of action that they get the entire team to buy into. Think about your business values and goals and then encourage your people to live them daily. Your mission statement is a good place to start.
- *Communicate.* If you communicate what you want and expect, if you listen to what your employees want and expect, and if you involve employees in the decision-making process, people begin to own the results. Communication could be a quarterly "state of the business"

report, or it could be a one-on-one meeting devoted to career goals. The important thing is that employees hear what is going on, know where things are headed, and feel free to offer feedback and suggestions.

- *Make employees feel that they are part of a team.* A sense of teamwork creates a superior business culture. Go to a game together. Help a charity together. At McCormick & Company in Baltimore, employees are encouraged to work one Saturday a year for the charity of their choice. When they donate the day's pay to that charity, the company matches their contribution dollar for dollar. Ninety percent of employees participate.
- *Reward your staff.* This chapter is about rewards. Whether the rewards are big (profit sharing) or small (a gift certificate), rewarding employees makes a big difference.

Tip: *1001 Ways to Reward Employees,* by Bob Nelson, is a great book that is chock-full of easy ways to reward your staff.

- *Demand excellence.* Demand the best of yourself and look for the best in others. Reward excellence. Do your best, help employees do their best, and work together to create results that everyone can be proud of.

Have Some Fun

The whole point of leaving the corporate world and striking out on your own is to create a business that you love. Sure, it can be serious and stressful and difficult and demanding. But do not lose the forest for the trees. Workplaces in which employees are encouraged to do their work *and* have fun are more productive than places where work is everything.

Example: Not long ago I was in Seattle with my family and we went to Pike Place Market, as we like to do. Aside from hosting the world's first Starbucks and the restaurant where Tom Hanks chatted with Rob Reiner in *Sleepless in Seattle,* the market is legendary for the giant fish toss, where fish market employees throw 50-pound salmon back and forth in front of bemused customers—and have a great time doing so.

That quintessential Northwest experience is the basis for the excellent business book *Fish! A Remarkable Way to Boost Morale and Improve Results*, wherein the authors explain how the fish toss is a metaphor for how and why having fun at work works. Here's why: although every small business has a culture, the vast majority of small business cultures are by default and only a few by design. And that is often a mistake because a company's culture is so important; it sets down the parameters and clues for how employees are expected to behave, work, and treat one another and the public. A company culture can be fun, or harsh, or boring, or whatever you deem important, but whatever your culture, make no mistake—it affects the bottom line. Your culture reinforces your most important business values, even when you are not around—especially when you are not around. A great culture fosters greatness.

As such, one value that you should definitely consider adding to your business's culture is that of fun. Why? Because it is good for business:

- *It results in better productivity.* Research has shown that people who enjoy their work and have fun at the office are also more productive. Makes sense, no? That is definitely one reason why such innovative, cutting-edge companies as Google and Facebook incorporate scooters, video games, and other tools that promote a casual, fun culture. Employees there work hard, but play hard too.

  For us, this sort of addition need not need be expensive or difficult to implement:
  - Install a basketball hoop in the parking lot.
  - Put a ping-pong or foosball table in the break room.
  - Put in an Xbox or other video game system.
- *It fosters creativity.* Play is creative and as such, employees who have a good time tend to be more creative.
- *It relieves stress.* All work and no play makes Jack a dull boy and Jill a dull girl, and no one wants dull employees.
- *It boosts morale.* When people work at jobs where the culture is one of tedium or overwork and stress, they generally are less happy. Unhappy employees are a drain on resources—they call in sick more, work less hard, and so on. Conversely, fostering fun at work boosts morale and makes employees happier. And happier employees means . . .

- *Happier customers.* Fun at work makes employees happier and more enthusiastic and customers usually love genuine enthusiasm. Consider: Would you rather buy from a store where the staff is bored silly and resentful or one where employees have a good time and like what they do? Right.

CHAPTER **30**

Exemplary Customer Service

A customer is the most important visitor on our premises,
he is not dependent on us. We are dependent on him. He is
not an interruption in our work. He is the purpose of it. He is
not an outsider in our business. He is part of it. We are not
doing him a favor by serving him. He is doing us a favor by
giving us an opportunity to do so.

—MAHATMA GANDHI

People can make or break your small business. The last chapter was about
caring for the internal people you work with—your employees. This
chapter deals with caring for the external people who make your business
possible—your customers. If you take care of both constituencies, then
small business success is yours.

CUSTOMER SERVICE

Great customer service is something we all hear about, something to which
many small businesses give lip service, but it is equally something that few
small businesses ever really incorporate into their daily way of doing business. Sure, they try to treat their customers well, but that is not enough.
For some, real customer service is impossible because the culture of the
business is so hectic that employees are too rushed to make the extra effort
with customers. For others, it simply is not important. Yet offering excellent customer service distinguishes you from the competition, and it need

not be expensive or cumbersome. By implementing a few changes, you may see increased sales and a more loyal clientele.

Say that you own a little coffeehouse. A customer who buys coffee and a bagel from you once or occasionally is nice, but nothing special. His share of your total revenue for the year is about $5. But what about that customer who comes in three times a week? If he spends even $10 a week at your shop, that translates into $520 for the year. The repeat customer is your most valuable customer for many reasons, not the least of which is that it does not cost much to keep him or her.

But what it does take is customer service. For people to patronize your business three times a week for a year, or to become a regular customer of any sort, they have to feel welcome and appreciated. Customer service means that people are treated as individuals, served well, and given respect and that they find your shop easy, not difficult. The café customer is rewarded for his or her patronage: by getting good coffee and tasty food, by being greeted by a friendly face, by someone knowing his or her name. According to Michael LeBoeuf, author of *How to Win Customers and Keep Them for Life,* "Fancy sales pitches, high-powered marketing strategies, and clever advertising can be very important attention getters. And they may persuade people to become your customer. But keeping customers for any period of time depends on how well you reward them."

Mystery Shoppers

Want to know how your employees treat your customers when you are not around? Hire a mystery shopper. A mystery shopper will come into your store, shop and buy, and then report on the experience.

If great customer service becomes part of your business culture, your business will be better for it. You know it when you walk into one of those stores where "We love our customers!" is more than just an empty slogan. Those small businesses treat you well, exceptionally even, and you enjoy the experience. It is not hard to turn any small business into that prototype, but it takes commitment. Teaching employees how to treat customers right should become part of your initial and ongoing training. It should be reinforced daily. You might also consider doing a few other things:

- *Reward customer service stars.* Consider the restaurant that has a plaque in the lobby listing waiters and waitresses who have learned 100 customers' names. LensCrafters gives employees bonuses for outstanding customer service.
- *Poll customers.* Ask your customers for feedback regarding your business's customer service and how it could be improved. In fact, hand out surveys and find out what your customers like and dislike about your business. Customer service is about more than saying "yes" or handling complaints—it is also about making your store the best it can be to serve the needs of your clientele, and getting feedback from them is one easy way to do that.
- *Just say "yes."* Whenever possible, do what customers ask. Saying "yes" keeps them around.
- *Encourage staff to "own it."* When employees run into an issue with a customer, it is essential that they have been trained to own the problem and have been empowered to solve it. Customers love that.

If They Want Mustard, Give Them Mustard!

Jeff and some business associates opened a Jewish deli. The food was great and customers loved the place, except for one curious thing: unlike other delis, there was no mustard on the tables. If someone ordered a pastrami sandwich, the restaurant decided how much mustard went on it. A minor issue, to be sure, but significant enough that people began to complain about it. Yet Jeff and his associates insisted: no mustard on the tables! Certainly they had a reason for doing business that way, although no one really knew what it was.

We all have ways of doing business and think we know our business better than anyone, especially better than some casual customer. And, of course, you cannot change the way you do business simply because of a few complaints from a couple of customers here or there. The customer is not always right. That said, if you are taking your customers someplace they don't want to go, sooner or later, they will leave and go elsewhere. Over something as silly as mustard on the table? You bet. Haven't you made comparable decisions for equally piddling reasons? Of course you have. We all have. You run the very real risk of losing your fan base when you stop listening to them. And, after you listen, you also have to be willing to be wrong about your business and make adjustments. What is the market telling you? If it's metaphorical mustard, you better give it to them.

Ignore Complaints at Your Own Peril

It is said that for every customer who complains about your business, there are six others who are equally unhappy but do not complain. That equals seven unhappy customers. On average, dissatisfied customers tell nine people about their bad experience. Those seven unhappy campers times nine friends equals 63 people who may have a negative impression of your business. When you consider that today, people don't just keep quiet but blog about their unhappiness, you can see that ignored complaints can multiply exponentially and threaten your business.

Customer Disservice

Just as there is a right way to treat customers, so, too, is there a wrong way to treat customers. Yet far too often, what I call "customer disservice" creeps in. Here, then, are the five commandments of customer disservice:

1. *Thou shalt not put phone calls ahead of real customers.* How often has this happened to you? You wait in line someplace, you get to the front, it is your turn, when suddenly the phone behind the counter rings and the person on the phone is suddenly more important than you. Actual people who visit your business in person are almost always more important than callers. Make sure your employees know that and are taught to treat actual customers with the respect that they deserve.

2. *Thou shalt not become a Nopey.* Do you remember Gumby? Gumby had a pal named Nopey. No matter what you said to him, no matter what you asked him, Nopey's answer was "No!" Sound familiar? Far too many employees flex their muscle by saying no. It gives them a

sense of power. But the Nopey is a problem employee. He is the one who angers already unhappy customers and turns customers into ex-customers.

3. *Thou shalt not be a strict constructionist.* In the law, a strict constructionist is one who says that laws and policies do not evolve but rather must be strictly interpreted as they were written. Although that might be a valid legal argument, it makes for poor customer service. Sometimes the smartest choice is to bend policy and make an exception. The customer will remember it, and your business probably won't suffer any harm by it.

Outback Steakhouse Does It Right

At Outback Steakhouse, if something is not to your liking, your waiter or waitress can fix it *without having to go to the manager.* He or she can give you a free drink, comp a meal, or take other actions to make sure you are happy. Bending policy to make customers happy is the norm, not the exception, at Outback.

---

4. *Thou shalt not have bad manners.* Your customers should not be thanking you; you should be thanking them. Common courtesy and good manners can go far toward leaving your customers with a good impression of your business.

5. *Thou shalt welcome complaints.* Feedback from your customers, whether positive or negative, is one of the most valuable things your business can get. An SBA survey found that 95 percent of dissatisfied customers would patronize a business again if their problems were solved quickly and satisfactorily. Solving the customer's problem is your job, even if you disagree with the complaint. When you get a complaint, the first thing to do is ask the customer how he or she would like the problem to be resolved, and resolve it that way if possible. If the customer wants a refund, it is usually in your best interest to honor that request. If an employee is involved in a dispute, trace the problem and provide the employee with training, if necessary. If you are convinced that your business is not at fault, apologize, offer

something to placate the customer, and explain how he or she can avoid similar situations in the future.

DEALING WITH BAD CUSTOMERS

It is all well and good to listen to your customers and try to treat them right, but there comes a time when you may have a customer who has become too difficult, too abrasive, or too demanding. What do you do then? You can try to smooth it over—and sometimes you can—but other times you simply cannot. Yes, you want to make the dough and keep the peace, but sometimes you have to take a stand. When you have customers who become such a problem that they are more effort than they are worth, what do you do?

Fire them, I say. Adios, sayonara, ciao, goodbye, so long!

Taking a stand is not easy. It will certainly anger your customer, and maybe a few of your employees. But guess what? You are the boss. It's your business, and one of the perks of the gig is that you get to work with whomever you choose. The good news is that by firing an unreasonable customer, you may end up with unexpectedly positive results. People might admire you for standing up for something bigger than the almighty dollar. You may attract a higher quality of customer. Firing that bad customer is a signal that you have standards and morals that are worth more than money.

CHAPTER 31

Negotiate Like a Lawyer

Everything is negotiable.

—LARRY STRAUSS

Deservedly or not, attorneys have a reputation for being, well, a bit smarmy. One of the reasons my old profession gets kicked around a lot is that they (we) get paid to be the jerk. People love to hate lawyers . . . until they need one. And then, when they do need one, one of the things people expect is that their lawyer will have the negotiation skills necessary to get the best deal possible.

Similarly, having good negotiation skills is vital to small business people because it is something we use every day. Whether it is asking a vendor to lower a price or getting a potential customer to sign on the dotted line, negotiations are part and parcel of small business life. Of course you do not need a lawyer to do the negotiating for you; not only would that be cost-prohibitive, but also it would take some of the fun out of the game. And if you do not see negotiating as a game, then pull up a chair for Lesson No. 1: don't take it too seriously, and most certainly, don't take it personally. Lawyers have a reputation for being good, tough negotiators precisely because they know that the whole thing is about getting the best deal possible, nothing more and nothing personal, thank you very much. It really is a game.

In this chapter, you will be offered a variety of tips, tricks, tactics, and strategies that attorneys employ to help their clients win the game. Some will pertain to you, others will not. Pick and choose those strategies and tactics that fit your style.

NEGOTIATION STRATEGIES

It is conventional wisdom these days that one should strive for a win–win outcome. But, as is often the case with conventional wisdom, it is not always right. Now, I am not saying that win–win negotiations and results are not good things—in the right circumstances, sure they are. But the point is, win–win is not always the way to go go.

Win–Win

A win–win negotiation is one in which both sides strive to understand the other and give the other what he or she needs, if not what is wanted. It is one in which tactics such as good cop/bad cop or storming out play no part. Win–win means that you work to come up with a mutually acceptable compromise that gives everyone as much of what they want as possible. The win–win negotiator does not try to talk someone into something; rather, the negotiator tries to get what he or she wants by helping the other party get what is wanted. As a result, win–win negotiations generally leave people feeling better about the negotiation, the other side, and often, the deal itself. This type of negotiation maintains relationships. For all of these reasons and more, there are many times when the win–win style makes sense and serves your best interests.

> **Creating Trust**
>
> Creating a win–win atmosphere requires creating a context of mutual trust. One way to do that is to ask for or offer help early on. Maybe it's a minor point that you need help with, or maybe it is a gracious offer on your part. Either way, making an early show that "we're in it together" fosters trust.

Win–Lose

As we lawyers know, there are times to worry about feelings and looking like the nice guy, but there are also plenty of other times when you gotta buckle down, go for the best deal, and handle whatever hurt feelings or other fallout may result. Having a win–lose mind-set also just fits some people better. Highly competitive people, litigators, and people who like to argue all may find that they simply want to go for it, not worrying about whether the other side accomplishes their goals or gets what they want or feels good. No *Kumbaya* for these folks—they just want to get what they want. There is no shame in this either. People have different styles and personalities, and it would behoove you to pick a strategy that fits yours. That said, the win–lose strategy usually works best when a great deal can be had if you push, or when you aren't worried (or don't care) about upsetting the other side.

The downside to a win–lose strategy is that, should you really have leverage and thus the ability to cram down a deal, the people on the other side may be more inclined to breach the agreement down the road, either because it left a sour taste in their mouths or because it was so one-sided they are unable live up to their end of the agreement.

Doing Your Homework

Before you begin any negotiation, you will need to do your homework. Not only do you need to decide which strategy you will employ, but also you need to decide which tactics, if any, you want to use to further that strategy. But beyond strategies and tactics, you first must decide what you really want out of the negotiation. Prior to any negotiation, then, you should settle on these things:

- *What would be a home run?* If the negotiation goes perfectly and everything breaks your way, what will the parameters of the ideal deal look like? What is your best-case scenario? Maybe your client will pay $10,000 for that new website that you are going to design.
- *What would you like to get?* Assuming the best-case scenario does not emerge, what things are more important than others, and what can you live without? Getting $7,500 for the site is not chopped liver!
- *What must you get?* Which issues are deal breakers for you? What price or terms must you get in order to make a deal? Anything less than $6,500 is not worth it.

The nice thing about prioritizing an upcoming negotiation in this manner is that it allows you to be creative and flexible. Knowing your bottom line, and knowing what a great deal looks like, means that you will immediately know a good deal when it is offered. And more important, you will be able to see when a decent deal is on the table, even if it is not the crème de la crème. Having done your homework, an offer of $7,000 is not half bad.

You also need to learn as much as you can about the other side, as well as any extrinsic factors that may be in play. Understanding the other side's motivations can make a huge difference. Here's an example: say that you have found a location you like for your business and are going in to discuss the terms of the lease with the potential landlord. Without doing some research, you would probably be inclined to pay whatever rent is proposed. But, if you learn first that the space has been vacant for two years, then you will also know that (1) the landlord is very motivated to rent it; (2) he or she will likely be amenable to a lower monthly rental payment just to get someone in the place; and (3) reading this book really helped! That is the power of research.

NEGOTIATION TACTICS

Tactics are used in negotiations very deliberately. They can break an impasse, create a good or bad impression (there are indeed times when it helps to have the other side be wary of you), move things along, stall, or even force a resolution. This section offers a wide variety of tactics from the negotiator's bag of tricks. The skilled tactician will have some at the ready before the negotiation ever begins, to be used as necessary.

Only Nixon Could Bomb Hanoi

In an attempt to strike a peace deal with the North Vietnamese, President Richard Nixon employed a novel negotiation tactic that he dubbed the *madman theory*. The idea was to force the North Vietnamese into a settlement by frightening them with the threat of nuclear consequences. As Nixon told aide Bob Haldeman, "I want the North Vietnamese to believe I've reached the point where I might do anything to stop the war. We'll just slip the word to them that, 'For God's sake, you know Nixon is obsessed about Communism. We can't restrain him when he's angry—and he has his hand on the nuclear button!'" The tactic didn't work.

The Opening Gambit

At the beginning of a negotiation, it is almost always smart to seem friendly, open, and reasonable. In that vein, these tactics may be helpful:

- *Use questions to obtain undisclosed information.* When you wander onto a car lot, what is the first thing the car salesperson does? That's right, he or she asks a series of seemingly mundane questions:
  - What kind of car are you looking for?
  - How much do you want to spend?
  - What is your time frame?
  - What will the car be used for?

    But far from being humdrum, these questions actually help the salesperson craft a pitch to you. It helps him or her figure out which cars to show you and what to emphasize. It's a tactic any of us can use in any negotiation, and we should because it works. Not only does it make you seem interested and cooperative, but it also often fosters the disclosure of useful information. Have a friendly little chat before things get started. You never know what juicy tidbit of information you may discover simply by showing interest.

- *Avoid making the first offer.* Although this tactic is Negotiating 101, it is still worth remembering. My brother gave me this advice when I was just starting out, and it has always served me well. I was applying for a job, and as he explained, "Steve, if you say you want $10 an hour, you will never get more than $10 an hour if you make the first offer. Certainly you won't get $12 an hour once you say that you want $10, will you? And what if they are actually willing to pay $15 an hour? Then your first offer of $10 really puts you in a corner." Whenever possible, get the people on the other side to make the first offer. What if they won't and you are forced to make the first offer? In that case, try being outrageous: "Well, if you really want me to tell you how much I want to make, I guess $50 an hour would be great!"

- *Ask for more than you want.* A corollary to the preceding tactic is that, no matter when you make your offer, be sure it is for more than what you want. Some people are so reasonable that they simply state what they want up front, forgetting that it is a negotiation. Big mistake. Not only will you be expected to lower your asking price (this is a negotiation, after all), but doing so shows how reasonable you are and thus creates goodwill. Starting out with an offer of more than you expect, therefore, has little downside.

- *Never accept the first offer.* Say something like, "You are going to have to do better than that!" You need not say it in an accusatory or snide way, simply be matter-of-fact about it. It could even be a joke. Even in a win–win negotiation, you want to get the best deal possible, and you do that by asking for more and negotiating down from there.

- *Don't act too interested.* When negotiating, remember the immortal words from the great musical *West Side Story:*

    Go man, go
    But not like a yo-yo school boy
    Just play it cool, boy
    Real cool!

It will really help you to stay, and act, a tad disinterested—just a bit above it all. You can take or leave the deal. When you seem less than totally invested in the outcome and can walk away at any time, you gain leverage.

Example: Jay was looking for a new office and found a place that he really liked. He learned that several other people were also interested in the space. So, very deliberately, when he was shown the property, instead of telling the landlord how interested he was, he turned the tables on her. He quizzed her about the property and acted as if the place was not good enough for his business. At the end of the showing, she offered him the space on the spot.

As Things Progress

Once begun, negotiations tend to have a life of their own. The smart negotiator will realize this and plan accordingly.

- *Don't fall in love.* When it becomes clear to the other side that you have to have something (whether it be a price, issue, or thing), you've tipped your hand—and your opponent will use it against you. If the car salesperson knows you just love that blue Beemer, watch out! And if you do fall in love, hide it. Play it cool!
- *Play good cop/bad cop.* We all know this old strategy because people use it, and people use it because it works. Decide up front who will be the good guy and who will be the tough guy; these are roles that will be used throughout the negotiation. The value of this tactic is that, as things progress, the other side will come to trust the nice cop and dislike the bad one (or at least not want to deal with him much). There are all sorts of advantages to be had once this routine is established:
  - The bad cop can deliver the bad news (the nonnegotiable items), thereby reinforcing his bad cop image, which also serves to reinforce the good cop's image.
  - Things the bad cop says are usually accepted as nonnegotiable. Why? Because the bad cop's a jerk and won't negotiate!
  - In contrast, things the good cop says are deemed reasonable. This allows the good cop to even take stances that, although possibly unreasonable, are nevertheless more acceptable because they come from the good cop.

> **Hint**
>
> For maximum effectiveness, it helps if the good cop says to the other side, "in confidence," that the bad cop is a jerk and he or she is very sorry about it. This establishes the good cop's bona fides as a reasonable negotiating partner.

- *Have a red herring.* Having something you do not really care about and are secretly willing to give up serves two purposes. First, it can create goodwill by making you seem reasonable when you do give it up. Second, it helps you get more of what you really want because you are faking giving up something of importance. And after giving up the red herring, there is a greater chance you will not have to give up other things that are more important. By giving up what you know to be superfluous items, you gain on the truly important ones.

- *Make unilateral concessions.* As an adjunct to the preceding rule, a carefully crafted unilateral concession, even a red herring, can create trust, especially when negotiating with someone you do not know well. It makes you seem reasonable and friendly and, moreover, creates the impression that you understand what the other side values. Better yet, it often forces the other side to give something up in return.
- *Be creative.* Lawyers know there are many ways to get the same result. Maybe you can't give your manager that raise he or she wants, but you could give time off for a few afternoons a month. The manager feels as if he or she got something, but really you didn't give up much at all.
- *Use the poker play.* We all know that good poker players never reveal their hand by the expressions on their faces. Try playing poker in your negotiation: when presented with an offer, have a stone-cold poker face. Say nothing. The uncomfortable silence that ensues will be broken by whoever gets more uncomfortable first. If it is not you, you will often hear the people on the other side upping their offer, worrying that they have insulted you.

Get Them to Negotiate against Themselves

Great negotiators love this trick: when given an offer, discuss it but do not give a counteroffer. Instead, tell the other side that the offer is not good enough and has to be increased. This is called "getting them to negotiate against themselves." If successful, you can get the other side to up the ante without ever having to do so yourself. Car salespeople are great at this. Think about when they come back in the room and say, "My manager says you have to increase your offer." They're trying to get you to negotiate against yourself.

The other advantage that silence gives you is that the other side may end up talking, just to fill in the gaps. There is a lot of valuable information that can often be gleaned from such ramblings.

Dealing with an Impasse

There are times in a negotiation when things get stuck, for whatever reason. Here are some techniques you can employ in these sorts of situations:

- *The calculated blowup.* I love this one and use it a few times a year. Here's why: sometimes it behooves you to have people dislike you a bit or, even better, fear you. Say that you bought a new computer system for the office and it just isn't working right. You have had the company that installed it out to fix it two or three times, and you always act reasonably. If the system malfunctions again, then it is time for the calculated blowup. Call the computer company and get mad—I mean really mad! Threaten to sue. Tell them that you are tired of being reasonable and are going to go to the press to tell everyone what a horrible job they are doing! Do not back down. Get them to think you have become a bit unglued.

  You can bet that they will not only try to calm you down, but more important, they will work to placate you. Later, you can apologize and say you are sorry for getting so mad. Everyone will make nice. But know this, too: they will not want to deal with you like that again. They will be nice to you for sure, but they also will be a bit afraid of pissing you off again. You will probably get what you want because they will want to avoid another confrontation.

  This technique can be used in almost any negotiation. It certainly gets people's attention and often moves them off a stubborn position. But know this, too: do it too often and they will decide dealing with you is more effort than it is worth. This is a technique that can be employed once, maybe twice, in a negotiation.
- *The walkout.* Similar to the blowup, the temporary walkout can also be very effective in getting a stalled negotiation back on track. When a union and a company are at an impasse, what will one side sometimes do? That's right, they will walk out and not come back to the negotiating table for a while. Again, it works, but it can't be used too often without seeming like the boy who cried wolf.
- *The ultimatum.* Another nuclear bomb sort of negotiation tactic—and one that often creates more problems than it is worth—the ultimatum

is an occasionally effective way to get what you want, especially when you think the other side may be tired or otherwise ready to buckle. But be forewarned: ultimatums get people mad, often leading the other side to employ the walkout.

Agreements

Remember that contracts are also called *agreements* for a reason: both sides have to agree to everything. Even so, too many people think that when offered a preprinted contract, the terms are nonnegotiable. Nope. Remember the rule stated at the beginning of this chapter: *everything is negotiable.* When given a lease or other contract, change the parts you do not like. Initial and date the changes, and have the people on the other side do the same (assuming they agree). Know this, too: contracts almost always favor the side that drafts the contract. It's a contract, but also an agreement, and you have to agree to it or no deal!

- *The gesture of goodwill.* A less confrontational way to create movement is to make a large, magnanimous gesture. Unilaterally give the other side something they really want, but explain that you are only doing so to move things along and fully expect that your generosity of spirit will be reciprocated.

Wrapping It Up

As things move toward a conclusion—either with a deal or without one—there are a few last tricks that may help you get more of what you want.

- *Make a last-minute demand.* Once you get to a point in a negotiation when the parameters of a deal have been hashed out and you are simply considering the final language, consider this tough but effective tactic: make a last-minute demand. At that point, everyone has invested substantial time and effort and wants the proposed outcome. Therefore, few people will be willing to rock the boat or scuttle the deal simply because you are being a jerk and making a new demand. They will probably be inclined to give it to you so as to salvage the deal. They will certainly dislike you for it, but you will probably get what you want, too.

- *Walk away.* The willingness to walk away from the table with no deal is the single most powerful weapon you have in your negotiation toolkit. To get the best deal, you have to be willing to walk away with no deal. Your obvious willingness to do so will likely force the other side to give in more than they would like and consider concessions they want to avoid. And what if your willingness to walk does not get you the deal you want? Then walk. (You can always come back. Even that is negotiable!)

Books to Get

- *Getting to Yes: Negotiating Agreement Without Giving In,* by Roger Fisher, William L. Ury, and Bruce Patterson (Penguin, 1991)
- *Negotiation Genius: How to Overcome Obstacles and Achieve Brilliant Results at the Bargaining Table and Beyond,* by Deepak Malhotra and Max Bazerman (Random House, 2007)
- *You Can Negotiate Anything,* by Herb Cohen (Citadel, 1983)
- *Negotiate Like the Pros,* by John Patrick Dolan (Penguin, 1992)

The bottom line: Everything is negotiable.

CHAPTER **32**

Legal-Ease I

It is easier to stay out than to get out.

—MARK TWAIN

Like taxes and insurance, law is one of those areas that entrepreneurs would rather not think about, and when they do, it is usually unpleasant. Yet you need to know what you need to know. There is a litigation explosion in this country, businesses are the prime targets (known in the trade as "deep pockets"), and you need to arm yourself with knowledge. Therefore, in this chapter and the next, you will get a primer on business law so that you know what to avoid and what to talk to your lawyer about if something does go wrong. One caveat: Although I am a lawyer, no book can take the place of an attorney who knows you, your situation, and the facts. So although the general information I provide can educate you, if you do find yourself in legal hot water, you are advised to meet with a lawyer in person.

CONTRACTS

Contracts are the easy stuff. A contract is like your personal set of laws. As long as you bargain in good faith and the subject of the contract is legal (e.g., you can't legally contract to open a house of prostitution), just about anything that you and the other side agree to will fly. However, not every promise is legally enforceable. To create a legally enforceable promise or set of promises, three requirements must be met that raise those promises to the level of a legal contract.

309

Offer

The first part of any contract is a clear and unambiguous offer. "I will buy 200 pounds of your flour at $8 a pound" is a clear and specific offer. It invites a clear and specific response. On the other hand, "I think I would like to buy some flour" is not an offer because it is neither a specific nor an unambiguous offer to accept specific terms.

Offers remain open unless they are accepted, but they may be revoked at any time. So, if you offer to buy the flour for $8 a pound but find it elsewhere for half that price, *and* if your offer has not been accepted, you can revoke the offer. However, if the flour seller has accepted your offer, you cannot revoke it.

Acceptance

Like an offer, an acceptance must also be clear and unambiguous: "I accept" is an acceptance, but "That sounds good, let me call you back in an hour" is not. The point of a contract is to allow a willing seller and a willing buyer to enter into a commercial transaction with clearly defined terms. Hence, the acceptance must be equally obvious.

Suppose the seller says, "I'll sell you the flour for $10 a pound." In that case, the $8 offer is deemed rejected and the seller has just made a $10 counteroffer, which you now have the power to accept or reject. This offer/counteroffer dance can go on ad infinitum. The exception is a commercial transaction between merchants in which there is an acceptance with minor changes that do not *materially* alter the original offer. In that case, pursuant to the Uniform Commercial Code, the offer is deemed accepted and the changes become part of the contract. What does *material* mean? That's what you hire lawyers for!

There are times when offers are not actually accepted but are enforceable. This occurs, for example, where the acceptance occurs as actual performance. For example, my offer to purchase 200 pounds of flour can be accepted by the delivery of 200 pounds of flour.

Consideration

To create a valid, legally enforceable contract, aside from the offer and acceptance, you also need a bargained-for exchange (legally, *quid pro quo,* or "this for that"), called *consideration.* In essence, this means that you have to give up something in order to get something: my money for your flour.

If I say, "I'll wash your car this afternoon," and you say, "Okay," no contract has been formed, even though there has been an offer and an acceptance. Why? Because there has been no consideration. You give up nothing for me to wash your car; it is just a promise on my part with none on your part, and therefore it is not legally enforceable. You need an offer, an acceptance of that offer, and a bargained-for exchange to create a valid, legally enforceable contract.

Tip: There is one legal tenet that can help you get around the need for consideration. If you make a promise that I rely on to my detriment, and if it was reasonably foreseeable that I would rely on that promise, I can get that promise enforced, even if we did not have consideration or a contract. For instance, if you say, "I will give you $5,000 if you drive my car to Los Angeles" and I do, I relied on your promise to my detriment, and I can enforce it in a court of law.

There are a few other things about contracts that you need to know:

- Although only certain contracts *have* to be in writing (most notably, those for the sale of land, for purchases exceeding $500, and employment contracts lasting more than a year), it is good business to get every contract in writing. Memories fade over time, and people choose to remember things wrong. If it's not in writing, there is no record of whose recollection is actually correct. Get it in writing. Avoid oral contracts.
- Remember, too, that standard or form contracts can be modified. A contract is also known as an *agreement* for a reason—you need to agree to it. If there is a clause in a standard contract you do not like, negotiate to change it or delete it.
- Be as specific as possible in your contracts so that nothing is left to chance. Ambiguity breeds litigation.
- The first one to breach a contract usually loses. Yes, there are legitimate reasons that may excuse performance (the contract was entered

into by mistake or by fraud, or it is impossible to perform), but usually the first breacher loses.

Do-It-Yourself Law

If you would like to draft your own contracts or otherwise act as your own lawyer, then check out a few sites: www.RocketLawyer.com, www.Legal Zoom.com, and www.Nolo.com are all excellent.

NEGLIGENCE AND LIABILITY

When ice on your walkway (ice that you asked your employee to remove but that he or she did not) causes a customer to slip, fall, and break an arm, in legal terms, that is called *negligence*. Being found negligent is one of the worst things that can happen to your business, as the damages can be astronomical. Whereas a breach of contract "merely" means that the loser has to pay the winner the value of the contract, a negligence suit can cost you hundreds of thousands, if not millions, of dollars, as you are obligated to pay the defendant for pain and suffering.

Here is the standard of care that you and your employees are obliged to maintain: *you must act as a reasonably prudent person would under the same or similar circumstances.* If you do not, and if that breach of duty causes someone damage, you must pay. In the case of the ice, a reasonably prudent employee would have removed the ice when the boss asked that it be done. The employee did not, and that caused the customer to slip and fall and get hurt.

This is why many small businesses enact standards, policies, and procedures for employees to do certain duties in a certain way. If the standards you adopt are adhered to, it is less likely that someone will get hurt, and even if someone does get hurt, it will be more difficult to prove that you fell below the standard of care if you have policies and procedures in place to avoid just this sort of accident. Your policies and procedures prove that you are a reasonably prudent business owner, see?

But accidents do happen, and people do get hurt. That is why you are strongly advised to buy liability insurance. Yes, your premiums will go up if claims are made against your policy, but it sure beats paying the damages out of pocket.

The Case That Made Me Want to Quit Law School

The most famous case in the history of negligence law is *Palsgraf v. Long Island Railroad.* In that case, Mrs. Palsgraf was standing at one end of the platform of the Long Island Railroad after buying a ticket. A train stopped at the station, and a gentleman carrying a package raced for the car. A Long Island Railroad employee on the car held the door open and reached out to help the gentleman in, while another guard on the platform pushed the man up from behind. The man's package dislodged and fell to the ground, causing the fireworks inside the package to explode. The shock of the explosion knocked over a set of scales at the other end of the platform near Mrs. Palsgraf, injuring her. Quiz: Did she win? Nope, the court ruled that the employees' actions, although negligent toward the man, were not so in relation to Mrs. Palsgraf.

The key to avoiding negligence claims is to maintain a safe place of employment. Set standards and enforce those standards.

PRODUCT LIABILITY

If you manufacture, wholesale, distribute, or sell retail products, you need to be concerned with a special subset of negligence law called *product liability law.* If a product that you manufactured, wholesaled, or sold injures a consumer, everyone in the supply chain between you and the buyer may be legally affected.

In the case of a defective product, there are three legal theories to be concerned about:

1. *Negligence.* Here again, the injured party must show that the seller or manufacturer breached the standard of care. For instance, if a car's wheel fell off because it was not bolted on properly at the plant, the manufacturer of the car would be found liable for any injuries that resulted.

2. *Breach of implied warranty.* If you, the small business owner, make an express or implied warranty or representation about what a product will do, and if the product fails to live up to that standard, thereby causing harm, you may be found liable for the injury under this theory. Many states have limited the use of implied warranty to business matters in which the buyer has suffered economic loss only.

Warning!

Whatever representations you make about your product, it must perform to that standard. One way to limit your risk is to avoid making representations in your advertising or marketing materials, as they may be used against you later.

---

3. *Strict liability.* This is the scary one. If an injured party can show that (1) the product was defective at the time the seller sold it and (2) the defect caused the injury, then you are on the hook. Unlike negligence, the injured party does not need to prove that you breached some standard; rather, he or she need prove only that the product was defective, for whatever reason. Your prudence and care is no defense. That is why they call this strict liability. When Firestone tires began to explode, you can bet strict liability was the theory the plaintiffs' attorneys used.

You can do several things to minimize your risk of being sued for product liability. First, try not to ship or sell defective products; inspect what you can. Second, warn customers whenever possible. Warning of dangers is a valid defense (and now you know why you see those crazy warning labels on products). Next—and this bears repeating—be careful about what you say and promise in your promotions. Also, consider using disclaimers. A conspicuous tag disclaiming any liability for damage caused by the product may protect you in some circumstances. Finally, specify the useful life of the product. Harm caused after the expiration of the useful life cannot be attributed to you.

INTELLECTUAL PROPERTY

An altogether different area of the law, but one that is no less important to your business, is *intellectual property law.* It has to do with intangible assets such as words, phrases, and pictures. These may, in fact, be your most important assets. Let's use Nike as an example. How important is that swoosh logo? That is intellectual property (a trademark). What about the name Nike? That is also intellectual property (copyright and trademark). And its tagline, "Just Do It"—yep, that is intellectual property, too.

Intellectual property is no less important in a small business. You need to know how to protect your business name, logo, inventions, and so on. Five areas of intellectual property may be relevant to your business: trademarks, copyrights, patents, trade secrets, and goodwill. Let's look at each.

Trademarks

A trademark is a word, phrase, design, or symbol that identifies your business and distinguishes it from the competition. (A *service mark* is essentially the same thing: it identifies a service that you provide.) Examples of trademarks are Dr. Pepper® and the Portland Trailblazers®.

Trademarking your business name or logo is quite easy. To get full trademark protection, you need to register your mark with the U.S. Patent and Trademark Office. Log on to www.uspto.gov and follow the directions.

Copyrights

A copyright protects the original, physical expression of a creative idea. For example, this sentence is a copyrighted sentence. To be copyrightable, an idea must be unique, it must be tangible (written or taped, for instance), and it must be a "work of authorship." Musical scores, magazine articles, choreographed dances, photographs, movies, and sculptures are examples of copyrightable expressions.

Copyrights last for the life of the author plus 75 years, and the creator owns the copyright, although if the creator made the work for someone else, the employer would own the copyright. You own the copyright to any works that your employees create in the fulfillment of their duties. This is called *work for hire*.

One of the best aspects of copyright law is that there is nothing to register. As soon as you create a work, it is copyrighted as a matter of law. This sentence is being copyrighted as I write it. Certainly you can register it with the U.S. Copyright Office, but it is not necessary. Instead, to put the world on notice that you have copyrighted material, affix the phrase "© All Rights Reserved" prominently to the work.

Patents

If you invent or discover a new and useful "process, machine, manufacture, or composition thereof," you can apply for a federal patent to protect your invention from being used by others without your permission. Utility patents protect machines and industrial processes and last for 20 years. Design patents protect the designs of manufactured items and last for 14 years. Plant designs protect new plant varieties and last for 17 years.

Patents are not inexpensive to obtain, and the assistance of a lawyer is almost always required. However, if you have invented a unique product or process, you will want to spend the money to patent it.

One good way to get the benefit of patent protection without actually spending the thousands of dollars a patent would cost is to apply for "patent pending." According to LegalZoom.com, "Filing a Provisional Application for Patent is the fastest, easiest way to start protecting your invention. As soon as your application is received by the USPTO, you'll

---

R. Buckminster Fuller

At one time, R. Buckminster Fuller had the most entries in *Who's Who*. An inventor, mathematician, author, and cartographer (among other occupations), Bucky is best known for inventing the geodesic dome. He once remarked that he owed his fame and success to his patent lawyer! Had it not been for the airtight patent that his lawyer obtained for the dome, Bucky believed that his beloved invention surely would have been stolen, and, he said, "No one would have ever heard of me."

receive a priority filing date and enjoy the right to label your invention 'patent pending.' Best of all, when you apply for a corresponding Non-Provisional Utility Patent, you can claim your original provisional filing date." The upshot is that a "patent pending" notifies potential product infringers that they could be on the hook for damages (including back-dated royalties) since the patent pending creates at least a patina of legal protection (and actual protection once the patent is issued.)

Trade Secrets

Most states have adopted the Uniform Trade Secrets Act. This law defines a trade secret as information that has independent economic value by virtue of remaining secret. A customer or vendor list might be a trade secret. KFC's "11 herbs and spices" would surely be a trade secret.

To be legally protected, you have to make an effort to keep your secrets secret. That is not to say you can never tell anyone the secret, but rather, you attempt to retain the secret and act appropriately.

Nondisclosure Agreements

If you want to share a trade secret with another party, make sure you have a nondisclosure agreement. Such an agreement states that you will be sharing confidential information and that it cannot be used by the other party for commercial reasons and cannot be disclosed to a third party without your prior written approval.

Goodwill

After some time in operation, your small business will have developed a positive reputation in the community and a valuable list of customers. This is called your goodwill. Goodwill is a business asset that usually relates to your exit strategy, when you are looking to sell your business. A significant asset to be sold at that time will be your business reputation, your goodwill. Protect it.

CHAPTER **33**

Legal-Ease II

> I can try a lawsuit as well as other men, but the most important thing is to prevent lawsuits.
>
> —CONFUCIUS

If you have ever been party to a lawsuit, you know only too well how true Confucius's words are. Lawsuits are a civilized form of war, pitting one side in a pitched battle against the other, both willing to do and spend almost anything to win, and both usually losing plenty in the process. Lawsuits are an expensive, time-consuming, exhausting, frustrating, and often ineffective way to resolve disputes. The point of the last chapter and this one is to help you avoid the dreaded lawsuit. The best way to do that is to know what the rules are and to do your best to follow those rules.

EMPLOYMENT DISCRIMINATION

Employment discrimination lawsuits usually arise when employees are fired or denied employment and they contend that discrimination is the reason.

At-Will Employment

When can you fire someone without repercussions? Although seemingly a simple question, the answer is not so simple. The basic rule is this: almost all employees are considered to be employed *at will*. An at-will employee can be fired at any time, for almost any reason. *Just cause* employees cannot—you need, as the term implies, a just cause to let them go. What makes a worker a just cause employee? Usually it is some sort of employment contract or promise of continued employment. If, for example, you have an employee handbook that promises job security, that could be construed by a court of law as a promise of continued employment, and thus your employees cannot be let go without a valid reason, such as stealing or some such thing. Tough times or the need to cut back does not count as just cause.

It is harsh but also smart, therefore, to have all employees sign a document acknowledging their at-will status. That way, it will be very difficult for them to come back and say that you had no right to fire them; a letter stating that they know they are at-will employees protects you.

Protected Classes

There are three instances in which even an at-will employee cannot be fired:

1. You cannot fire someone in retaliation for the exercise of a statutory right, such as filing a workers' compensation claim.
2. You cannot fire someone in retaliation for the exercise of a legal duty, such as jury service or military service.
3. Most important for this topic, you cannot fire people on the basis of their color, sex, religion, age, ethnic background, or disability. Membership in the armed forces cannot be a reason to fire someone, and neither can past debts or bankruptcy. In the law, these are called *protected classes.*

Warning!

When interviewing prospective employees, avoid asking questions pertaining to protected class status. Why? Because if you do, and then you do not hire the person, the candidate may sue for employment discrimination, claiming that is the reason you did not hire him or her—that your nonchalant question about his or her age, for example, is evidence that you discriminate on the basis of age. Ask only questions related to the candidate's competence and qualifications for the job.

For workers, most employment discrimination cases made against businesses fall under the category of *disparate treatment:* they claim that the employer treated them unfavorably compared with other employees because of their membership in a protected class. Plaintiffs in employment discrimination cases sue under Title VII of the 1964 Civil Rights Act.

If you are found guilty of not hiring someone for discriminatory reasons or of firing someone for discriminatory reasons, the penalties are harsh. If an ex-employee wins, he or she might be awarded back pay, reinstatement, attorney's fees, money for emotional distress, and even double damages as a way to punish you.

Preventing Claims

There are a few things you can do to protect your business from employment discrimination claims:

- Have an employee handbook that explains what is expected of employees, what at-will employment means, and how the disciplinary system works. Also explain that nondiscrimination is your policy and that discrimination claims will be investigated promptly and thoroughly.
- Document, document, and document some more. Conduct regular written performance reviews. When you do have problem employees, *warn them in writing. Have them sign the warning. Have them sign any second warnings.* The more documentation you have that the reason the employee was fired was legitimate and not discriminatory (poor performance or whatever), the less chance there is that any discrimination claim will stick.

SEXUAL HARASSMENT

Needless to say, the most prominent sexual harassment case in recent history is *Jones v. Clinton.* In that case, Paula Jones alleged that then-governor Bill Clinton invited her to a hotel room and groped her. She sued, claiming sexual harassment. In the end, her case was tossed out of court. The judge in the case ruled that even if the event did happen as alleged, Jones suffered no damages. She never went to a psychologist, was never treated unfairly at work afterward, was never denied a promotion, nothing. One of Jones's main arguments—that she didn't receive flowers on Secretary's Day, as others in Arkansas government did (although she was not Clinton's secretary), was almost laughable to the judge: "Although it is not clear why plaintiff failed to receive flowers on Secretary's Day in 1992, such an omission does not give rise to a federal [case] in the absence of some more tangible change in duties or working conditions that constitute a material employment disadvantage."

There are two types of sexual harassment cases to be concerned with at your small business. The first is a *quid pro quo* case, literally, "this for that." In this type of case, the victim is forced to have sex in exchange for a job benefit. If you promise your secretary a raise in exchange for a sexual favor, you have committed quid pro quo sexual harassment.

The second type of case is called *hostile work environment.* In this kind of case, the employee must prove that a supervisor or coworker made unwelcome sexual advances or physical conduct and that such conduct was pervasive enough to poison the employee's work environment and create an abusive workplace. Note that a same-sex sexual harassment claim under this theory is equally applicable in many jurisdictions.

Policies at Work

Just as you should adopt an antidiscrimination policy in your workplace and in your employee handbook, you should so adopt and make known to employees your anti–sexual harassment policy. Creating a written policy that everyone knows about is both the right thing to do and good business. Investigate claims promptly and discipline any offenders.

UNFAIR TRADE PRACTICES

Here, there are two issues to be concerned with: treating consumers fairly and legally and protecting your business from ex-employee competition.

Consumer Protection Laws

The first consumer protection law to be concerned about is deceptive or fraudulent advertising. Your advertising must be truthful. You can boast, but like George Washington, you cannot tell a lie. If you do, not only can you be sued by consumers who claim damages, but you can also get in trouble with the Federal Trade Commission (FTC), which investigates false advertising claims. The FTC can issue a "cease and desist" letter or sue.

Gone Bananas

Consider the case of the car dealer who promised in an ad to sell a car for "1,000 bananas." Of course he meant $1,000, but when a customer came in with 1,000 bananas, the dealer would not sell the car. The consumer sued the dealer and was awarded $1,000 in compensatory damages (the value of the car) and substantial punitive damages to punish the dealer for misrepresentation.

Aside from false advertising, you also need to avoid phony price comparisons. For example, there is nothing wrong with proclaiming that at your sale this weekend, the price for a particular $250 item will be "$100 off—$150!" However, if your normal price is not actually $250 but really $200, then the sale price is only $50 off, and you have broken the law.

Similarly, be careful when you use the word *free*. In your ads, free had better really mean free. "Free Printer!*" (with the asterisk explaining that the printer is free with a purchase of $1,000 or more) won't fly in most places. For instance, New York law states that "any limitations or conditions imposed on a 'free' offer must be disclosed in advertising . . . a description of the condition must be near the word 'free' (an asterisk plus footnote are not good enough), and in type at least half as large."

The upshot of all of this is that you need to avoid deceptive advertising and pricing and treat consumers with honesty.

Ex-Employees

When an employee leaves, a concern arises as to whether and how that employee can compete against you. Employees often learn confidential information in the course of their employment—information that would be useful should they decide to go into business for themselves or jump to a competitor. Of course, you will want to prevent former employees from using that information, but can you? It may be an illegal restraint on trade. Usually you can stop former employees from competing against you, at least for a while. Here is how: have employees sign some or all of these four documents when they come to work for you:

1. *A confidentiality agreement.* You need a document that specifically spells out what you consider to be your confidential trade secrets— customer lists, wholesale costs, that sort of thing. It should state that the employee agrees to keep this material confidential, and then have the employee sign it. Both of you should keep a signed copy.
2. *An assignment of inventions.* Any invention that an employee creates while at work is the property of the employer—that is the general rule. To be safe, however, it is wise to have all appropriate employees sign an agreement stating that they understand the business will own anything they invent as part of their employment. If they invent something on their own time, that is different.
3. *A noncompete agreement.* This is the trickiest of the four, legally speaking. Our free enterprise system means that courts are loath to infringe on people's right to work. Yet courts also understand that there are times when competing would be unfair, and so a balance between these two interests is required. Noncompete agreements that are limited in length and geography sometimes fly. A noncompete agreement may state, for example, that the employee agrees not to join a direct competitor or start a directly competing business for a set time (usually two years is the maximum a court would allow) and in a specific geographic region (e.g., the greater Albuquerque area).
4. *A work for hire agreement.* This agreement states that any documents that an employee creates while at work are, along with the copyright, the property of the employer.

State laws treat these agreements differently. In California, for example, noncompete agreements are frowned upon and enforceable only in limited circumstances. Again, in most places, as long as the time is reasonable and the contract is limited to a specific geographic area, such agreements are acceptable.

When staffers do leave, make sure during the exit interview that they remember they signed these sorts of agreements. It is far better to head off a lawsuit than to litigate one.

FINDING A GOOD ATTORNEY

A lawyer can help you out of a jam, but a good lawyer can also help you avoid the jam in the first place. Attorneys can help with incorporating, contracts, leases, hiring and firing, and a host of other issues. But this begs the question, where do you find a lawyer who knows his or her stuff and is trustworthy? The best way is through a referral. A satisfied client will tell you far more than any commercial. So, if you know people who have businesses and business lawyers, find out how they like their lawyer. You need to find out:

- *Does the lawyer get good results?* Ask your colleagues, did their case settle successfully, was their contract beneficial, were their taxes reduced? Results are what count.
- *Is the attorney accessible?* Too many lawyers are hard to reach and fail to return phone calls quickly. A call should be returned within 24 hours.
- *Are the fees reasonable?* Of course you need to be concerned about fees when hiring a lawyer, but fees are not the most important thing to be concerned about. As in life, with attorneys, you usually get what you pay for. In this case, cheaper is probably not better.
- *Who does the work?* Many lawyers (especially at big firms) use underpaid, overworked associates to do a lot of their work. That is usually fine, as associates are typically quite bright, and this helps keep fees down. But know, too, that many associates are young with little experience, in both life and law. You need to know that when it counts, the person you hired will be doing the heavy lifting.

If you can get a referral for an attorney who meets these criteria, call to schedule a meeting. As you are looking to start an important long-term relationship, expect to spend a few hours with the lawyer. Get a feel for his or her personality. Make sure he or she knows what you expect. Ask about the lawyer's background. Get referrals and call them. And certainly, you should not be billed for this meet and greet with the lawyer. If you are, that is a bad sign.

Barring a referral from a friend or business associate, there are a few other ways to find a good attorney. Look in the Yellow Pages; most lawyers advertise today. In the back of the attorney section of the Yellow Pages is a listing for lawyers by specialty. Look under "business law." Find a few who look good and set up a few meetings. You need someone who is smart and experienced and with whom you feel comfortable.

Finally, call your local bar association. Lawyers are listed by their areas of specialty, and the bar can usually refer you to a few of its members with good reputations. As bar associations are nonpartisan, you can rest assured that the recommendation will be trustworthy.

PART

IV

Technology

CHAPTER **34**

Managing Your Technology

To err is human, but to really foul things up requires a computer.

—*THE FARMER'S ALMANAC*

Whether it is hardware or software, there is no doubt that running a small business today requires that one be, if not technically savvy, at least technically proficient. That competence will enable you to keep your computer systems and other technology up and running and, when things get beyond your ken, to be able to hire helpers and know what the heck they are talking about. In this chapter, we explore how to manage your technology and how to fix what will probably someday ail you.

TOP TECH TERMS

Just so that we are on the same page, and so that you will be able to speak geek when necessary, here are some essential small business tech terms that you might need to know.

- *B2B, B2C, B2D, B2E, B2G.* Acronyms that describe relationships, websites, or applications that are business to business, consumers, distributors, employees, or the government, respectively.
- *Bandwidth.* The transmission capacity of the lines that carry electronic traffic. The greater the bandwidth, the more data that can be

transmitted at one time. In popular slang, bandwidth has also come to refer to one's resources: "We don't have the bandwidth to deal with that problem right now."

- *CMS*. An acronym for a content management system—software that allows you to manage large amounts of website content. Popular CMS systems include WordPress, Drupal, and Joomla.
- *CRM*. An acronym for customer relationship management—software that allows you to identify and target your customers.
- *Data mining*. Analyzing and extracting information, insights, and trends from the numbers, statistics, and information within a database.
- *DNS*. An acronym for domain name server. A DNS converts domain names into IP addresses and vice versa.
- *FTP*. File transfer protocol; a set of rules that allows two computers to communicate while transferring files.
- *HTML*. Hypertext markup language; the basic coding language of the web.
- *IP address*. Every computer that transmits information over the Internet has an IP address. Think of it as the telephone number for your computer.
- *Java*. Created by Sun Microsystems, according to Webopedia.com, "Java is a general purpose programming language . . . well suited for use on the World Wide Web. Small Java applications are called Java applets and can be downloaded from a web server and run on your computer."
- *LAN*. Local area network, a computer network for a specific area and number of computers.
- *OEM*. Although this acronym stands for original equipment manufacturer, it is almost an oxymoron because OEM products do not come from the original manufacturer. In reality, an OEM is a customer of the original manufacturer who buys a product and then resells it under its own name and brand.
- *On-demand*. Having content available to users that can be accessed at any time, as opposed to content that is only available at certain times (a webinar, for example).
- *Organic search results*. Actual search term results, as opposed to paid-for listings.
- *Paid search*. Buying placement on search results.

- *Peripheral.* Any external device attached to a computer, such as a printer or monitor.
- *SaaS.* Software as a service; a business model that allows users to access software over the Internet. Cloud computing. It typically costs much less because users pay only a monthly fee and do not buy a full license.
- *Scalable.* The ability of hardware or software to adapt to increasing demands. If a website can grow as the business grows, it's scalable.
- *Search engine optimization, or SEO.* The process of creating web pages to increase the likelihood that the pages will rank high in a search engine query. SEO uses keywords and links to create higher rankings.
- *Virus.* There are all sorts of Internet bugaboos out there: *Trojan horses,* programs that conceal their evil purpose; *worms,* programs that replicate themselves; *viruses,* software that takes over and slows down systems; *spyware,* programs that gather and transmit private information; *adware,* software that displays random advertisements; and *phishing,* e-mail attempts to fraudulently get you to release confidential information.
- *Web 2.0.* Describes a new Internet era that is more collaborative and interactive. Online communities, streaming video, podcasts, webcasts, and shared information—these are the hallmarks of Web 2.0.
- *WYSIWYG.* "What you see is what you get" (also sometimes called Wissywig). This means that what is on your monitor is what you will see in real life.

Top Text Terms

According to Netlingo.com, these are some of the top text terms used in business:

    BHAG—Big hairy audacious goal
    CYA—Cover your ass
    DD—Due diligence
    DQYDJ—Don't quit your day job
    EOD—End of day
    IANAL—I am not a lawyer
    KISS—Keep it simple, stupid

LOPSOD—Long on promises, short on delivery
NWR—Not work related
P&C—Private and confidential
RFP—Request for proposal
SME—Subject matter expert
TIA—Thanks in advance
TWIMC—To whom it may concern
WIIFM—What's in it for me?

ADOPTING NEW TECHNOLOGY

Technology is supposed to make your business life easier and more productive. But too often, it has the opposite effect. Whether it is the challenge of learning new software, computer crashes, or e-mail snafus, technology is not always the panacea it is made out to be—or should be. That said, if implemented properly, new technology should be more of a help than a hindrance. The secret is to implement it properly. Here's how:

- *Choose right.* There is nothing worse than laying out big bucks for a new technology solution, only to find out that you made the wrong choice. Buying everyone an iPhone is a big mistake if a BlackBerry or Android smartphone is the better choice. So do your homework, comparison shop, get feedback, and choose wisely.
- *Create buy-in.* Employees resist new technology either because they don't see the purpose behind the switch or because they do not want to put in the time necessary to learn new tricks. It is your task, then, to show them how the new technology will make the business better and their jobs easier. They also need to understand that the new way is going to be the only way and that using the new technology (or software or whatever) will be required. So, although buy-in is important,

"For a list of all the ways technology has failed to improve the quality of life, please press three."

—Alice Kahn

so is leadership. You're the boss, so it's okay to boss your employees around sometimes.

- *Take time.* Often the biggest barrier to new technology adoption is time. Solo entrepreneurs especially may be loath to put in the time to really learn how the new thing works and how it can make them more productive. That's a big mistake. If you are going to shell out money for new technology or software, it is shortsighted not to take the time needed to learn how it works. Make a commitment to spend a few hours, or days even, and learn it. Remember, the companies that create products for small businesses put a lot into their research and development; these products are built with you in mind. It would be a shame if you did not take full advantage of all that is offered.
- *Train.* Almost all small business software and hardware solutions now come with some sort of training, either embedded or online. Partake. Beyond that, if you are implementing a big change across a wide spectrum, don't skimp on the training you offer your staff. Weekly sessions may be needed. E-mail and other assistance should be offered. Training should be experiential as well as theoretical. If cost is a concern, consider your local community college—most offer a wide array of computer classes, and at fees any small business can afford.

SECURITY

Technology security can mean many things.

Internet and Computer Security

The basics of prevention and Internet security include these elements:

- *Passwords.* Using the same password everywhere invites trouble. Try this instead: use the same password, but add the name of the site as a prefix. For example, if your normal password is 4444, then use Gmail444, MSN4444, and eBay4444.
- *Firewalls.* As the name implies, a firewall is a wall between your computer and the outside world. It does two things. First, it hides your computer from the Internet at large so that hackers and viruses can't see you. Second, if a virus does infect your computer, the firewall

warns you and lets you stop it from transmitting to other computers via the Internet. Zonealarm.com has a fine free firewall that you can download. Windows also has one that you can turn on.

- *Software.* There is no shortage of software protections available for unauthorized Internet intrusions.
- *Automatic updates.* Be sure to turn on automatic updates for Windows, as security patches are issued regularly.

Reformatting the Hard Drive

When getting rid of an old computer, merely deleting files is not enough. All of your old information remains on the hard drive, even if you do not see it. Before disposing of that old computer, then, reformat your hard drive to wipe it clean. The method for doing so differs depending on your operating system, so do a Google search for "reformatting a hard drive" and your operating system, and you will get instructions for how to do so.

Social Media Fraud and Security

In this day and age, it is not enough to merely protect your base technology; you must also be vigilant about protecting your online identity. If you aren't careful, if you don't take some simple but necessary precautions, your Facebook account can get hacked, your Twitter account can get usurped, even your bank account can be robbed.

Indeed, according to the FBI, in 2008 and 2009, crooks fraudulently transferred more than $100 million out of small business bank accounts. How? They were able to obtain bank login information by hacking social media accounts. I recently spoke with Kevin Haley, the Director of Security Technology and Response for Symantec, the world leader in information protection, to get some expert advice on this issue.

Haley confirmed that getting hacked can be as simple as clicking on a bad link, one corrupted by the crooks. When Barack Obama first ran for president, his official Obama for President Twitter account was hacked, telling people they could "possibly win $500 in free gas" by taking an online survey (with link).

Here's how these schemes work: Say that someone you know on Facebook or wherever instructs you to follow a link. So you trustingly click over to the site, which looks every bit as normal as a real site, and you click the link, except that it is infected with malware. Once you click the link, the malware is installed onto your computer without you ever knowing it. That malware might be, for example:

- Key logging software that records your keystrokes and that in turn allows the criminals to login to your social media accounts—or even your bank.
- Software that sends out fake social media messages as if it were you (Tweeting Viagra tweets would likely be bad for your business).

According to Haley, the danger is that with social media, we generally trust the information we receive from people. But your friend's links can be infected and they might not even know it (e.g., "watch this cool video!") or the bad guys themselves could send you a message, trying to fake you out ("Someone from the class of 2000 is looking for you, click here to see who asked about you"). Whatever the case, once you click the bad link, according to Haley, "Bam, you're owned!"

So what do you do and how can you protect yourself? The first thing is to get the right software. You want an integrated suite that will block intruders and viruses, detect and prevent the installation of other sorts of malware, and protect your privacy.

Protect Yourself

Symantec offers plenty of smart and affordable ways to protect your business and online work. For example, Symantec Endpoint Protection, Small Business Edition "protects your computers and servers with the most effective antivirus, anti-malware technologies available in a single, integrated solution."

Additionally, it is important to institute policies and educate employees about the dangers of using file sharing programs and free programs and updates downloaded from the Internet. Also, if you don't already, monitor your social media output. Infected accounts can send out ongoing malicious messages without you ever knowing if you are not watching.

Finally, change your passwords often.

Data Security

Computer security also means not losing your data. For starters, you should have an uninterruptible power supply (UPS) so that if you have a power outage in your area (or a spike or a surge), you will not lose any data stored on your computers. A UPS gives your system enough power to save your data and power down properly—a typical UPS will give your computer about 5 to 10 minutes of power. A UPS is essentially a large battery that plugs into the wall, and all of your computer components then plug into the UPS, just as they would with a power strip. Choose a UPS with an Underwriters Laboratories rating.

Another way to ensure that you don't lose your data is to back up your computers on a regular basis. There are two kinds of computer users: those who have never had a crisis that caused them to lose data and so don't back up (yet!) and the rest of us. Try losing two chapters of a book you were writing because you didn't back up, and you learn the hard way. The fact is, you never know what might cause you to lose important computer files—a fire, a power outage, even someone kicking a cord. According to ADR Data Recovery, businesses lose more than $12 billion per year because of data loss, and the vast majority of that is from hardware or system failure. Other causes are software corruption, natural disasters, and, of course, human error. So the only real protection you have against losing vital information is to back up your important files, as they say, "early and often."

You can back up your computers a few ways:

- Manual backups require that you regularly copy your data to an external hard drive.
- Backups to an external hard drive can also be done automatically using software.
- Automatic backups can be accomplished using an online backup service. The nice thing about these services is that they copy your data onto remote servers, so if there is a natural disaster, your data is stored

far away. Make sure that the company storing your data keeps it secure and confidential.

Stupid Google Tricks

Movie times and locations: Type in the name of the movie and the city.
Weather: Type in "weather" and the city.
Tracking FedEx, UPS, or Post Office shipments: Type in the tracking number.
Flight times: Names of cities, for example, "New York to Dallas."
Measurement conversions: For example, "teaspoons in a tablespoon."
Calculator: Type in the equation.
Word definitions: "Define ____."
Times in other cities: "Current time in ____."
Convert currency: "$5 USD-Euros."

TECH SUPPORT

Most small businesses do not have an information technology (IT) person, yet as the business grows and as the network grows, the need for a network administrator of some sort grows, too. At a minimum, there should be one person in your office who knows how the system is set up and the basics of how it works. This person should be in charge of:

- All passwords and product keys, although you, too, need to know where they are stored in case this person should leave unexpectedly
- Regular system backups, if done manually
- Basic repairs and updates

Another option is to schedule a monthly maintenance and service call. There are companies that offer tech support for small businesses for a small monthly fee. This also gives you access to tech support online, over the phone, or in person, as needed. Some services to check out are:

- Geeks on Call, www.geeksoncall.com
- Gurus 2 Go, www.gurus2go.com
- Geek Squad, www.geeksquad.com

By putting in the time to learn how your technology is supposed to work, you ensure that you are running it and it isn't running you (too much!).

TOP FIVE TECH MISTAKES

Whether we like it or not, being an entrepreneur these days also means you have to be a techno-geek. Computers, hardware, software, e-commerce, smartphones, dumb phones—there is a lot that can go wrong. Here then are the top five tech mistakes that small businesses tend to make and how to avoid them:

1. *Looking small.* Of all of the great things the Internet has brought to small business (the ability to sell anywhere, anytime for starters), maybe best is that there is no need for any business to look small, ever. No matter how small your small business, the Internet has leveled the playing field. In fact, while you may be small offline, the technology trick is that online you can look every bit as big and professional as your biggest competitor—and you should. If you do not already look big online, then it's time to fix that. Getting a great website is simply a matter of using one of the many online site-creation services available or hiring a designer. Craigslist and Elance are excellent options for that. Either way, you would be smart to take advantage of this amazing opportunity to be small but look big.

2. *Lack of security software.* Of course you know that you are supposed to have computer security software in place to thwart potential online crime, malware, and scams. Your customer lists, account numbers, passwords, data, contracts, and other vital documents are the lifeblood of your business, but far too many small businesses act like the threat is not real. But it's real, very real. So get some great security software. Now.

3. *Not scheduling regular data backups.* You know that you are supposed to back up your data, but do you? Maybe not. Take it from me—I lost two chapters of the rewrite of this book because I had not signed up for an online backup service. I won't make that mistake again. So learn this lesson the easy way—from your pal Steve. He learned it the hard way for you.

4. *Never really learning the software.* Most software is not unlike the brain: people tend to use only 10 percent of it. And that's a mistake. Software companies spend tons of time and money adding bells and whistles on their software, much of which is ignored. You would be wise then to surf on over to the software maker's website and check out the many tips, tricks, and tutorials you will find there.

5. *Not disposing of old technology properly.* There are two problems with not disposing of your technology the right way. One, if you simply throw that computer away, it adds potentially toxic materials to landfills. Two, improperly disposing of your technology potentially exposes your valuable, sensitive data to being accessed by others. To get rid of your old technology properly, check with the manufacturer, your local department of waste management, or donate it to charity for a tax deduction.

CHAPTER 35

Mobility I: Small Office Mobility

Any sufficiently advanced technology is indistinguishable from magic.

—ARTHUR C. CLARKE

My first job out of law school was with a large firm in San Francisco. The year was 1992. I had interned between my second and third years of school there, and they had wined me and dined me in an effort to get me to join the firm once school ended the next year. They took me on river rafting trips and to wine and cheese parties, not to mention soirées at partners' homes—I was duly impressed and couldn't wait to join the firm. I went back and finished my last year of law school, and then I walked into the office in early September after a summer of studying for, and passing, the bar exam.

That very first morning, the managing partner of the firm walked in and said: "I have a little story I want to share with you." He went on: "A young man was driving down the street when he got into a car accident. He slipped into a coma and suddenly found himself at the Pearly Gates. God said to him, 'You may die soon. Would you rather go to Heaven or Hell?' 'Could I see them both?' asked the young man. 'Yes,' God replied." The partner had a strangely ominous tone to his voice. He clearly relished telling this tale. "So first the young man walks through the Pearly Gates and into Heaven. Everything is soft and beautiful and very peaceful. Next, he is transported to Hell, and he's surprised at what he sees. Everyone is dancing and partying, music is playing, drinks are flowing, and everyone is having a great time! And then, just as suddenly, the man whooshes back to earth and back into his body. He fully recovers and goes on to live a long, healthy life."

The partner was leading up to some seemingly sinister punch line. "Many years later, the man finally dies and finds himself back at the Pearly Gates. Again he is given the same choice by God. Remembering his experience from many years before, he says, 'I choose Hell!' The man immediately finds himself in Hell. It's 120 degrees! Everyone is toiling away, carrying bags of rocks on their backs, groaning, working, and sweating. 'But, what about my fun youthful vision?' the man stammered. 'Oh that,' said the partner, playing God, "'that was our summer internship program.'"

Happily, it turns out that the partner's bark was worse than his bite. The firm was a great place to work, even if I never got to go to another party at one of the partners' homes. Unfortunately, for many reasons, my wife and I were unable at that time to move to San Francisco, so I ended up commuting more than 100 miles a day. After a while, exhausted by the commute, I asked the firm whether I could telecommute two days a week. Although such an arrangement is commonplace now, it was a most unusual request then—1993—bordering on bizarre. There was no Internet, no laptop computers, no e-mail, and nary a cell phone. But to its credit, Long & Levit let me. It worked just fine, but even so, not long after, I ended up following my dream and started my first business, my own law practice.

Today, not only would my request to telecommute *not* be thought of as odd, it is routine because the technology to make it work exists in abundance. The computer/Internet/information technology revolution that has occurred over the past 20 years has radically transformed business in general and small business in particular. Indeed, if there is one event in the last generation that has changed small business, the computer revolution is it. Today, small businesses have the tools and technology to look big, act big, yet be mobile.

MOBILITY BASICS

Today, the average small business employee spends about 25 percent of his or her time working outside the office—be it on the road, at home, or in Starbucks. It really is an amazing transformation of the workplace. But somewhat surprisingly, many small businesses are not set up to make their mobile workforce as effective as it could be. By connecting your mobile employees to your network and giving them the right mobility tools (small business servers, remote access, smartphones, laptops, wireless access, and broadband technology), you empower them to be more effective.

What Mobility Means to You

Having a connected office means that you always have access to your office computer's files, programs, and desktop. It means controlling your office desktop from home or from the road. It means that employees can work from home when necessary, allowing them to balance their work and home lives. It means that when a fax or a call comes into the office, you can receive it on the road. It means that your team is able to collaborate on projects while working in different places using cloud-based technologies.

The first step in creating a connected office is being able to connect to your main computer from anywhere. There are three basic ways to do this:

1. *Remote PC access software.* Software programs such as LogMeIn or Laplink Everywhere allow you to securely access your home or office computer from any web-enabled device.
2. *Cloud-computing.* Online services such as GoToMyPC.com enable you to access computers connected to the Internet using a web browser. Once you log into both computers, you will be able to transfer files back and forth, print from your remote PC to a local printer, collaborate and work with others, and so on.
3. *Windows.* Remote Desktop is a feature that allows you to connect your computer using the web from any computer or smartphone. Once you are connected, Remote Desktop gives you control over the remote computer.

These tools offer one way to connect to your main office computer. The other way is to do so through a small business server.

Servers

We all know that a server has something to do with the Internet, but what, exactly? When two or more computers log into the same Internet site, that site sits on a server. It is a sort of master hub that connects other computers. For a business, you might want to think of it as the central nervous system—the place through which all business information flows and, more important, is shared within the business. Most offices these days have information stored on many computers. Key contacts might be on your computer, whereas important e-mail addresses might be on your secretary's, and your client list sits on the computer of your vice president of sales. It's not the most efficient system, but this is how many small businesses work.

Imagine instead that you have a master computer to house and store all of your vital company information, a computer that can be accessed equally by everyone in your office from wherever they may be in the world. This is your server. A small business server is a centralized place to store business information, keep you better organized, and keep your staff better informed.

But small office mobility goes far beyond simply being able to access your computer remotely. It involves a variety of tools and strategies that not only free you from the office but also help you work more effectively.

YOUR WIRELESS NETWORK

We all know how great wireless is—we probably couldn't work today without it. Not only does wireless allow you and your employees to work in any office or area, but it is equally appreciated by visitors who expect to be able to be plugged in anywhere, anytime. Yet, even so, some offices still remain tethered to the morass of wires poorly hidden behind desks. So the question (aside from WHY?) is, if wireless really is the way to go, how does one go from wired to wireless? Here are four easy steps:

1. *Do your research.* First, read up. Wireless equipment comes in at many price points, covers distances great and small, and offers speeds of varying degrees, so you really have to know what you need before you shop.

Tip: A great site to compare prices and quality of any technical product is www.cnet.com.

2. *Understand your options.* There are many ways to get your office computers online wirelessly. The most common follow:

- *Wireless broadband.* Wireless broadband allows your computers to connect to the Internet using a high-speed network. It is typically lightning fast with broad range because you are basically piggybacking on the wireless signal of your mobile phone carrier. Essentially, what you do is buy a PC card or laptop card and connect to the Internet via cell phone towers. Check out carriers such as Verizon and Sprint.
- *Wi-Fi.* The main difference between wireless broadband and Wi-Fi is coverage. Because wireless broadband uses the signal of your cell phone carrier, its coverage area is broad. Wi-Fi is much more limited in range. The coverage area, called a *hotspot*, can be as small as a single room or as big as a building.
- *Bluetooth.* With even less range and power than Wi-Fi, Bluetooth is a connectivity system with limited range, used basically for small peripherals.

3. *If necessary, hire experts.* If your networking needs are complicated, then an off-the-shelf solution may not be for you. Instead, consider hiring a pro. The larger your network is (that is, the more users), the more difficult it will be to create and maintain. In that case, it is smart to hire an information technology (IT) expert to set up your network properly from the get-go.

4. *Don't forget the basics.* Place your base station router in the middle of the desired wireless network area so that you will have even coverage. Keep it secure by requiring passwords. Update your software periodically. Use virus protection.

MOBILITY TOOLS

Wireless networking is just one of the many (and ever-increasing) tools in the arsenal of the mobile business warrior.

Laptops and Netbooks

As laptop computers become lighter, ever smaller, and less expensive, and as e-mail and Internet use are always increasing, the tool of choice for mobile small business people is, of course, the laptop or netbook. What is making laptop use even more attractive these days is that not only has battery life increased but also laptops are becoming ever lighter while more powerful.

Of course, it is impossible to offer a laptop buying guide—not only are your needs unique, but the options are always changing. Instead, here are some things to consider:

- You will never be unhappy with a faster system—more memory, a bigger hard drive, a faster processor, etc.
- Do not worry too much about weight. The difference between a 3-pound laptop and a 4-pound one is minimal, especially when you consider that, for the typical business traveler, a cell phone, documents, and book add an extra 10 pounds to the briefcase!
- Smaller notebook = smaller battery.
- An extra battery comes in very useful.
- The more ports, the better.
- Bigger notebooks tend to be sturdier.
- A glossy screen is better for viewing movies and photos. A matted screen is generally better for word processing and web browsing.

The iPad and Other Tablets

The late, great Steve Jobs did it again when he unveiled the iPad in 2010. Until then, tablet computers were a niche market that seemed to be going nowhere, but as he often did, Jobs made the technology cool. Not long after that, a slew of imitators hit the market from the likes of BlackBerry and Dell, but none hit the mark quite as the iPad did; that is, until Amazon introduced the Kindle Fire. It seems that there is at least one legitimate competitor now in the tablet computer wars.

But that begs the question: Are there actual business uses for tablet computers? Using them to watch videos at home or in a plane makes sense, but beyond that, what? A recent survey of 1,641 business people by ChangeWave answers that question with interesting results. The survey asked them if they were planning on buying tablets, and if so, for what purposes.

Here are the results:

- 7 percent said their company provided them with a tablet computer.
- 14 percent more were actively planning on buying one. Of those, 78 percent intended to buy an Apple iPad.
- 73 percent planned on using the tablets to go online and handle e-mail.
- 46 percent planned on using them for "sales support."
- 45 percent planned on using them for "customer presentations."
- 33 percent said that their tablet was a "laptop replacement."

Tip: More than a half a million laptops are stolen every year. Protect yours. First, always keep it near you, especially in airports, where thieves look for laptop cases that are unattended. Especially in airport restrooms, be sure to keep your laptop case close by. (More than a few businesspeople have had their laptops stolen, snatched by the strap while they were, well, indisposed.) Consider insuring your laptop as well. A policy can be had for less than $100. And, as damage to your laptop is more likely than theft, and such policies cover most damage, buying one is even smarter. Finally, you can purchase software that tracks your laptop to its new Internet connection if it is ever stolen. If you would like to protect your laptop or tablet, encrypt your data, track a stolen laptop, and get it recovered, then check out MyLaptopGPS.com.

VoIP (Voice-over Internet Protocol)

Rather than using a traditional phone line, VoIP uses the Internet to make and receive phone calls, and thus it is incredibly inexpensive. VoIP is simple, easy to install and use, and can be integrated with your PC and Microsoft Outlook. You can even convert voice mail into e-mail and check messages by using your browser. And maybe best of all, no one will ever know you are using a practically free VoIP system.

Cell Phones and Smartphones

The only thing hotter than tablets is smartphones and their copious amount of apps. Products such as the RIM BlackBerry, Apple iPhone, and Google's Android are revolutionizing business generally, and mobile business specifically. See the next chapter to learn more and to discover how you can take advantage of this revolution.

CHAPTER **36**

Mobility II: Mobile Mania

Smartphones are reinventing the connection between companies and their customers.

—RICH MINER, COFOUNDER, ANDROID

There is no doubt we are living through a revolutionary technological time that is changing the way people work. More and more, business people are becoming untethered—untethered to their desktop and desktop computer, untethered to the office, untethered even to the old 9 to 5 hours. Owners and employees are increasingly working where they want, how they want, and when they want. And while laptops, netbooks, notebooks, and iPads are a big reason, probably the biggest reason and change is the advent of the smartphone. As a result, today small businesses are on the march—out of the office.

Recent surveys back this up, indicating just how much the workplace is changing and how significantly smartphones are affecting that change. A 2011 survey by the firm RingCentral indicated that 56 percent of those surveyed said that forgetting their smartphone at home was worse than forgetting their wallet. Other interesting results included:

- Although only 22 percent said they checked their phone for business once or twice a day, 62 percent said they check it multiple times a day. In fact, more than half surveyed said they were "addicted" to their smartphones.

- Only 21 percent said the best thing about their phone was never missing an important call, whereas 49 percent said it was the ability to e-mail anytime, anywhere.
- A full 60 percent said they used their phone for business more in the last 12 months alone (15 percent said they used it 75 percent more).

Another survey called the Small Business Technology Poll surveyed 2,000 small business owners. Its results are also interesting: 40 percent of the respondents said that they allow and encourage employees to use smartphones away from the office, and 49 percent said that maps and other mobile navigation tools are their favorite and most used apps. Although the poll did not include an analysis of other ways small businesses are using their smartphones, it is probably safe to say that they are getting and receiving e-mail, texting, making appointments, and calling customers. Some even will be tweeting and monitoring their mobile marketing campaigns (although that must be a fairly small number still).

We really love our smartphones.

It is no wonder why they are becoming so popular. More powerful than ever, small and handy, with apps galore to run a business (and kill some time), smartphones are on pace to outsell PCs in the near future, according to Gartner Research.

> What exactly constitutes a "smartphone"? Although there is no one definition, typically a smartphone is considered a mobile device that makes calls, can send and receive e-mails and texts, has Internet access and a web browser, and allows one to work on documents and spreadsheets—basically, a mini computer on which you can chat.

All of which is to say—this is a trend that warrants your attention. Smartphones, tablets, and apps are changing the way people live, and increasingly how they do business too. And if they haven't already changed the way you do business, they will, sooner or later.

GETTING STARTED

This section is for those readers who do not yet have a smartphone (who are you?) or who, although maybe having one for their personal use, are not deploying them in their business yet. If this does not describe you—if smartphones are already a part of your business—then jump to the next section.

Choosing a Network

Maybe you want an iPhone and are ready to get some for your business. Great. Or maybe the BlackBerry or Android is your cup of tea. Fine choices, all. But whatever phone you pick, the important thing to understand is that you are not just buying a phone or phones, you are also choosing an operating system and carrier as well. What you should look for is a carrier that offers:

- *The latest and fastest sort of data connection*—whether that is 3G or 4G in your area (*G* stands for *generation*).
- *Coverage.* You need a carrier who is able to provide coverage in the physical locations you require for your business. You may want to check the site DeadCellZones.com to see how a certain carrier works or does not work in your area.
- *Customer service.* Not all cell phone carriers are created equal.

Internet Access Anywhere

Have you ever wanted to connect your laptop to the Internet but were in a spot that had no wireless Internet connection? Of course—we all have. Well, that's where your smartphone can come in handy. Many carriers offer an option called "tethering," which allows your phone to act as a wireless modem. Although it costs extra, tethering is an excellent option to consider if Wi-Fi is important to you.

Choosing a Smartphone

Although iPhones are all the rage, these things tend to ebb and flow. Once Palm was king. Then it was BlackBerry. Other current choices include Android and Windows Mobile. And we also know this much to be true: something else amazing will come along too—what it is, we don't know yet, but it will. So choosing a phone on a flavor-of-the-month analysis may not be the smartest idea. Instead, it is wise to really check out the various phones, systems, and data plans before jumping in.

The different phones have different strengths and weaknesses, although all are powerful of course. The iPhone has an easy interface. Windows Mobile works great with Windows and Office, of course. The Symbian platform from Nokia is a popular international choice. Androids tend to be more affordable, and since they are made on Google's operating system, work best with Google Mail, Calendar, and so on. There are many variables to consider.

Another consideration is what sorts of apps you want to run on your phone system and for your business. Although Apple still has the most apps right now, other systems are very robust and offer many equally powerful app choices. (In one of the following sections I discuss how to use apps in your business.)

Creating Your Network

Larger companies tend to choose a phone and system and then create an internal system for safeguarding, tracking, and maintaining the security of the system. One reason that BlackBerry is so popular among larger businesses is that its Enterprise Server enables information technology (IT) departments to easily control the system. For the smaller business, it is often a matter of figuring how to manage the employees' personal choices between the iPhone, BlackBerry, Droid, and Windows Mobile. In that regard, setting companywide policies regarding security, usage, and so forth, is what is required.

If you decide that you want to create and maintain your own system with phones that you buy, the important thing to understand is that all phones and carriers now have some form of system and software that allows your IT person the ability to manage the system.

Creating an iPhone Security System at Work

The iPhone Configuration Utility gives IT administrators various tools to manage a companywide iPhone system, including passcodes, e-mail security, ability (or inability) to log on to iTunes, and so on.

RUNNING YOUR BUSINESS WITH YOUR SMARTPHONE

The reason that it is smart to consider running your business with apps is that that is where things are headed. You are on your smartphone far more than you ever used to be, right? Well, the same is true for your staff, vendors, and customers. iPhones and smartphones are where the eyeballs are, and as such, it is where you need to be too. It is how people are gathering information these days.

The old Apple commercial "There's an app for that" is truer than ever. There are hundreds of thousands of apps available on all sorts of platforms, so finding the ones you need to run your business effectively is more a matter of sorting through the options than finding an option. Here are just some of the ways you can take advantage of this apptastic revolution so as to whet your appetite:

- *Tasks.* There are a ton of great task management tools available. David Allen has a popular one called Getting Things Done. Other popular choices include Tooledo, Things, Remember the Milk, and for we Outlook users, Outlook Mobile.
- *Track expenses.* No one likes making expense reports, and that's why an app like Concur Breeze is a wonder: you can snap photos of your receipts with your phone and the receipt can then be downloaded into an online expense report. Credit card payments can also be inputted automatically.
- *Take credit card payments.* Many apps let you accept credit card payments through your smartphone. Check out Square for example.
- *Make presentations.* mbPointer turns your smartphone into a Power-Point remote control. MightyMeeting allows you to save your PowerPoint presentation remotely, thereby also allowing you to access it remotely.
- *Keep track of your time.* Many apps, Harvest, for example, are available to track the time spent on various projects.
- *Document review and creation.* Microsoft offers Office Mobile, and there are similar apps for Google Docs. You might want to also check out Documents to Go.

Of course, these are just some ideas to get you started. I certainly could never tell you which apps would work best in your business. There are simply so many out there these days, doing so many different things for businesses, that it is impossible to say which you need and would like. But you can figure out fairly quickly which you should check out by:

- Doing a Google search
- Reading industry magazines, websites, and blogs
- Getting recommendations from writers and bloggers you like (personally, I like and use recommendations from SmallBizTrends, CNET, and SmallBizTechnology)

The important thing is to find some apps that fit your business and try them out. Undoubtedly you will find some amazing tools out there that will help you run your business easier, faster, and better.

CREATING AN APP FOR YOUR BUSINESS

It should follow from the previous conversation that if so many different companies are creating and offering apps, it might just be a smart thing for you to do the same. And you might think this is a nice idea, but too expensive. Well, not necessarily. Creating an app for others to buy, or a free app related to your business, can actually be a very affordable proposition, and maybe even a free one.

There are many reasons why you might want to create an app for your business, but the main one is this: it can help you get more business. People are on their smartphones more, a lot more—that's a fact. So by marketing your products through an app, you give your business not only another shot at making a sale but a good shot at it because that is how people are accessing information these days.

There are basically two ways to create an app for your business. You can either pay for and develop an app or create for almost nothing an app version of your website.

Creating a Professional App

1. *Have a good idea.* Your app idea has to be something that people need or want and serves a market need.

2. *Analyze the idea.* Who is going to use it? Why? Will they pay for it? How much, if anything?

3. *Hire a developer/designer/programmer.* Hiring a developer/programmer to create a fairly simple app can cost anywhere from, say, $1,000 to $10,000 (although people have certainly spent more). If you want to do it yourself, Apple has an iPhone Developer software program that you can buy.

Finding a Developer

You can compare rates and get quotes from app developers at iPhoneAppQuotes.com. You can also get bids at Elance.com.

4. *Submit the app to iTunes.* This is something your developer should help with, as it actually is a fairly technical process.

5. *Market your app.* Just as you must market your business, so must you market your app.

Free and Cheap Apps

There are all sorts of sites out there that will help you create a simple app that mimics your website. SwebApps does this for around $200, as does MyAppBuilder.com. With this sort of service, you point, click, drag, and create an app. It's easy. Your app could include:

- Content, blogs, and podcasts, etc.
- Your e-commerce store
- Maps and contact info
- YouTube, Facebook, and Twitter buttons

Creating an App on the Cheap

Another good option for building an inexpensive app is Magmito (www .Magmito.com), which aims to be to mobile content creation what Blogger was to website creation. With Magmito, do-it-yourself developers can create rich and engaging apps to promote products, services, events, companies, and so on. The apps are free with advertising or $99 without ads.

Creating a simple app is actually a very easy way to go, allowing you another way to stay in front of your customers. But whatever way you go, it's probably time to hop on the app bus, Gus.

MOBILE MARKETING CAMPAIGNS

The last, and maybe best, way to hop on the app bus is to create a mobile marketing campaign, that is, a text or Twitter or mobile app campaign. For example, in Los Angeles, gourmet food trucks are all the rage and can be found all over the city—except that a truck may not be in the same place two days in a row. They use Twitter to announce their location. So if you want to find, say, the Kogi Korean Barbecue trucks one day, you must follow Kogi on Twitter. Not only does that get people to follow Kogi on Twitter, but it also engages their customers daily via their smartphones. Smart indeed.

Mobile marketing is hot because that is where people are getting their information today. We have gone from radio, newspapers, and television to wired computer desktops to wireless laptops to now small smartphones and tablets. So it should be no surprise that small businesses are getting in on the mobile marketing act. Here's how you can too:

Tip: Contests, polls, sweepstakes, discounts, coupons, games, and promotions work best in mobile marketing campaigns.

---

1. *Create a good list.* What you want to do is create a list of opt-in customers who give you permission to text or tweet them specials, and you do that by asking people you know to sign up for your campaign. They will if you explain that they will get special deals if they do so, deals that others won't get. Solicit people:

   - In your shop
   - Through your e-newsletter
   - On your site
   - Via e-mail
   - Via social media
   - In your advertising

Your pitch could be something like, "Sign up for our text alerts and get 20% off on your next purchase." Or "Follow us on Twitter to get our daily Twitter deal of the day." Creating your own opt-in list beats any list you could buy from a broker.

2. *Choose a service*. There are more and less affordable text message service providers. As with most things, you get what you pay for. They will help you craft a campaign if needed.

3. *Go for it*. Come up with a special, blast it out, and watch the results. Tweak as necessary.

Technology and mobility are changing business. Let it change yours.

CHAPTER **37**

Small Business Software

Buying the right computer and getting it to work properly is no more complicated than building a nuclear reactor from wristwatch parts in a darkened room using only your teeth.

—DAVE BARRY

The point of software is to make your business more effective. It is supposed to save you time and make things run more smoothly, although we all know that is not always the case. With the wide variety of software available, it is sometimes hard to know what to buy. In this chapter, we will look at what software your small business really needs and give you an idea about your options.

A caveat: It would be impossible to analyze every product available. A good web search will allow you to compare scores of products and prices. What I want to do here is to give you an idea about the products that are the market leaders and how these leaders compare. That is not to say they are the only products available, because they are not. However, I have found that when a few products dominate a field, it is for a good reason—they are usually the best.

OFFICE SUITES

Almost all computers now come with some sort of basic office suite preinstalled that allows you to draft simple documents and so on. Although these are nice products, if you are serious about running a successful

359

small business, you will likely need to upgrade to something more robust. A good office suite should be an integrated program that allows you to create documents and spreadsheets, produce marketing materials, manage e-mail and contacts, and much more. As your office suite will become your essential daily tool for organizing and running your business, you should not shy away from buying a good one. This is not the place to skimp.

Microsoft Office

Microsoft Office is the leader, and for good reason. It is a bundle of essential programs: Word (word processing), Excel (spreadsheets), Outlook (contacts, contact manager, calendars, and e-mail), Publisher (graphics), and PowerPoint (presentations). Office is not inexpensive, but be aware that if you have an older version of Office, upgrades are much less expensive than buying it new out of the box.

Software in the Cloud

Increasingly, software is moving to the cloud, meaning that the actual program is not sitting on your own computer but is instead hosted on a remote server by the company that created the product. The advantage is that (1) you do not need to pay for updates and (2) you can access the software and your files from any computer anywhere. Many of the programs on this list are being offered that way.

For example, Microsoft has a new/old product in the cloud called Microsoft Office 365. Essentially it is your old standby, Microsoft Office, in the cloud. According to Microsoft.com, "Microsoft Office 365 for professionals and small businesses is an easy-to-use set of web-enabled tools that you can use to access your email, important documents, contacts, and calendars from virtually anywhere and on almost any device. Office 365 includes public websites and web hosting along with much more."

Corel WordPerfect Office

Corel WordPerfect Office comes with WordPerfect (word processing), Quattro Pro (spreadsheets), Corel Presentations (presentations), and

Corel Central (appointments and e-mail). Like Microsoft Office, this is an excellent product for handling your daily office tasks. The question is whether you want to work in a Microsoft environment or a Corel environment.

Google Docs

If the idea of an online, cloud-based, free office suite is appealing to you, then you should check out Google Docs. The online suite of applications allows you to create documents, spreadsheets, and presentations and then store them online on Google's servers. They can also be saved onto your computer and sent via Gmail.

Tip: Cloud computing is also known as software as a service (SaaS).

BUSINESS CONTACT MANAGEMENT SOFTWARE

Contact management software is intended to help you keep track of clients, leads, and prospects and turn those leads into customers. A good contact management program should be able to import contacts from other programs and integrate with e-mail programs.

Sage ACT!

ACT! is a powerful program that has been around for quite some time. It allows you to:

- Manage contact information in one place, including name, business name, phone numbers, addresses, and so on
- Manage leads, customers, and vendors
- Track each relationship
- Create sales forecasting models

ACT! can be shared, thereby keeping everyone's notes about customers and vendors in a central location.

GoldMine

Another granddaddy in this field, GoldMine is a popular choice. Its interface is similar to that of Microsoft Outlook, with taskbar and menu options, including the ability to create custom taskbars. The program easily integrates with Outlook, Microsoft Exchange, Lotus Notes, and Lotus cc: Mail. GoldMine's contact management tools are powerful. For instance, when you create and send a letter, fax, or e-mail, the program automatically records your interactions with the contact. You can also forecast sales, complete transactions, assign quotas for employees, and easily create reports and charts analyzing sales data.

Microsoft Business Contact Manager

Beginning with Office 2007, Microsoft integrated its contact manager program, Business Contact Manager, with Outlook. As with similar programs, it tracks leads and prospects and allows you to create custom reports, which can then be exported to Excel or Word.

TAX SOFTWARE

Greatland

When you are in business, one thing you must deal with is the maze of forms that make up W-2 and 1099 reporting. The good news is that there is one company that specializes in this—Greatland. Check out Greatland. com for everything you need in this area, including e-filing software.

ACCOUNTING SOFTWARE

A good accounting software program is also a must for any small business. All of these programs offer similar tools—accounting, after all, is what it is, and so all offer budgeting, accounts receivable management, payroll, inventory control, and so on. The key is to find a program that offers the bells and whistles you want and the functionality you like.

Sage Simply Accounting

This popular program is easy to use and affordable. It is a good choice for the small business that has accounting needs and a tight budget.

Peachtree

Peachtree is another solid choice. It is especially good at handling e-commerce and has a host of usable financial features. Some of the best options are the inventory control function, which lets you track products based on size or color, and the daily register report, which is a snapshot of your daily activity.

Office Accounting

Microsoft's accounting software is as good as any here.

QuickBooks

QuickBooks has an easy-to-use, intuitive interface and powerful tools that should please both the new and seasoned entrepreneur alike. Sure, it handles all of your basic accounting needs, but it also has more sophisticated functions such as loan management, cash flow forecasting, tracking of fixed assets, and vehicle mileage tracking. Again, like most other makers of programs on this list, Intuit has also moved versions of its popular Quicken software to the cloud.

Concur Breeze

Although not an accounting program per se, Concur makes a product directly related to accounting: expense reporting and tracking. Concur Breeze is a great program that automatically helps you track receipts and expenses and thereby takes the pain out of this tedious task.

BUSINESS PLANNING SOFTWARE

Business plans are not just for startups that need capital. They are an essential tool for anyone running a small business who wants to think strategically, plot a course of action, and then follow up to see how well the plan is being followed. A good business planning program will walk you through the steps necessary to create a usable, powerful business plan.

Business Plan Pro

The best-selling business planning software for a reason, Business Plan Pro is useful to the novice and experienced businessperson alike. It easily helps you work through each category in the plan (executive summary, sales forecasts, etc.), and contains more than 400 sample plans. With excellent templates, charts, and graphs, the program is also easy to use. The business plan you'll find through Appendix B of this book is taken from Business Plan Pro. It's an excellent choice.

> ### Marketing Software
>
> Palo Alto Software, the makers of Business Plan Pro, also offers a great product that can help you create a marketing plan, called Marketing Plan Pro.

ANTIVIRUS, ANTISPAM, AND ANTISPYWARE SOFTWARE

The technological plagues of the modern era—computer viruses, spam, spyware, and adware—must be controlled if you are to be productive at work. As a virus can ruin your computer, and spam and spyware can slow work to a crawl (or worse), containing these problems is vital. Although spam control is being built into many office suites nowadays, you still may need extra help.

Symantec Antivirus

Symantec is the industry standard when it comes to powerful protection against viruses and spyware.

Cloudmark Spam Blocker

A network of more than 1 million people use the software, and whenever a piece of spam gets through to any one of them, a simple click of the mouse marks that e-mail as spam, and it is thereafter blocked for the rest of the community. It is very effective.

McAfee AntiVirus Plus

Using filters, lists, and reports, this program also blocks much unwanted spam, monitors your e-mail, and quarantines spam that does get through.

Mailwasher

This is another good program, and free. Go to www.mailwasher.net.

AVG Anti-Virus Free Edition

Another free antivirus software solution.

Spybot Search & Destroy

A very effective, free, antispyware software. Says *PC Magazine*, "Only one . . . Spybot Search & Destroy actually managed to destroy the spyware and adware it detected."

Ad-Aware

Another very good antispyware solution, and also free.

Iolo System Mechanic

Even though you may run your antivirus and other software protection programs religiously, files still get corrupted, diminishing computer performance. System Mechanic is a great tool for finding those bugs, fixing them, and making your system hum again.

BLOGGING SOFTWARE

Blogs, as you know, have become an essential tool for communicating in a more personal way with your clientele. The following are a few good blogging software choices.

WordPress

WordPress is possibly the most popular blogging and website creation program out there. (Confession: A few years ago, wanting to redo my own site, I received bids as high as $75,000. Sticker shock led me to rethink the project, and my assistant extraordinaire, Vivian, convinced me that we should use WordPress. It turned out to be a very smart business decision. I love WordPress.)

Creating a blog or website with WordPress is surprisingly easy. There are literally hundreds of themes to choose from, and most are free. These themes can be completely customized and installed quickly. Additionally, adding content with its content management system (CMS) is simple and intuitive. It is designed to make adding or changing content to a site a breeze.

Blogger

Blogger.com is the place to go for the first-timer wanting to create a basic, simple blog.

TypePad

Similar to WordPress, TypePad offers a full range of features and management tools. Its WYSIWYG (what you see is what you get) editing system makes it easy to create and post a blog in minutes.

E-COMMERCE SOLUTIONS

Although creating a great website and/or a corresponding e-commerce platform used to be a fairly complicated matter, simple solutions are now available. This is discussed in detail later in this book.

Growing Your Business

PART

I

Advertising and Marketing

CHAPTER 38

Basic Advertising Strategies

Early to bed, early to rise, work like hell, and advertise.

—TED TURNER

Not advertising is like being alone in a dark room with the door closed. *You* know you are there, but no one else does. You absolutely have to advertise if you are going to succeed in business, because it is the main way new customers learn you are out there. Yet it is surprising how many small business owners assume that their great idea, ideal location, big sign, good looks, or *whatever* will bring people in the door. This is what brings new people in the door: advertising. Sure, marketing is very important, as is networking, customer service, and word of mouth, but advertising is the route with potentially the biggest payoff. Advertising turns the lights on.

THE PROCESS

The problem for many small businesses is that there are a lot of advertising choices, many are not inexpensive, and a costly mistake can cripple the budget. Absolutely understandable. And, as discussed earlier, one trait of great entrepreneurs is that they reduce their risk to the extent possible. That is what we want to do here. Few small businesses have the cushion to absorb a costly mistake, so here I will outline a process that allows you to greatly reduce the possibility that you will bet on the wrong horse, advertise in the wrong place, and lose a bunch of money. What should happen instead is that you will create a winning ad with less risk.

The good news is that creating a successful advertising campaign is a joy. An ad that works will become a tried-and-true friend that your small business will rely on. Once you have one, you can breathe a little easier, knowing that when you roll it out, you will get predictable results. The ad that the travel company runs in the travel section of the Sunday paper is probably its bread and butter—it knows that ad will bring in x dollars every time it runs. It may be a monthly ad in a magazine, a regular radio buy, or a cable television campaign—a smart, well-thought-out ad campaign can be your ticket to success.

The key is to bet on the right horse, to pick the right ad and the right vehicle. How can you be sure of that? Creating an (almost) risk-free, winning ad campaign* is a five-step process:

1. Think ahead. What is the purpose, size, and budget of your campaign?
2. Decide what medium (or media) works best for your business, brand, and budget.
3. Create an ad that builds on your brand and gets attention.
4. Test the ad.
5. Once you are convinced that you have an ad or campaign that works, roll it out.

BRAINSTORMING

The first thing you must do is decide on the purpose of your ad campaign. There are basically two types of ad campaigns. The first is a branding campaign that is intended to publicize your name and corporate identity so that people will remember it when they need the product or service you offer. Take the ad in the paper that says, "Divorce for Fathers." This is a branding ad. Of course, the purpose of the ad is to get customers, but unlike the second type of ad, which has an immediate hook and call to action ("Sale!"), this type of ad is a bit subtler, as it is intended to build awareness of the business as well as get customers today. The plan is to have people

---

*When I say "campaign," I am referring to an ongoing advertising presence. Your campaign may be a multimedia plan that is organized six months in advance and utilizes both electronic and print media, or it may be an overnight radio buy that lasts a week. Either way, the process is the same.

see the advertisement again and again, so that when the time comes that some dad needs a divorce lawyer, he remembers which firm to call.

A branding campaign takes time, but if you have the time and money, it can be very rewarding. By branding your business, you create long-term viability. Branding is not done in a week or a month. It is an ongoing process that pays more and more dividends as time goes by, but you must remember this: fundamental things apply. Branding, when done right, will make a long-term difference, but it will not yield immediate rewards.

This brings us to the second type of ad campaign, the one intended to generate sales *now*. This type of campaign is usually shorter and more intense. Several media sources may be used to reinforce the same message. Whether you want to let people know about your sidewalk sale this weekend, or a free drawing for a digital camera, this type of campaign is intended to create immediate dividends with a noticeable increase in sales. If a branding campaign is a marathon, this ad campaign is a sprint. It will be more periodic, maybe once a month or so.

How much do you need to spend on advertising? The Small Business Administration (SBA) suggests that you earmark 2 percent of your gross annual sales for advertising. Others believe the amount should be closer to 5 percent. If you gross $500,000 a year, assigning 5 percent of that figure—$25,000—to an annual advertising and marketing budget is probably not far off. That $25,000 yearly is roughly $2,000 a month. If you want to continue to generate half a million dollars in sales each year, $2,000 a month for advertising is a small price to pay. This process, then, requires that you look at your gross sales and earmark an appropriate percentage of that amount for your monthly ad budget. Your income determines the budget. This is called the *cost method*.

If the cost method sounds too formulaic to you, there is another method to determine the right budget. It is called the *task method*. Here, you look at how many customers you need to acquire or how much product you need to sell in order to hit your sales goals for the year, and then, based on past sales from advertising, calculate what you need to spend this year. If you spent $15,000 last year generating $300,000 in sales, and you want to grow 10 percent this year, you will need to spend more, maybe $17,500 or so. Your goal creates the budget.

So that is your first assignment: deciding what sort of campaign best suits your objectives and needs and what sort of budget you can afford.

CHOOSING THE RIGHT MEDIUM

Different media outlets have different strengths and weaknesses. Your campaign may utilize only one medium, or it may take several to accomplish your goals. The most important thing when advertising generally, and when choosing your medium specifically, is zeroing in on your target audience. Earlier in this book, I suggested that you need to know exactly who your customers are. What is your target demographic? What do they watch, read, and listen to? Your earlier research and business plan should be consulted. Knowing who your potential customers are takes a lot of the guesswork out of choosing the right medium. If your customers are men in their 20s, then a magazine such as *Maxim* or an alternative rock radio station would be an excellent choice. If your target customers are business travelers, then *SkyMall* would be a great choice. Without knowing *exactly* which people you are trying to reach, figuring out where to advertise is a shot in the dark. Do your research.

Here are your main options.

Newspapers

The world of print media is changing radically. There are fewer customers and readers, fewer ads and options than even a decade ago. Let me suggest however, that those very changes might offer the savvy small business person some tremendous opportunities.

For starters, one of the main things you want from your advertising is the chance to STAND OUT. It used to be that advertising in the print media made that very difficult because there was so much competition. But because there are in fact fewer businesses advertising in print, and fewer ads in those publications, your ability to stand out has increased. Fewer ad pages mean your ads can be stars.

In addition, because print media need advertisers, there are some very good deals to be had out there. As such, a half-page ad in a magazine or large ad in the paper not only will offer you some great exposure due to less competition but also will cost less than you probably expect.

But that's not all. Print advertising continues to offer some great benefits not shared by its online counterparts:

- *It is highly targeted.* Print advertising offers you the chance to catch people by their interests, religion, hobbies, work, age, etc. Targeting your marketing to the right demographic is fairly easy by advertising in the right place, and it can be highly profitable.
- *It does not evaporate.* Magazines stay in homes for months. Newspapers may be around for days. But web pages come and go. In addition, people reading web pages digest information far quicker—and move on—than do people reading print content.
- *It is great for branding.* A print ad is a physical thing; it can be copied and placed in your store, or on your website even, for years. E-ads do not have the same cachet.

All of this is not to say that online advertising is not important; of course it is. But by the same token, as we rush to understand and embrace this new world of e-advertising, let us not forget that print can play a significant role in the mix.

Ad Synergy

Ideally, your print ads can and should empower your online ads. Research indicates that a not insignificant portion of online searches stem from offline ads—people see an ad in a newspaper or magazine and then search that topic on the Internet. As such, aside from your URL, print ads today should contain product names, keywords and key phrases, taglines, and so on. By using your print ads to drive people to your website, you essentially get a twofer, benefiting from both offline and online exposure.

Television

Although television might be the most powerful advertising medium ever invented for many businesses, television can be both cost-prohibitive and unnecessary. Here's the deal: you must be willing to make a substantial commitment of time and money, you must be willing to wait a few months for a payoff, and your small business must have regional appeal for a television campaign to be worth the cost. A stand-alone bakery has no need to advertise on television, but a chain of baker-ies might. If you have a regional business or product, and you have the money and commitment to make a significant television buy, the payoff can be huge.

TV Success

What makes a good television ad? First, it must be highly visual: television is a visual medium. Because of remotes and competition, your ad must GRAB THEIR ATTENTION quickly. Be sure to repeat your phone number and the name of your business several times. Finally, do not make the mistake of creating an ad that is more interesting than your business or product, or so amusing that people fail to remember what you are selling. Finally, do not be afraid to copy a good commercial that works.

To be effective, television advertisements must be aired repeatedly. How often? A lot. Here is a way to figure out how often: a GRP is a *gross ratings point*. It refers to 1 percent of the television households in a broad-cast area. If there are 2 million television homes in your city, one GRP would be 20,000 households. To make a television buy worth your time, you would need to buy at least 150 GRPs a month. The price you will pay for each GRP relates to the stations you want to advertise on, the size of your city, and the competition. In a city such as New York, you might expect to pay $2,500 per GRP. In a smaller place, say, Raleigh, it might be $100.

TV Tips

- *Advertise during off-peak hours.* Prime time has the most viewers and costs the most.
- *Go with cable.* Cable allows you to advertise on a station that targets your desired demographic and is much less expensive than the major networks.
- *Consider a media-buying service.* Television salespeople will quote you their standard rate card, maybe negotiate down a bit, but that's it. Media buyers charge a 7.5 percent fee but can easily save you more than that because they buy millions of dollars of advertising a month and have a lot more pull than you do.

The bottom line is that television makes sense for only a few small businesses. But if yours is one of those and you have both the time and war chest to do it right, you can reap tremendous rewards.

Radio

Radio is another medium that can allow you to target your audience, and therefore it can be a very effective advertising tool. However, like newspapers, it too is changing because of the Internet, as people increasingly listen to podcasts from iTunes and on Pandora and other sources. That said, radio is still radio, and radio still works. The following chart outlines what you might expect to pay (per minute) in the top 16 markets on top-rated stations (top three or so), secondary stations, and tertiary stations.

Market	Top Tier	Secondary	Tertiary
New York	$1,500	$1,000	$350
Los Angeles	$1,500	$1,000	$350
Chicago	$1,200	$ 800	$250
San Francisco	$1,000	$ 750	$250
Dallas	$1,000	$ 750	$250
Washington, DC	$1,000	$ 750	$250
Seattle	$1,000	$ 750	$250
Atlanta	$1,000	$ 750	$250
Boston	$ 850	$ 600	$175
Denver	$ 850	$ 600	$175
Philadelphia	$ 850	$ 600	$175
Houston	$ 750	$ 500	$150
Minneapolis	$ 750	$ 250	$150
Phoenix	$ 750	$ 250	$150
Baltimore	$ 500	$ 350	$100
Portland	$ 500	$ 350	$100

It is estimated that people have to hear an ad six times before it sinks in. So the key is repetition. The key is repetition. The key is repetition. What is the key? See? And, of course, repetition costs money.

The other key with radio, as with any media source, is that the station you pick must deliver your desired demographic audience. Speak with your sales rep and get verifiable information regarding the station and particular shows' audience size, rating points, listeners, age, and income.

The Internet

The number and types of ads that you can run online is almost dizzying: pay per click, banner ads, Craigslist ads, search engine ads, and so on. It is a topic worth its own chapter, and so it has. See Chapter 43 later in this book.

Magazines

Other than websites, magazines are the one medium that can target your audience best. There are simply so many magazines today that it should be easy to find one that your customers read. Magazine ads are not inexpensive, but magazines tend to stick around a house for months and are often read by many people. Therefore, you might get more bang for your advertising buck by advertising there.

Yellow Pages

Even with all of the changes wrought by the Internet, service businesses such as plumbers and locksmiths would probably be silly not to advertise in the phone book. That said, if your business model does not compete on price, the phone book may not be your best choice.

CREATING A WINNING AD

Knowing your objectives and media options helps you create an ad or series of ads that builds your business and allows you to fulfill your mission. There are many different theories about what makes a good ad; whole books have been written on the subject. But the truth is, if you are like most small business owners, you probably do not have the time to read yet another book. Here is an easy ad creation method that works. It is the

---

Yellow Pages Tips

- *Ask for a discount.* First-time advertisers should get as much as a 40 percent discount their first year.
- *Create a memorable ad.* Look through your phone book. Which ads catch your eye? Often, it's the ones with color, a picture, or a lot of white space. The problem with the Yellow Pages is that you are competing against a lot of ads for the same eyeballs, so you have to make your ad stick out.
- *Consider your category.* There might be several different sections in which you could place an ad. Figure out a few different categories for your business, and then see which one has the most ads. The odds are, the largest section is the one that is read the most.
- *Read.* A good book that you might want to get is *Yellow Page Advertising: How to Get the Greatest Return on Your Investment*, by Jeffrey Price.

---

tried-and-true AIDA method: Attention, Interest, Desire, and Action. The AIDA formula serves as a blueprint for creating a winning ad—any type of winning ad, be it online, in a magazine, or on radio, television, or wherever.

Attention

THE FIRST THING YOU HAVE TO DO IS GRAB THEIR ATTENTION! Once you do that, you can get potential customers interested in what you are selling, but if you do not get their attention up front, they will never hear a thing above the din of headline news, sports stories, and full-page ads. So first, you must hit your prospect with a powerful, benefit-laden headline.

An attention-getting headline (either print or electronic) must quickly capture potential customers' attention, get them to want to know more, and do so in a few seconds. For example:

- "Amazing New Technique Relieves Arthritis!"
- "Free Pamphlet Makes Your Computer as Easy to Use as a Telephone!"
- "Save 50% on Office Supplies—Today Only!"
- "The Lazy Man's Guide to Riches!"

The idea is to tease them enough to want to know, read, watch, or listen more.

Interest and Desire

So, you've grabbed their attention. Great. Then what? If a potential customer is reading your ad, it had better sell them or else your great headline will go to waste. You can do so by making a compelling offer in the body of the ad—describe the benefits of what you are selling in simple and interesting terms. To work, the interest and desire section of your ad must be well written, clearly explain the benefits to consumers, and keep their attention. You must explain, in easy-to-understand language, how your product fills the customer's need. If you solve some problem that customers have, and your ad explains that simply, bingo!

Action

Having grabbed their attention and shown them the benefits of buying from you, you must now ask for the order. Give incentives for customers to buy now, and make it easy to do so. This might involve a coupon, a toll-free number, an e-mail address, an online order form, a fax order line, or some other means to make it easy and simple to buy or call.

Here's an example of an AIDA ad:

Bankruptcy?
Free Seminar! Free Advice!
[*This headline captures the attention of someone who is in debt. Remember that "free" is the most powerful word in advertising.*]

This Thursday at 8:00 p.m. at the downtown Holiday Inn, local bankruptcy attorney Dave Rosenberg will be conducting a *free* bankruptcy seminar. All of your questions will be answered, and there is no cost and no obligation. [*Interest and desire*]

Seating is Limited. Call 448-9000 for Reservations.
www.freebankruptcyseminar.com
[*"Limited seating" is a call to action. The website can give more details.*]

If you follow the AIDA formula, you should find that your ad will work, no matter what medium you place it in.

TESTING THE AD

After coming up with your game plan and designing your ad, you need to be sure you are not making an expensive advertising mistake. Test the ad and make sure that it pulls. Testing the ad could mean many things. It may mean running a smaller version of the ad in print, then enlarging it or buying better placement once you are convinced that it pulls. It might mean running your radio spot on a less expensive station, or on a less expensive show, until you know it works.

Consider running the ad in different media sources at the same time, each with a different code that people need to use when responding ("Mention code 1122 when calling and get 10% off!"). That way, you will be able to track which ad in which source works best.

The important thing is that you avoid sinking a lot of money into an ad campaign until you know for sure that your ad and strategy work. After that, go for it!

The Worst Business Decision Ever?

In the history of bad business decisions, perhaps the worst of all was Coca-Cola's decision to scrap Coke and introduce New Coke. How could this have happened? If you are going to toss out "old" Coke, you might as well ban mom and outlaw apple pie while you are at it. At the time, Coca-Cola was being challenged by Pepsi. Nervous, executives at Coke began to secretly experiment with new formulations until they finally found one that beat Pepsi in taste tests. Convinced they had a winner, Coca-Cola triumphantly rolled out New Coke—to huzzahs and ridicule. The problem was, Coca-Cola never test-marketed New Coke. The marketing wizards at Coca-Cola never took batches of New Coke and tested them in stores in, say, Des Moines. Testing is key to avoiding expensive, painful belly flops.

ROLLING IT OUT

If you have created an ad that works, it is time to roll it out, for it is your meal ticket. Run it as often as you can afford, avoiding oversaturation of the market. Maybe you recall an infomercial a few years back in which an entrepreneur talked about how placing a "tiny little classified ad" could make you millions. The strategy was to find a product or service to sell, create a small, inexpensive classified ad, test it, and when the ad pulled, to roll that same exact ad out to hundreds of newspapers across the country. This is essentially what you should do. Once you find an ad that works, use it in as many places and as often as you can.

As you start this process, you will begin to meet and discuss pricing with a variety of media outlets. The first rule of media is this: *never pay the rate card*. The rate card is the price you will be quoted from the media outlet's book. Yes, sometimes inventory is tight and you will have to pay the rate card, but just know that is not always the case. If you will be buying a lot of time or space, or the outlet needs advertisers at that time, you can negotiate the rate card rates down. If you cannot negotiate down, see what else the outlet might offer you. It might be free response cards, better position at no extra cost, free color, or ads in a special edition.

Advertising is one of the most important things you do in business. If you do it right, your small business should reap the rewards.

CHAPTER **39**

Marketing Muscle

Marketing is not an event, but a process. . . . It has a
beginning, a middle, but never an end, for it is a process.
You improve it, perfect it, change it, even pause it. But you
never stop it completely.

—JAY CONRAD LEVINSON

Small businesses do not have unlimited funds—indeed, quite the opposite is true. Just as you need to be thoughtful about how best to use your
advertising dollars, you need to be equally intelligent about your marketing efforts. Both must clearly reinforce your business identity. Marketing,
advertising, and branding are the threads that make up the tapestry that is
your business image. Together, they constitute your most powerful weapons for getting people to notice you and buy from you. If these threads
are disparate, if your advertising does one thing while your marketing
does another, and neither reinforces your brand, your tapestry will be,
well, ugly. But if these threads reinforce one another, if they communicate a unified message, then your business image will be a tightly woven
fabric with a clear identity that people can recall. That is the plan. There
are so many small businesses out there competing against you for the
same customers that it is the ones with a rich, memorable tapestry that
get people to remember them above the din.

MARKETING OVERVIEW

Marketing, boiled down, is the combination of all your efforts to get people to remember your business. It includes everything—from how you

383

answer the phone to how you deal with complaints to how you design your signs, logos, letterhead, and promotions. Whereas advertising aims to bring in new clients, marketing not only does that but also helps keep them around. Marketing, more than anything else, is what builds your brand, and an identifiable brand is the hook that gets people to remember your business. And if they remember you, they will likely buy from you. That is why marketing and branding are so important.

Think of it this way: your business identity, your brand, is your business personality. It is what people remember. Just as we sometimes meet people with blah personalities who are easily forgettable, we all run across far too many small businesses with little, if any, personality. Forgettable businesses—what a waste. But by the same token, when you meet someone with a large, identifiable personality, you remember that person, just as you do when you run across a business with a distinctive personality.

Starbucks

Does Starbucks have a personality? You bet—hip, a bit laid back, and friendly. How did Starbucks create that brand? By consistently reinforcing it with everything it does. From the decor of its stores to the personality of its baristas to the choice of music played and sold in its stores—oh yes, and its coffee—Starbucks consistently tells you that it is a cool place to hang out, even if it does cost a bit more. That is what you want. You create that distinctive personality, that memorable brand, by marketing a consistent theme.

Peter Drucker, the guru of modern business, says that marketing is what your business looks like through the eyes of your customers. What do your customers see when they look at your business? A law office must appear stately because the matters that people need lawyers for are serious. Legal clients want to see excellence, so a law office needs embossed letterhead, a prestigious address, and a proficient receptionist, for starters. Its marketing materials must be professional and elegant. All are different aspects of an interwoven marketing campaign that is intended to get clients to believe in the firm enough to hire it.

Marketing is the process of getting customers and potential customers to perceive the value of what you offer. So many different marketing methods are available that it would be impossible to cover them all in a single chapter. This chapter is devoted to some of the most powerful, easily implementable ones. Chapter 19 covers scores of other ways to promote and grow your business with little money.

THE MARKETING PLAN

A marketing plan should not be new to you, but it probably is. If you drafted a business plan, your marketing plan made up a major section of that document, and it should be reviewed. However, the fact is, if you are like most small businesses, you have neither a business plan nor a marketing plan. That is fine. It is not required. The five-step process discussed in the previous chapter can easily be adopted here as well:

1. Think ahead. What is the purpose, size, and budget of your marketing campaign?
2. Decide what medium (or media) works best for your business, brand, and budget.
3. Come up with marketing materials that build on that brand.
4. Test the materials.
5. Once you are convinced that you have a marketing method that works, roll it out.

Just as you were advised to come up with an ad campaign and test it out before expanding it, you should do the same thing here. Review the myriad of marketing tools listed here, pick the ones that make the most sense for your business, test them out, and then go for it.

TOOLS YOU CAN USE

If you are like most small business people, you have already figured out a few marketing methods that work for you. It might be a stall at the Saturday market, a monthly seminar, a regular sale, or an incentive program for referrals. That is good. But if you are also like most small businesspeople, you have one or two or three methods at most. What I want you to do is think big. There are so many ways to market your business and get new customers that it would be a shame if you did not consider and implement some new options. Although your methods may work well now, the danger is that marketing materials eventually get stale and stop working. And even if they don't, the smart entrepreneur has many ways to bring in business, so that if one income stream slows down, others are in place to keep the money pumping.

> "If you're attacking your market from multiple positions and your competition isn't, you have all the advantage and it will show up in your increased success and income."
>
> —Jay Abraham

The Elevator Pitch

I do a lot of public speaking about business issues. A few years ago when I was beginning, I was talking to another speaker, lamenting how slow business was, and he asked what I talk about. "Well, small business success, basically," I replied. He was silent. After a pregnant pause, I finally asked, "What do *you* talk about?" He said something like, "I speak to organizations that want to energize and excite their employees, get them working together, help them understand their core values, and allow them to realize what it means to be a team. My speeches are dynamic and funny, and I leave audiences invigorated, committed, wanting more, and I usually get a standing ovation." Given our respective answers, which of us would you hire if you were planning an event and needed a speaker? I knew the answer, and it was not me. Ever since that illuminating encounter, I have been working on my elevator pitch.

We are all asked to explain what it is that we do. Having a quick, interesting, powerful answer is the simplest of marketing tools, yet it is also one of the most effective; it may lead to opportunities that we did not even know existed. As they say, you only have one chance to make a good first impression. You want to prepare a pitch that will spark someone's interest and have him or her saying, "Tell me more!"

Here are a few questions you must answer in order to create a great elevator pitch:

- *What problem are you trying to solve?* Every great business solves a problem for someone. Why do you go to the local store to buy bread? Because you have a need for bread, and the store solves it. What problem does your business solve?
- *Can you keep it simple?* Use plain English, be intriguing, and speak with conviction.

Example: There once was a Silicon Valley entrepreneur whose product protected digital signals. His original elevator pitch went something like this: "We utilize the latest 20–50 key exchange using Duffle transponders, blah blah blah." After getting some help, he ended up with this: "We protect communications."

- *Why would people want to know more?* Instead of saying, for instance, "I am a graphic artist," you might start with, "I help people get more business by illustrating their dreams."
- *Does it accelerate your heart rate?* A great pitch is a passionate pitch.

Here's your basic pitch: "Hi. I'm Mara Sydney, president of Jillian Publishing. We publish architecture books." Here is an elevator pitch: "Hi, I'm Mara Sydney, president of Jillian Publishing. We publish books, newsletters, and video programs designed to help architects, drafters, and urban planners become more successful. Our best-selling title, *How to Become the Recognized Expert in Your Field*, was named Specialty Book of the Year by *Architecture Magazine*."

Networking

Of course you should network, you know that, and most of us probably believe it. But sometimes that is easier said than done. First of all, networking takes time, second, it is not always easy, and third, social networking may be taking more and more of your time. Yet even so, some of your best prospects will undoubtedly still come from networking in person, face to face, whether it is at a chamber of commerce social, a meeting of a group like LeTip, or some other social situation.

Much of business is about relationships. Indeed, it is not what you know but *who* you know, and networking ensures that you know more people. Is it occasionally uncomfortable to make chitchat with people you do not know? Sure. But here is some motivation. According to the book *The Millionaire Next Door,* most self-made millionaires network all the time, wherever they are: at the car wash, on the golf course, or at a business conference. They recognize that they never know which contact may be a big deal or lead to a big deal.

Here are two tips for making networking easier:

1. *Use your elevator pitch.* Having a prepackaged, snappy opener is a great segue into a more meaningful conversation.
2. *Pretend you are the host.* Rather than sitting back and waiting for something to happen at the event, flip the situation around and pretend you are the host. How would you act? That's right—gregarious, self-assured, and positive.

Form a Strategic Partnership

We are not called *small* business owners for nothing. According to the SBA, of the roughly 29 million small businesses in this country, 23 million have no employees. Of the remaining 6 million with employees, the vast majority have 10 or fewer. The point is that we often need help. A large corporation has plenty of resources that we do not have—marketing departments, accounting—you know the drill.

One of the best ways to get around this dilemma and to grow your business (that, after all, is the purpose of marketing) is to team up with other businesses that are after the same customers and with which you have some synergy. With the right strategic partner, you can combine and leverage—*for very little extra money*—your respective distribution networks, infrastructure, and knowledge for greater success. The teamwork could, for example, entail cross-promoting each other's product or jointly creating new products. For instance, a veterinarian and a local pet store might agree to cross-promote each other in their respective establishments.

To make a strategic partnership work for you, consider the following:

- *Is the other business congruent with yours?* Do you have the same goals? You need to discuss and agree on the purpose of the partnership and what each side expects.
- *What are the downsides to the deal?* Brainstorm both the positive and the negative.
- *Is the deal a win-win?* Negotiate viable commitments that both sides can live with. How will disagreements be resolved?
- *What is the exit strategy?* Having a set of definable objectives allows you to know when the partnership is and is not working. What will trigger an end to the deal?

Marketing and the Self-Employed

If you work for yourself, be sure to check out my site TheSelfEmployed. com, where you will find all sorts of strategies specifically designed for the solopreneur.

Direct Marketing

Direct mail is one of the oldest and most tried-and-true marketing methods around. Using direct mail letters, flyers, coupons, and reply envelopes, you can sell your products or services to qualified prospects, increase awareness of your business, and create new customers. For instance, if you own an Italian restaurant, you could send out a flyer to all homes within a 3-mile radius offering a free glass of wine with dinner. No doubt that would create some new customers in the process.

Using the mail, you can announce a big sale, offer a new product, or provide a 10 percent off coupon (insert your idea here). The point is, direct marketing allows you to get your business noticed.

Creating a successful direct marketing campaign is a threefold process. First, you must find a letter, offer, flyer, or coupon that works. This is a matter of testing, testing, and more testing. Again, start small, tinker, and analyze the results. A restaurant might try sending that free wine offer to one-third of the homes in the area, a 10 percent off coupon to another third, and a free child's dinner to the last third. After tabulating the results, the owner would then know which coupon pulled best and could then send it out every four months or so.

The second step is to obtain a usable list. One of the nice things about direct marketing is that not only is it a chance to attract new customers, but it is equally valuable in helping you stay in contact with present customers. Your list could be self-generated, if the goal of the campaign is to get old customers back into the store. If the goal, however, is to find new business, then you need a broader list. You can buy lists from list brokers and you can be very specific about the type of audience you are trying to attract when you buy your list: "I want a list of homeowners in the surrounding five counties," or "I want a list of men aged 25–34," or any other criteria that describe your target market.

The final step in a successful direct marketing campaign is to get people to read your offer and respond. Here is how:

- Depending on the size of the mailing, consider hiring some high school kids you know to address the envelopes. Are you more likely to open an envelope addressed by hand than one that is computer generated? Your potential customers are, too.
- Put something chunky in it. A bulky letter is more apt to be opened as well.
- Remember that an effective offer answers the question that is foremost in the reader's mind: "What's in it for me?" You must offer something that customers want; saving time or money often works.
- Remember, YOU MUST GRAB THEIR ATTENTION, QUICKLY.
- Use a conversational tone, deliver credibility—customer testimonials are great, as are guarantees—and give them an incentive to act. An expiration on the offer works well.
- Be patient. Often, several letters are needed to get a response, and even then, remember that a good direct mail campaign response rate is about 5 percent. But think about it. If you send direct mail to 1,000 potential customers, it will cost about $500. How much will you make with 50 new customers?
- P.S. Always include a P.S. because they are almost always read. The postscript is a great place to reiterate the offer.

Have a Sale

What will you be announcing in your direct mail piece? Often it is a sale. A sale is one of the most powerful tools in your marketing tool chest. It reinforces your good name with old customers, helps attract new customers, gets rid of unwanted inventory, and creates a buzz, all at once. Not bad!

As with a direct mail campaign, obtaining a good list is critical to a successful sale. The most important thing you can do to create a successful sale is to develop your customer mailing list. An up-to-date, good list of even 500 people is far more valuable than, say, an unqualified list of 5,000. Begin creating your list by asking your regular customers to fill out a preferred customer card. Add them to your list. When customers write you checks, even if they don't fill out the preferred membership application, copy their names and addresses onto your list. Obtain membership lists from local organizations such as clubs and churches. Finally, buy a list if you must. When buying a list, make sure that you do not overspend for unqualified names. Be selective. And of course, don't forget to tap your social media contacts list as well.

Sales are loss leaders. You need to mark down enough items for the sale to be worth your customers' time, but not so many that you lose money. Markdowns are critical to the profitability of your sale. Generally, product that is less than four months old should be marked down no more than 30 percent. Product that is less than eight months old should be marked down no more than 50 percent. Items older than eight months can be marked down 75 percent. If you have product that is eight months old, move it—it is taking up valuable space for product that can be turned over again and again. Because sales allow you to convert inventory to cash, be aggressive when pricing old merchandise.

Before the sale, you need to get your store ready. Of course you need to spruce things up, but beyond that, be sure to:

- Mark everything clearly with the reduced price. Make it easy for your customers to buy
- Put everything out where it can be seen and touched
- Organize everything and have it arranged by size and category
- Get signs ready

During the sale:

- Know that the first week of the sale will always be the busiest. Be sure that you have plenty of inventory and that the shelves are stocked.
- Continue to keep displays full. Customers will not buy if they think the best deals have already been had.
- Watch for slow-moving merchandise and mark it down more if necessary. Something is better than nothing, and space for better-selling merchandise beats the clutter of old merchandise.
- Create a buzz. Talk about what a great deal this or that is. Have big signs or balloons. Your outdoor "Sale!" signs are vital. Use different signs to attract attention.

The Entrepreneur

At Carpet World in Los Angeles, the owner (my dad) put up a huge sign in the middle of the store that proclaimed, "Our Word of Mouth Advertising Starts with You!"

Brochures

When you leave a new car showroom, what do you leave with? A beautiful, glossy brochure. For the right business, a brochure can be the most important marketing method. It is a chance to put your best foot forward, proudly display who you are, what you offer, why it is unique, and why people should buy from you. If a customer asks for a brochure, it is a rare chance to present your best offer, so be sure that you create a top-notch one. Here's how:

- *Brainstorm.* Meet with your team and get their input. Find out what they think is important to have in the brochure. What do your customers need to know? What sells them? What needs do they have that you can fulfill, and why can you fulfill it best?
- *Decide on the purpose of the brochure.* What is the role of the brochure in your overall marketing efforts? Will it be a tool for your salespeople? Will it be used at a trade show? Will it be offered at the point of sale?

- *Consider the competition.* If your competitors have a slick brochure, can you legally use some of their ideas? At the very least, know what your competitors' brochures look like and strive to best them.
- *Determine your budget.* Creating a brochure used to be an expensive proposition: graphic artists, layout and design, and printing costs were not inexpensive. But today, things are much different. If you have (or buy) the right software program and learn to use it yourself or assign that task to a staff member, creating a brochure in house should not be expensive at all.
- *Create a mockup.* You do not have to, and should not try to, get every important fact crammed into the brochure. This may be a case in which less is more. People are busy and do not like reading a lot of copy. Get the essential ideas across. Get them to want to know more. Use color, words, and pictures to spark interest.
- *Print it.* Even if you do not have access to a color printer, you can always go to FedEx Office or the like. Of course, you can always use a commercial printer. In this case, you will be dealing with a professional and should get excellent results. It is good to remember that you do not have to anymore.

Publicity

A newspaper, magazine, or online article about your business or a radio or television segment can do more than almost anything to market and build your business. If you want to know how small businesses become big businesses, here is a trait they all have in common: at a critical moment in the growth of the company, the business invests in public relations and gets a lot of publicity. That publicity is then parlayed into additional business and more publicity, and a boom is born.

But even if growing large is not your goal, you should not bypass the opportunities that await by getting some timely publicity. That article or story is independent verification of what a great business you have created. For starters, the people who see the story will be tempted to patronize your business and check it out for themselves. Even better, however, is that you can tape or copy the show or article and use it forever in your marketing materials. Say that you own a chain of flower shops, and you get your local TV station to do a story about your business. Maybe the hook is Mother's Day or Valentine's Day—it does not matter. What matters is that the video can be posted on your site and mentioned in all your shops. A quote can be pulled and used in subsequent advertising: "Beautiful stores with a great selection," says the *Chronicle*.

To top it off, getting publicity is quite cost-effective. What would it cost to get on the front page of the business section, even if you could? What would it cost to get a 3-minute segment during the local news? Now compare that with the cost of hiring a public relations firm, or even just doing it yourself, and you begin to see the bargain that is publicity.

Tips From the Pro

One of the top PR firms in the country is Emanate, with offices in Los Angeles, New York, and Europe. The CEO is the smart and savvy Kim Sample. According to Sample, one thing that small businesses should really consider is the use of publicity in the area of "thought leadership." For example, if you sell solar panels, a thought leadership area would be trends in solar power for homes and businesses. By positioning yourself with the media to be the go-to person on a given issue, by becoming a top thought leader in your field, you can set yourself apart from the competition. According to Sample, doing so is a 6-step process:

1. Analyze what thought leadership topics can benefit you and your business.
2. Look at the media options in that area; who covers this topic?
3. Figure out where you and your business fit into that media landscape.
4. Figure out what you have to say that is unique and valuable.
5. Contact the media with your message. Be consistent, stay on message, and follow up.
6. Once you have some success, use your social media and other online assets to multiply your effectiveness, output, and reach.

Kim also suggests that it is important for the small business to know when they can do their own PR and when it is time to hire an agency. The questions you need to answer are: Do you like to promote your business and are you good at it? There are times when hiring a professional can make a huge difference, especially if PR is not your forte. When hiring a firm, "Make sure you explain what PR success will look like to you so your PR partner understands what you expect them to accomplish," she says. When choosing

(continued)

a PR agency, Sample suggests that it is often smarter for a small business to go with a single practitioner or smaller agency as opposed to a bigger one, so that you won't be a small fish in a big pond.

Finally, if you do decide to do it yourself sans agency, Sample suggests the following:

- Shoot to get coverage in trade journals and local media—they are easier to get.
- Create relationships with local reporters, editors, and producers. You may even suggest meeting them at some community event.
- Remember, it takes time to get results, so stay committed.

Editors, bloggers, writers, and producers have to come up with new stories every day. There is no reason why you or your business shouldn't help them feed the hungry monster that is their daily story requirement. The way to do so is to give them a new hook. They are not in the promotions business; they do not care whether your business gets publicity or not. They are in the news business, and what they do care about is finding a newsworthy story. So if you are going to succeed in getting on the air, you need to couch your desires as news. You must give them a hook and get their attention.

How do you do that?

First, think like an editor. That is, consider things from their perspective. Like most of us today, they are busy, too busy. So you must craft a pitch that is quick, simple, and which has a unique hook or angle. Personally, for me, I find that an informal pitch via e-mail is the way to go. Yes, we are taught to draft a who-what-where-when-and-why press release, but mostly I think those get ignored these days—too wordy, too formal, too old school. An e-mail addressed to the writer in question, which clearly indicates that you know the person's writing and beat, is what works best.

There are several ways to intrigue your reporter:

- Indicate that you are doing something in the public interest (e.g., sponsoring a beach cleanup day).

- Pitch an innovative product or service that can help the readers or viewers.
- Have something significant to say or share.
- Create a publicity stunt. GM gave Oprah's audience members a new Pontiac. Priceless publicity, that.

So the essential steps are these: Research and locate the right reporter who covers stories like the one you want to pitch. Craft a hook and pitch that is newsworthy. Send the writer a personal, short, snappy e-mail. Be friendly and accessible. Follow up, but don't be a pest.

The next chapter dives into all of these strategies in more detail.

CHAPTER 40

Advanced Marketing and Advertising

Advertising is the "wonder" in Wonder Bread.

—Jeff I. Richards

There's an adage about advertising and dogs that is pretty true, and once, I had the dog to prove it. Her name was Gert. A wonderful black Lab, she was sweet, smart, beautiful, and gentle—everything you could hope for in a dog. But, like most dogs (and cats for that matter), Gert hated it when she had to swallow a pill. She would spit that pill out as fast as she could. Then I got wise and learned that the only way to get Gert to swallow a pill was to wrap it in something tasty. I usually stuck it in a hunk of cheese. She would gobble the cheese up, pill and all—a spoonful of sugar and all that.

Well, as the tale goes, your advertising is not unlike that pill. Customers don't really like ads. They try to avoid them and spit them out by turning the page or zapping through them. So what do you do? You need to wrap your ads in some sort of tasty metaphorical cheese, of course—then they become much more appealing. Your cheese may be a great benefit, or humor, or maybe a catchy jingle. Whatever it is, the idea is to make your ads appetizing. Do that, and they will get noticed, and your business will grow.

ADVANCED MARKETING

Increasingly, business marketing is moving online using a variety of new tools: social media, YouTube, Facebook, and e-newsletter and search engine advertising, for starters. All of these new e-tools will be discussed later in this book. This chapter is devoted to a detailed examination of more old-school methods for marketing and advertising your business.

Getting More Referrals

Want more referrals and word-of-mouth business? Then ask for it! Create a referral form and give it to satisfied customers and clients. Then give them an incentive to return it to you—a discount on a future purchase, a trinket, something. Then use the referrals in your other marketing endeavors: post them in the shop or online, use them in ads, and so on. Presto! Instant word of mouth.

SUCCESSFUL ADVERTISING

What works in advertising? Well, ask yourself this question: What works on you? Begin to notice what sorts of ads catch your fancy. Open newspapers and magazines, review websites, listen to and watch ads on television and radio, and begin to notice which ads stick out, and then ask yourself why. Usually it is a combination of the following factors.

The Medium Matches the Message

Great ads begin when you know exactly which people you are targeting. Once you know that, your job is much easier, and conversely, if you don't know, you are wasting your money. Too many small businesses, especially early in their life cycles, try to appeal to everyone. A few expensive lessons later, they learn that they only have to reach a few key people—their niche, their market. Begin by figuring out which people, exactly, you are creating this advertisement for: their age, sex, income level, what they want from you, and so on. Once you know your market, choosing the right medium is much easier.

Benefits, Benefits, Benefits

Think about those times when you are looking to buy a certain model car. All of a sudden, you begin to see that car everywhere, right? The reason is psychological: the brain filters a lot of information every day, but when you focus on something new, whether it is a car or whatever, it's a signal to the brain that the information need not be filtered out anymore. The benefit of the new thing is allowed to seep through.

Writing Better Ads

Beyond the AIDA method outlined in the last chapter, here are some other techniques for making your ads pop:

- *Use creative visuals.* Not everyone likes to read.
- *Be unpredictable!* No: "Anderson's Market is having a sale." Yes: "Tomatoes Shocked by Low Prices! Vine-ripened tomatoes at Anderson's Market were justifiably upset Thursday when they learned they were being sold for $1."
- *Use words and phrases people will remember.* Bad: "Anderson's is the Place for Vegetables." Good: "Anderson's: Where Tomatoes and Potatoes are First-Rate-O." Rhymes, alliteration, and creativity work well.

That's how good advertising works, too. You may never notice an ad, even if that ad typically runs again and again . . . until you have a need for what the ad is selling. So it is incumbent on you to stress the benefits of what you are selling, not its features; people zero in and remember benefits.

It's Been Tested

As indicated, it is always smart to test an ad first to see whether it works and then tweak it as necessary. Testing can improve:

- *The headline.* Because the headline is the most important part of any ad, testing to see what works is important. Try different words or graphics.
- *The cost.* Does a big ad pull that much better than a small ad? You might be able to keep a big headline with a smaller ad and save money.
- *Success rates.* Throwing a lot of money at an untested ad is risky business.

There are a few ways to test an ad:

- *"Mention this ad."* Of course, the most tried-and-true way is simply to ask. "Bring in this ad and get an additional 10 percent off."

- *Use a lower price.* Offer those tomatoes for a quarter on a certain day and see how many you sell. This loss leader strategy helps you learn who is seeing your ads.
- *Use two prices.* Mention one discount in one publication or station and a different, albeit similar discount, in a different one. The prices can't be too different because that will skew the results.

Frequency

When it comes to advertising, as I have said repeatedly in this book, repetition is the key. How much repetition? The short answer is *as much as you can afford.* If you want people to notice that ad, then it simply has to be repeated and repeated and repeated. Of course it depends on your budget, but just know that buying an ad and not repeating it is a waste of money.

How these factors play out in different media varies a lot. So let's look more closely at those media discussed in Chapter 38 and see how they work.

NEWSPAPERS

Yes, the newspaper business is, if not dying, at least pretty darn sick. Like everything else, advertising is increasingly moving online, and newspapers are bearing the brunt of that shift. But many people still read the newspaper, and companies still advertise there. The reason is simple: when it works, newspaper advertising is great. You reach a large number of people, and you can specifically target your ads to the right section. Generally, newspaper advertising these days is best for reaching people aged 40 and older who are still in the habit of reading the paper daily. That simply is not true for Generation X and those younger.

So there are pros and cons to newspaper advertising.

Pros and Cons

The pros are that:

- Newspapers have quick deadlines, which means quick responses.
- People don't avoid newspaper ads as much as they do, say, television ads, which they can fast forward through with their DVRs. In fact, some people buy the paper for the ads.

- Your ad could be big or small, expensive or inexpensive, in color or black and white.
- You are not limited to 30 to 60 seconds to get your point across.

The cons are that:

- There is lots of competition for eyeballs. Between feature stories and other ads, it may take a lot to get your ad to stand out.
- It can be cost-prohibitive to do it right.
- The ad is obsolete as soon as the next edition comes out tomorrow.

Creative Newspaper Ideas

How do you make newspaper advertising work given the changing nature of the business and our changing lifestyles? Here are some options:

- *Weekend editions.* People read more leisurely on the weekend and take more time reading the paper. Papers are increasingly aware of this and are beefing up their weekend offerings. Bonus: Saturdays are less expensive.
- *Neighborhoods.* Advertise only in areas where you get the most business.
- *Special sections.* Throughout the year, the paper will print special editions devoted to gardening, entertaining, or whatever. Find the one that fits you; they are scheduled long in advance.
- *The Internet connection.* Use your ad to drive people to your website, where they can really see what you are offering. Also, advertise on the paper's website for a fraction of the cost.

Words That Work

Best words for getting your ad noticed: *free, sale, last chance, guaranteed, secrets, supply is limited, new.*

MAGAZINES

Much of the advice given for newspapers applies equally here, especially with regard to the graphics of the ad. There are, however, some significant differences. First, magazine advertising is usually more expensive than newspaper advertising because magazines have a longer shelf life and, often, a larger circulation. Second, because there are so many magazines and they are so specialized, it is fairly easy to pick one that will put you in front of your target market.

Prices vary a lot. At one end of the spectrum, you might expect to pay well in excess of $100,000 to advertise on the back cover of a national magazine. Alternatively, advertising in the regional edition of a smaller magazine can easily be done for less than a grand. How much you will spend and how big your reach will be depends on the circulation of the magazine. As with newspaper advertising, you will pay less if you sign a contract and agree to run in multiple issues. That's smart (repetition being the key and all), *but only if you test the ad first and make sure that it works.*

The Web Connection

When advertising in magazines, inquire about running your ad on their websites, too. Most magazines offer very reasonable rates for concurrent magazine advertisers.

Although magazine advertising is an excellent way to target an audience and create sales, consider these other benefits of magazine advertising:

- *It builds the brand.* The same ad, run again and again, creates an impression in the minds of readers. By listing national products in your ad, not only are you eligible for co-op dollars (see Chapter 19), but also you will be cobranding with national brands.
- *It creates legitimacy.* Running an ad in a magazine is considered more prestigious than ads in some other media, and because the ad can be reproduced and displayed later, the legitimacy has a long shelf life. This also means you do not have to compete as much on price, which is always good.
- *It can remove obstacles.* Words such as "100% Guaranteed" or "Checks Accepted" make people more willing to shop with you.
- *It can make you look bigger than you are.* Advertising in, say, a regional edition of a national magazine gives you gravitas.

RADIO

As indicated, radio is changing, too. With the advent of satellite and Internet radio, people have far more choices when it comes to what they listen to. Nevertheless, traditional radio remains a valuable tool in your advertising arsenal because, despite all of the competition for attention, people still listen to the radio—at work, in the car, and at home.

If you want to succeed in your radio campaign, here are three rules to follow:

1. *Pick the right station.* It does not matter how great your ad is, how clever it is, or even whether you're "giving them away!" If you pick the wrong station, the ad is dead on arrival. The people who need to hear it, who might buy what you are selling, will never hear it. It is a waste of money. So you have to know whom your ad is targeting and find stations with the same demographic. You discover this by calling the station, speaking with an ad rep, getting a sales kit, and looking at the listening audience's demographics.

2. *Have a creative ad.* As you have seen repeated throughout this chapter, your headline is vital. After that, the key with radio is to be engaging and creative. Radio is a medium that takes place between the ears; people must use their imaginations to make it work. Whether that means telling a story or using wacky sound effects is up to you. It is important to be creative, engage people, and capture their interest. And, although it is vital that your ad be memorable and clever, the ad also must answer the basic question in the minds of the listeners: "What's in it for me?"

3. *Buy as much frequency as you can afford.* More than almost any other medium (save television), radio requires frequency. It is said people have to hear an ad six times before they really *hear* it. In addition, listeners change stations, tune out ads, and talk on the phone while listening, so you have to repeat the same message again and again to get it heard above the din. How many ads do you need to buy? As a general rule of thumb, on any given station, no fewer than 15 is preferable during a week, and 25 or more is desirable. And, if you do pick your station carefully, then the right people will hear your ad every time it runs, month after month, year after year even.

Getting the Best Rates

Radio advertising rates are usually more affordable during the first and third quarters of the year. The fourth quarter is expensive because the time is snagged by holiday advertisers. Election seasons are also expensive.

TELEVISION

Television is the 800-pound gorilla of traditional advertising because it works. That said, it most certainly is not for everyone. Like other forms of media, one of the best things about television advertising is that it is fairly simple to match your target market to a station's or show's demographics. When you get that right, and you have a good ad that people notice, the results can really be terrific—television is not the big gorilla for nothing. By the same token, when it does not work, it can be a financial disaster, so tread carefully.

The challenge and opportunity of television has to do with its reach. Because you will be reaching a large audience when you advertise on television, you should expect that it will cost accordingly. How much? One 30-second spot in the afternoon may cost $250 (depending on the station and city, of course). That same ad during the evening news may cost $750 or more. During prime time, it may be double that. Overnight, it could drop to $50. It all depends on how many people you will be reaching. Then, multiply that number by the required frequency you will need, and you begin to see how much this can run you.

The first thing to consider is whether you need to reach that many people. Ask yourself:

- Do I have a business that has regional appeal?
- Would people be willing to drive across town to come to my business?
- Can I afford to advertise often enough to get people to notice, remember, and act on my ad?
- Is there a better, more cost-effective use for my advertising dollar?
- If my ad works, can I handle the increased traffic that will result?

Like radio, frequency is an important element of successful television advertising. You simply must air your ad a lot to get people to act on it. This is even more difficult in this age of DVR, when people zip past the commercials. It is also expensive to produce a good ad, so the costs add up. Between creating the ad and buying enough time to make the ad work, expect to pay tens of thousands of dollars. How can you keep your costs down? Here are some ways.

Test

The first thing to do is to test your ad to make sure it works before rolling it out. Try it on cable television for starters. Overnight television, although a vastly smaller audience, is also vastly less expensive. Testing your ad at inexpensive times allows you to get a feel for it and avoid making an expensive mistake.

> **Quiz**
>
> How many stations do you think most people watch? Despite the glut of choices, the answer is fewer than 15. Of those, most are network stations, and the rest are top cable stations, such as CNN and ESPN.

Negotiate

Everything is negotiable, even the television rate card. You can also get a better deal if you sign a contract, say, for 6 or 12 months. But do that only after you are sure the ad works.

Cable and Other Inexpensive Options

Cable television rates are far less expensive because the audience is much smaller. If you decide to advertise on cable, make sure you specifically choose which stations and shows you will be on. Ending up on the "broad rotator" schedule, although cheaper, means that your ads will be placed anywhere, anytime, and thus you won't get the frequency you need in front of the people you desire to make a difference you will see. Also consider overnight and weekend ads.

Have a Good Ad

A good ad is de rigueur. Here's how to get one:

- *Hire a good production company.* Make sure the company you choose is professional and established. Shop around, look at the ads they have produced, compare prices, and get references. Tell them what you want and get their feedback and ideas.
- *Be creative and unique.* Why do people remember those Super Bowl commercials? Because they are clever.
- *Repeat vital info.* Always repeat your phone number, website, and other branding tools (logos, catchphrase, phone number, etc.).

DIRECT MAIL

Start by figuring out what you want to sell and coming up with a strong mailer. The mailer you use must incorporate all of the ideas presented in this chapter: strong headlines, benefits, a call to action, good graphics—the works. Then send that mailer to that great list of potential repeat customers.

Here's the deal on buying a list: most lists have a 5,000 name minimum, and costs can range from $40 per 1,000 to more than $250. Given that, you can see why creating a new, repeat customer is important; doing so will help pay for that list many times over. Direct mail lists are divvied up by age, race, gender, household income, geography, and a whole host of other factors. A list broker will help you figure out which demographics to target with your mailing.

Other things to consider when choosing a list include:

- How recently it was compiled
- How often it has been purchased

A good direct mail list will allow you to make a compelling offer to a potential customer who has a recent, specific history of buying or needing the product or service you have to offer. Do that, and a whole new world of potential customers is yours.

CREATIVE AD PLACEMENT

Lester once had unique business cards printed. On one side was his regular card. The other side was printed to look like a folded $20 bill. He would then hire kids in the neighborhood to drop the fake $20s around town, and people would get $20 off when the cards were "redeemed." Hokey? Sure. But memorable.

Unconventional advertising is great because, not only is it usually different, but also it need not cost a fortune. In Tokyo, Apple lined the main train station with huge posters containing hundreds of cardboard iPod cutouts. Commuters were encouraged to peel them off and take them home. Or what about wrapping your car (or paying to wrap other cars) in your business name and logo?

The unusual can be as simple as advertising where you don't normally advertise. What about renting a hot air balloon or using a smaller rooftop balloon to draw attention to your short-term promotion or advertising campaign? The Internet casino Golden Palace once won an eBay auction for the right to print "GoldenPalace.com" on 100 cows grazing by the side of a major highway. Or consider these ideas:

- Putting your logo in sand at the beach (yes, companies do that)
- Having your logo projected onto any surface
- Advertising on golf carts or hospitality carts
- Having signs at health clubs and spas

Obviously, there are plenty of creative advertising ideas. Check them out and try something new.

PART
II

Your Website

CHAPTER **41**

Creating Your Website

Give a person a fish and you feed them for a day; teach
that person to use the Internet and they won't bother you
for weeks.

—Anonymous

In the first edition of this book, I began this section by stating, "I am assuming you have a website." That was a wrong assumption in the first
edition, and it still was in the second edition in 2008, and even here, in
the third edition of this book, at least 25 percent of small businesses still
do not have a website. Unbelievable. At a time when it is easier than ever
to market your business online to people far and wide, when getting a site
has never been cheaper or easier, and when having a site is as essential as
having a business card or phone number, not having a website constitutes
small business malpractice.

Why, then, do some businesses insist on *not* having a site, or, if they
do have one, not having a good site? The usual answer is that it is too
expensive, too time-consuming, or unnecessary. All are faulty assumptions. As I will show you in this chapter, these days it is incredibly easy to
create a great, professional website, and often it is free. And as for
whether it is necessary or not, just consider this statistic: 8 in 10 Americans now spend as much time online as they do watching television.

Or consider this anecdotal experience: Recently, my wife called and
asked me to pick up dinner on the way home from the office. She mentioned a restaurant we like, so I jumped online to look at its website and
check out the menu. But I couldn't find the menu because I couldn't find

411

the website—it didn't exist. I ended up going to a different restaurant. Multiply that experience by many customers, and you can see why even the smallest of businesses must have some web presence, even if it is only a limited one. These days, a website has become a basic way, and in some cases *the* way, for people to get a hold of you and learn more about your business. It is the twenty-first-century equivalent of putting up a sign.

PRELIMINARY CONSIDERATIONS

One of the best things about the Internet, from a small business perspective, is that it levels the playing field. Offline, small businesses look, well, small. People can see how big (or small) your business really is, how many employees it has, and so on. But the Internet is the great equalizer. Online, there is no reason whatsoever to look small. Your site can be every bit as powerful and professional as that of any huge conglomerate. On the web, you can have a great-looking site that impresses all who see it, and no one ever needs to know that you run your business out of your spare bedroom. The Internet is the great equalizer.

Example: Tim Carter started his e-commerce site, AskTheBuilder.com, in 1995, when few people were online. On his fourth sales call, he sold a banner ad for $12,000—and that was before the site was even launched!

That creating a nice site is increasingly easy means that there is simply no excuse for not having a site or, maybe worse, for having a bad one. You don't want one of those sites that looks as if your teenager created it. You know the ones I am talking about: the home page scrolls on forever, the graphics are jarring and amateurish, and it seems as if no one has visited the site since 2000 or so. No, you don't want that. What you want is an elegant, professional, aesthetically pleasing site that impresses customers—would-be and actual customers alike.

Having such a site offers multiple benefits for your business:

- *It creates credibility.* People will think more of your business if you have a professional site. It fosters legitimacy. More and more, people check out business websites right before becoming a customer—as part of the decision-making process or right after—to confirm that they made the right decision. Conversely, like the restaurant I chose not to go to because I couldn't find its site, bad sites or no site create the exact opposite effect—people may assume that your business is not professional, or at least not the type of business they want to frequent.

- *It is a marketing bonanza.* Everything is trending online, and if you are not there, you are going to miss out on the action. Recall the statistic I mentioned at the beginning of this chapter—most people spend as much time online as they do watching television. And because your website is essentially a very affordable e-billboard, the opportunity to market your business through your website is one you cannot miss out on.
- *It is a potential new profit center.* Your site can easily become a 24/7 source of new business.

If you want to take advantage of these potential benefits and others, then there are a few decisions you must make up front:

- *What type of site will it be?* There are basically three types of sites you can have:
  1. *Informational.* An informational site is the most basic type of website. It tells the world what your business is and does. This sort of site has a home page and a few inner pages: "About us," your location, contact information, and so on. It is your e–Yellow Page ad.
  2. *Marketing.* More extensive than a site that just dispenses information, a marketing site gives more detailed information and offers content that engages the visitor. You use e-marketing tools to drive customers to the site, and once people get there, the site endeavors to sell them on your product or service.
  3. *E-commerce.* Think Amazon.com, a site devoted to selling to you. Your e-commerce site, although smaller, would essentially do the same thing. E-commerce sites are profit centers unto themselves.

Example: Coastal Tool and Supply was a small local hardware store in Hartford, Connecticut, when it opened in 1980. After going online in 1995, it became one of the largest discount tool outlets in the country. Check it out at www.coastaltool.com.

- *How much time, money, and effort are you willing to put into the site?* Of course, a smaller site requires less effort and almost no money. On the other end of the spectrum, elaborate e-commerce sites can be very costly and may require all of your resources. Most small business sites will fall somewhere in between.

As you begin to plan your site, keep in mind that it is pretty easy these days to get a beautiful, simple site up and running in less than an hour. Of course, that is not always the case; my site, MrAllBiz.com, for instance, took several months and iterations before we were able to relaunch it. The question is, how extensive do you want your site to be?

Begin by looking at sites that you like or that are similar to the one you want to build. Make a list of what you like and dislike. What is the content like? What products are sold? What about the aesthetics of the site—what can be improved and what can be borrowed? (Legally, of course.) You do not need to reinvent the wheel. Figure out what you like and think will be attractive to your customers and start there.

Keep in mind that in this era of Web 2.0, what people expect from and like in a site has changed. Passive reading is out, and interactive participation is in. Internet users want to read, watch, listen, chat, comment, post, and play. The more interactive tools you have on your site, the greater the likelihood that people will stick around for a while and even come back. Among the sticky tools to consider are:

- Articles and other content
- Blogs
- Videos
- Polls and quizzes
- Excerpts and reviews
- Webinars

- E-newsletters
- Products and services
- Podcasts
- Forums and message boards

Sticky

The term *sticky* comes from Malcolm Gladwell's book *The Tipping Point.* What does he mean by that term? According to Gladwell, the term was used to describe television shows such as "*Sesame Street* and *Blue's Clues* . . . [which] started epidemics of learning among pre-schoolers by creating 'sticky' programming—programming engineered in such a way that children were able to remember and understand what they saw on the screen."

CREATING YOUR SITE

Once you know what your site will do and what you want it to look like, the next step is to get it built. You have three choices, but by far the last one rocks the others for most small businesses.

Do It Yourself

There is no shortage of software out there that you can buy and learn that will help you get your business online. The key word is *learn*. If you are savvy with this sort of thing, then by all means, go for it. But if you have never before used a graphics program, expect a steep learning curve. This is certainly not the best way to go for most small businesses. It will take too long, and the results may be sketchy.

Hire a Web Developer

If yours is going to be a more complicated site or needs special attention, then one way to go is to hire a web designer, which can be a very smart move if you get the right one. You can find web developers by doing an online search, of course, but also check out Craigslist as well as Elance or ODesk which are sites that allow you to post your project and get bids from freelancers.

Next, find some developers you like and check them out—I mean *really check them out.* There are plenty of irresponsible ones out there. Look at:

- Their background
- Their track record (get references and call them)
- Their portfolio
- What sort of program they will be using to create your site;
- Whether you will own the copyright
- Whether you will be able to take what they create and easily update your site

I cannot stress enough how important it is to find a reliable web designer with a solid track record. Dropping thousands into a site that does not work or, worse, never gets finished is not a pleasant experience.

So, what should you expect to pay to have a site designed for you? I received bids that ranged from $2,500 to $75,000. So it really helps to shop your project around. And consider this: web design is one of those things that can easily be done remotely, so you're not stuck hiring someone in your area. In fact, you will probably find that you can locate qualified people at a lower price if you open your search nationwide, or even worldwide. I have a business associate who lives in San Francisco (the city's unofficial motto: "Home of expensive web help!") who went to Craigslist and found a web developer in New York who created the exact site he wanted for a tenth of the bids he had received in the Bay Area.

Either way, if you choose to create your site yourself with software or have a web designer create it for you, the next step is to get a web address (URL) for your site. It is hard these days to find a .com address that has not already been taken, so you will probably have to be very creative if you want to go that route. But if you can find a workable .com, take it. A dot-com address is still considered more trustworthy and legitimate for businesses, so even though it will be far easier to find a good .biz URL, for example, it is far less attractive.

You can search for and register a web address by going to sites such as NetworkSolutions.com, GoDaddy.com, Register.com, and 1and1.com. Prices vary.

Most Common Website Suffixes

.com: Commercial
.edu: Educational
.gov: Government
.net: Network
.org: Organization
.biz: Business
.info: Information
.pro: Professional

You will also need to find a host for your site. Your website will eventually sit on the host's computers—its servers—so you will need a reliable host with a lot of bandwidth and great customer support.

Do It Yourself Online

By far the best website creation solution for most small businesses can be found in the suites of do-it-yourself tools offered by various online services. These point-and-click options are easy to use and offer superior results. Typically, this is how these services work:

- First, you get a web address and site registration.
- Next, you can easily and quickly point, click, and design an elegant, professional website. These services even offer templates for different professions to give you a head start (real estate, law, restaurants, and so on).
- The site also serves as your web host.
- Also, you get help with your e-marketing, such as e-newsletters and e-mails that match the look of your site.
- The service helps you with your search engine optimization, as well as your search engine advertising.
- Finally, for a small fee, an e-commerce service can help you sell on your own site or on eBay, Amazon, etc.

Whether you use this sort of service or design it some other way, there really is no reason not to have a website, and a great website at that. As advertised, creating one is easy, quick, and essentially free.

Other Online Options

One other way to build a site is to use a prepackaged template. Check out WordPress, Drupal, Joomla, and Mambo.

A FEW LAST TIPS

When creating your website, keep your design simple and uncluttered. If you are going to have content, update it frequently so that the site doesn't get stale. To establish credibility, use testimonial letters and guarantees, and let people know how to get in touch with you.

CHAPTER 42

E-Business Essentials

The Internet is a marketing medium.

—Jay Conrad Levinson

What do you do with that pretty new website once you get it up and running? You use it to drive business and to make more money, of course. How? In this chapter, we will discuss how to get people to come to your site, what they should find when they get there, how to conduct e-commerce, how to fulfill the orders you receive, and how to use the power of the Internet to create even more business.

SEARCH ENGINE OPTIMIZATION

Pop quiz! What do you think might be the most cost-effective way to grow your business right now?

1. Start a Facebook business page
2. Buy some pay-per-click ads
3. Search engine optimization (SEO)

Option 1 is increasingly a good answer because let's face it—it's Facebook's world and we are just living in it. But that said, it takes work and won't produce immediate results (although it will eventually create results; check out Chapter 45).

Option 2 is a fine answer, but it will cost money and, again, usually takes some trial and error to be effective.

419

No, for my money, option 3, SEO, is the best choice. If you're not familiar with the concept, SEO is simply the process of making your website as relevant as possible to search engines like Google, Yahoo!, Bing, and so on. With just a little SEO knowledge, you can dramatically improve the chances of people finding you and your site through a search result, and nothing beats having people buy from your site because they did a search and found you because your page ranked high. It's practically free advertising.

Yet SEO is also one of those things that has a bit of a learning curve. But it need not be too steep. Here then are some easy and quick SEO tips to help you help your business grow.

UNDERSTANDING SEO

Search engines rank websites by sending out automated "spiders" that analyze the sites. The spider visits a site and reads the web pages. This information then goes into the master index, which catalogs the site; this is why search results are so fast—the sites have already been spidered, analyzed, indexed, and cataloged. So the trick is to have the spiders look at your site, find it relevant to some topic, categorize it appropriately, and thereby have it ranked high.

Here's how: different sites use different methods for ranking web pages. To some degree or another, each uses a different set of complex algorithms that analyze the keywords and phrases used most on your site and home page, They also take into consideration the number and quality of the links going to a page to figure out what you offer. After all, a page that has a lot of other sites linking to it must be a relevant, valuable page, right? Right. Links are critical.

Getting Links

How do you get good links to your site? Here is one way: go to your favorite search engine, type in your keywords, view the results, and then visit the sites that are ranked highest. Send an e-mail to the sites and find out whether they are interested in a link exchange.

Get Your Site Ready

Insofar as keywords go, search engines also rank sites based largely on several keyword and key phrase factors (although please note that these factors change):

- The keywords that appear in the title of a page (the specific page URL)
- The frequency with which keywords appear in relation to other words
- Their distinctiveness

Maybe you think that you can surreptitiously have your keywords written 100 times at the top of a particular page and be assured of a high ranking. Wrong. That is a type of spamming that will ensure you receive a low ranking. And in any case, the link analysis also plays a large part in how high you will be ranked.

So what can you do vis-à-vis keywords to improve your rankings?

- *Pick them carefully.* The words that you think people will use to find your site are your keywords. For me it might be "small business success" or "small business writer." What about you? Each page on your site will be spidered and indexed, so you need specific keywords to reflect each page's specific content.

Finding Keywords

Another way to analyze keywords and phrases is to google your key phrases and see how the competition uses these terms.

- *Have URLs that reflect the keywords on the page.* If you have a page about skiing in powder in Utah for example, then the URL might be www.YOURBUSINESS.com/skiing-in-Utah-in-the-powder. The keywords must be part of the URL.
- *Have specific pages.* Create pages with content and keyword placement that are specific enough to catch a spider's eye.
- *Get linked up.* It is important to reiterate that getting other sites to link to your specific keyword-rich pages is one of the best ways to get better rankings.

Content Is King

It should go without saying that you need great content if your site is going to be interesting to anyone besides yourself. That content could be articles by you and your staff, or your blog, or videos . . . you know what constitutes great content. (For an in-depth discussion on content, please see the next section on Social Media.) The important thing is that you have some of it on your own site; otherwise all of your fancy keyword analysis and linking strategies will be for naught.

The question may arise: Aside from your own efforts, where can you get that great content? Plenty of places:

- RSS feeds
- News feeds
- Free content websites
- Users (Encourage your site visitors to comment on articles or have a contest that has them create online content to win.)
- Pay for it

Bottom line: SEO is a very valuable and important, albeit complicated, subject. It would behoove you to delve deeper into this subject.

Buy Good Rankings

No, you cannot buy a high ranking, but you can do something that is pretty close. Think about Bing or Google for a second. When you get your query results, what do you also see? To the far right are the small ads, right there at the top of the listings. So if you are willing to pay, you can buy exceptional placement.

Pay-per-click search engine ads are also great because, aside from the top of results placement, you pay for them only when someone clicks on them. With pay per click, you bid on search term results. You might pay 25 cents or $2 for every person who sees your ad and clicks on it. The important thing is that by agreeing to pay, you can be assured that, although you may not be ranked the highest in the "organic" results, you can still end up on the first page people see when they type in the keywords that you paid for. Given the ever-increasing use of the Internet by shoppers, this can be a very good use of your marketing dollars and a powerful way to increase sales.

According to Google, here is how the pay-per-click process works:

- *"You create your ads.* You create ads and choose keywords, which are words or phrases related to your business. (Google gives you a keyword generation help tool.)"
- *"Your ads appear on Google.* When people search Google using one of your keywords, your ad may appear next to the search results. Now you're advertising to an audience that's already interested in you."
- *"You attract customers.* People can simply click on your ad to make a purchase or learn more about you."

Caution

When doing pay-per-click advertising, make sure to limit how much you will spend each month. This dollar number can be programmed into your online campaign, and it is vital to ensure that you do not bust the bank on any one campaign.

E-COMMERCE ESSENTIALS

Getting people to your site using SEO and pay per click is good, but in order to make money online, they have to buy something. The process is not all that different from when customers purchase something from you offline: they enter your store, see your products, pick what they like, put it in a shopping cart, proceed to the checkout, and then pay with a credit card. The only difference online is that it all happens virtually. But the idea is exactly the same. That is e-commerce. It should follow, then, that to conduct business over the Internet, your website will need to be equipped with a few special things:

- A shopping cart and related software to allow you to display your products using formatted templates, manage your inventory, take orders, and make shipping arrangements

- Credit card processing to allow you to process payments online
- Products
- A web host capable of furnishing back-end support

A good turnkey, e-commerce web-hosting solution should offer you a package that includes all of these features. In addition, 24/7 live customer support should be a priority. Again, the web-hosting solutions discussed in the previous chapter all offer these e-commerce options.

The actual logistics of conducting e-commerce are as follows:

- *Products*. If you are selling your own products from your offline store, each one has to be photographed digitally so as to be displayed online. Your shopping cart software will allow you to create an online catalog of thumbnail photos of your products.
- *Credit card processing*. Almost all Internet purchases are made with credit cards, so you must have the capacity to accept them. This requires having a merchant account with a financial institution. A merchant account allows you to take a credit card, authorize it, accept the funds, and get the money. A Google search will turn up many merchant account providers.

PayPal

Probably the most widely used online payment option is PayPal, an online service that allows you to accept credit cards, debit cards, and checks.

- *Shipping charges*. Do not underestimate the cost of shipping products. It may not be insignificant. If that is the case, consider charging your e-customers less than your actual shipping cost. Why? Discounted shipping can create bigger orders—just ask Amazon. E-merchants usually ship using UPS, FedEx, or the U.S. Postal Service, with shipping costs calculated by weight, distance, and dimensions.
- *Security*. Customers want to know that their transactions are secure, so you will need some sort of encrypted security solution. This, too, should come with your e-commerce shopping cart.

DROP SHIPPING

Fulfilling orders online through your shopping cart is fairly simple. After a visitor goes to your site and clicks to make a purchase, you will get a notification of the purchase, and if you have a merchant account, the money will be deposited directly into your bank account. You then ship the product as you would any other order.

What if you don't want to go through the hassle of actually physically fulfilling orders? One of the best things about having a viable e-commerce site is that you do not have to have stock physically on hand to sell merchandise. *Drop shipping* is an arrangement between you and a wholesaler or distributor whereby you virtually stock your online store with their products and take orders. You then inform the wholesaler or distributor of any sale, and it ships the merchandise. In essence, you are just an intermediary (although no one knows that—it looks to the entire world as if the merchandise is stocked and sold by you). Using drop shipment, you can sell first-rate merchandise on your site and make a healthy profit, without actually having to stock and ship product.

Here is an example: Say that your athletic shoe site carries a product called "The Best Tube Sock Ever," and a package of 10 sells for $44, plus $6 for shipping and handling. When a visitor clicks and purchases this item, you get an e-mail notification. You then send the tube sock manufacturer an e-mail message (in some systems, this, too, is automatically generated by the sale), the manufacturer ships the package—using your label—and sends you a bill for its cost, say, $35. PayPal takes the money and deposits it into your account. You make $15 on every purchase, and all you have to do is take the order.

If you think this is a great business model, you're right. You do not have the labor expense for shipping and handling, you can stock name-brand items, you can easily add and delete items to your e-store, and you do not have to buy inventory. You start this process by deciding which products you want to carry and then speaking with the manufacturer of those products to see whether it has a drop shipping system. If it does not, then work on finding a distributor. A distributor is a business that has an inventory of products from other businesses and distributes them.

As with any business deal you make, you need to negotiate the best deal you can. When you find a wholesaler or distributor you want to use, you need to find out the following:

- How do their wholesale prices compare with retail? This allows you to calculate your profit.
- How and what do they charge for shipping?
- How will they bill you?
- How do they deal with returns and refund requests?

Drop shipping is an easy, affordable way to sell online. Avoid companies that want to charge you a fee for selling their products (they are out there, so beware), and be sure to choose quality products that reinforce your image and brand and afford you a healthy profit margin.

eBAY

If you already have products to sell and do not need a drop shipper, one of the best, easiest, least expensive ways to create another profit center is to begin an eBay business. Moreover, if you have old merchandise that you have not been able to sell, you might be surprised to find a ready market for it on eBay. Selling online through eBay costs very little; if it works, great, and if not, all you have lost is some time.

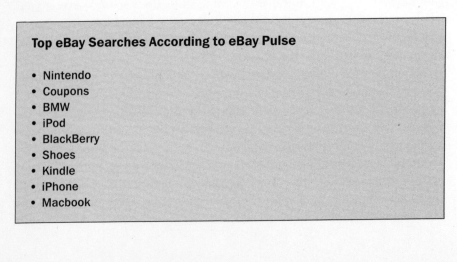

Top eBay Searches According to eBay Pulse

- Nintendo
- Coupons
- BMW
- iPod
- BlackBerry
- Shoes
- Kindle
- iPhone
- Macbook

One secret to selling on eBay is the old dictum to buy low and sell high. Remember the motto of our antiques dealer, "It's all in the buying." He knew that if he could buy items at a cheap price, reselling them for a healthy profit would not be difficult. That is especially true on eBay.

There are several things you can do to increase the likelihood of eBay success. First, be sure to set a proper, hidden "reserve price" for your auctions. The reserve price is the lowest fee that your auction will accept for your product, thereby assuring that you will make a profit on the sale (if you sell it). Second, focus on customer service. Potential customers will e-mail you questions, and those questions need to be answered promptly. Similarly, once you make a sale, stand behind your product, and be sure to ship it promptly. Here are a few other things you can do to make sure your foray into eBay is successful:

- *Use photos.* People want to see what they are buying.
- *Write a great headline.* Redundant but true: headlines grab people's attention.
- *Be thorough.* Giving a full description of the product can make a big difference.
- *Accurately estimate your shipping costs.* Even though eBay buyers usually pay for shipping, you will eat into your margin if your actual shipping fees are more than what you are charging your buyers.

Learning how to sell on eBay is not difficult. Visit www.ebay.com/ education to get a full tour of how the process works, or check your local bookstore—there are several good books on the process. All in all, eBay is a great, low-risk way to grow your online business or to start a potentially lucrative small business with very little money.

CHAPTER **43**

Advanced E-Marketing

My formula for success is rise early, work late, and strike oil.

—J. Paul Getty

Strike oil, eh? No, you will not strike literal oil. But figurative oil, why not? Today, there is no better place to tap a gusher than online. Just ask Jeff Bezos whether he feels as if he struck oil when he discovered in 1992 that the Internet was then growing at 2,300 percent *a year*. And what about Google founders Larry Page and Sergey Brin? They probably feel as if they struck oil, too. But they are not the only ones who have struck oil online—millions of businesses have, and you can, too.

WHAT WORKS ONLINE?

To really tap the power of the Internet, it helps to first understand what makes it unique and how to use that uniqueness for maximum advantage. Bezos is as good an expert as there is on this subject. Here is what he says makes for a great business website. Ask yourself:

Does the website harness the unique characteristics of the Internet to create a strong value proposition for customers, one that could not be easily duplicated in the physical world?

According to Bezos, the reason Amazon.com took off like it did was that it did something online that could not be duplicated offline—namely, it

429

offered every book in print for sale. Because it was impossible to duplicate in the physical world what he created in the virtual one, his business became a hit. So the question then becomes, what other unique characteristics of the Internet can you use to your advantage? Essentially, there are three:

1. *Low overhead.* Web-based businesses have a distinct advantage over their brick-and-mortar cousins in that it is, or should be, far less expensive to do business online. There is no rent required for a store, labor costs are usually far less, and there is no sales tax. Getting a bargain is the culture of the web. That is what people expect.

Tip: The most successful online businesses are the ones that offer their services for free or allow consumers to buy goods at a steep discount: Google, eBay, YouTube, Facebook, Amazon, MSN, Wikipedia, Craigslist, Huffington Post.

---

2. *A chance to excel.* Aside from simply being able to look as good as the big boys, the Internet also affords you the opportunity to compete with them on a far more level playing field. First, the cost of entry into the market is low; for example, drop shipping means that you need not even stock actual products. Next, because you are small, your customer service should be better. Advantage, you. Thus you have a better chance of competing against big retailers online than you ever would if they actually moved down the street.
3. *New markets.* Because you are not stuck selling to people only in your area, as small businesses have been doing for eons, you have a unique opportunity when you take your business global. You can become the new East India Trading Company.

The East India Trading Company

Formed in 1600, the East India Trading Company was created when a group of merchants was given a monopoly to trade with the East Indies. The company's

(continued)

first ships arrived in India in 1608, and trading posts were soon established throughout India. The company became a ruling power in the 1750s.

However, discontent with the company grew, culminating in an Indian peasant rebellion in 1857. The company was dissolved in 1858. Thereafter, the British government ruled India until Mahatma Gandhi led the movement to set the country free.

Keep these three things in mind as you grow your site and online business. Use the uniqueness of the Internet to your advantage.

GROWTH STRATEGIES

There are many ways to get more people to come to your site. Here are some of your best bets.

E-Mail Marketing

One of the easiest ways to grow your business using the Internet is through e-mail. No, not spam, but rather targeted e-mails to qualified customers and prospects. Personally, I have used this method with great success to syndicate my *USA Today* column to small business sites all over the world.

The idea is to offer goods or services to specific customers by e-mail. In this sense, it is not unlike traditional direct marketing—the difference is that you find your list of potential recipients through a web search, and your communication is electronic. For instance, say that you are an architectural drafter. You could e-mail architects across the country, explain who you are, tell them how good yet inexpensive your services are, and offer to create a virtual partnership. If the architect is interested, he or she will e-mail you back, and you just may have a new client.

The challenge is that the one thing that really can help you make or close a sale—rapport—is more difficult to create online than it is offline. In the nonvirtual world, you create trust and rapport the old-fashioned way: you meet people, look them in the eye, find something in common, and so on. But online, you cannot do that. So what do you do, especially when you are essentially cold-calling someone with your unsolicited marketing e-mail? Here is what works:

- *Use names.* If you begin your e-mail with "Dear Sir/Madam," your e-mail is going to be deleted immediately. You have to find the name of the appropriate person to whom you should address your inquiry and e-mail that person by name.
- *Write a super subject line.* Think of the subject line as the headline of an ad. It must be catchy and intriguing enough to get people to want to know more and open the e-mail.
- *Keep it short.* We are all too busy these days, so your e-mail must get to the point quickly.
- *Be impressive.* You are trying to create a business relationship. One way is to impress the person to whom you are writing. Have a great website the prospective customer can check out. The use of testimonials, either in your e-mail or on your site, also helps a lot.
- *Give a reason to respond.* Discounts always work, as do giveaways. And of course, be sure to make your initial query compelling.
- *Offer a guarantee.* Especially online, a guarantee helps reduce the risk factor in your prospect's mind.

Words of Wisdom

I spoke with one Director of Marketing and asked him about the secret to his success with solicitation e-mails. He said, "The e-mails don't have to be too short, but they do need to be catchy, succinct, and to the point. Have an attention-grabbing intro, use examples and links, and make it easy to respond via e-mail or phone."

E-Newsletters

There are all sorts of reasons that you may want to create and offer an e-newsletter for your site, but here is the main one: it captures data. By creating an e-newsletter and making it intriguing enough that people sign up for it, you are getting them to opt in and give you their e-mail address.

Consider how powerful and incredibly useful that small act really is: these are people who *want* to hear from you. It's a very valuable list. You can use it for follow-up marketing: tell your opt-in membership about upcoming sales and promotions, special events, and so on. By getting people to opt in and sign up for your e-newsletter, you create a list of potential customers who have given you permission to market to them. Fantastic!

This idea—getting people to opt in and give you their e-mail address—is such a powerful Internet marketing tool that in the next section, I will offer you six additional ways to get people to opt in. For now, let's concentrate on how to make your e-newsletter work.

Your e-newsletter offers you numerous benefits:

- It allows you to stay in touch with prospects and customers.
- It creates credibility and helps develop brand awareness.
- It builds your business because you can use it to announce sales, promotions, and other news.
- If it becomes popular, you can sell advertising in it.

To create this sort of successful e-newsletter, it has to be well written, engaging, easy to read, and useful. If you are unable to write it yourself, have an employee do it. The content must be top-notch and not generally available elsewhere. Pick a topic related to your business that people want to know more about.

Once you have created the newsletter and started to get people to sign up for it, you will need to manage your list. Using a web service makes it much easier. Here are a few good choices:

- Constant Contact (www.constantcontact.com)
- Topica E-mail Publisher (www.topica.com)
- AWeber (www.aweber.com)

Six More Ways to Get People to Opt In

1. *Offer free articles and information for people who register.* Offer people who register with your site content that they would not otherwise get. Make it something desirable.

2. *Offer a free webinar.* Webinars are all the rage and easier than ever to produce and show online. Again, come up with a topic of interest and have people opt in to attend (for free, of course).

3. *Offer a free e-book.* An e-book need not be lengthy to be an effective e-mail capturing tool. It can be short—even a dozen pages will work. The important thing is that you have a great topic, one that would entice people to opt in—something like "Valuable Report Lists 14 Ways to Get Money for Free!" The e-book captures valuable e-mail addresses for later marketing.

4. *Offer other freebies.* By working with other sites that offer free software, you can offer people who visit your site free downloads if they register. Maybe you can swing a deal whereby you offer free screen savers or wallpaper. You can also offer for free something that your business creates.

5. *Create a "members only" area.* Offering premium content to people who register is another way to create a valuable list. That is what AOL did for years.

Example: One person who knows more about the Internet than almost anyone is radio talk show host Kim Komando. Her site, Komando.com, offers basic computing information, but if you really want to access the good stuff—message boards, podcasts, archives, and the like—you have to become a Kim's Club member.

---

6. *Have fun.* Have people opt in to:

- Participate in a contest to win a free prize
- See the results of today's survey
- See the answers to today's quiz

Blogging for Business

Yes, blogging has become mainstream, and it is a great way to build the visibility of your site. Because the very nature of a blog is that it is informal, having one on your site offers you a more personal way to interact with your crew. In addition:

- *Blogs boost your SEO.* By their very nature, blogs incorporate links and keywords, and as people respond to your blog, more keywords show up. That really helps your search engine optimization.
- *Blogs let you plug products, gently.* A good post allows you to share business products in an informal way.
- *Blogs give you valuable feedback.* When customers respond to your posts, you are getting precious feedback, almost like a focus group.
- *Blogs make your business more human.* Let's face it, business can seem quite impersonal sometimes. The very nature of blogs counters that.

Blogging Tips: Be informal. Give insights into your business that people would not otherwise get. Write in a conversational way. Give good tips.

Four Ways to Make a Great e-Impression

What is marketing if not a way to get on people's radar and impress them? But what happens when you do get on their radar but don't impress them? You have wasted your time, energy, and money, that's what. If you go to all of the effort to get people to find you online, then you simply cannot miss the opportunity to wow them, and their first impression of you is critical.

Back in college I had a friend who had an interesting work philosophy. "Whenever I start a new job," he told me, "I always work extra hard the first month. That way they view me as a hard worker, even later on when I slack off a bit." Although his reasoning was skewed, his logic was impeccable and his point is well taken: you really do never get a second chance to make a great first impression. People often view you and your business through that first lens they see you through. It is also equally true that in this 24/7, interconnected, wired world, there are a lot of different ways to make (or break) that great first impression. Here are four:

1. *Have a great and up-to-date website.* If your site says © 2008 at the bottom, that's a mistake. If you have broken links, that's a problem. If your site still looks like it was built in 2002, you are blowing it. More than maybe even your storefront, today your website is often the first thing people see. What do they see when they check you out online? If your site isn't beautiful and professional, people likely are not going to take you too seriously.

Here's what not to do: I have a colleague who consults with people on their businesses, yet he still has a website that says "under construction." You have got to be kidding me. I can't believe he gets business.

2. *Remember that content really is king.* One of the first pages people click when going to a new site is the About page. What is on yours? And what about the rest of your site, do you offer some free tips or valuable product information? Do you have testimonials on your site? Do you have some brands to show off? The friendlier, more helpful, and more impressive your site, the more people will trust you from the get go.

3. *Have a decent social media presence.* This issue is so important that the whole next section of the book is devoted to it. For now, suffice to say, you need to have at least some sort of social media presence if you want to make a good e-impression, No, you do not have to have 5,000 Twitter followers but you should have a respectable social media presence if you want to be taken seriously. If people try and find you through social media and cannot, they will wonder why.

4. *Remember your e-mail etiquette.* Use proper English and grammar. Don't use emoticons or refer to yourself as "i." And be sure to respond to e-mails promptly, because if you don't they may conclude that you are either too busy or too disorganized to give them your time.

The Internet is continuously changing, and new ways of plugging your business online are emerging even as I write this. The key, then, is to stay engaged. Learn the tricks discussed in this chapter—because they work—and keep your eyes open for new ones as they come along. You will be happy you did. May the e-force be with you!

PART

Social Media

CHAPTER **4 4**

Social Media Overview

How can you squander even one more day not taking advantage of one of the greatest shifts of our generation?
How dare you settle for less when the world has made it
easy for you to be remarkable?

—SETH GODIN

Back in the day networking used to be so much easier . . . or was it
harder? It was different, that's for sure. Back then, you would trudge off
to the ol' chamber mixer with a stack of business cards in your jacket or
purse, have your elevator pitch ready, eat some rubber chicken, make
some small talk, pass out your cards, follow up, and hope that someone,
somewhere looked at your card, remembered you, and was interested
enough to want to do business with you. It's exhausting to even think
about, and even writing about it makes it sound like a shot in the dark,
which of course is what it was.

But then again, is networking today—social networking—any better?
What you have to do now is create an online presence and profile; figure
out which social networking site is right for you; log on daily (or more);
offer up some consistent, excellent content; find friends, followers, and
fans; become a friend, follower, and fan; and hope that you impress someone enough to make an online connection such that someone remembers
you and is interested enough to want to do business with you. Writing
about it makes it sound like a shot in the dark, which of course is what
it is:

- If you don't know what you are doing
- If you don't use your time wisely
- If you have no plan of action

But if you do know what you are doing and do have a plan, and if you do figure out how to use your valuable time and the tools available wisely, then social media networking and marketing should be an incredible boon to your business. The fact is, social media is one of the biggest transformative events for business in many years and any small business that is not taking advantage of the incredible opportunities that social media affords is making a big mistake.

Here is a simple example: Jenny was 55 when she lost her job as a middle manager at a Fortune 500 company. She looked for work diligently, was grateful for her unemployment benefits, but grew petrified as the time for them to run out approached and she still had no new job. Jenny finally decided she had no choice but to become an entrepreneur. The problem was, she had never started a business before. She knew nothing about it.

But what she did know was LinkedIn. Jenny had mastered the social media site both at her old job and then during her long stint of unemployment (using it to try to find a new job). In any case, once she decided that she had to become a small business owner to survive, Jenny turned back to LinkedIn.

- She joined various groups dealing with start-ups.
- She participated in them consistently—posting and sharing and meeting and, well, linking-in.
- She followed and got introduced to people who had started their own businesses.
- She read blogs relating to business.

Slowly, Jenny learned the ropes. Although it was difficult, and although she was working out of her spare bedroom alone, she felt that she was part of a larger community because of her favorite social networking site. Six months later, as her business started to take shape, Jenny concluded that she needed a board of advisors. So she put the word out to her network. The result? 50 highly qualified people from around the globe offered to sit on her board, for free. Today Jenny attributes her success in her business to social media, the people she met there, and her related efforts.

So yes, social networking can work big time for business if you know what you are doing, but if you don't, it's basically a waste of time. A fun waste of time maybe, but a waste of time.

So let's look at how to make it work big time for you.

SOCIAL MEDIA OVERVIEW

In all likelihood, you know more than a little about social media already. You probably have a Facebook page and maybe even a LinkedIn profile. Maybe you are on Google+ or whatever else is the hot social media flavor of the month. No doubt you have watched videos on YouTube. But that said, being a casual participant on social media in a personal way is a lot different than actively and purposefully using it to grow your business, and that is and should be our goal—to use it to grow your business.

The problem is that social media is a double-edged sword. On one hand, it offers a vast sea of possibilities and people to meet; people and opportunities you otherwise would not meet and have in the physical, real, nonvirtual world. But on the other hand, it is far too easy for many people to get lost in that vast social media sea, or to spend too much time there because being at sea can be more fun than working. You can even drown in this sea if you end up wasting your time, marketing efforts, energy, and precious capital chasing leads that never materialize.

Or maybe you are of the other ilk. Maybe you think that social media is not for you and your business and so are reading this chapter out of curiosity and not much more. If that is the case, then I say to you, my friend, that you are missing the boat as much as the people who are spending all day tweeting and posting and updating their Facebook status with nothing to show for it.

Let me suggest that the best way to think about this thing called social media is as a conversation. People are already online, on these sites, having conversations about everything imaginable. They are talking about your industry, your products, your competitors, maybe even your business. There are strangers having these conversations, but so are your customers, associates, colleagues, friends, and competitors. You can be part of these conversations and help guide and influence them, or you can keep your head in the sand, convinced that your participation makes no difference. Which sounds more accurate?

Now, do you *have* to become part of this social media revolution? Does your business really need a Facebook business page? Of course not. You can survive just fine without jumping in. But that said, does it not make a little sense to join the conversation and see where it leads? What about joining in if for no other reason than to be part of the online conversation with your own, current customers? What about using it to build your brand, prospect, and make more sales? Do you see how powerful it might actually be for your business? I bet it leads to new opportunities. It should.

Benefits

It should be apparent that there are all sorts of benefits of becoming engaged in social media, more than just the aforementioned ability to make new relationships. For instance, by becoming a font for valuable content, you are creating and enhancing your brand; that is, by consistently posting the right content, you will get more people to think of you in a certain way. And after all, isn't that the whole purpose of branding? Added benefit: It costs you nothing but time.

According to the 2011 *Social Media Marketing Industry Report,* of all categories of users, small business owners are seeing the greatest benefits from social media marketing. Indeed, the report found that 67 percent of the self-employed and 66 percent of small business owners said that social media was "important to their business," mostly because of the increased exposure created by the platform.

According to the *Social Media Examiner* (April 2011), the main benefits that small businesses are seeing from their social media efforts are these:

- "The self-employed and small business owners were more likely to report new partnerships, with at least 59% noting a benefit."
- "Small businesses were twice as likely to find qualified leads than other types of businesses."

- "48% of self-employed and small business owners saw improved sales as a direct result of their social media efforts."
- "The self-employed (59%) and small business owners (58%) were more likely than others to see reductions in marketing costs when using social media marketing."

The *Social Media Examiner* concluded that "the 2011 study proved that time is a key success factor for social media marketers. Spend more time (wisely, of course) and you're likely to see greater results." How much time? It depends on your experience. "Those with 3 or more years of experience in social media marketing are seeing the greatest results [but] only 25% of those just getting started in social media saw new partnerships form, as compared to 80% or more of those with 3 or more years of experience."

> **Time Commitments**
>
> Fortunately, social media need not be all-consuming. In the *Social Media Marketing Industry Report,* 75 percent of those "spending as little as 6 hours per week on social media marketing saw increased traffic."

Other benefits of your social media efforts should likely include:

- *More traffic.* This could mean more people reading your blog, more hits on your website, more people shopping in your e-store, or more people coming into the physical store.
- *More relationships.* Although having a lot of Twitter followers or people who like your Fan page is nice, the real value in social media is that you can actually meet and get to do business with some new folks; people you would not otherwise normally meet. The people who really make money with social media and who have figured out how to use it to grow their business in fact use it to meet and create relationships.
- *Better brand awareness.* Although real relationships are a valuable way to measure your social media ROI it is nevertheless also true that another valuable benefit is that more people will learn of your business. Having a lot of fans and followers, or having your tweets retweeted, increases brand awareness. Social networking, when done right, builds your brand.

Getting Started

As indicated, social media for business is different than social media for you. The first thing you need to decide then is which site best fits your business; which one offers you the best chance to meet new people and get some business? There are no shortage of social media sites out there, but of course the big three are Twitter, Facebook, and LinkedIn. In case you don't know, each does something a little different:

- **Twitter** allows for short bursts, or tweets, of only a few sentences (140 characters). As such, it is great for having back-and-forth conversations with people and posting short nuggets of information. People who follow what you do on Twitter are, of course, your "followers." One benefit of Twitter is that it allows you to see what people are saying about your business publicly, giving you an easy way to find and engage with those people.
- **Facebook** allows for a more robust interaction by allowing businesses to create fan pages where they can post videos, articles, contests, events, and the like. It is also where most of your customers and likely customers congregate. It has the eyeballs.
- **LinkedIn** allows you to link to all of the people you know on the site, create a network, and then make connections to your network's network, creating an even more vast network.

A Partial Current List of Other Social Media Sites:

Google+, BizSugar, Del.icio.us, Ning, Squidoo, YouTube, Xing, Tagged, Orkut, Care2, Gather, Tribe, Ziggs, Plaxo, Digg, Badoo, Bebo, Meetup . . .

So you begin by spending some time on each site and getting a feel for how they work and how you and your business might participate.

1. *Set up accounts.* Create accounts at all three. Be thorough and add enough information to make you and/or your business relevant and interesting. On LinkedIn, be sure to add all of your contacts. On Facebook, create a Fan page (see next chapter). If you know of any

niche social media sites that specifically cater to your industry or business, definitely consider setting up shop at those as well.

2. *Choose.* Although I am suggesting that you cast a wide net at the beginning, what people often find is that, with this sea as vast as it is, it helps to narrow it down and, sooner rather than later, concentrate on one site in particular. Social media takes time and effort, especially in the beginning, so concentrating on one social networking site will enable you to most efficiently master that site. After that, if so desired, you can tackle another site.

3. *Get involved.* Whatever site you choose, the secret is to immerse yourself in it. If you like LinkedIn, join a group, create new connections, add apps to your home page. On Twitter, the key is to create useful content that people like, tweet it, follow, and get followers. As opposed to the misconception that Twitter users tweet mundane things about their life, the fact is that most small business people tweet articles and content that are quite interesting. The point is, you must do more than merely sign up if you are to make a go of this. You have to find the social media site that is best for you and spend time there. Meet people. Make connections.

4. *Stick with it.* Mastering social media takes time, and getting business results from it takes even more time. Spending an hour a day on it is not uncommon in the beginning, and as you really get into it, that may increase multifold. Don't get discouraged. The trick is to begin to meet and engage people, to become part of the conversation, and get your business out there. The more you do that, the more your network will grow, the more you will build your brand, and the more business opportunities you will get.

What Works

Once you sign up and get started, then what? The thing to understand about social media is that it has to become more about *them* and less about *you.* Your job is to become added value to their day, and you do that by tweeting or posting content that you think your friends (old and new alike) would find interesting and useful. If all you do is post what you have on sale that day or other such mundane stuff, you will not go far. If on the other hand you learn to post interesting, intriguing, smart, valuable, funny, quirky, or insightful content (either by you or others), you will attract attention, impress people, and forge new connections.

A study by the tech company Roost looked at how small businesses can best engage their social media audience. The survey found that the following types of content offer maximum social media value:

- *Photos.* Publishing photos on your Facebook page generates 50 percent more impressions than any other type of post. Photos are great because they are friendly, engaging, easy, and quick. Pictures of your business, your products, your people, all would work.
- *Questions.* Posting a question on Twitter or your Facebook or LinkedIn page is an excellent way to engage people and get them to begin to chat with you, and each other. The survey found that questions generate almost two times as many comments as any other type of post. Added bonus: Questions that foster discussions equal comments full of keywords that boosts SEO.
- *Quotes.* The study found that quotations drive an average of 54 percent more retweets than any other type of tweet.

This is just for starters. Other things to post: articles of interest, free e-books, resources, links, and contests.

Using Social Media for Lead Generation

The previous section suggests that although there are plenty of benefits that come from participating in social media, hopefully the biggest benefit to small business should be increased sales. As opposed to using it to build your brand or attract a ton of Twitter followers (both of which can be useful in their own right), using social media to create leads and sales can happen immediately, and you don't even have to be a social-media expert to do it. Here's how: use the various search functions on the different sites.

The first method is to use the search function within each of the main social media sites to search for and locate people who would likely be interested in what you sell and do. That is, you can use these search tools to instantly create a list of viable leads.

- On Facebook, simply search for the relevant keywords (like, say, "sporting goods stores" in "San Antonio").

- On LinkedIn, check out the "advanced search" function. By using this tool, you can find people with a specific job title or who work for a specific company. You can also search professions, businesses, industries, and so on.
- On Twitter, use hashtags (#) to locate discussions around certain areas, or simply use the Twitter search function to find people in your field.

Then, once you have your list of potential leads from these three sites, whittle it down, and away you go.

The second method takes a little more time but is also useful. Here, like Jenny who began this chapter, you join relevant groups on the sites. You can search for and join groups of which you know your potential customers would be a part. Engage them, get to know them, and before long, pitch them. On Twitter, you can use hashtags to find relevant discussions and approach the participants. Either way, by searching for and finding relevant groups and discussions, you can get in front of your targeted audience quickly,

---

The New Marketing

According to the Mobile Marketing Association, the way to measure the success of a marketing campaign today requires a new sort of analysis, which includes "The number of eyeballs, shakes and finger swipes. The number of blogs, articles, tweets and diggs. The number of acquisitions, conversions, calls, responses or purchases. Total basket size, consumer recall, loyalty and recommendations. Check-ins on foursquare and check-outs on Amazon."

SOCIAL MEDIA MARKETING

Clearly all of this takes time, and if there is one thing that small business owners tend not to have a lot extra of, it is time. That said, there are ways to manage your social media efforts intelligently and efficiently and not spend your day tweeting and meeting and posting and boasting. For example, in the excellent book *30-Minute Social Media Marketing*, author

Susan Gunelius argues that you actually can handle it all by implementing a daily, 30-minute social media strategy.

Gunelius breaks down the social media marketing process into four "pillars," each of which can become part of your daily marketing habit:

Pillar 1—Reading and research. "A successful social media campaign starts with research and the research must be ongoing." The book suggests that you check out industry websites and periodicals, blogs, e-books, Twitter feeds, and online videos and podcasts.

Pillar 2—Create. "Success in social media marketing comes from developing online conversations about your business, brand, products, and promotions." As such, the "cornerstone of any social media marketing strategy is creating amazing content." What is amazing content? It is content that "truly adds value to the audience and online conversation." Your content could be almost anything: articles, videos, blogs, podcasts, links, presentations, and so forth.

Pillar 3—Share. There are two forms of sharing when it comes to social media marketing. First, share the best content you find during your Pillar 1 research, and second, share the great content you create. But as you share, keep our old friend, the 80–20 rule in mind. Gunelius suggests that you "spend 80 percent of your time on the social Web interacting and 20 percent of your time self-promoting."

Pillar 4—Discuss. What you want to do through all of this research, content creation, and sharing is to create a loyal following and to meet people with whom you can do business. You are not getting thousands of Twitter followers for your ego's sake, but for your business's sake.

Might this take more than 30 minutes a day? Maybe, but it also need not take three hours a day. Bottom line: "Amazing content" engages and connects you with people and adds value to their efforts. As such, if I did my job right, then the following might make sense for you: you can follow me on Twitter: @SteveStrauss, become my colleague on LinkedIn, or my friend on Facebook.

CHAPTER **45**

Facebook for Business

A million dollars isn't cool. Know what's cool? A billion dollars.

—Justin Timberlake as Facebook's first president,
Sean Parker, in *The Social Network*

To call Facebook a phenomenon is an understatement. Consider how long it took each of these different things to get to the 50 million user mark:

- Radio—38 years
- Television—13 years
- The iPod—3 years
- Facebook—less than 1 year

Today, Facebook is verging on 1 billion users. About one-seventh of the planet. Know what's cool? A billion users.

Something that gets that much bandwidth, that much attention, and that is that big and growing that fast deserves our attention. Your business has to remain in front of people; it needs to be where the eyeballs are, and if that is Facebook, then so be it.

That certainly is what Dan Kim, CEO of Red Mango Frozen Yogurt concluded. Opening its first store in 2007, Red Mango quickly caught Facebook fever. Not only does Kim advertise on Facebook, but it is what he does after that that is interesting and valuable. Red Mango's Facebook ads drive people to the Red Mango Facebook page, a page that is fun,

449

interactive, and full of good content and that offers specials and coupons. It is no wonder that the page went from 4,000 fans near the beginning to the more than 300,000 people who "like" it now as of this writing. (Like it yourself and get a $2 off coupon.)

Tip: In 2010, Facebook replaced its "Become a Fan" button with the "Like" button. Even so, business pages are still unofficially called Fan pages.

The reason the Red Mango Facebook page is popular is that they are doing it right:

- They refrain from posting boring content that would be of no interest to their customers. For instance, they learned that "company news" is not compelling content, and therefore, they don't post it.
- Coupons are popular, as are gift card contests, videos, and articles.

Like Red Mango, building a business page on Facebook may be a very smart idea for your small business too. The key for the companies that have had success driving interest and business from their Facebook pages is that they create pages that are, for the most part, friendly and interactive, and which add value to people's Facebook experience by maybe saving them money (coupons and specials are popular) or being fun (contests and videos are also popular).

Another example: Tillamook County Creamery Association is a dairy cooperative along the gorgeous Oregon coast that makes lots of great products, but a summer in the Northwest would not be complete without a trip to coast to the Tillamook Cheese Factory, where the ice cream is fresh and decadently creamy. Not long ago, the dairy started airing their first-ever television commercials, which consisted of real customers talking about their first time eating Tillamook Ice Cream. And where did they find those customers? You guessed it: Facebook. On their Facebook page, Tillamook asked people to share their experience of their first taste of Tillamook Ice Cream. Fans posted some fun stories, which became the basis of the TV ads.

The entire campaign is a great example of how any business can use social media generally, and Facebook specifically, to market and grow their business, even on a small budget. There are two key takeaways from the Tillamook example that are applicable to any small business that wants to hop on the Facebook bandwagon:

1. *You have to engage people.* Online, on social media, there are countless choices when people surf around. They will stay with you only if they find your site engaging, interesting, fun, and/or otherwise rewarding. On Facebook that means having contests, posting polls and quizzes, posting videos, offering coupons, asking questions and responding to comments, and so forth.

2. *If possible, get users to create content.* User-created content is the best because it inherently has a lot of veracity, and it is free. Sure you have to figure out what is and is not usable, but that is still easier than creating it all yourself. Tillamook used real customers who created real content and real customers starred in the ads. Talk about savings. You get people to create content just as Tillamook did—by asking them to.

By interacting with the people who visit your Facebook page and even getting them to create some of your content, you too can have some yummy results.

GETTING STARTED

Creating a Facebook page for your business is a bit different than creating your own personal account. Here is how you do it:

1. *Secure your username.* The first thing to do is to capture what is known as your Facebook vanity URL (or username), that is, www. Facebook.com/[YourBusinessName]. You do that by registering your page, setting it up, and getting 25 people to "like" it. Once you do that, Facebook allows the vanity URL to be established. Be sure that the name you pick for your vanity URL is either your business name, a name associated with your business, or something closely related to your brand as your fan page becomes a de facto website for your business.

> Whereas a person can have a maximum of 5,000 friends on Facebook, no such limit exists for the number of people who can like your Fan page.

2. *Create your page.* Facebook will first ask what sort of business you have. After that, you click over to the Facebook page template where you will begin to customize the page. Add in all relevant data:

- Company description
- Business bio and background
- Mission
- Awards
- E-mail and website
- Photos
- Products

Once the basics are out of the way, then the fun (and work) begins: you need to create that page we keep talking about—you know, the fun, interesting, interactive one that is full of articles, coupons, contests, and other valuable content. Facebook actually makes this process fairly easy as you can add apps and tabs for all sorts of these things.

3. *Grow.* Once your page is up and running and your vanity URL is established, it is time to get people to notice the page. You begin by telling your extended network about the page and getting them to like it. After

---

Apptastic!

There is no shortage of Facebook and third-party apps you can add to your Facebook page to make it more valuable. Here are a few you might want to check out:

- YouTube: Allows your visitors to watch your YouTube videos on your Facebook page.
- Promotions: Makes it easy to create contests and promotions.
- Social RSS: Allows you to add the content from your other online properties (like your blog) to your Facebook page.

- Polls: Allows you to get feedback. Engage. Post a poll.
- Extended Info: Allows you to add extra info to your profile, such as favorite movies, what you're currently reading, and so on.
- Twitter: Make it easy to find and follow your tweeting Facebook friends.
- SlideShare: Allows you to share presentations.
- My Flickr: Displays photos from your Flickr account.
- Upcoming: Allows you to post upcoming events.

that, it is really a matter of engaging with your customers and extended audience. Much of the rest of this chapter explains how to do that.

HOW TO ENGAGE

Probably the easiest way to begin to get more people to like your page and engage with your audience is simply to consistently update your status. Share tips and ideas, mention specials, and promote events. By updating your status time and again, you end up top of mind because your updates go to the Wall or News Feed of your friends. Updates are an easy way to stay front and center.

Another way to make your Facebook site valuable is to, as mentioned already, offer specials via the site. But the secret here is not to offer just any old special, but a special that is available to your Facebook friends only. This serves two purposes. First, it is a way to reward them for liking your page. Second, it is a very specific way to measure the success of your page and plans. That is, one challenge with social media is that it is often difficult to quantify the return on investment (ROI) of your efforts. Building a brand, after all, is inherently an amorphous thing. But by creating and offering a unique special only for your Facebook fans, you can very specifically quantify the success (or failure) of your page. You can see how many people respond to the promotion and how much money it makes you.

Next, you will want to offer the sort of "amazing" content mentioned in the previous chapter. On Facebook, the content should be light, breezy even. Videos especially are a great way to engage your audience. Now, why is this? Well, think about Facebook for a moment. Most people who go there are going there to chat with friends, see what is going on, that sort of thing. It is a casual place, a friendly place. So you have to be casual and friendly there too if you don't want to be ignored. As such, videos and other easy-to-digest content fits the bill; they dovetail with the mood of Facebook.

Another key strategy to Facebook success is encouraging community interaction and interacting with your community. Obviously, if yours is just some static, boring business page, you are not going to have much success on Facebook because the whole idea of the site is to share. So share you must. Don't be boring. Ask questions of your fans. Answer questions. Start conversations and participate in those conversations. Even better: By giving voice on your Facebook home page to your fans, your page looks active and that fosters even more interaction and activity.

Small Business Rules!

According to Pagemodo.com, 85 percent of the companies that use Facebook are small businesses. Most of those businesses use it only to share business information, although 62 percent also share content like articles, pictures, and videos.

Ways to foster this conversation include:

- Ask your folks questions, for example, "What are you doing to give back this holiday season?"
- Post interesting articles.
- Ask for feedback on some business issue or new product.
- Post pictures.
- Ask users to post pictures and content.

Earlier I mentioned polls and quizzes. The idea there is the same; these sorts of tools give people something to do when they come to your site. Additionally, polls are an excellent way to garner customer feedback and conduct some informal market research.

ADVERTISING ON FACEBOOK

Aside from creating your own Facebook page, another way to take advantage of the popular site is to market your business on the site. For example, Chris Meyer is a wedding photographer. Wanting to try something new to grow his business, Chris decided that he would try a Facebook ad campaign. One of the best things about advertising on Facebook is that you can very specifically target who will see your ad. That means that you only (generally) pay for highly qualified leads, which is good for your budget. So Chris created an ad for his wedding photography business and chose to have it be seen by women in his area, aged 24 to 30, whose Facebook "relationship status" was "engaged." Brilliant.

Chris spent $600 on the initial ad buy. And how much did he make? How does $40,000 over the course of a year sound? Today, Chris says, "I have found Facebook ads [very] effective. My business wouldn't be anywhere close to where it is today if it weren't for Facebook, and the ads campaign."

Creating a Facebook ad campaign of your own is really very easy:

1. Log on to the Facebook advertising center. Facebook.com/advertising.
2. Use the point-and-click design tools to create and design your ad.
3. Target the ad. Facebook will ask you to target your audience. That's the best part. Your target audience can be as large or small as you like, but the greater the reach, the more you will pay. You can choose to either pay per click (CPC) or pay per impression (CPM); that is, you pay either only for the number of people who click on your ad or for the gross number of impressions of people who see it.
4. When prompted, create a budget, review your ad, and get started.

Once that is done, the trick is to track your results in real time to see who is clicking and change your ad as needed. That last point is important. It is unwise to simply create an ad, check out, and come back a few weeks later to see what happened. I once did a similar Google ad campaign, seeking people looking for "small business speakers." I ended up paying a lot of money for clicks, not from people looking for a keynoter, but from people looking for Bose speakers.

Facebook for Business

Not long ago, Facebook launched a new page called Facebook for Business (Facebook.com/Business), which offers step-by-step tutorials on how to use all of Facebook's various marketing features. It's a Facebook marketer's user manual. Four marketing tools are highlighted:

- *Pages.* This area explains in more detail how you go about creating a business Facebook page.
- *Ads.* As discussed earlier, Facebook ads can be an excellent way to reach your desired demographic.
- *Sponsored Stories.* This feature helps you foster word-of-mouth advertising from your fans.
- *Platform.* This shows you how to add plug-ins and custom apps.

CHAPTER **46**

Twitter and You

Twitter is a broadcast marketing tool.

—G<small>UY</small> K<small>AWASAKI</small>

Of all of the social media platforms out there, Twitter is probably the most challenging one to grasp—and certainly the hardest to master from a business-use perspective. For small business people especially, both Facebook and LinkedIn make sense and are intuitive. But Twitter is different and takes some getting used to. The stream of tweets scrolling down your timeline, the hashtag conversations (#), having followers you never met—it all can seem a bit out of context until you get the hang of it.

Certainly that was the case for me when I first came across Twitter and started writing about it in my *USA TODAY* column. That was in April 2009, a time when Twitter was at the tipping point, what with everyone talking about it, Ashton Kutcher trying to get a million followers, and so on. Back then, I infamously wrote a column in which I suggested that small business people should not tweet. I immediately knew that I had struck some nerve (which nerve exactly I was not sure) when my editor gave the column the following headline: *Ask an Expert—Should Entrepreneurs Twitter? Uh, No.* Not a good sign, that.

Here is a portion of what I wrote:

"Twitter is all the rage. Everyone is either tweeting or talking about it or following someone, and so yes, I get that Twitter is the flavor of the month. But know what else I know? Sometimes you don't want or don't need the flavor of the month; sometimes you

457

need chocolate or vanilla. Sometimes newer isn't better. Here are some reasons why your small business should not Twitter:

1. **You are in business:** Yours is not a club, or a group, or a sorority, or a party. Yours is a business. And the business of your business is to sell products or offer services that people want at prices they are willing to pay. You have to impress them, offer them value (especially today), and deliver on your promises. But what you don't have to do is be their friend. Sure, some customers are friends. That's great. But that is not the purpose of your business . . .
2. **It offers just too much information:** Do people really want to know what you are doing at 3:47 tomorrow afternoon, what you are thinking, who you are meeting?
3. **It requires too much time:** When you tweet, or follow someone's tweets, that means you are not doing something else. If you are on Twitter for fun, great, but if you are on there to drum up business you better be darn sure that it is going to pay off, because it is not a quick indulgence."

If you know anything about Twitter, what you may notice is that I actually knew very little about Twitter, and boy were the Twitteratti more than happy to set me straight. Nothing I have ever written set off a firestorm quite like that Twitter column. Of all of the people I heard from, easily the most compelling was a woman who had turned to Twitter when the economy faltered and had used it to grow her business 21 percent the next year as a result. So I reconsidered Twitter in a following column:

"First, where I was wrong: What really surprised me about the column was just how much play it was getting. I had never had so many people comment on a column. Then one of them explained that it was because the column had been transplanted onto Twitter. Aha! So I saw firsthand what a powerful tool Twitter can be for spreading a message and creating instant feedback.

Mea culpa. I did not get that before. Score one for the Twitter nation."

I then wrote about the woman who grew her business with Twitter and explained that:

> "She says that what ol' Strauss didn't get is that Twitter is a fantastic tool for networking, building a brand, and prospecting. 'Twitter is great for creating intelligent conversation, leads, and tips,' she says. Score two for Twitter. Used properly, I see now that Twitter can be a great business-building tool for the right business."

So where I missed the boat, and where I was appropriately called out the most, was in not understanding just how powerful a marketing tool Twitter can be for most small businesses. It turns out that Twitter is often a great way to:

- Get your message out
- Make more contacts
- Become an influencer
- Build your business
- Make more money

But where I still think I was right is that Twitter takes commitment and has to be used intelligently and with a plan if it is to help you grow your business. Just spending time reading tweets and chatting with Twitter friends may be fun, but it isn't productive. That said, I personally have become a convert and Twitter has become an essential part of my marketing and branding strategy. But the question is, Is it right for you? What I want to do in this chapter is answer that question and discuss whether you should even use Twitter for your business, and if so, how to do so the right way.

TWITTER 101

When people go to Twitter for the first time, it seems strange. There are no real explanations of what you are looking at, what a follower is, how you get them, what to tweet, and so on. Let me suggest then that the best comparison is to think of Twitter as a river. It is a continuous stream of tweets, links, information, and conversations floating by. So when you log on to the River Twitter, you are actually walking into the middle of that information flow—that's why it can seem confusing and makes little sense. But what you have to do then is get your feet wet and wade in. Eventually, your job, should you choose to accept, is to be able to navigate your way down and through the river, stopping in for a chat here, making a new contact there, adding your links and thoughts and messages to the stream of information, jumping into new canoes and inviting people into your own.

You begin this journey by signing up for the service and picking a Twitter handle. It is important that you pick one close to your own name or business name so as to not confuse people. Mine is @SteveStrauss. My friend Rieva Lesonsky is @Rieva (there is only one Rieva). You will then set up a home page and create a profile of yourself. As with the rest of Twitter (and the part that is the most infuriating) is that you can use only so many characters in your description (160 to be exact, as opposed to the 140 character limit in your tweets), so you have to be brief and bold. You can also customize your page and you should, branding it with your colors, photo, logo, and so on.

Once you set up your account, bio, and home page, you will want to begin to do the following:

1. *Follow people who interest you.* That is the easiest way to get a feel for the site. Read what they tweet. Follow the links they provide. And once you follow someone, they will likely follow you back.

2. *Begin to tweet.* In a following section I discuss in detail what to tweet, but at the beginning you can tweet introductions, compliments, or articles of interest. Tweet things you find interesting. Tweet videos. By tweeting, you begin to broadcast your message and grow your network. Even better—and the ultimate goal—is that by tweeting you will get retweeted, and that is Twitter gold; it is someone saying to their own followers, "Hey, I found this person's stuff valuable and think you will too." Getting retweeted is how you grow your brand on Twitter.

3. *Network.* Twitter is a networking platform whereby you can easily connect with new people. So connect.

> **Whom to Follow?**
>
> Don't know whom to follow? Then check out WeFollow.com to get some ideas. Or follow famous people you like (but don't expect a follow back). Follow industry experts and leaders. Follow your competition.

Once you are on the site, you will see that there are many different ways to get value out of it. Twitter works for many small businesses for all sorts of reasons:

- It is a great way to network and brand your business. By tweeting the right info to the right people, you can make connections and get to know new people. That is why Twitter is also, of course, a fantastic networking tool.
- It is an excellent resource for staying abreast of news you need to know. Following people and seeing what they tweet is one way, of course, but just as important, follow hashtag conversations. That is, on Twitter, people will use the symbol # in a tweet to direct that tweet to a conversation about similar topics. For example, I always read the #smallbusiness stream. Find the streams that interest you and fit your business. Finally, watching what your competition tweets and whom they follow is, well, interesting.
- Tweeting can also allow you to get branded as an expert: by tweeting your specialized knowledge, you can become the go-to guy or gal on that subject.
- Twitter is a great tool for prospecting—by searching for people, industries, or gigs in the Twitter search box or at Search.Twitter.com, you can look for, find, and meet people who can help you get ahead.
- It is an easy way to grow your online brand equity. Let's face it: having 10,000 followers looks good.

But whereas there is plenty good to be said for Twitter, as indicated, it is far less popular than Facebook for a reason. On Facebook, you will have a direct connection to your friends and fans. Twitter is different. One reason it can seem odd is that you often tweet your tweets into an open Twitterverse of followers, not really knowing who sees what you tweet and often never getting any feedback on it. On Facebook by contrast, the feedback can be instantaneous and personal.

Another reason Twitter is a less popular social media platform is that it is more difficult to generate specific leads and/or see specific results. My friend Tim Berry, the founder of Palo Alto Software (the makers of Business Plan Pro, the source of the business plan in the appendices of this book), is also a social media expert. Tim made the following points in a column for OPEN Forum (September 22, 2011). He notes the following caveats about Twitter as a tool for small business:

1. *It's not really free.* Tim says that, although a Twitter account is free, "to make tweeting effective you need to dedicate time and effort. Just throw a few tweets into the mix every so often and you have nothing but wasted time." And since time is money, Twitter is not as free as it looks (which is true for all social media actually).

2. *Twitter is inherently fuzzy and hard to measure.* "Because of Twitter's inherently social nature, a lot of the business benefits are by their very nature hard to measure. Your Twitter strategy might be about brand awareness, generating leads, validating your expertise or handling complaints . . . but how will you measure the impact of the people you've affected who don't click, or go to a website later, or keep you in mind?"

Top Twitter Tools

- TweetBeep: TweetBeep allows you to set up keyword alerts on Twitter.
- TwitterFon and Tweetie: These iPhone Twitter apps allow you to tweet and notify you of new tweets, replies, and messages.
- TwitPic: TwitPic enables you to share pictures with your followers.
- URL shorteners: Since Twitter allows you only 140 characters, and since people often tweet web pages of interest, it makes sense then that the URLs need to be shortened to fit into a tweet. Plenty of services offer this; I like TinyURL.com.
- TweetDeck: This is one of the most popular third-party Twitter applications out there. A desktop application, TweetDeck is a dashboard that allows you to control your Twitterverse in one place.

So is Twitter right for you? If you are willing to put in the time to learn how it works, follow, get followers, find great content, tweet it, and meet new people, then it can be a powerful networking tool. If all of that sounds like too much work, that's fine too. There are plenty of other places to place your social media efforts. Assuming you want to delve deeper into Twitter, the next question you probably have is this: What to tweet?

What to Tweet?

Throughout this social media section of the book, I have stressed the need to create and/or post great content, content that brings value to others. It is content your customers, viewers, friends, fans, and followers would find interesting and useful. It is content that is fun, funny, intriguing, quirky, or fascinating. It is an article that would help people in their own businesses, a video that they would find appealing, or a free e-book. It is that which makes you a valuable and worthwhile online addition to their busy day. That said then, here is what it is not: another tweet about you and what you are doing or another post that does nothing more than promote you and your business.

So where do you find all of this great content? Here are a few places:

- *You.* You can post interesting blog posts you write, articles you post, or videos you make.
- *Your favorite websites.* As you surf around the web, be sure to mark those articles and pages that you find interesting. It could be industry news or a column you found interesting, whatever the case, you know what you like and what your people will likely like. Trust that.
- *Business Insider, Harvard Business Review, Smart Brief, USA TODAY Money, and so on.* You can find all sorts of great articles of general business interest at sites like these.
- *StumbledUpon.* This cool site lets you sign up and indicate the areas of interest you would like to know more about, and then it helps you stumble upon sites that are about those things.
- *Alltop.* This site is an online version of a magazine rack, except that it has 900 subjects and is free.

But posting articles and other interesting content is only one thing you can and should do with Twitter. The other main idea is to forge connections and engage your audience, and to do that, you need to do more than just post articles. Consider some of these ideas:

- *Offer a freebie.* What about tweeting out a special of the day? People will sign up to follow you just to find out and get the daily deal. You could offer something free or a discount, but the important thing is, using Twitter this way forges a connection and gets people thinking about your business.
- *Retweet.* On Twitter, there may be no bigger compliment than a retweet. A retweet happens when you like someone's tweet so much that you click the retweet button and thereby send it out to all of *your* followers. It is the ultimate twenty-first century word-of-mouth shout out. So, not only can you retweet other's tweets, but you can also know when you are on the right track by seeing which of your tweets get retweeted.

Making It Personal

Another great thing about social media is that it personalizes your business, giving it a more human face. So although mostly people do not care what you had for lunch, it is also smart sometimes to let them peek behind the curtain a bit. By sharing where you went on vacation for instance, or live tweeting the event you are attending, you allow people to have a more personal connection to you and your business.

Getting More Followers

There are many reasons to want more Twitter followers: so you can meet more people and have more conversations, so you can have a farther reach and, let's face it, so you can establish your online brand and credibility; after all, the more followers you have, the stronger your online presence, right? So then the question becomes, How do you get more Twitter followers?

The basic answer, the one you may have heard before and even the one I have given, is that you have to be a great tweeter of great content. Do that and potential followers will organically find and follow you. That said, the quality of your tweets is only one factor. It turns out that there is a lot more to it, and it's not rocket science. Using the techniques that follow, I have quadrupled my own Twitter following in a little more than a year. Here's how:

1. *Follow more people*. The quickest and easiest way to immediately get more Twitter followers is just to begin following more people. There is an unwritten twittiquette that you should follow people who follow you. Therefore, if you follow more people, you will get more followers.
2. *Follow people in your industry who have a high likelihood of following you back*. Here's a personal example of how this works: As I write about small business, I watch and follow the best, most followed small business tweeters I can find. Then I look at their "followers" list and see which people there I would like to follow and then follow them, figuring that if someone follows one of these folks, there is a high chance that they would like to follow me back as well. (Note: I strongly suggest that you do not simply follow all of their followers. This will not only create a bad list for you but will also likely lead to a Twitter terms of service violation.)
3. *Use hashtags to find the good followers*. People who follow your favorite hashtag conversations would be great followers, so meet and follow them. Additionally, it is good practice to add appropriate hashtags to your tweets so that they will show up in those Twitter streams and thereby increase your chances of getting retweeted and followed.
4. *Get retweeted*. As I said, having your followers retweet your content is the best word-of-mouth advertising today. It is like getting an unsolicited endorsement. How do you get retweeted? Tweet great stuff of course, and then . . .
5. *Ask*. It never hurts to ask, right?

Using Twitter to Generate Business and Leads

All of this may be well and good you say, but does it actually lead to more business? That is a good question, because if it is not, what really is the point? Here's how to use Twitter to grow:

1. *Use it to prospect*. There is a search function at the top of your Twitter screen. Use that to search for relevant terms, keywords, people,

industries, and gigs. Find people tweeting about those things and get to know them. Voila! Insta-prospects.

2. *Foster relationships*. The woman I wrote about in my *USA TODAY* column taught me that the key to succeeding with social media is not the quantity of your contacts, but the quality of them. Use Twitter to meet new people, forge new relationships, and thereby potentially grow your business. That is what works. No, it's no magic formula, but it is a real one.

3. *Offer exclusive deals*. Tweeting a special out to your Twitter followers only makes them feel special and can get them to (1) patronize your business to get the special and (2) retweet the deal and thereby expose your business to a lot more people.

Bottom line: No, Twitter is not for everyone, but when used correctly, it is a great weapon in your social media arsenal.

CHAPTER **47**

Link in with LinkedIn

Twitter is like a bar, Facebook is like your living room, and LinkedIn is like the Chamber of Commerce.

—B. S. STOLTZ

Although today Stone Melet is a serial entrepreneur in San Francisco, back in the late 1990s he was a local television anchor/reporter in Charleston, West Virginia. But Melet's life changed significantly after he was afflicted with a disease that was quickly spreading across the globe. *Internetius Start-upitis* was a fast-moving virus causing people of all walks of life to stop what they were doing and head west in search of Internet gold.

Certainly that's exactly what Jeff Bezos did in 1993, after he learned that this thing called the World Wide Web was growing at 2,300 percent a year. Bezos quit his job on Wall Street and pounded out a business plan in the car as his wife drove them across the country to their new home in Seattle. Bezos's plan was in fact brilliant, evidenced by his site Amazon. com. But as we know all too well, plenty of other people were not as savvy and, although they may have even received their share of venture capital

---

Burn Rate

Burn rate is a term used in the start-up world to indicate how quickly a company spends its investment capital, that is, the rate at which a company burns through its money. Needless to say, a high burn rate is usually a very bad sign.

(VC money), not a few flamed out with little to show for their efforts except maybe an impressive burn rate.

Like these other Internet pioneers, back then Melet also thought he had a great idea for a new online business, but unlike most of them, he was right. He raised his VC money, got to work, and actually created a valuable e-product, business, and website. And even after the Internet boom went bust in 2000, taking down thousands of businesses in the process, Melet and his team persisted, survived, and in fact thrived. In the end, the product they created was valuable enough to be bought out by a major on-line player (the terms of which, unfortunately, prevent me from describing further the product, terms, or buyer, but suffice to say, it was significant).

Since then, Stone Melet has created several other successful busi-nesses. So when he says that he has a secret for succeeding in business, I listen. And indeed he does have a new secret these days (and its even one I can share): LinkedIn.

LinkedIn

Today, Melet owns a business called Best Of Legacy, a company that takes media clippings, videos, and other highlights of people in the public spotlight and compiles them into a gorgeous, custom leather book and DVD—the "best of" that person's work that year. Most of the clients are, not surprisingly, athletes, but it could be anyone in the public eye. Far from an ego or vanity thing, the Best Of Legacy books and videos are a great way to pass on a proud legacy to one's children, to generate busi-ness, and so on.

In 2009, Melet had a brainstorm for Best Of. With the election of Barack Obama recently concluded, he realized that the public might be interested in a Best Of Legacy type book of the historic election. But in order to create it, Melet needed to find the right media partners with whom to work—newspapers, magazines, TV stations, and so forth—to ob-tain both the media clippings and the rights to use that media.

That's where LinkedIn came in; that's how Melet found his partners. By tapping into the social media website, by looking at his network and extending it to the people they knew, and even the people his networker's network knew, Melet was able to get introduced to and meet exactly the right people to work with on the project. Before long, Melet and his partners at the *San Francisco Chronicle,* released "Barack Obama: Road to the White House"—Best Of Legacy's first product for sale to the public. "It's because of LinkedIn that the book ever came to be," Melet says.

He adds that, "I still use LinkedIn all of the time. It's my favorite social networking site. Whenever I have a new idea or project and need to find the right person to team up with, LinkedIn is by far the easiest way to locate and meet them."

LinkedIn 101

Let's face it, Twitter is a little weird. Facebook too takes a little getting used to. But LinkedIn? LinkedIn makes sense. LinkedIn is easy. And in all likelihood you have already checked out LinkedIn and may even have an account there. But even if you haven't and don't, the idea is so simple to understand that I need not spend much time explaining it, so here it is in a nutshell:

Step 1: Sign up. On LinkedIn, you start by creating a personal profile in which you list your background, education, career, place of work, specialties, interests, and so on.

Step 2: List your connections. Once you sign up, LinkedIn will ask you to create a log of all of your desired connections, importing the names you choose from your e-mail program of choice. It will then send out an individual e-mail to each person you choose, for example, "Spencer Paulson listed you as someone he has done business with at Paulson Parties and would like to add you to his connections. Click here to accept Spencer's invitation."

Once someone accepts your invitation, that person becomes part of your LinkedIn network. Thereafter, you can contact him or her directly for whatever purpose you may have.

Step 3: Link in. It's not called LinkedIn for nothing. The great thing about LinkedIn is just how vast, and how quickly, your network can become. Consider this: if you have 100 LinkedIn connections and each one of those people has 100 of their own connections, your extended LinkedIn network is suddenly 10,000 people (100×100).

Thereafter, the beauty of LinkedIn is that you have fairly direct access to those 10,000 people. If you want to meet a party planner, you can do a LinkedIn search, and if one pops up as a connection of one of your 100, then all you need do is contact your contact via LinkedIn and ask for an introduction. Nothing beats that sort of personal intro, right? That's how Stone Melet finds the right people for his projects and how you can meet the people you want or need to know for your business.

Pros and Cons

The obvious and first benefit of creating a LinkedIn account and listing your connections is that you will be building an online network that is far more vast, and far more easily and quickly accessible, than anything that you could create in the offline world. Networking is something small business owners do all of the time, something we innately understand. So LinkedIn is great because it gives the small business owner the ability to network on steroids. Whatever your business needs or desires, by using LinkedIn you will be able to network and find people who can take you one step closer to meeting them.

Now, whether you will be able to woo them once you connect with them is another matter. But at least LinkedIn gives you a very good shot at locating and getting to meet the right people. Aside from giving you the ability to be networking to your heart's content, LinkedIn also offers great benefits, discussed next.

Make Connections

By spending some time on LinkedIn and growing your contact list, you will be able to get introduced to and meet a lot of people who may not know you. If you really drill down, you can find not only good contacts generally but those specific people who may need you and your business.

Build Your Business

This, of course, is the key to the whole thing. By vastly extending your network, you have an opportunity to connect with people who can help you take your business to a whole new level. You can:

- Solidify old contacts
- Get introduced to new contacts
- Prospect

Build Your Brand

Like all social media sites, LinkedIn allows you to create and build your own profile. That is actually an incredibly beneficial thing. You can list and highlight what you want about yourself—such as your business and your career—the way you want. The brand you seek to create should be reflected in your profile, and when it is, and when people find you, the impression you create is the one you intend to create.

Additionally, LinkedIn gives you the chance to have people endorse and recommend you. By getting these sorts of independent reviews, you increase your brand equity.

It really is difficult to find many negative things to say about LinkedIn, but here are a few.

Time Commitment

What does not work on any of these social media sites is to simply sign up, and as the old infomercial goes, "set it, and forget it." Nothing comes from that. No, what works on LinkedIn (as well as Twitter, Facebook, and the rest) is making a real commitment to the platform. That means posting and updating your profile, linking up, searching and finding new connections, joining groups, participating—the whole ball of wax.

If you are not ready for that, if you give the site only a half-hearted effort, you are likely wasting your time. You will see few results from that. Social media takes time to see payoffs.

Time Wasting

The flip side of the previous discussion is that it is far too easy to get obsessed with social media and spend far too much time on the various sites, whether that be Facebook or LinkedIn or whatever. If you are spending all of your extra time posting to your LinkedIn groups, for instance, but not seeing a corresponding uptick in business, you are doing something wrong. For small business, social networking should be about the bottom line.

Using LinkedIn to Generate Business

So all of this necessarily begs the question: How do you actually use LinkedIn to grow your business and make more money?

Start with a Great Profile

Your LinkedIn profile is one of the most powerful weapons you have in your social media arsenal. When you Google your own name, you may have noticed that your LinkedIn profile is often near the top of the listings. Because it has such a strong SEO pull, your LinkedIn profile needs to be not fine, not good, but great. It should be:

- Professional
- Well written
- Clear
- Specific
- Chock-full of keywords

That last part is really important. You need to infuse your profile with keywords that broadly explain who you are and what you do. If a main purpose of LinkedIn is to create a vast network (and it is), it makes sense then that you want to be able to be found by people interested in what you do.

Here then is a great trick: list as many specialties and keywords as legitimately possible in your profile. What keywords and key phrases would people in your industry use? For instance, a PR person, instead of just listing public relations, might use "public relations, PR, media, media strategies, media relations, publicity, advertising, communications, PR campaign, publicist." The likelihood that they will be found in a search is much higher the more keywords they use.

Not sure which keywords to use? Try using the Google AdWords Keyword Tool. There is no need to guess—this tool will tell you what terms people search.

Do Something

One of the cool things about LinkedIn is that every time you do something—make a new connection, update your profile, post something—LinkedIn lists it on your home page, which can be added to and sent out as an automatic weekly LinkedIn e-mail blast. By doing something, therefore, you stay top of mind.

Make It Easy

Services that allow you to update all of your social media feeds automatically at once include HootSuite, Yoono, Twitterfeed, and Ping.fm.

Join a Group

Again, the whole point of LinkedIn is to get noticed and make connections that can lead to opportunities and business. Given that, it really helps if you join and participate in some of the many groups on LinkedIn. There are thousands of LinkedIn groups, and by participating in some, you will gain valuable exposure to people in your line of business. By chatting with these folks, posting and answering questions, and posting articles, you can make an online LinkedIn name for yourself.

Tip: If you are a blogger, you can also gain valuable traffic to your blog by posting your posts to your LinkedIn groups.

Prospect

The obvious way to use LinkedIn to get business is by searching, networking, and connecting. The key to that is to tap into the power of the "advanced search" function on the site. Using this tool, you can do a lot more than search for people—you can search industries, professions, businesses, specific job titles, alma maters, zip codes, and more.

Another great way to prospect with LinkedIn is through online recommendations. We all know that satisfied customers are the best source of new customers. On LinkedIn, you can generate online word-of-mouth referrals by asking your happy clients and trusted associates to write you a recommendation. Not only will they be published and seen on your own LinkedIn profile, but—even better—they will be broadcast out to the author's LinkedIn network as well (e.g., "Spencer Paulson just wrote a recommendation for John Johnson").

Other LinkedIn Tricks

Here are some other cool things you can do on LinkedIn:

- *Save searches.* To the far right of your search result is a link that says "save this search." You can save up to three searches.
- *Create a poll.* Your LinkedIn home page need not be static. The polls application is a great way to interact, make your page more interesting, get feedback, and learn what people are thinking. Maybe even more useful is that your poll is a form of shoestring market research.
- *Find out what people are saying about you and about your business.* LinkedIn has a cool tool that allows you to monitor the buzz about your business, called Company Buzz.

CHAPTER **48**

Videos and YouTube

You can't do today's job with yesterday's methods and be in business tomorrow.

—Anonymous

Of all of the things you can include on your website and Facebook page to attract and retain viewers, it turns out that adding video is just about the best, most effective, and most engaging option. It makes a site, as they say, sticky; that is, video is that magic thing that causes people to spend more time on a site—to stick around. And after all, that's what we want—to have people spend more time on our website. By getting people to stick, you have a greater chance to make an impression.

How sticky is video? Consider that almost two in three Americans now watch videos online every month. In addition, according to the online video production site TurnHere.com:

- You are *50 times more likely* to appear on the first page of Google with video on your home page.
- 26 percent of video viewers will visit the physical store.
- 21 percent of video viewers will make a purchase.
- YouTube ranks behind only Google as the world's most popular search engine.

Now, why is video so popular and powerful online? If you think about it for a moment, it makes perfect sense. Web 1.0 was a static place where all you could do was read a website. Most small business sites back then (circa 2000) were nothing more than an e-version of the company's Yellow Page ad. But the Web 2.0 world we are living in now is very different. People expect to interact with a site these days—to respond to a blog post, answer a poll question, and yes, probably most of all, watch a video. People like and watch them and they give your site, and by extension your business, paradoxically, both a more polished image and a more friendly face. Not many other media can offer that. So yes, adding video to your site is almost an imperative.

The questions then becomes, What sorts of video should you make, what can you do with them, and how do you make a great one? Let's find out.

SIX WAYS TO USE VIDEO IN YOUR BUSINESS AND ON YOUR WEBSITE

If you have spent any time on YouTube or otherwise watching video online, you know that the variety of videos available is exhaustive:

- How tos
- Comedy
- Music videos
- And of course, cute cats!

But what works for a small business? It turns out that there are all sorts of different videos you could create to help promote your business and connect with your web visitors.

Top Five Most Popular YouTube Videos as of this Writing

5. Charlie bit my finger - again!—383,893,985 views
4. Eminem - Love The Way You Lie ft. Rihanna—397,807,852 views
3. Shakira - Waka Waka (This Time for Africa)—413,596,535 views
2. Lady Gaga - Bad Romance—424,295,064 views
1. Justin Bieber - Baby ft. Ludacris—649,844,003 views

1. *Provide introductions.* What is the most important page on your website, aside from the home page? Could it be the About page? Maybe. People want to know who you are and click this page to get the answer. So consider putting an introductory video on the About page. Because video is statistically clicked more than almost anything else on a web page, the odds of your About video getting clicked are fairly high. Do you see what a tremendous opportunity that is? An introductory video on your About page can give you that all-important friendly connection; it can create rapport. Maybe you could have one of your kids interview you, or you could interview your staff. Whatever the case, a friendly video allows you to make an impression that simply is almost impossible to duplicate with the written word.

2. *Demonstrate something.* Product demonstrations are almost always inherently interesting—you only need to turn on late-night infomercials to see that. If you can offer a snappy demonstration of some product you sell, then you will have a video that people will likely stick around to watch.

3. *Show off your expertise.* What is it that your business does that others who come upon your site might find enlightening and interesting? For instance:
   - An accountant can discuss the Top Three Mistakes That Trigger an Audit.
   - A pool service can offer Tips on Weatherizing Your Pool or Spa for the Winter.
   - A gift shop can post How to Gift-Wrap Like a Pro.

   The point being, showing off what you do is also subliminally showing why you should be hired. (Tip: When people come to a website, sure they want information—but if you can also make that information entertaining, that is all the better.)

4. *Tour your facility.* A video tour of your office, business, shop, store, or other significant location is an excellent way to engage, interact, and forge a connection with your potential new customer.

5. *Create a web series.* This one is a little more challenging but the payoff may be bigger, too. If you can come up with a multipart series, then what you have created is a way that will, ideally, cause people to come back to your site or Facebook page or YouTube channel time and again.

For instance, on Will Ferrell's comedy site, *Funny or Die,* Zach Galifianakis has a web series called *Between Two Ferns.* Often hilarious and always odd, the series brings people back to the site time and again to see the latest installment. And although you are, of course, not Will Ferrell or Zach Galifianakis, by the same token, they are not you either; you know things they do not.

6. *Include testimonials.* Testimonials generally from happy customers are always valuable because, rather than it being you saying your business is great (in an advertisement or whatever), a testimonial is independent, third-party verification that your business is in fact special. Because it comes from someone else, a testimonial is given greater weight by the reader or viewer.

And in the case of video, that already-significant power of testimonials geometrically increases because the testimonial can be viewed. There is a greater gravitas to video testimonials—people will automatically view both the video and the statement therein as more credible since they can see the person making the statement.

HOW TO CREATE A GREAT SMALL BUSINESS VIDEO

No matter what sort of video (or, ideally, videos) you choose to make for your site or to post on YouTube or your Facebook page, there are certain Internet conventions your videos must conform to if they are to be successful. As you well know, online videos are a breed unto themselves; some are great, many are awful, others are boring, and a few go viral. Fortunately, for the small business, you need not create the World's Greatest Video for yours to be effective. Rather, what you need to do is create video content that can be easily consumed, which is useful; video that is somewhat memorable; and video that puts your business's best foot forward. Yours should contain some or all of the following elements.

Great Content

The phrase is not "content is prince" or "content is duke." No, they say "content is king" for a reason—because it is, and it is as true for your video as it is for your blog posts, your tweets, or the articles you write.

For your content to be worth someone's time, then it needs to be worth someone's time. You have to put some forethought into it and consider what it is that you think your customers, fans, and followers would find interesting. What is it you can offer in video format that your people would like? If you have some specialized knowledge, that of course would work. If you can be humorous, great. The important thing is that you present the information in your video in a way that is accessible and which promotes your brand to the best extent possible.

But you also need not create a basic, down the middle video either. For instance, if you want to create a video that people forward to one another—that has the chance to go viral—then a how-to or product demonstration video won't do. Instead, what works is laughter or tears. If you can create a video that makes people either laugh or cry, you are on the right track for a video home run. (That said, keep your audience and brand in mind. You probably do not want to create a comedic video if yours is a serious business.)

Not Too Long

Not only are we living in a time of shorter attention spans, but people have come to expect that videos online will be no more than a few minutes in length. Longer, and people generally tune out. This means that your videos need to be short and snappy for the most part. How short? It is normally accepted that about three minutes is an ideal length for online videos. Yes, four minutes can work, but five is definitely pushing the limit. Notice the length of the videos you watch online, and at what point you start to lose interest. It is likely around the 4-minute mark if you are like most people.

Context Is King, Too

Context is also king. Three minutes is a fine length for a lot of videos, but it also depends on the subject matter and your goals. An online course will necessarily require longer videos than a funny bit about your shop. It all depends, but always keep in mind Shakespeare's notion about the matter (someone I think we can all agree is an expert on the subject of content, right?): "Brevity is the soul of wit."

Make It Accessible

Fortunately, in this era when it seems that anyone and everyone is creating some sort of online content, your content need not be perfect to be useful. Videos in particular can be fairly informal, and that offers you a great opportunity to make a great impression. How often do you get someone's undivided attention for three minutes online? Rarely. If you make your videos stiff and formal, you are probably missing out on an excellent opportunity to bond with your viewer.

So consider making your videos:

- Friendly
- Funny
- Quirky
- Positive, etc.

Of course, you will want to come across as smart and knowledgeable too, but to the extent you can be less formal, it probably behooves you to do so.

Break It Up

If you ever analyze a television news segment (and for our purposes here, I suggest you do), what you will notice is that there are many edits and cuts; the action rarely stays on one subject for more than, say, 30 seconds or so, and most cuts are just a few seconds long. The same is true for TV shows and movies—the action moves (unless, of course, you are watching *Star Wars, Episode I: The Phantom Menace,* but I digress).

Keep that in mind as you consider the video(s) you will be making for your small business. For instance, people are not used to watching someone speak into the camera nonstop for four minutes. They will surf on long before that. What works, what keeps people engaged, what holds their interest, and what makes you look like a pro (even if you are not one) is to break it up. Here are some ways to do that:

- Shoot from different angles.
- Shoot indoors and outdoors.
- Insert some stock footage into the segment, that is, if you are discussing food, cut in some pictures of food. In the industry, this is called B-roll.

- Have more than just one person in the piece.
- Insert slates with bullet points.

All of this may sound difficult, but the opposite is actually true. Computer technology and software make editing videos a breeze these days. Even if you can't do it, your teenager probably can. Or hop onto Craigslist and find a pro. You can likely get someone to shoot and edit your videos for a couple of hundred bucks, or less.

Be Transparent

On all of your videos, be sure that the name of your business and/or URL is obvious. You never know who may see it or where, but you want them to be able to find you when they do. So be sure to insert your vital info in the beginning, or as a watermark in the middle, or as an ending credit.

Don't Spend a Lot of Money

Aside from the ease by which technology makes making a video today, a corresponding fact is that you do not, and probably should not, spend a lot of money producing your videos. What you need is a good (but not necessarily great) digital video camera, some lighting, and some editing software (versions of which come pre-installed on operating systems now). A few hundred bucks and you are good to go.

VIDEO, YOUTUBE, AND YOUR BUSINESS

Once you have created your cool videos, there are a few places to post them:

- Your website
- Your blog
- Your Facebook, LinkedIn, and Twitter pages
- YouTube and the like

Going Viral

Want people to forward links of your videos on to their friends and associates? Of course you do. Then try this nifty trick: add a link to the video, along with a catchy description, to your e-mail signature. Not only will your recipients likely click on it, but once they like it, it is easy for them to forward your e-mail on with the link to their network.

Indeed, when people think about online video, they automatically think of YouTube, although, of course, there are many similar places to post your video content. But because YouTube is the standard, let's look at that site and its possibilities a little more in depth.

Here are just some of the ways you can combine video and YouTube to get ahead in business:

- Upload your videos: YouTube gets more than a billion views per day. That is one big audience.
- Post presentations you have given.
- Post interviews with experts.
- Post customer testimonials.
- Upload videos of business events.
- Answer customer questions.

Another option, and one you have seen if you have spent any time on the site, is to create your own, branded YouTube channel. On YouTube, a channel is really nothing more than a home page for an account. The channel will give the account name and type, the public videos that have been uploaded there, as well as essential user information. Additionally, a channel will also display friends, comments, subscribers, and so on.

For the small business, there are several benefits to creating a YouTube channel. First, they are another affordable way to stake out some social media and Internet real estate. Channels can also help you prospect, build a list, and extend your brand. And if your channel becomes popular, you can make a lot of money with advertisements on your videos.

How to Post to YouTube

"Click the Upload link at the top of any YouTube page. Click the Upload video button to browse for the video file you'd like to upload to our site. Select the file you want to upload and click Open. As the video file is uploading, enter as much information about your video as possible in the relevant fields (including Title, Description, Tags, and Category). You're not required to provide specific information, but the more information you include, the easier it is for users to find your video! Click the Save changes button to save the updates you've made to the video file."

—YouTube.com

Here are some tips on successfully creating your own YouTube channel:

- *Understand that it will take time and effort.* To create a popular channel requires that you create valuable content, upload it, tag and describe it, and search engine optimize it, let people know it is out there, and then repeat. That all takes time. So in that sense building a successful YouTube page is not that much different than creating any other popular social media page. It takes planning and effort.
- *Remember, it's not just about watching videos.* YouTube, like any social media site, is social. People post and comment and chat and share. You have to be part of that conversation if you want to influence it.
- *And remember too, it's also a search engine.* You have to optimize your videos with the right keywords and key phrases and links if you want to be found.

VIDEOS AND SEARCH ENGINE OPTIMIZATION

Aside from posting to YouTube, posting videos to your own site make a great impression, helps you connect with your customers, and affordably gets your message out. But maybe better than all of these is this: by posting video to your site the right way, you significantly increase your chances of ending up on page 1 of search engine result rankings. Yes, that's right: page 1—the Holy Grail of SEO.

In this book, I have talked plenty about SEO, keywords and key phrases, incoming links, and so on. The problem is, plenty of people know a lot about SEO too, and there is a lot of content available, and that is why their articles end up on the first page of a Google search instead of yours (or many of mine for that matter). With so much written content out there, and so many people who know how to optimize it, the competition is incredibly tough and the chance to end up on page 1 increasingly small. That then begs the question: Is there anything you can do to even the playing field? Yes. That is where SEO video comes in.

What I am not talking about is simply putting a video on your site with an embedded YouTube player or posting your videos to YouTube. Those are different strategies and a fine way to get your videos viewed, but neither will generate great Google results for your site because they are not search engine optimized, and using a YouTube player will result in SEO results for YouTube.

Here is why video SEO is an amazing page 1 generator: First, search engines now use "blended" search results, where they don't just list articles or web pages but also videos, pictures, and other content. So video gets more play because there is less competition for video results as opposed to article results. And that is the second, and more important, reason. Because there is so much less of it, and because only very little of all online video is properly search engine optimized, there is a disproportionate bias towards properly optimized video. You end up being a big fish in a very small pond.

So here is what you do:

1. Create some great video.
2. Post it prominently throughout your site.
3. Search engine optimize it and submit it. First, you must optimize the video. That means that keywords and phrases must be used in the file name, in the page URL, in the video's captions, and so on. Second, once you have posted the video on your site, you need to then submit it using XML tools to Google and the other search engines. That last part sounds geeky because it is, but it need not be. There are some great online services that will submit the videos for you. For example, Fliqz.com will properly index and submit your videos to the various search engines.

The upshot is that your videos and video pages should end up at or near the top of relevant search results. In fact, according to Fliqz, by using its "SearchSuccess" tools, "more than two-thirds of all videos submitted produce a first-page Google search result, and up to 25 percent have resulted in a number one Google ranking."

Well, what are you waiting for?

CHAPTER 49

Groupon and Other Deal-of-the-Day Websites

Businesses use Groupon because we deliver a ton of new customers to their door.

—ANDREW MASON, GROUPON FOUNDER

Which one of these quotes is real?

"The response was fantastic. Our phone has been ringing nonstop and we've gotten new customers who heard about us through Groupon but missed the deal."

or

"I take full responsibility for my decision. Please do not attempt to interpret this post as me blaming Groupon or our customers for anything. I am merely sharing the experience. The decision to run a Groupon campaign was my own decision, and one I regret. [In fact] it has been the single worst decision I have ever made as a business owner thus far. . . . "

Would you be surprised to learn that both quotes are real, from real business owners who decided to sign up for the burgeoning phenomenon that is Groupon? The first quote, the happy one, if from Greg Major of

487

Bulldog Bootcamp & CrossFit. His business ran an incredibly successful Groupon campaign for his 6,000-square-foot fitness center.

The second quote comes from Jessie, the owner of Posies Bakery and Café in Portland, Oregon. Although the Posies Groupon campaign did in fact expose the business to a ton of new people, the structure of the deal (as explained later in this chapter) made it such that, among other things, Jessie was unable to meet payroll at one point due to the burden of the Groupon deals she was obliged to honor and as such she had to pull $8,000 out of her own savings to meet payroll that month.

Are Groupon, LivingSocial, and the explosion of similar deal-of-the-day sites a winner or a loser for your business? Are they a way to make a lot of money or lose a lot of money? Are they a chance to get exposure to a vast amount of new people or a way to attract nothing but cheap looky-loos?

Yes.

OVERVIEW

In all likelihood you have not only heard of Groupon, LivingSocial, and the like, but you have probably bought a deal or two from one or more of these sorts of sites. And why not? The deals are amazing. My wife bought a series of yoga classes last month that penciled out to be four bucks each. So, with daily deals like that, it is not hard to understand sites like these have had nothing short of explosive growth. In fact, a report conducted by Groupon, and as reported in *Forbes Magazine*, states that the site is projected to "make $1 billion in sales faster than any other business, ever."

It's certainly not hard to understand why these sorts of daily deal sites have been growing by leaps and bounds. Especially in a tough economy, people like to get a good deal, and that's exactly what you get when you sign up and buy a deal from a site like Groupon or LivingSocial:

- One of the most popular of these kinds of deals in history occurred on January 19, 2011, when Amazon.com made an amazing offer through LivingSocial: purchasers could get a $20 Amazon gift card for just $10. The deal attracted 1.4 million purchases.
- On March 2, 2011, Fandango and LivingSocial teamed up to offer two movie tickets for only $9. More than 1 million tickets sold in two days.

Deals like that are just about impossible to beat, and that is why such sites have become so popular so fast. Not surprisingly then, a slew of copycat daily deal discounts sites have also recently come online, looking to cash in on this modern day gold mine (a gold mine for the deal-of-the-day sites at least, if not for the small business owners who too often learn the hard way the meaning of the phrase "loss leader," but we will get to that in a moment). Walmart started experimenting with a deal-of-the-day business model as have many other retailers and online stores.

Not surprisingly, each service is a bit different, but not all that much. Let's look at how the main two work:

Groupon

The word *Groupon,* you may have surmised, is an abbreviation of "group coupon." It often works like this: The small business owner contacts Groupon and works with a rep to craft a deal. Typically, Groupon likes offers that are at least 50 percent off of the retail price—so BE CAREFUL! You don't want to lose money in the deal. Groupon reps work with you to schedule the offer and then they do the rest—write up the deal and blast it out on deal day. You don't pay Groupon a dime, but they do take a percentage of all sales.

Then, in your city, if a certain number of people sign up to buy that deal, it goes "live" and becomes available to everyone. Groupon takes approximately 50 percent of all revenue received from the deal, so it might work out something like this: You own a restaurant and offer a steak dinner for two for $20 (normally $40). Of the $20 received for the Groupon, Groupon gets $10. You, the restaurant owner, will be on the hook to sell a $40 meal for $10.

So yes, a lot of people will buy your amazing deal and learn about your business, and yes, it can also be a big risk.

LivingSocial

With LivingSocial, the consumer needs to subscribe via e-mail for the service and then receives an e-mail each day describing the offer of the day for his or her area. Unlike Groupon, there is no minimum threshold number of purchases necessary to partake in the offer (and for all practical purposes, the Groupon deal almost always goes live), but in any case, as with Groupon, LivingSocial subscribers can then buy the discount deal via LivingSocial and save a bundle.

Time Magazine Q & A with Groupon Founder Andrew Mason (June 24, 2009)

Q: Why should anyone use Groupon?

A: Groupon features an unbeatable daily deal on great stuff to do in major cities across the United States. We feature the things you're doing already, but for way less. So in that sense, Groupon is a couple hundred extra bucks in your pocket each month. On top of that, we take those things you've maybe always wanted to try and offer them at prices you can't refuse, giving you the extra push to get out there and do them.

Q: The goods featured on Groupon tend to be splurge-y sorts of items—spa treatments, dance classes, baseball tickets. They're not exactly things people need. What sort of more practical, essential items have been on Groupon?

A: Definitely a big part of Groupon is taking some of those nicer things that are hard to afford these days and bringing them back within reach. But we also try to use our membership's collective buying power to negotiate great deals on stuff everyone needs. We've had Groupons for teeth cleaning, eye exams, discounted apartment leases, dry cleaning, car washes, chiropractors, and transportation services like Zipcar, to name a few.

It should already be fairly clear that there are both big risks and big rewards when thinking about whether offering a Groupon sort of deal is right for your business. Let's look at both the upsides and downsides so you can make a smart, informed decision.

THE GOOD NEWS

Groupon in particular has exploded in popularity for a very good reason: it gave consumers what they wanted, namely, discounts—great big, fat, amazing discounts—at a time when there was clearly a significant unmet need for that sort of offer. Specifically, in a recessionary economy people want, nay need, to save money. That is why in such times people flock to discounters and sales, clip coupons and look for deals. Given that, there are not many better deals out there than what people can find on deal-of-the-day sites like Groupon.

As I said previously in this book, one tried-and-true success strategy for business growth is "ask them what they want, then give them what they want." That philosophy supersized is essentially what you get with Groupon.

So up front what you know is that if you do a deal with Groupon, you are going to get some significant attention. New people, people who have never been exposed to your business before, will hear about you. That's nothing short of fantastic. Small business owners try all sorts of ideas, tricks, and strategies to get heard above the din (the rest of this book is evidence of that), so it cannot be ignored that Groupon, LivingSocial, and their ilk have hit upon a definable, reliable, repeatable way to reach and catch the eye of a lot of consumers. That's tough to find fault with. In an era when there is just so much darn competition out there, the ability to make an impression on a lot of potentially new customers is not to be taken lightly.

Other benefits of doing your own deal of the day include:

- *Sales.* The correlation to getting all of this new exposure is that you will definitely sell more—maybe a lot more. Now, will you be able to make a profit? That is the question.

Hyundai Nets 1,300+ Customers with Groupon Deal (*Motor Trend*, April 26, 2011)

"Last week Hyundai became the first automaker to use the online coupon site to attract dealership service customers. 10 Hyundai dealers in the Chicago area offered a $29 Groupon promotion for an oil change, tire rotation, a multipoint inspection and a basic car wash, which . . . is worth up to $79.95, a savings of 63 percent. More than 1,300 customers took advantage of the deal. Said Brian O'Malley, general manager of Hyundai Motor America's Central Region, Based on initial response, we can clearly call the pilot program a success in driving traffic. The question now is if the automaker will use the site to drive up sales leads with possible leasing or financing deals."

I mentioned loss leaders earlier and, at the risk of being redundant, the risks and rewards they offer bear some reiteration here. Groupon works because businesses are willing to take a steep discount in exchange for vast exposure. In that sense, as discussed next, one way to think of Groupon is as an advertising medium. If you do that, you would likely be looking less at the immediate profit (or as the case may be, loss) and more at the long-term beneficial ramifications from the exposure.

That said, a loss leader is still a loss leader. You have to be darn sure that the price you end up getting (e.g., $10 for a $40 steak meal) will at least cover your nut. Losing money on a sale—or worse, on many, many sales—is neither a pleasurable experience nor a savvy business move. So the ideal way to offer a daily deal is to price it just high enough so that, even after the site gets its cut, you at least break even, or at best, make a small profit. That is the win–win–win–win: Groupon gets its cut, your new customers get a great deal, you get that all-important exposure (and you even make a little money to boot).

- *Advertising and marketing.* As indicated, another significant factor when considering the Groupon model, aside from a boost in sales, is that it can also be viewed as a unique way to advertise, market, and/or brand your business. I always say that being in business is like being in a room without the light on—no one knows you are there. You turn on the light by marketing and advertising your business—this is how new people discover your business. So in that vein, if nothing else, a Groupon-type campaign will turn the light on and expose your business to a lot of new people.
- *Looky-loos.* In business, looky-loos get a bad rap. You know who these folks are, right? These are the people who sample the food at Costco but never buy the product. They are the ones who think nothing of having their real estate agent show them 42 homes, and then end up buying the 43rd . . . with a different agent. These are the people who come into your store, look, and leave.

So sure, these people get a bad rap for plenty of good reasons. But there is also something good to be said about looky-loos, especially insofar as discount group buying sites go, and namely it is this: They are looking. They are open. They want to discover something new. How great is that?

We all love our old customers for many reasons, but we especially appreciate their loyalty and longevity. We can usually rest assured that they are *our* customers, even if a bight shiny new store opened down the way. Regular customers are the bread and butter of any business.

But even so, customers do leave; even reliable, regular, long-term customers leave, and they do so for all sorts of reasons—good and bad alike. Given that, and given that we all like to grow, it turns out that looky-loos might be just as valuable as the long-term customer. Why? Because we need someone to take their place. We need people who have open minds and are not set in their ways with regard to a product or service. The fact that they are looking means that we have a great chance to impress them and turn them into our new, hopefully soon-to-be old customers.

Okay, so there is plenty of good to be said for Groupon: A lot of new people will hear about your business and will pay a discounted fee to be able to check it out. You will gain incredible exposure and be afforded the opportunity to impress, sell to, and hopefully convert, a slew of potential new customers.

But that all said, there is a lot of bad to be said as well.

Top Sites

Top five daily-deals sites, by percentage of visits, according to *USA TODAY* (September 2, 2011): Groupon (47 percent), LivingSocial (30 percent), Eversave (11 percent), Dealfind (4 percent), and Bloomspot (2 percent).

THE BAD NEWS

The bad news when it comes to Groupon and its kin is not insignificant, and in many ways, it outweighs the good news. For starters, let's look at this idea of conversions.

Conversions? What do you get when you offer a steep discount to the masses? Masses looking for a steep discount. Very few people in fact woke up this morning looking for your auto detailing service, but then they came across your incredible LivingSocial offer of a $99 detailing for $49 and figured, "Why the heck not?" It was too good of a deal to pass up.

The problem is, will you be able to convert that bargain-hunter into a real, ongoing customer willing to pay your normal prices when what he or she was more interested in was the discount and one-time deal and not your service?

Hopefully, but not necessarily. These people, these discount hunters, will come in, try out your business, and take their spoils. But the question is whether you will be able to impress them enough that they would re-up, and at actual, retail prices no less? That is a tough sell—not only will they have to like you enough to want to stick around, but after being spoiled by your LivingSocial prices, they will have to like you so much that they will be willing to pay about double to stay with you.

Because that is such a challenge, not a few small businesses have found that converting deal-of-the-day customers into real customers is very, very difficult.

Capacity. I once had a colleague who really wanted to get his pizza restaurant reviewed by the local paper. So we put together some press materials and lo and behold, the restaurant critic bit and came out a few weeks later. That next Friday, there was a five-star glowing review in the paper.

Marketing gold, right? Wrong.

It was a total disaster for my friend. He was completely unprepared for the onslaught of customers that stormed his establishment that night, and that weekend. He ran out of dough early, did not have enough wait-staff on hand, the line grew to be an hour and a half long, and people got impatient. In the end, he angered a lot of customers—new and old alike. What a wasted opportunity.

That is the same risk businesses take with Groupon. If you are not ready for the masses, if it is going to overwhelm your business, don't do it. Many Groupon participants hire extra staff to handle the overflow. Will that pencil out for you?

Current customer issues. By the same token, what will your current customers think and do while you are busy servicing all of these new people who are paying less? Hint: They will not be happy. I recently heard of a salon that got so overwhelmed by Groupon customers that the owner had to start to book appointments for old customers four months out. Needless to say, she had a lot of damage control to do once the promotion ended.

Staffing Issues

Consider too the effect of a deal-of-the-day offer on your staff. They will know that the looky-loos are not their real customers and will likely act accordingly; it's human nature. And in that case what do you get? Overworked employees who are ambivalent about this new crowd and a new crowd that will probably be getting less than 100 percent effort from your staff.

Branding. You have carefully cultivated your brand, and unless you are a discount warehouse or Taco Bell, I can safely bet that your brand is probably not based on being a discounter or "the low cost leader."

Except now it is. When you advertise a deal on Groupon or Living-Social, what you are saying is that, despite everything else you offer and do right, low prices are your calling card. No matter what else you have done to build your business and create your brand, when you get into the cutting prices game, you not only cut into your margins but also slice up your carefully cultivated brand too.

Possible loss of money. There are plenty of stories out there about how entrepreneurs love and made a lot of money with Groupon, as well as just the opposite—people who have lost money and would never do it again. With Groupon taking a cut of roughly half (sometimes more and, yes, sometimes less), it is easy to see how the numbers don't crunch for some businesses.

Here then, in her own words, is an excerpt from a blog written by Jessie Burke, the owner of Posies Bakery and Café in Portland Oregon, and the woman whose negative quote opens this chapter, explaining why Groupon was her worst business decision, ever:

Groupon, In Retrospect

For months I've been thinking about whether or not to write a blog post about Groupon, and sharing the kind of experience it has been for the business. I've been weighing the possible reper-cussions of such a candid post as well, but after today, and having to decline a longtime customer's Groupon for being past the expiration date, she asked that I share with everyone the reality of Groupon.

Today one of our most loyal customers, Lucinda, came in and asked if she could use her Groupon that had expired the day before. I felt terrible, but I had to say no. . . . So I explained to Lucinda, and now to all of you, how Groupon works for the businesses, and why it has been the single worst decision I have ever made as a business owner thus far.

I heard about Groupon, and after doing my research, I thought the idea was pretty clever. I, the business owner, would offer a discount to the consumers utilizing Groupon's social network, and we would get noticed by many who may never have seen us otherwise. A great marketing opportunity and way to increase future foot traffic! I assumed Groupon would take a percentage, but that it wouldn't be that huge . . . maybe 5–10 percent?

I spoke with John, a Groupon rep, and . . . we talked pricing. We were going to offer a $6 for $13 (pay $6 and get $13 worth of product) because John told me people really respond to deals that are over 50 percent discount. John told me that when the consumer pays less than $10, Groupon usually takes 100 percent of the money. What?! He reassured me that most customers buy more than the $13, and that we would never have to advertise again after taking advantage of their network. I said, "Ok, let me think about it."

I hung up and thought it over. I called him back and said we would have to get at least 50 percent to cover our costs of product; to this day I don't know why I thought even 50 percent would be a good deal for us. Maybe because I thought since we were covering our food costs. What I didn't think clearly enough about was that that margin we mark up is what covers all of our other costs . . . like staff, rent, utilities, etc.

Against my husband's advice, I decided to do it knowing how many other businesses I admired had utilized Groupon. We were featured on March 9th and sold nearly 1,000 Groupons. When I talked to Lucinda today, she asked if there was a cap on how many were sold to help protect the business from too much loss, and the simple answer is, no. When you sign up for Groupon, you are agreeing to sell as many as get sold . . . and why would Groupon want it any other way? They get half of the earnings.

We were bombarded the first weekend after our feature. Over the six months that the Groupon is valid, we met many, many wonderful new customers, and were so happy to have them join the Posies family. At the same time we met many, many terrible Groupon customers—customers that didn't follow the Groupon rules and used multiple Groupons for single transactions, and argued with you about it with disgusted looks on their faces, or who tipped based on what they owed (10 percent of $0 is zero dollars, so tossing in a dime was them being generous). Or how about the lady that came in the day of Groupon and asked for the Groupon discount without an actual Groupon in hand because she preferred to give us all $6 rather than half of it to Groupon.

After three months of Groupons coming through the door, I started to see the results really hurting us financially. There came a time when we literally could not make payroll because at that point in time we had lost nearly $8,000 with our Groupon campaign. We literally had to take $8,000 out of our personal savings to cover payroll and rent that month. It was sickening, especially after our sales had been rising. So the experience jaded me, and the interactions with the few bad Groupon customers we had jaded our staff. After all of this, I find myself not even willing to buy Groupons because I know how it could hurt a business (side note: service industry businesses do quite well with features like this because it is just the cost of time—you are not paying for a product for resale. Resale, in my opinion, get hit the hardest).

In short, to dear Lucinda and anyone else that comes in with a Groupon in hand, please know that our respectful decline of your coupon is not personal. It's because we cannot afford to lose any more money on this terrible decision I made, and the only saving grace we had was an expiration date. (www.posiescafe.com)

So, as they used to say in *Hill Street Blues:* Be careful out there.

PART

Growth Strategies

CHAPTER 50

Developing New Channels and Multiple Profit Centers

Do the one thing you think you cannot do. Fail at it. Try again. Do better the second time. The only people who never tumble are those who never mount the high wire.

—OPRAH WINFREY

To grow your business, you are going to have to try new strategies and tactics, meet some new people, and do things that you have not done before. There will be a learning curve, and you will make some mistakes along the way. Although that is all true, as always, I want to help you increase the likelihood of success. In this section, we will look at what it takes to get your business to the next level—whether it is increased sales or finding new and bigger clients. In this chapter specifically, we will look at how adding multiple profit centers and bigger clients are smart steps.

PRELIMINARY CONSIDERATIONS

The first step in deciding how to grow your business is to figure out what is your *core competency*. That's business jargon for understanding and doing what you do best. When you know your core competency, you can begin to add revenue streams that are logically related to that strength, but when you don't, finding new ways to grow your business becomes more of a crapshoot. What you do not want to do is put a lot of time, energy, and money into plans that have little chance for success because they are outside your area of expertise. Defining what you do best allows you to better analyze opportunities that come your way.

So what is your core competency? What does your business do best? You want to define your core competency broadly enough to allow for opportunity but narrowly enough that you do not get distracted chasing leads that can become time-consuming, expensive, and possibly even disastrous. It does you no good to pretend that you can run a restaurant if you are really in the grocery store business. The core competency for my business is the ability to accumulate and disseminate useful small business information. This means that opportunities that come along for speeches, books and columns, or media make sense for us. But creating a retail product is something we know nothing about, and so even though such an opportunity might someday present itself, the time and effort it would take us to move from concept to product would be too great, and we would likely miss opportunities that do fall within our specialty.

I once heard a radio interview with the CEO of a cellular phone company whose business had recently bought the naming rights to a baseball stadium. The interviewer asked him whether he could foresee a day when his business might buy the team itself. The CEO answered that he knew what his company's core competency was—providing great cellular phone service—and that meant he was not in the business of buying baseball franchises. That is the value of understanding your core competency.

What is it that you do best? As you begin to think about additional profit centers that you could add to your business, keep in mind your core competency.

MULTIPLE PROFIT CENTERS

Once you have decided what your core competency is, then it is time to begin to find additional ways to make money by leveraging it. The first strategy I want to share for doing this is adding *multiple profit centers,* a term coined by my friend Barbara Winter in her great book *Making a Living without a Job.* The basic idea is that, although most small businesses have one basic way to make a buck, the best ones have several. They have multiple profit centers.

The advantages of having multiple profits centers are twofold:

1. *It fosters growth.* Additional profit centers create additional income.
2. *It evens out your cash flow.* Anyone who owns a business knows that the money tends to come in the door in cycles. When the money is flowing, you are able to pay all your bills on time, try some new advertising, even sock some cash away. But when the cycle turns, as it inevitably does, things get challenging. Having multiple profit centers evens things out. When one part of your business is down, another part may be up. A smart stock investor does the same thing. He or she knows not to buy just one stock. That stock may go up, but it may also go down. Having more than one stock ensures that when one stock does go down, the likelihood of taking a big financial hit is remote because other stocks are going up; thus, the investor's portfolio is diversified. Having multiple profit centers offers similar protection for your businesses.

This is what all great businesses do. Amazon began selling books, and then—wanting to be able to continue to sell when book sales dipped—added music, electronics, pet food, and more. Money continues to flow in the door despite the business cycle.

There are five steps to creating your additional profit centers.

Step 1: Build on Your Brand

At the risk of sounding redundant, your new profit centers must fit in with and complement what you are already doing. By adding logical profit centers, you build rather than dilute your brand. A store that sells spas can extend into other recreational products—barbecues, pool tables, backyard furniture, and so on. But the Chinese restaurant down the street that is now advertising "American Breakfasts!" seems to be missing the point. You need to choose a new endeavor that does not confuse your customers or diminish your brand.

Step 2: Look at New Products and Line Extensions

Offering new products or services to your existing business, or creating what are known as *line extensions,* is an excellent way to create additional profit centers. For example, Tom's of Maine started out selling natural toothpaste. It then added logical line extensions: natural floss and mouthwash, shaving cream and soap, deodorant. But notice that Tom's does not sell clothing. That wouldn't fit.

The key, then, to extending your line is to assess which products or services you can add that will complement and expand your current offerings. If you sell handmade jewelry, you most certainly do not want to start selling schlocky costume jewelry. Remember, a good brand attracts some people and repels others. That's fine. That is the idea. McDonald's is not for everybody.

Step 3: Consider New Markets or New Locations

One way to create an additional profit center is to add new products to what you already offer. Another is to target a new market altogether. These days, there is no shortage of markets available, thanks to the Internet. There are markets, both physical and virtual, available to you that have never been available to any small business before in history. Sell on eBay. Start an online store on your website. Export to India. Open a new location. Try a new market.

Step 4: Start Small, but Think Big

Start small and test, test, test. You want to be sure that the idea really works before committing significant resources to it. If your tests show that the idea is not as good as you thought, then you haven't lost much. If, on the other hand, your test indicates that you have a winner, you can roll it out in a big way. One time at the law firm, I wanted to start another new practice area. I began by simply sending a letter to old clients announcing the new practice, just to see what the reaction would be. That one $100 mailing ended up generating six-figure revenues. Once I saw that the new profit center had real potential, we jumped into it in a big way—with advertising, training, and so on. But it started with a simple and inexpensive mailing to test the waters.

Step 5: Take the Leap

Having brainstormed ideas that fit within both your core competency and your brand, having considered both line extensions and new markets, and having tested various ideas to see which have the greatest likelihood of success, the next step is to stop testing and jump into the deep end. I recommend all of that homework and slow going so as to avoid an expensive mistake—to minimize the inherent risk involved. But once you are convinced that you have a winner, then it is time to go for it. Commit the money, resources, and time necessary to give it your very best shot.

Example:
- A restaurant could begin to offer catered, delivered lunches to all of the office buildings in the area. It could offer catering to the public. In off-hours, the chef could teach a cooking class. What about selling that famous cheesecake online?
- An antiques dealer could begin to offer wares on eBay. The dealer could start an antique restoration service. What about selling at festivals? He or she could consign his antiques to other stores.

One of the great entrepreneurs ever is billionaire Richard Branson, owner of the Virgin Group. Branson had the multiple profit center strategy in mind from the moment he opened his first business—a record store above a shoe shop in London where he bartered his rent. That is why he named his business the Virgin *Group*. Virgin Music was eventually joined by Virgin Atlantic, Virgin Megastores, Virgin Books, and most recently, and maybe most improbably, Virgin Galactic.

"When we start a new venture, we base it on hard research and analysis. Typically, we review the industry and put ourselves in the customer's shoes to see what could make it better. We ask fundamental questions: Is this an opportunity for restructuring a market and creating competitive advantage? What are the competitors doing? Is the customer confused or badly served? Is this an opportunity for building the Virgin brand? Can we add value? Will it interact with our other businesses? Is there an appropriate trade-off between risk and reward?"

—Virgin.com

SELLING YOUR PRODUCT TO BIG STORES

A strategy that is related to the multiple profit centers concept is that of selling to big business. Corporations not only look to buy from small businesses but also have the budgets to make your life easier. Here's how to create a new profit center by landing the big fish.

Although getting your product into major chain stores is not easy, it can be done. Many small businesses have done it—just witness the thousands of products already on store shelves—and if they did it, so can you. How? Here are a few methods.

Start at the Top

All chain stores have buyers who decide what the store will stock. These are the people you will have to woo in order to get your product into a large chain. They are not easy to reach, but you must reach them if you are to sell your product in their stores. You will probably have to start with underlings and sell them on the idea before being able to reach the head honcho, so your sales skills have to be sharp and your product has to be first-rate. You will also have to be able to convince the buyer that you have the capacity to produce the product or purchase enough of the item in question to keep the shelves stocked.

This last point needs to be underscored. Do you have the capability to fulfill an order for, say, 50,000 widgets? If so, great—pass Go and collect $200. But if not, do not waste your time trying to sell to the big boys. And what if the widgets do not sell? Can you handle a lot of returns? You simply have to be at a level at which you can handle the needs of a large client if you are going to make a play for them.

Start Small

Barry Bonds, baseball's home run king, hit a total of 762 home runs. Pete Rose, baseball's all-time hits leader, had 4,256 hits, 3,215 of them singles. Lesson: You have a much better chance of getting a hit when you go for a single than when you swing for the fences. (Second lesson: Maybe it helps to be a schmo if you want to really succeed in baseball!)

Aside from targeting a big buyer who buys for the entire chain, it may be a smarter strategy to go after individual stores, each of which usually has some leeway insofar as what is sold. You will have to contact the store's buyer or manager, but either way the idea is the same: get in one store and prove that your product sells. If you can do that, and if you can show that you can handle the orders you get, you will have a far better chance of getting your product carried by the whole chain. That track record will serve you well.

Start at a Trade Show

I have a colleague who is a buyer for gift stores. Trade shows are the key to her business: she is constantly on the lookout for new products to add to her line, and she finds them at industry trade shows. By attending a trade show with your product, you can get your wares in front of a lot of people in a short amount of time. The downside: It is expensive to attend and display at a trade show, and there is a lot of competition.

SELLING YOUR SERVICE TO BIG BUSINESS

Big business needs small business. Not only do big businesses sell to us little guys, but they also buy a lot of goods and services from us. But big business is much different from small business. If you are going to try to crack the corporate market, keep these tips in mind:

- *You have to solve a problem.* The first step (after identifying your target, of course) is to show the company in general, and the manager to whom you are making your pitch specifically, that you have a product or service the company needs and that by buying from you, you will be solving a problem it has. So before ever even making that first phone call, educate yourself about the company. Find its pain points and be ready to explain how you can alleviate them.
- *Know whom you are dealing with.* Corporate managers are busy people who have to justify the decisions they make to higher-ups. You will need a dynamic presentation and you will need to follow up and then follow up some more. Show them that you are the best choice for this expenditure so that they can explain it to their manager (and their manager's manager). A proven track record helps, as do testimonials from other companies with which you have worked. They also work

for businesses that are big and professional and thus expect you to be, if not big, then at least very professional.

- *Appreciate budgets.* All departments and all managers have budgets. When they buy from you, it means they will not be spending their money elsewhere, so you need to be able to show them that this expenditure is the best use of their limited budget dollars.
- *Have a dynamite proposal and presentation.* A good business proposal explains your idea simply and logically. It is easy to read and understand. It explains to the reader, who may know nothing about your idea, what the proposition is and how it will work. It also avoids jargon and hyperbole. More important, a good business proposal is a sales tool that shows readers how it is in their self-interest to agree to what you are proposing. Therefore, the proposal must be persuasive, well written, and compelling. Don't overhype, but don't undersell either. And remember what I said about time: these people are busy. So keep your proposal sharp and to the point. To be taken as a professional, your presentation must be professional.

Avoid Clichés

In your business writing, especially in your proposals, you want to avoid business clichés. Here are some of the worst offenders:

- Interface: You interface with a computer screen, not a person.
- Face time: When you speak with another human being, that is called *talking*.
- Incent: Apparently an offshoot of *incentive,* this is not a word.
- Think outside the box: This phrase has become such a cliché that it is itself in-the-box thinking.
- Giving 110 percent: Not possible.

At the end of the day, let's strive to become change agents who put these clichés to bed!

- *Check out supplier diversity programs.* Many corporations have what are known as *supplier diversity programs.* These are efforts to increase the purchasing of goods and services from selected small businesses, typically those owned by veterans, women, people with disabilities, and minorities. In fact, many of these companies have offices dedicated specifically to helping small businesses enter their diversity programs, so check them out.

Book Recommendation

Another book you might want to read is *Bag the Elephant: How to Win and Keep BIG Customers,* by Steve Kaplan (Bard Press, 2005).

CHAPTER **51**

Secrets of Sales Superstars

For every sale you miss because you're too enthusiastic, you will miss a hundred because you're not enthusiastic enough.

—ZIG ZIGLAR

You probably know a thing or two about sales by now, or else you would not be in business. But even so, sales is one of those areas in which even the smallest little trick or new idea, once implemented, can reap surprising rewards. Brian Tracy, maybe the world's best salesperson, tells the story of how his first sales job was selling soap door to door to earn his way to YMCA camp. He heard rejection after rejection until he ever so slightly rephrased his sales pitch. Instead of asking, "Would you like to buy a box of soap?" he said instead that he was selling soap, but that "it is only for beautiful women." Thereafter he said getting to camp was a breeze. So yes, the smallest sales secret can often make the biggest difference.

SALES SECRETS

Let's look at some sales secrets and strategies that may make a difference for you.

Rapport

Rapport, once established, will make your sales almost effortless. Once you create rapport with people, they begin to trust you, and with trust, walls and reasons melt away.

There is a sales strategy that suggests that if you quietly mimic your customer's intonation and physical movements, you will subconsciously create rapport. This may or may not be true, but it sure does seem sneaky. Consider instead building rapport the old-fashioned way: by being your best self, by finding things in common, and by being friendly and helpful. People rarely buy from someone they do not like, and, conversely, they will go out of their way to buy from someone they do.

Tip: According to one successful salesperson, "Your job is to create rapport, inform them about the product, avoid pressuring them, let them make an intelligent decision, and if they leave before buying, make sure they have everything they need (your phone number, e-mail address, brochures, and so forth) so that they can easily make the purchase later on."

One of the best ways to build rapport is by focusing on the needs of your customers. They are there, wanting to buy, for a reason. Customers have needs or wants that they think you may be able to fill. If you can focus on those, and if they understand that what you are really interested in is fulfilling those needs or desires, then the sale becomes that much easier.

One way to do this is to ask questions, and then actually listen to the answers. Salespeople often make the mistake of falling in love with their own voice, convinced that if they spin just one more angle, the sale will be theirs. But in actuality, the opposite is usually true. If you listen at least as much as you talk, sales usually increase. In fact, master salesman Tom Hopkins says, "The human body has two ears and one mouth. To be good at persuading or selling, you must learn to use those natural devices in proportion. Listen twice as much as you talk and you'll succeed in persuading others nearly every time." When asking questions, keep these points in mind:

- Questions that require a yes or no answer do not add much to your knowledge or your rapport.
- Similarly, questions that relate to price or to the technical aspects of the product do little to help.

- Asking open-ended questions, which invite customers to explain their needs and motivations for buying, do help.
- Asking follow-up questions and requiring more explanation helps even more.

Going the Extra Mile

Because it costs so much more to create a new customer than it does to keep an old one, it behooves you to foster your relationships with your current clientele. Part of that is doing your homework and keeping up to date on where your customers are and what they need. Putting a little extra effort into learning about a customer, for instance, by studying trends in their industry or knowing a bit about a competitor, can go a long way toward impressing that customer and keeping him or her around.

The Pickle Jar

Visualize a pickle jar for a moment. Think about that first pickle. Getting the first one out of the jar takes some work, right? But once you get the first one out, all the other pickles come out easily. So, too, in sales. Getting that first sale from a customer takes a lot of work, but once you get it, all subsequent sales to that customer are much easier.

Similarly, going the extra mile for potential customers can reel them in. There is the story of the sports agent who flew cross-country just for the chance to have a brief meet and greet with a potential client. The sports star was so impressed that he signed with the agent, concluding that that kind of personal service was what he wanted from an agent.

Remember this, too—it can take up to *six interactions* to close a sale. Going the extra mile means being willing to see a potential customer again and again, continuing to build rapport, until the sale is made.

Finally, going the extra mile also means following up. Thank-you notes, checking in to see whether the product is working out, and that sort of thing builds rapport for future sales.

The moral of the story is that all sales are built on relationships.

Effective Cold Calling

One of the hardest things to do in sales is making an effective cold call, precisely because you have not yet established rapport. Here are a few tips to make cold calls easier:

- Begin with the right attitude. Know that cold calls are not easy, but they are valuable. Cold calling requires a competitive spirit.
- Before calling, smile. It puts you in the right frame of mind.
- Remember that cold calling is a numbers game. Smile and dial, smile and dial.
- The purpose of a cold call is *not* to make a sale. It is to engage the customer and create rapport. It is to set an appointment.
- If the customer balks at setting up a meeting, say something like, "All I need is 10 minutes of your time. I wouldn't waste my time coming all the way out to see you for 10 minutes if I didn't think it would really benefit us both."
- When asking for an appointment, do not say, "Can we meet next week?" Instead, be specific. Say something like, "How is next Thursday at 11:00 for you?"

Golf Lessons

If you have ever played even a little golf, you know that the harder you try, the less successful you are. But when you ease off the throttle a bit and trust your natural abilities, when you stop trying so hard, that's when you make great shots. To a certain extent, the same is true in sales. It is a paradox: just as you make the great golf shot by not caring about the great golf shot, so, too, can you get the sale by not worrying about the sale. A customer can sense when a sale is your priority and will back off accordingly. But once the customer is convinced that you are more concerned with helping to solve the problem than with making the sale, you will birdie the sale. Stop trying so hard.

Solve Problems

If you want to succeed in sales, you must focus on the benefits to the customer, on how your product solves their problem. *Do not* focus on your product's features. Selling benefits, not features, is Sales 101. When customers come in to buy a drill, what do they really need? They need a hole. The drill is a means to that end, and to that end, if you focus on the features of the drill (for example, its aluminum casing), you will miss the sale. The customer does not care about your drill's aluminum casing (or cares little); instead, he or she is concerned with fixing his need for a hole. So if you focus on the benefits to the customer, if you show how well this drill can solve the need for a hole, the sale is yours.

This is true in any sales situation. Sure, the cool functionality of your product is nice, but that alone will not make a sale. Those things come into play only once the customer sees the product as a way to solve his or her problem.

Once the customer sees that a product like yours can solve the problem, the next question inevitably is, why your product and not someone else's? Once the customer has settled on this sort of product, he or she will buy from you if it is in his or her self-interest to do so. This usually means that your product has to be less expensive, faster, more convenient, or of higher quality. The smart salesperson will have several reasons ready when the customer gets to the "What's in it for me?" stage.

Effective Sales Meetings

The purpose of a sales meeting is to help your sales staff sell more, yet too many sales meetings are boring lectures and time wasters. The key to a successful sales meeting is to make it interesting, useful, and positive. Have an agenda, pass it out, and stick to it. Do not ramble. Start by congratulating and thanking your staff for something. Avoid chastising people. Do not make threats. Keep it upbeat. At least one positive war story should be a part of every meeting. Ask your staff for their opinions and find out what they are hearing from customers. Attendee participation in some form is a must. Employees want to feel respected. Also, consider bringing in a customer occasionally to explain why he or she buys from you. Finally, keep the meeting short and sweet. Meet for more than an hour, and watch them fade out.

Secrets of the Car Salesperson

Who better to learn sales from than a car salesperson? Despite their unseemly reputations, car salespeople know how to sell, almost better than anyone. So do they have some secrets to impart? You bet.

The first thing to understand is that to the car salesperson, selling is a game, and it is a game they play for a very good reason—it works. The goal of the car sales game is to sell you a car at the highest possible price, today, and salespeople do so by enlisting you in their game and getting you to play by their rules. That is the first valuable lesson: the best salespeople consider selling a game, not a chore. The right attitude can take you far.

How is the game played? By following several preplanned steps.

First, the car salesperson gains your trust. A car salesperson is nice and friendly because creating rapport with you is essential. Once rapport is created, trust begins. Then the salesperson starts to ask some seemingly innocent questions. But innocent they are not. In only a few minutes, the salesperson can learn:

- Whether you are ready to buy, and if so, how much you have to spend
- How much you know about the product
- How much you know about the game

Next, the salesperson starts to get you excited. That small talk and those "innocent" questions allow him or her to learn some valuable things about you—in particular, what benefits you think are important. Like the Tiger Woods of sales, the salesperson casually takes you to a car thought to be a good fit and does the "walk-around," discussing the things he or she has concluded are probably important to you—safety, color, roominess, whatever.

Next, the salesperson invites you to sit in the car. Why is that? There is a phenomenon in the car business called "taking mental ownership." The longer you sit in the driver's seat, smelling and touching it, the more invested in the car you become.

The next step is critical: the salesperson gets you emotionally invested in the car. How? You know. He or she asks whether you want to take a test-drive. Test-driving a car is fun and exciting. The salesperson knows that when you get excited about a car, you are more apt to make an

Falling under the Ether

Some real estate professionals have their own name for this same concept, called falling under the ether. Once a real estate agent learns what a client is looking for, he or she immediately schedules tours of appropriate properties. Before long, during a walkthrough somewhere, the client usually finds a house he or she loves and becomes invested in owning it. The client has fallen under the ether.

emotional rather than a logical decision. Sure, the car may be nice, and yes, it may be the one you want. But even so, making a $20,000 decision based on a 10-minute test-drive is illogical. Yet it happens every day because car salespeople get patrons excited about the purchase.

Finally, the salesperson creates a sense of urgency. You may be told, "The boss wants this car off the lot," so a special deal is available, or "Someone is coming by this afternoon to look at it again." Whatever the case, the point is, you would be foolish not to buy *now*.

Yes, some car salespeople are too pushy, but not all are, and most know what they are doing. By playing the game to some extent, they sell cars, lots of cars. You might want to learn the game, too. It is as simple as creating rapport, finding out what the customer wants, getting the customer emotionally invested in the sale, and then giving an incentive to make the purchase today. Try playing the game and see whether you don't sell a few "cars" in the process.

The Closer

What about that step in the car buying process when the salesman goes to talk to his manager? Usually, they are just discussing strategy—trying to figure out how to get you to raise your offer. The "manager" then comes out and explains why your offer is too low. This authority figure becomes the person who can make the deal happen, and usually does. The lesson for you is that it might help sales, too, if you add a "closer" to your sales process.

The Sales Presentation

Of course, selling the car salesperson way works only in certain situations. Just as often, a more professional approach is required, and sales presentations are the standard method. The typical sales presentation is a fivefold process:

1. Create rapport.
2. Introduce the topic or product.
3. Ask questions to find out what the customer needs.
4. Highlight the product's benefits.
5. Ask for the sale.

Although the process is simple, what makes it work is preparation. You need to organize your presentation, prepare your selling points, and consider possible objections. Creating rapport at the start may be the most important aspect of the presentation. Here is an easy way to create that rapport: within the first few minutes of your presentation, ask the audience or group some questions that they can easily answer. That dialog builds rapport quickly. During the presentation, be sure to take plenty of notes, listen, and deal with negativity by countering with positivity. "There is always a solution" should be your motto. Finally, ask for the sale. It might be as subtle as "Well, how should we proceed?" or it might be more blunt; it depends on your style and how the presentation proceeds.

The Close

Here are two excellent ways to close a sale at the end of a presentation: First, offer a one-time incentive: "If you want to do this today, I will throw in an extra hour of my time for free." Second, offer a 100 percent money back guarantee.

EVEN MORE SALES SECRETS

Here are a few more ideas to put into your sales tool chest.

Make a Wish List

I once attended a seminar by master salesman Chet Holmes. Although he offered plenty of good advice, one piece that I thought was really smart was to make a wish list of your potential best customers. The idea is to think *big*. Bigger clients mean bigger paydays. Ask yourself: Which people or companies could have a huge effect on my business? Figure that out and then begin to target them. Give it the full-court press. Really go after them.

I have a pal who is a real estate broker. Selling duplexes and fourplexes, he was happy making around $20,000 a deal. But his mom kept nudging him, telling him to think bigger. Mom's advice: "It takes the same amount of work to sell a 50-unit apartment building as it does to sell a triplex." So my pal finally listened and made a list of the largest apartment owners in the area. He then began to court them and finally got that first pickle out of the jar. He now sells nothing but large apartment complexes, and yes, he makes *a lot* more money now. He also works less.

Know the Two Most Important Questions to Ask

In his great book *The Little Red Book of Sales Answers,* author and salesman Jeffrey Gitomer says there are two questions that are most critical to sales success:

1. "When I say [name of your product], what one word comes to mind?" This tells you what the customer's hot button or pain point is and allows you to deal with it.
2. "When buying [name of your product], what are the three biggest mistakes people make?" People do not want to make mistakes, which is why this question helps. Gitomer says you may want to substitute "opportunities" or "reasons" for mistakes. It will still yield good info.

Note, Gitomer also says that one of the dumbest questions you can ask is, "What will it take to get your business?" You should know.

Be Happy to Hear "The Price Is Too High!"

Why is that? Because it means that the customer is interested and wants to buy. Your job, then, is to show the value of the product and the intelligence of the purchase. Explain why the price is actually quite fair. Explain how price should be just one of many considerations, and not even the most important one at that.

Know What Motivates Customers to Buy

Gitomer says that five things can be in play when someone decides to buy:

1. Your product is different.
2. You offer a better value.
3. There is no risk buying from you.
4. The buyer has confidence in you.
5. Your price, if not the lowest, is at least reasonable.

Avoid Common Mistakes

- *Ask more questions.* People who have a hard time with sales often do not ask enough questions or do not listen to the answers.
- *Take responsibility.* It is your fault. It is also your success. No one is in charge but you.
- *Don't sell too hard.* Sales is not about talking someone into something. It is about solving problems, making connections, asking questions, and helping the customer buy.

Don't Forget to Say Thank You!

As you should always be aiming for the second sale, a short, personal, handwritten thank-you card is a great sales tool.

CHAPTER **52**

Small to Big

You will either step forward into growth or you will step back into safety.

—Abraham Maslow

Business and growth go together: the stock market is a daily reminder of which businesses are growing and which are not. The business section of the newspaper analyzes it, television shows debate it, and websites obsess over it. This is as true for small business as it is for big business. We are all supposed to want to grow our businesses—from wherever they are to whatever is the next level.

But not all small businesses want to grow. Many are content to stay just where they are, happy in the knowledge that they've got a good gig going. And there is nothing wrong with that. If this describes you, then skip this chapter, because this is the place where we look at the traits necessary to take a business from one level to the next. Whether it is taking your one-person business to a five-person business or going from $1 million to $5 million in sales, let's see what it takes to grow from small to big.

FIRST, A CAVEAT

Growth is all well and good, *if* you want it and *if* you are ready to grow. Reluctance is understandable. Growing pains are real. Taking your business to the next level will require new people and systems, new ideas and expenditures, some strategy, and maybe a bit of luck. You just need to be sure that you are ready for both the joys and the pains that you will encounter along the way.

Example: Several times in this book, I have mentioned my favorite entrepreneur, my father. He and his partner started small, with just one carpet store. He loved that time, when the business was small, when he got to do all of the hands-on entrepreneurial stuff: strategizing, selling, scheming, and generally making an immediate difference. Their business grew slowly until they reached a tipping point about seven years in, and then the business just took off. Dad and his partner were opening a new store every year, eventually topping out around 16.

But things were not as rosy as they seemed.

- It was expensive to open new stores, so much of the money they were making was eventually plowed back into the business.
- Dad and his partner differed as to how to run what had become a fairly large enterprise with a lot of employees. The bigger it got, the more they fought.
- And the more the business grew, the more unhappy my dad became. He no longer felt like an entrepreneur. Rather, he had become, in his mind, a boring middle manager.

Eventually, inevitably, dad sold out to his partner and went back to his roots, opening up a single carpet warehouse. He never grew it past that one store again, yet that was the happiest I ever saw him in business.

The moral of the story is that you have to be careful as you prepare to grow your business, because when that tipping point comes, there is no turning back. You, and your business, will be different. It might go great, or it might all go to pot. You might be unable to fulfill the big order, you might get sued, you might make a million, who knows? So, like a boy scout, to the best of your ability, be prepared!

Rapid growth can lead to rapid problems when your company is not ready to handle all of the issues that the big deal will bring, such as increased capital demands, the need for more labor, demands on resources, the need to be more organized, and so on. The big deal can become a big boondoggle if you are not ready. So the lesson is to plan for extra growth and be as ready as possible when it comes. If it is a natural next step, go for it, but if it feels more like an unnatural leap, think twice.

GOING BIG

If you want to play in the big leagues, or at least the bigger leagues, then you need to know the rules of the game. When yours is a very small business, you know how things run. But as you grow, the way business operates and the way you need to operate your business changes. Bigger, more mature companies are more structured, more organized, and less freewheeling than their smaller cousins. Here, then, are the top small-to-big rules.

Create a Team That Is Bigger Than You

The fatal flaw for many small businesses is that, too often, they work in a vacuum. I have a friend who is a solo architect. One day, as we were driving down a quiet stretch of the road, he remarked to me, "Hey Steve, do you notice there are no office buildings here? I think I will build one." He was serious, and within a week this new project was well under way. I thought it was a fairly dumb idea—the reason there were no offices in that particular area was that it was mostly residential. But he would not be dissuaded. He saw the small office park that he envisioned as his ticket to bigger and better things, but in the end, he dropped the idea for lack of financing.

The problem my friend had is the problem many small business owners have—namely, when you work alone, or even with a small group, you don't get a lot of perspective or feedback. Large corporations, on the other hand, have built-in feedback systems. Plans and ideas are disseminated, shared, examined, and vetted. And because there are plenty of people involved in the process, the bad ideas typically get tossed and the good ones usually remain. Not always, of course, but often enough.

This is why it is so important for the entrepreneur to have a board of directors or advisors, or even a "mastermind" group. If you want to grow, if you want to run your business more like a big business, then the first thing to do is take a page out of the corporate playbook and surround yourself with folks who will be honest with you and who want to help you play a bigger game. Feedback is important.

The other thing that adding teammates does is that it creates more expertise, a division of labor, more hands, and increased productivity. For instance, if you do not have an assistant, guess what? You are an assistant. Hiring even your first employee can make a huge difference in how productive you are, freeing you to spend your time growing the business rather than working every moment running the business. Can't afford it? Then think again. By hiring your first employee, you will be free to make even more money, thereby justifying the expenditure—in fact, thereby making it affordable.

Consider Hiring Interns

Bringing in interns from your local college is a great way to beef up your workforce without breaking the bank. Although some are free, most receive a small stipend, and almost all interns are so grateful for the opportunity that they will work their tail off for you. Here's how to find one:

- *Draft a job description.* Describe the duties, hours, who the supervisor will be, what skills are necessary, and what the student will get out of the project.
- *Contact colleges.* Next, call or e-mail some local schools and locate the internship coordinator's office. Send the coordinator the job description and have him or her get the word out.
- *Interview.* Gather resumes and interview your best prospects.
- *Give them real work.* There is nothing worse for interns than an internship in which all the intern does is make copies and get coffee. Give the intern some real work to do. You will both be happier.
- *Give feedback.* Interns are there to sharpen their skills, and it is your job to help them do that.

Commit to a Growth Strategy

This entire section of the book is populated with ideas and strategies that can help you grow your business from small to big. The important thing is to find some that make sense for you and then create a long-term growth plan, test it, implement it, and see it through. That is what growth companies do. No, it is not simple or easy to grow your business significantly bigger, but it is doable, very doable. All of the companies on the New

York Stock Exchange or the NASDAQ started out as a small business. If they did it, so can you.

- Ed Lowe owned a small factory that made a kiln-dried clay that was supposed to be an industrial absorbent. It was only when his neighbor came by one day and asked to use some for her cat that Kitty Litter was born. Being the first to market helps you go from small to big.
- Bette Nesmith was a terrible typist but a good painter. She would bring small tubes of paint to the bank where she worked in order to cover up her typos. Playing with various concoctions, she eventually invented Liquid Paper at home on her kitchen table. The business grew only after getting some great publicity; that, too, helps you go from small to big.

What are some other successful small-to-big strategies? First, *innovate*. Creating a new product or a way of doing things is a tried-and-true way to grow from small to big. Innovation gives these companies what is known as the *first mover's advantage*. Like Ed Lowe and his Kitty Litter, they are the first to market with this new product, so they become almost synonymous with the emerging industry. That is the power of innovation and the first mover's advantage.

Second, *form a strategic partnership*. When you work alone, as many small businesses do, or even if yours is a company of, say, eight people or so, there is only so much you can do by yourself. Your institutional knowledge is limited to what you do, your reach is limited to whom you know, and, of course, your resources are limited. In that case, growth, although a laudable goal, is often one that can understandably be out of reach. So what do you do?

Find a partner, that's what. Partners can bring your business to a whole new level. They have contacts you do not and resources that are different from yours. They also will have ideas that are new to you and offer unique ways to implement those ideas. So, in order to grow, look for strategic partners who offer some synergy: They need what you do and you need what they do. Together, you can accomplish more than what you could do alone.

Partnerships of any kind offer both risks and rewards. The good news is that working with new people and businesses with different backgrounds and skill sets often creates that desired synergy. You may be a financial genius but know nothing about marketing, and you might know someone who is a marketing wiz but knows nothing about money. Together, you just might make a great team. On the downside, partnership is a big commitment, not unlike a marriage. You must pick a person or a business that you trust and like. It is often best to start by doing a project or two together to make sure your styles and goals mesh.

Caution

When looking at potential partners, be wary of partnering with family members. Your venture may or may not succeed. Owing money to a family member or close friend—or worse, blaming each other for the failure of the business—is not a pleasant experience.

Be Unique

If you want to take your business to the next level, you should concentrate more energy on your "X factor," that is, *the one special thing that sets you apart and makes you stand out from the crowd*. Think about the businesses you like best, the ones you frequent most often. Don't they do something special, unique, different, something out of the ordinary? Figuring out what your X factor is and then putting extra effort into it can go a long way toward taking you from small to big.

- There is a bookstore in Portland, Oregon, called Powell's City of Books. The store takes up a full city block and sells used books right next to new ones. That is a unique X factor.
- The Pioneer Pharmacy in Erie, Pennsylvania, is the busiest pharmacy in town. Why? One reason is its X factor: free delivery. Every day, it has two full-time drivers delivering prescriptions for free, often to elderly customers.

The X factor—what's yours?

Plan Big

No, I did not say "think big." Most entrepreneurs have no problem thinking big. But what growth companies do *is plan big*. They create a team, figure out their X factor, find strategic partners, come up with a plan, and execute those big ideas. That is how you go from small to big.

CHAPTER 53

Exodus

Be prepared.

—BOY SCOUT MOTTO

There may come a time in the life of your business when you want to move on, when you have given it as much as you can. People leave businesses all the time—to start another business, to cash out, to let a child finally take the reins, to retire—the reasons are many. But any exit strategy requires preparation, preparation that many entrepreneurs are loath to do. In this chapter, we tackle getting out, made easy.

SUCCESSION PLANNING

No one likes to think about his or her own death, but should you die without a plan, what would happen to your business, to your family? Succession planning is your way to ensure the continued viability of your vision, and therefore it should be part of any small business plan. If something does happen to you or to other key team members (should someone die or leave unexpectedly), would the dream live on? Succession planning ensures that it will. Not only do you need to create a succession plan for your own sake, but it is also something you owe your employees, vendors, shareholders, and investors. They all depend on your business to some extent for their livelihood. Succession planning is the process whereby replacements are identified and groomed, not only for the chief executive officer (CEO) or president but possibly for key managers as well.

Consider the cautionary tale of Marty, the owner of a successful small business. As he got older, Marty decided that he needed a succession plan, so he created what he thought was a foolproof one. Then the unexpected actually happened: at the age of 50, Marty died suddenly, and his plan had to be implemented. When Marty's will was read, everyone discovered that Marty's right-hand man was given 25 percent of the business and was to take over running the business. The other 75 percent was equally divided among Marty's three children, two of whom were still minors. What Marty had never imagined was that his plan would create more problems than solutions. His oldest son wanted to run the business, but Marty's will specifically gave that responsibility to his employee. Then, after a year or two, the employee came to resent working full-time but having to give 75 percent of the profit to Marty's kids. In the end, the children sold their shares of the business to the employee, and Marty's master plan, and dream, like Marty himself, died prematurely.

As you start to create a succession plan, you need to answer three questions. First, what is your vision for the future of the business in your absence? Second, who can best implement that vision? Finally, what plan will you create to see that your vision is carried out?

Start by deciding what you want for the business should something happen to you, your partner, or other key people. Do you want the business to continue? Would that signal instead that it is time to wrap things up? Legally speaking, the death of a partner ends the partnership unless some other arrangement has been agreed to. In an LLC or corporation, death does not necessarily end the business. If the business does continue, who will own the deceased's share of the business, and how much say would he or she have in running it? These are questions you need to answer.

Caution

Whatever plan you create needs to be memorialized in two places. First, it should become part of the operating agreement for the business. Second, if ownership shares are being transferred, that must be handled in your will or living trust.

Next, if continuing on is appropriate, you need to decide who is capable of replacing the person in question, whether it is you or someone else. You and your team have duties. Who can best handle those duties? Look around your business and think about who might best replace key individuals. You do not necessarily want a clone of yourself but rather someone who can step in and lead. Examine skills, personality, leadership ability, and intelligence. You may even want to give potential candidates a self-assessment test to see how they view their strengths, weaknesses, skills, and vision. They do not need to know the reason for this test if you do not want them to.

Finally, once you have identified the person you think would be the best candidate to fill the position—say, for instance, your position—you need to speak with the person about this and get his or her perspective. If it is your son, for instance, who is going to take over, you not only need to broach the subject of succession but also discover whether he would like to become the boss. If the answer is affirmative, you need to actively begin to groom him for the position. Teach him what he needs to know. Answer questions. Expose him to all aspects of the business, your vision, and the plan. But be careful as you do this. Choosing a successor can also create hard feelings. Qualified candidates who are not selected may leave, and the process itself may cause companywide anxiety. Your best political skills will be required.

Jack Welch

In 1991, General Electric chairman Jack Welch said the thing that preoccupied his mind, the thing he spent the most time on, was succession planning. This was *nine years* before he stepped down.

Finally, you should put your succession plan in writing so that there is no mistake regarding what you want.

SELLING YOUR BUSINESS

It may be that you want to sell your business because you are unable to locate a successor or simply because it is time to move on. The important thing to know is that a business sale requires forethought, as it is a complicated, time-consuming transaction. Finding qualified buyers, going through your books and inspections, transferring real estate, and closing the deal can be a protracted process. Certainly it could take a year or more, all told. So, to make sure that you are able to find a viable buyer and close in a reasonable amount of time, a few tips are in order.

Line Up Your Ducks

Like the sale of a home, the sale of a business requires that you increase the business's "curb appeal," among other things. You will want to paint what needs to be painted, fix what is fixable, clean up the back room, and otherwise get the place ready to show.

- *Get a business valuation.* A lot of small business owners overestimate the value of their business, especially their goodwill, thinking it is worth more than it is. It is wise, then, to pay for a professional business valuation early on in this process so that you know what to expect and can honestly evaluate the offers you receive. The value of your business is based on its profitability, goodwill, assets, and liabilities. A business broker will be able to accurately assess the value of your business as part of his or her services.
- *Get your house in order.* One reason buyers buy businesses is that they want to reduce their risk, and the only way they can see whether your business is risky or safe is by looking at your books. All records—profit and loss statements, tax returns, contracts, permits, leases, everything—need to be in order.
- *Boost your profits.* People buy businesses because they are profitable. It follows, then, that one of the best things you can do to ensure a lucrative sale is to increase sales and profits to the extent possible.
- *Speak with your advisors.* Your attorney and accountant may have some good ideas about the sale of your business, and they may even know of potential buyers. You need to talk to them beforehand, tell them your plan, and then have them review the deal as it nears completion.

Hire a Business Broker

Having decided to sell your business, and having spruced up the office in preparation, the inevitable question is, where do you find buyers? You have two options. You can advertise the sale yourself, or you can hire a business broker. Should you decide to sell it yourself (akin to selling a home without a real estate agent), you should advertise in the following places:

- *Craigslist.* Under the "For sale" section on Craigslist, you will find a category called "Business."
- *Sunday paper classifieds.* Look under "business opportunities" to list a business for sale.
- *Magazines.* Most trade magazines have a section in the back for business owners who are selling their business.
- *Online.* If you type "businesses for sale" into your favorite search engine, you will get a list of sites that broker business sales.
- *Sites.* Sites like www.BizBuySell.com are an excellent source.

Although you might do just fine selling your business without a broker, consider what it would be like to sell your home without a real estate agent. You would not have access to the agent's expertise and experience, access to the multiple listing service, or contacts and colleagues. So, too, in the world of business sales. Brokers have a listing service and associates, both of which are excellent ways to find buyers. So the first advantage of hiring a business broker is that you will have access to many more qualified buyers than you could find on your own.

Although they are not cheap (usually they are paid a percentage of the sale price), business brokers can be an invaluable resource when selling a business. A good broker will help you decide on the right price, be an important sounding board, negotiate a good deal, and handle the closing. Maybe best of all, a good business broker will separate the real buyers from the looky-loos, bring in more qualified prospects, and thereby garner a better price for the business.

Business Broker Background

If you are considering hiring a business broker, be sure to find out the following:

- *What is the broker's experience?.* Good brokers need to know business valuation, sales, business financing, negotiations, and more. You want someone with experience who really understands the world of business.

(continued)

- *Is the broker certified?* You want a Certified Business Intermediary, a broker who is accredited by the International Business Brokers Association.
- *What services are provided?* Will the broker help you value the business? Will the broker do more than negotiate the deal? A good broker should be an overall financial advisor for your end of the transaction.

The upshot is that the purchase of a business is a major event, and a good business broker can help make sure it is a successful one.

The Price

How much should you expect to get for your business? It is a fair question, although not an easy one to answer, as every business is different. When it comes to price, there are four basic questions to answer:

1. *What does the business own?* A business with assets is obviously more valuable than a business without. Of course, assets include things such as trucks and equipment, as well as contracts, intellectual property rights, "goodwill" (i.e., the reputation that the business has in the community), and so on.
2. *What does the business owe?* The value of your business is offset by its liabilities. Less is more, of course.
3. *What is the business's profitability?* Again, the same principle applies: bigger profit equals a bigger price.
4. *What about the intangibles?* What makes the business unique? Do you have a great location, a favorable lease, or valuable employees? These can make a difference.

These four items are taken into account and used to determine the value of your business. There are three ways to go about doing so. The first is called *price building*. The second method is called *return on investment*. The third is the *multiplier*.

Book Recommendation

To learn more about how to sell your business, pick up a copy of *How to Sell Your Business,* by C. D. Peterson.

Price building is a valuation method that simply looks at the hard numbers—assets, profits, accounts receivable, goodwill, leases, and so on. For example, yours might look like this:

- Real estate: $400,000
- Equipment: $100,000
- Inventory: $50,000
- Goodwill: $50,000
- Subtotal: $600,000
- Less liabilities: $100,000
- Total: $500,000

Return on investment, or ROI, looks at the profit per year to help determine what a buyer's return on investment will be. For example, say that you decide on an asking price of $500,000. Is that fair? Using the ROI method, and assuming some numbers, we would see:

- Net profit: $200,000
- Business sale price: $500,000
- Return on investment ($200,000/$500,000): 40 percent

Using ROI, and these numbers, the buyer would be getting a 40 percent return on his or her investment. Given that a good passive investment may return a yield in the teens, a 40 percent return for an active investment may be a bit high. Thus, a higher price for the business may be in order.

The last method, and a common one, is the multiplier. Here you would again look at the earnings, but you would then multiply that number by some factor—it varies depending on the industry—to get a final price. A factor of three would result in a $600,000 asking price. Of course, the battle is what that factor should be.

If all of this is too complicated, and it can be, then consider simply getting an appraisal or hiring a business broker. (Look in the Yellow Pages under "business brokers.") It will probably be worth it to ensure that you get a fair price.

BANKRUPTCY

Sometimes, the decision to get out of the business is a necessity, not a choice. Many things can precipitate a bankruptcy: illness to you or a partner, divorce, losing a big customer or contract, a growth strategy gone wrong—it could be anything.

Bankruptcy is the big bad monster in your business movie; I get that. But in reality, the bankruptcy monster is more like that big sweet blue creature in Pixar's *Monsters, Inc.* than that mean, scary thing in *Alien*. Why? Almost every area of the law is about revenge, except for bankruptcy. Criminal law is about putting people behind bars; lawsuits are about getting money. But not bankruptcy. Although the rules were recently toughened (more on *that* idea in a minute), the basic tenet of bankruptcy is about forgiveness, not revenge. It's about giving people a break when things get out of control and helping them start over. The bankruptcy code calls it a "fresh start." A fresh start—sounds nice, huh?

You should also know that many of the greatest entrepreneurs had to file for bankruptcy protection at one time or another:

- Before Walt Disney created the animation studio that bears his name, his first animation studio filed for bankruptcy.
- In 1994, Donald Trump's Trump Hotels and Casino Resorts filed for bankruptcy.
- Before Henry Ford started the Ford Motor Company, his first automobile business filed for bankruptcy.

So bankruptcy happens in business. That's a fact. When the bankruptcy laws were restricted in 2005, the idea was to cut back on bankruptcy fraud—that is, to prevent people who are not *really* in over their heads from legally escaping their debt. But the fact is, bankruptcy fraud was never really a big problem. Most people want to pay their debts, but because of business problems, divorce, illness, or something, things changed and now they can't.

So should you file bankruptcy if your business is in trouble? Well, I hate to sound like the lawyer that I am, but it depends. If your business is a sole proprietorship, then you and it are one in the same, legally speaking. You could file for Chapter 7 bankruptcy and possibly wipe out your unsecured debt and get a fresh start. I say "possibly" because the 2005 changes to the law made filing for Chapter 7 bankruptcy much more difficult. You will have to check with a lawyer to see whether you qualify. But if you do, then it really is a chance for that fresh start. And you will be getting credit again within two years or so—expensive credit to be sure, but credit nonetheless.

If you do not meet the stringent Chapter 7 requirements, you will need to file for Chapter 13 bankruptcy. This is a repayment plan. The amount you repay may be anywhere from, say, 10 percent to 100 percent. The repayment time is between three and five years. It just depends on the facts.

If your business is a corporation, then your options are as follows:

- Chapter 7 bankruptcy, which acts as a liquidation. Your business closes its doors, and all assets are sold to pay off creditors.
- Chapter 11 bankruptcy, which is a corporate repayment plan.

If you do have to file, here is what I can say: no, it is not ideal, but then again, the only thank-you cards I ever received when practicing law were from Chapter 7 clients whose lives were easier after it was all done. Good luck!

P A R T

Strategies for Small Business Success

CHAPTER **54**

Small Business Success Secrets

I think it is an immutable law in business that words are words, explanations are explanations, promises are promises—but only performance is reality.

—HAROLD S. GENEEN

What counts is what works. Small businesses come in all shapes and sizes. Some are good and some are not. Some make a lot of money and some do not. Some foster happy, productive, meaningful workplaces and others do not. What is it that separates them? In these last two chapters, the distinguishing characteristics of the best small businesses are explored.

SWIMMING WITH THE BIG FISH

It is easy to fall into a rut, especially when it is a comfortable rut. If your business earns a nice profit and it is a good place to work, everyone might easily settle into a routine in which growth is less important than maintaining the status quo. You know what you know, and what you know works. Why upset the apple cart?

But if you want to take your business to the next level, to make more, do more, and have more fun, then you will you need to (1) break the routine and (2) begin to associate with people who can help you to get where you want to go. Tried and true is nice if that is what you want, but the best small businesses strive to become even better.

541

Board of Advisors

Bob Vukovich is an entrepreneur who has started two very successful businesses, acts as a mentor to many aspiring entrepreneurs, and serves as a judge at Moot Corp., an internationally acclaimed business plan competition hosted by the University of Texas. Vukovich knows a thing or two about small business success. He says, "The worst thing you can do as an entrepreneur is to think you know everything. When I need advice, which is very often of a general nature rather than technical, it's very important to have a great board to turn to."

A Generous Gift

In 1992, Allegheny College in Meadville, Pennsylvania, received the largest gift in its almost 200-year history: $22 million from Bob Vukovich and his wife, Laura.

The "great board" Vukovich is referring to could mean your board of directors if you are incorporated or, if not, then a less formal board of advisors. This is something that all small businesses can benefit from. A board of advisors is a group whose purpose is to help you guide and grow your business. A great board can offer you advice, feedback, expertise, perspective, and contacts.

Contacts are especially important. When you are a small business owner, your sphere is what it is. Any of us can have only so many contacts and colleagues. And if it is true that "it is not what you know, but whom you know" (and it is), then a board of advisors helps you know more people. There is no telling what opportunities, contracts, or other sales might come from having the right board members.

But even beyond this, a good board is an important sounding board. By recruiting experts and colleagues, you expand your small business IQ. So, when looking for board members (five is a good number), look for potential members who:

- *Have experience.* You want to stock your board with business-savvy individuals. Putting your brother-in-law on your board negates its purpose, unless he offers some unique expertise. The more "heavyweights" you can get, the better. Not only will this vastly increase your small business acumen, but also these are the kinds of players who can steer business your way. Good board members will have contacts they can reach out to: investors, strategic partners, even potential customers. An experienced board also impresses the outside world if you need a loan, for example, or if you are trying to nab that big contract.

- *Have diverse skills.* None of us has all of the necessary knowledge, experience, or skills required to run every aspect of our business (although we might like to think we do!). There are so many different facets of a small business—sales, finance, marketing, legal—that having board members with a variety of business skills ensures that you will have someone around who can answer questions and help solve problems when they arise.
- *Are independent.* You want people who are willing to be the devil's advocate, who will give you their honest feedback.

Board members are often compensated for their time, either with money or stock, although some may be willing to assist for free. The opportunity to be involved in an interesting business, plus teaching what they know, may be satisfaction enough. The important thing is that you find people who share your vision for your business and get them committed to helping you get where you want to go.

Contracts

The federal government contracts out $240 billion of business to private businesses every year, and by law, 23 percent of those contracts must go to small businesses. That means that there is roughly $60 billion in government contracts available to small businesses every year. You say that you have no idea how to even start finding, let alone bidding on, those contracts? You are not alone. But now there is help.

Hector Barreto was for many years the head of the SBA. When he was first appointed to run the agency, he quickly realized a fundamental truth: "What small business wants is the same as what big business wants—more business!" The question was, How could he help facilitate that? According to Barreto, although the 23 percent, $60 billion set-aside seemed like a great opportunity to help small businesses get more business, most of these contracts went to small businesses "inside the beltway." He thought that small businesses throughout the United States should have an equal opportunity to bid on, and get, these contracts. "They have the know-how," he told me, "but not the know who."

Business Matchmaking

To fix that, the SBA and HP teamed up in 2002 to create a program called Business Matchmaking (www.businessmatchmaking.com). Business Matchmaking matches small businesses with government and private procurement officers who are looking to buy what the small businesses have to offer. As Barreto puts it, the program "matches small companies with federal, state, and local government agencies, and large corporations that have actual contract opportunities for products and services."

In order to facilitate this matchmaking, the SBA and HP created a traveling event that goes to different cities around the country, bringing together those looking to buy goods and services with local small businesses looking to sell such goods and services. It is sort of like speed dating for small business. And, whereas it began as a program to help spread the 23 percent of government contracts set aside, Business Matchmaking now includes many large private businesses that also need and use small business vendors.

According to Barreto, these events have been an unqualified hit, both in terms of the number of participants and the billions of dollars of contracts that have resulted. "In one or two days at one of these events, a small business can see more contractors with real contracts than they could in a year on their own," Barreto says. "It's better than a trade show because at our events, buyers who are ready to buy are meeting small businesses ready to sell. We are matching supply with demand." To date, these meetings have resulted in several billion dollars in contracts for small businesses around the country.

So, if you have a product or service that you think might be useful to the government or large corporation, then go to www.businessmatchmaking .com and sign up. What you will find when you attend an event is what Barreto calls "a meaningful opportunity."

What to Expect

The leading organizations at the Business Matchmaking events are from both the public and private sector. The Departments of Homeland Security, Commerce, State, and Interior are on hand with the military buyers. On the private side, American Airlines joins HP, Lockheed Martin, and several larger firms in each city visited.

BREAKTHROUGH COMPANIES

What makes a company break out and jump to the next level? Author Keith McFarland wanted to know the answer to that question, too. A former Inc. 500 CEO, McFarland spent years researching thousands of successful companies in order to figure out the secrets to breakthrough business success. Here are his top five tips:

1. *Happy employees create great businesses*. Top management in McFarland's breakthrough businesses spent ample time and effort figuring out how to create a positive, happy workplace and workforce. A great place to work begets a great business.
2. *You can do it on your own, and most do*. The top nine breakthrough companies that McFarland identified were started without big-bucks investors. They figured out how to raise the money in other creative ways.
3. *Trust your people—they are more capable than you know*. Breakthrough companies created a context that allowed otherwise ordinary employees to be extraordinary. Great systems and confidence from the top down encouraged people to do their best.
4. *Trust your gut*. Breakthrough companies were led by people who bucked the conventional wisdom and instead took risks and ran their business their way.
5. *You don't need to be cool to be successful*. These breakthrough businesses were found in every sector imaginable. One distributed nuts and bolts; another processed payroll.

The lesson for the rest of us seems clear enough: Breakthrough business growth can happen to almost any company *if it is run properly*, *intelligently, and compassionately.* It is a matter of doing the right thing, taking smart and calculated risks, and treating your people right. In that sense, we are almost back to where this book began, with the basic tenets of entrepreneurship. Have big goals. Treat your people right. Listen to the market. Follow your passion.

High Praise

Stephen Covey, author of *Seven Habits of Highly Effective People,* says of Keith McFarland's book, *The Breakthrough Company:* "It will inspire those in charge to become true leaders by rejecting 'small' goals rooted in ego and embracing visionary values that impart moral authority up and down the organizational ladder."

THE SYSTEM

In order to make more money and be more successful, the successful small business should be organized in such a way that the owner or owners are free—free to spend time networking and marketing, free to go after big contracts, and free to spend time on the parts of the business they enjoy and less time on the parts they do not.

One would think that would be the case. After all, a very big reason entrepreneurs create their businesses in the first place is for the freedom—freedom from the boss, from the grind, from being an employee. But if you have owned a business for any length of time, you may not be all that free. The demands on your time are great—indeed, that is probably the chief complaint among small business owners. If you are like other small business owners, you likely spend so much time handling issues and putting out fires that time to think and plan is lost. It is a paradox: you may have busted out of one prison only to create another. You are likely not as free as you would have hoped.

Is there a solution? You bet, and it is a solution that, if implemented, means you will enjoy your business more and make more money. In his great book *The E-Myth: Why Most Small Businesses Don't Work and What to Do about It,* author Michael Gerber explains that most small businesses can be divided into two parts. First, there is the technical part of the business—the baker bakes the bread; the web designer designs the websites. Second, there is everything else associated with running a business: advertising, payroll, money . . . you know, the program. The problem is that knowing how to make a great croissant or website does not mean you know how to run a great business. Therefore, the second part of the business is often the trouble spot for many small business owners, taking up far too much time and energy and preventing them from growing their business.

Gerber says that the solution to this common dilemma can be found by looking at one of the most successful businesses of all time—McDonald's. Whether you go into a McDonald's in Moscow, Russia, or Moscow, Idaho, you can expect the same thing. The restaurants are clean and affordable, and the food tastes the same wherever you go because founder Ray Kroc created a system. Any franchisee who follows the system should get the same result, profits and all.

In *The E-Myth,* Gerber suggests that by creating a system (as opposed to haphazard individual efforts and decisions), your small business can become a machine that runs itself. If you systematize it, a bit or a lot, you enable your employees to do their jobs, thereby freeing you up to do yours. Gerber says that you will know whether the system you have created works "if it works without you to work it." Doesn't that sound nice?

Take a look at your business. What works? How could it be more efficient? Think of your business as a prototype for 100 more that will be just like it. What would those other businesses need to know, and what processes would they need to have to create optimal results?

"Does it work? [The] answer is a resounding 'Yes!' it does work. Every time it is applied. And it will work for you. It works because it requires the full engagement of the people working it. It can't be done half-heartedly. It can't be done frenetically. It can only be done intelligently, systematically, and compassionately."

—Michael Gerber

Who needs to do what, and when? How can the work be made predictable and accountable? How can you get employees to take pride in the results? Answering these sorts of questions will help you start creating a system.

If you can create a step-by-step guide to running your business, much as any franchisor would, a guide that will allow others to deal with details, then you, the owner, will be able to concentrate on those things you most enjoy, think strategically, and have far more free time. Or consider this: if you are really good at creating a system, you could hire a manager and employees to run the business for you altogether. You could become an absentee owner who collects the profits and pays for labor. Many small business owners do just that: their businesses are turnkey operations that simply make money for them while they do other things.

This is a seven-step process:

1. *Identify your primary aim.* No, not your aim for your business, but your aim for yourself. How do you want your life to look? What do you really want to do on a daily basis? Gerber says until you know what you want your perfect life to be like, you cannot figure out how your business should be organized.

2. *Create your strategic objective.* "Your strategic objective is a very clear statement of what your business has to ultimately do for you to achieve your Primary Aim," says Gerber. What is your vision for your business? Who are your customers, how much money should the business make, what is its purpose?

3. *Create your organizational strategy.* Based on your answers in the first two steps, how would you need to organize your business? What would your business look like if you were not forced to handle every little thing? Would you need to add or delete staff? What job descriptions and training would they need? How could you turn your business into a turnkey operation?

4. *Create your management strategy.* In the best franchises, they say that "the system is the solution." You need to create that system for every part of your business. A great system is essentially a series of checklists. Anyone should be able to look at his or her checklist and know what to do. It should be the same process as creating the same French fries time and again.

"The path you're now on, this entrepreneurial path, winds around corners that will amaze you at times, and even shock you at others. That's why it's so exciting! It's the path of surprise. It's the path of constant engagement. And because it's all of those things, it's truly the path of life, or, as Rollo May puts it, 'the path of freedom.'"

—Michael Gerber

5. *Create your people strategy.* The danger of creating this system is that employees may feel like they are nothing but cogs in the machine. A people strategy prevents this. Your people strategy is what you want your business culture to be and how you plan to implement it. Your way of doing business becomes part of your operations manual and your system.
6. *Create your marketing strategy.* Your marketing strategy examines who your customers are and how they fit in with your new business model.
7. *Create your systems strategy.* You have three systems: Hard systems (computers, cash registers), soft systems (people), and information systems (inventory control, sales, and so forth). Your business process needs to integrate all three systems.

Tip: For more information, pick up a copy of *The E-Myth,* by Michael Gerber.

By systematizing your business, you just may find that you will be freed up to make more money and have your business live up to its full potential.

YES

A final secret that separates the good from the great small business is as simple as one small word: yes. No matter the question, yes should almost always be the answer. Here's why: whatever your business, you are in the service business. You serve your customers and in a sense, you even serve your employees. How well you serve them will, I suggest, largely determine how successful you are. So no matter what the question, the answer usually should be yes:

- "Can you stay open 15 minutes extra so that I make it there before you close?" Yes.
- "I see you have some empty rooms tonight. Can you give me an upgrade?" Yes.
- "Can I have some mustard on the table?" Yes.
- "Can you rush this and get it to me by tomorrow?" Yes, I'll do my best.
- "Can I have an extra afternoon off this week?" Yes, we can make that work.

It is this willingness to make your people happy (within reason, of course) that makes the difference. Is there a risk that by saying yes you might get burned? Sure. The check may bounce. That customer may never show up. But the alternative is usually worse. By being a contrarian, or simply by not caring enough to put in the extra effort required to make someone happy, you are creating a mediocre business. What does it cost for you to say yes instead of no? Usually not much—probably some inconvenience.

But no? No is stagnant. No is negative. No is obstinate. And, too often, no is a power play. Do you remember the old Gumby cartoons? Gumby had a friend named Pokey, and another named Nopey. No matter what you asked Nopey, his answer was "No!" He did that because it put him in charge of the situation. The same is true in business. Too many businesses are either run by, or employ, Nopeys. For whatever reason, these folks seem to enjoy the power that saying no gives them. Telling people no usually means that you prefer policies over people and currency over customers.

But yes? Yes is friendly. Yes is positive. Yes creates goodwill. Yes is flexible. Yes cements customers and relationships. Yes creates growth. Saying yes to your employees fosters loyalty and hard work. Think about the sorts of businesses you like best. Don't you prefer proprietors who are friendly, helpful, easy to work with, and accessible? People who don't hide behind policies and who try to make you happy? When given a chance, I say that we would rather give our business to businesses that say yes. Here's the secret: if you want to succeed in your business, just say "yes."

CHAPTER 55

The Visionary Small Business

What you can do, or dream you can, begin it.
Boldness has genius, power, and magic in it.

—GOETHE

Owning a small business has much more to do with vision and boldness than it does with profits and losses. Profits and losses are a means to an end. In fact, the business itself is a means to an end. We start a business because we have a dream, a destiny that is fulfilled by creating a sustainable, beautiful business that we love. No, we are not always successful, but it is this vision of creating something special, of making the world and our world better, that drives us. Which begs the question, How can we better realize this passion? Are there business traits that the best of the best can teach the rest? Indeed there are. The best businesses are beacons illuminating the path so that as we continue our entrepreneurial journey, there is light showing us which way to go.

THE BEST BUSINESSES

In their excellent book *Built to Last,* authors James C. Collins and Jerry I. Porras sought to answer the question, "What makes the truly exceptional companies different from other companies?" The results of their exhaustive research and analysis are fascinating, and they apply to businesses both small and large. More than a desire for profits, more than a plan to produce pleasing products, the best businesses are founded on, and driven by, vision.

It helps to remember that every amazingly huge, Fortune 500, NAS-DAQ-traded, stock-splitting, name-branded, well-known company you can think of once started out as a small business. Yet by adhering to their vision, they were able to grow beyond their humble roots and become something special. And when I say special, I am not referring to money or profits, although money and profits are nice. I am talking about a business that makes a difference—for its shareholders and owners, for its employees, and for its customers. A special business, a great business, solves problems, creates value, is enviable.

The Business Is the Thing

To start a successful business you need not be a genius, you do not have to invent the Next Big Thing, and you do not have to start out with a Big Idea. Walmart began as a single five-and-dime store in Arkansas. Founder Sam Walton told the *New York Times,* "I had no vision of the scope of what I would start, but I always had confidence that as long as we did our work well and were good to our customers, there would be no limit." His big idea, to create a chain of rural discount stores, did not come to him for quite some time: "Like most overnight successes [Walmart] was about 20 years in the making."

Slow starts are okay. Bill Boeing's first plane was such a failure that his aircraft company sold furniture for a few years. Microsoft lost money for its first two years. One of the largest electronics companies in the world began in the bombed-out basement of a department store in Tokyo right after World War II.

If it is not the great idea that gets the motor running, what sustains the small business in the early years? It is the dream. It is the business itself. As Collins and Porras put it in *Built to Last,* "Never, never, never give up. Be prepared to kill, revise, or evolve an idea, but never give up on the company." They site HP as a classic example: "Bill Hewlett and Dave Packard kept tinkering, persisting, trying, and experimenting until they figured out how to build an innovative company that would express their core values."

It is not your great idea that will sustain your business; it is your great business that will sustain the idea. The business is the thing. A slow start can be handled as long as a strong foundation is being laid. Creating a great small business requires that you create an organization with values that matter and processes that last. A visionary organization creates visionary products and profits, not the other way around.

There Is More to Business Than Profits

To start a small business, you have to be idealistic; if you were not, then fear, criticism, the unknown, or the naysayers would have stopped you. So we know you are idealistic. The trick to sustained business greatness, then, is to transform that idealism into a set of core business values. The best small businesses have core values and live by them. These values guide owners and employees alike in their everyday activities.

In 1945, Japan was a country in ruins. Devastated by war and two nuclear bombs, Japan had a long, long way to go. It was there, in the remnants of Tokyo, that Masaru Ibuka decided to start a new company that he would call Sony. Begun in that bombed-out, deserted department store I just mentioned, Sony was started with the last $1,600 of Ibuka's personal savings. Aside from initially creating some forgettable products (for example, sweet bean-paste soup), Ibuka quickly created a code for his nascent company:

- "A place of work where engineers can feel the joy of technological innovation."
- "To pursue dynamic activities . . . for the reconstruction of Japan."
- "We shall welcome technical difficulties."
- "We shall eliminate any unfair profit seeking."

That last point is critical and illustrative. Everyone loves profits, but evidence indicates that the best businesses mix profits into the values bag, treating them equally with other important business attributes.

Henry Ford's Innovations

Henry Ford is widely credited with helping to create the middle class by introducing both the five-day workweek and the $5 a day wage (roughly double the prevailing wage in his day). The *Wall Street Journal* denounced this last action, stating that Ford had "injected spiritual principles into a field where they do not belong."

The point to take away is that great companies value values. They are not just enterprises created to make a buck. These businesses have a core ideology of which profit is but one ideal. As Collins and Porras point out in *Built to Last,* in 1960, David Packard of HP gave a lecture to a group of employees. There, he said:

> "I want to discuss why a company exists in the first place. Many people assume wrongly that a company exists simply to make money. . . . As we investigate this, we inevitably come to the conclusion that a group of people get together and exist as an institution that we call a company so that they are able to accomplish something collectively that they could not accomplish separately—they make contributions to society."

Each small business must decide for itself what its core values are. They should be simple, guiding principles on which to build. You do not need a reason and do not need to justify them. They are *your* core values. Figure out what they are and live by them.

A corollary to this is that the visionary small business should recruit people who can buy into the value system; that is certainly something that should be discussed during the interview process. Real values, to mean something, must be lived, and if an employee is unwilling to adopt your way, then it should be the highway.

Xerox

When he died, Joe Wilson, founder of Xerox, was found with a small blue index card that he apparently had kept in his wallet. It said, in part, "To attain serenity through the leadership of a business which brings happiness to its workers, serves its customers, and brings prosperity to its owners."

Think Big

The most successful small businesses create clear, specific, big goals and then organize to achieve them. The goals serve as a focal point for the efforts of the participants. When Ruth Handler decided that her small toy company would create a doll modeled on a shapely woman, not a baby, as all girls' dolls had been up to that point, the goal was huge. The company had to invent new processes to manufacture the doll, and it took eight years. It changed the entire direction of her business. But her business— Mattel—and her invention—Barbie—transformed an industry. Setting the bar high raises expectations—of yourself, of your staff, and of your business itself. A great, big, audacious goal can get everyone excited. It crystallizes efforts.

But a goal alone is not enough. Your business has to be committed, financially and emotionally, to achieving the goal. A goal without commitment is like a basketball without air. It's empty. Set goals for your company. Commit to them. Enlist your team in them. Achieve them. And then set more.

Experiment

Before inventing Tupperware, Earl Tupper created a variety of forgettable products: knitting needles, egg peelers, compact mirrors, and flour sifters, to name just a few. He kept plugging along until he finally hit on a product that worked in the marketplace. This is true for many successful small businesses. Grand visions and strategic plans are wonderful, but it often takes plain old trial and error and plenty of experimentation before the magic combination hits.

Failures happen, but you have to keep throwing stuff against the wall to see what sticks. R. W. Johnson, Jr., of Johnson & Johnson famously said, "Failure is our most important product." He knew not only that failure meant his company might learn something new but also that it should prod them in the proper direction. If you continue to experiment and try new things, opportunities will eventually avail themselves.

Teflon

In 1938, a DuPont scientist named Roy Plunkett was experimenting with a substance known as TFE. He stored a canister of the material in dry ice at the end of the day to preserve it. The next day, the canister was empty. When he
(continued)

cut it open, he discovered that the TFE had transformed into a silky substance that lined the inside of the canister. Plunkett had inadvertently created Teflon. Despite efforts to commercialize the product, DuPont found only industrial uses for Teflon. It took a Frenchman named Marc Gregoire, who had heard of the material and experimented mightily, to finally figure out how to stick the world's greatest nonstick substance to frying pans. The company he created to sell the pans, Tefal, is still the standard in the industry.

THE COMPETITOR IS YOU

Sure, capitalism is cutthroat, but the best small companies do not necessarily look to their competition to figure out what to do. Instead, they look to their own values and successes and try to top those. It is like the sports team, playing for the championship, that says, "We do not care what our opponent is going to do, what their defensive scheme is, or what plays they will run. This is not about them; it is about us. Are we up to it? How well will we carry out our plan? Will we be our best? If we are our best, no one can beat us."

Be your best. Have a vision. Dare to dream big dreams and have big goals. Commit to them and then chase them. Enroll your team in your cause. Try something new, and then try something else. Make sure your small business stands for something; if it personifies your best values, you will have created a business of which you can be proud.

Be bold, for boldness has genius, magic, and power in it.

Appendix A
How I Became an Entrepreneur

TO PETER CLEVENGER,
WHEREVER YOU ARE

No one hated his or her job more than I. I mean, I disliked just about everything I could dislike about the last job I ever had—the boss from hell, the horrible hours, the boring, oh so very boring work—everything. The funny thing was, on the surface, it all looked great. But it's what is below the surface that really matters, eh?

Back then, I was a young lawyer fresh out of law school, working for a big firm in the big city making the big bucks. But it turned out to be fool's gold, and I was the fool: I had a pregnant wife and a baby at home whom I seldom saw because the hours were so tough. I was making more money than I ever had, but between student loans, diapers, and formula, we were still sharing one car. Maybe the worst part was the mind-numbing work. I spent all day, every day, in the law library by myself, researching and drafting memos and motions for cases I knew little about and would never get to argue. The firm figured we needed two years of seasoning before we were ready to cook.

And then there was my boss. A story is illustrative: One day she called me into her office and pointed to two huge boxes containing thousands of pieces of paper. "Those boxes are my client's paperwork for the past five years," Linda said. "I want you to take them, go through them, and make a chronology of what happened when, with a document referencing each event." "Sure," I replied, adding, "when would you like it?" She replied, "Tomorrow."

I left her office in shock. There was simply no way I could read all of those documents, let alone analyze them and reference them, in less than a week, probably three. I walked into the office of another associate who had worked for Linda for six years and explained my dilemma. She told me, "I wish you luck. Chronologies usually take a month. Working for Linda is very difficult. In fact, it will probably be the toughest challenge of your legal career." "But what if I'm not ready for the toughest challenge of my legal career yet?" I stammered. "I've only been out of law school a year!"

As I left, the associate added—for good measure, I suppose—"Linda has fired the last three lawyers who worked for her." I spent the next 18 hours reading and writing furiously, barely stopping to eat or sleep. The next day I went into Linda's office, unshaven and disheveled, and gave her a pathetic document that outlined the major events of the case, saying, "I really need a lot more time if I am going to do this right." Said Linda, "Of course, you do. I was just testing you."

I really hated that job.

I had spent my twenties trying to be a writer, wanting to get published. No offense to me, but no one cared what I had to say. Then I met my future wife and stepdaughter, and suddenly I wasn't a child anymore. Law school seemed like a good backup plan. It turned out that I was pretty good at it and even liked it.

But even after I graduated, while working for Linda, I still had the writing bug. I sent off a slew of query letters to publishers far and wide, proposing that I write a series of small legal books for the layperson. I received a slew of rejections. Stuck, sad, and frustrated, I tried to make the best of my time at the firm, but the truth was, I was a lousy employee. Having grown up in an entrepreneurial family, I had always longed to be my own boss. I had my own ideas, hated taking orders, and wanted to make my own hours. And now I wanted to be a writer, too? Good luck, kid.

And then I received the letter that changed my life. "Dear Mr. Strauss," it began. "A long time ago you sent us a query letter for some legal books. We would like to explore this idea. Could you come to New York to discuss?" The letter was from the editor in chief of a major publisher. I couldn't believe it! Literally, the only thing I had published at that time was a letter to the editor.

The problem was, I couldn't afford a trip to New York: the credit cards were maxed out, there were bills to pay, yada, yada, yada. Then I remembered that I had a ton of frequent flier miles from a post–bar exam trip to Thailand. I called the airline and discovered that I was 90 miles short of a free roundtrip flight anywhere.

So I hatched my escape plan. I told Linda I needed a few days off (she was unhappy with me, natch), bought a ticket to Reno, which was about 100 miles away, and also booked a flight to New York. A week later, I flew to Reno as my wife and baby drove in our Volkswagen van over the pass to meet me. She picked me up at the Reno airport, and I drove home. Yes, the van did conk out once going back over the pass in the snow, but we made it.

With a free flight now mine, I flew to New York the next day, met the editor, and came home with a four-book deal. For the next year, I continued to work at the firm during the day, and every night I wrote my books. Late in December of that year, right before Christmas, and after the books were written and on the verge of being published, I was called into Linda's office. Said Linda, "We are going to have to let you go." (No surprise there!) "But, why?" I asked. "You don't write well enough," she told me.

You know that you are really an entrepreneur when you have a wife and three children at home, get fired, lose your paycheck, health insurance, and other benefits, and you are ecstatic.

Armed with a book advance to help me get started, along with a little help from my friends, I started my own law firm a few months later. I made a profit the very first month and never looked back. And if you think I am petty enough to have autographed and sent to Linda my books once they came out, you are right. "To Linda," my inscription read, "I hope I wrote my books well enough for you!"

Sure, there have been rough spots since then, especially when I decided to retire from the practice of law altogether and concentrate solely on my career as a small business writer and speaker, but I love being my own boss even more than I imagined I would. As I always like to say, there's no business like your own business.

Postscript: A few years ago, I ran into that editor, the one who changed my life, and asked him why he decided to publish me. He explained that every few months, they have an intern comb through all of the unsolicited book queries they receive to see whether there is anything interesting in the so-called slush pile. That year, the intern riffled through the slush pile and pulled just one query letter—mine. "What was that intern's name?" I asked. "Peter Clevenger," he said.

So Peter Clevenger, a man I never met, is the reason you are reading this book today.

Appendix B

To view Appendix B: Sample Business Plan, please go visit: http://www
.mrallbiz.com/small-business-expert/books/small-business-bible-3rd-ed-
appendix/.

Index